## About The Author

Joe Pettitt is a freelance high-performance automotive journalist, photographer, and car-fi guy. He's written hundreds of articles for the performance press including *Hot Rod, Sport Compact Car, Drag Racer, Car Craft, Circle Track*, and *Motor Trend*. His adventures as a high-performance journalist include piloting IROC cars around the famous ovals of Daytona and Talladega and strapping into the world's fastest open road race record holder vehicle as a journalist/passenger. This mind-warping experience offered 27 minutes of sheer terror at over 220 mph while making the 90-mile Silver State Challenge run from Ely to Lund, Nev., with an average speed of over 194 mph. As a car audio journalist he wrote for *Autotronics* magazine, where he indulged his passion for great cars and great music.

An avid do-it-yourselfer, Pettitt modified and tuned numerous sports cars, hot rods, and street machines, installing sound systems in all of them. His favorite was a '59 XK 150 Jag. "I didn't have the most expensive gear in that car," said Pettitt, "but I installed it right and it made wonderful music as it moved swiftly through the turns and twist of the canyons of Southern California. "Every time you build a car," says Pettitt, "you learn something new. You learn how to do it a little smarter and a little easier; you learn how to find the right people to answer your questions. Finding good information isn't easy; but once you have it, it makes your high-performance projects run much smoother."

That's why SA Design had Pettitt write this book—to help you cut through all the marketing hype and get to the truth of the subject. He knows how to find the best experts in the field and get the real high-performance story.

Pettitt currently lives in his own virtual reality in Southern California with wife Patricia, stepdaughter, Vanessa, and their baby daughter, Jordan. In addition to this volume, Pettitt has written SA Design's *High Performance Honda Builder's Handbook Vol. 1, How To Install Nitrous Oxide Injection,* and *How to Install High-Performance Car Stereos.*

# By JOE PETTITT

All rights reserved. No part of this publication may be reproduced or utilized in any form or by any means, electronic or mechanical, including photocopying, recording, or by any information storage and retrieval system, without prior permission from the Publisher. All text, photographs, and artwork are the property of the Author unless otherwise noted or credited.

The information in this work is true and complete to the best of our knowledge. However, all information is presented without any guarantee on the part of the Author or Publisher, who also disclaim any liability incurred in connection with the use of the information and any implied warranties of merchantability or fitness for a particular purpose. Readers are responsible for taking suitable and appropriate safety measures when performing any of the operations or activities described in this work.

All trademarks, trade names, model names and numbers, and other product designations referred to herein are the property of their respective owners and are used solely for identification purposes. This work is a publication of CarTech, Inc., and has not been licensed, approved, sponsored, or endorsed by any other person or entity. The publisher is not associated with any product, service, or vendor mentioned in this book, and does not endorse the products or services of any vendor mentioned in this book.

# High Performance Honda Builder's Handbook Vol. II

**By Joe Pettitt**

Copyright © 1999, 2002 by Joe Pettitt. All rights reserved. All text, illustrations and photographs in this publication are the property of Joe Pettitt, unless otherwise noted or credited. It is unlawful to reproduce — or copy in any way — resell, or redistribute this information without the expressed written permission of the author. Printed in U.S.A.

EDITED BY
**MONICA DWYER ABRE.**

PRODUCTION BY
**TAMARA BAECHTEL**

ISBN 978-1-61325-113-3
PART No. SA58P

---

**CARTECH, INC., 39966 GRAND AVE., NORTH BRANCH, MN 55056**
www.cartechbooks.com

# CONTENTS

INTRODUCTION ...................................................................4

**CHAPTER 1 - HOW TO DRAG RACE** ...............................8
- TIPS FOR DRIVING A SMARTER, QUICKER RACE ........8
- PASSING TECH INSPECTION .........................................8
- SELECTING A CLASS ......................................................8
- THE STAGING LANES .....................................................9
- THE BURNOUT .................................................................9
- STAGING AND REACTION TIME ...................................10
- THE LAUNCH ..................................................................12
- DRIVING THE RACE .......................................................13
- SHIFTING ........................................................................13
- SHIFT RPM TELLS YOU HOW TO TUNE YOUR ENGINE ........13
- WHAT IF... ......................................................................13
- SHUTTING DOWN AND TURNING OFF .......................13
- HOW TO CALCULATE SHIFT RPM ...............................14
- QUARTER QUANDARIES BY PATRICK HALE .............15
- ENGINE DYNO TESTING ...............................................17
- QUARTER JR. SIMULATIONS .......................................19
- RPS PERFORMANCE PRODUCTS CLUTCHES ...........19

**CHAPTER 2 - CURVE CARVING ESSENTIALS** ............20
- TIRES AND HOW THEY WORK .....................................22
- STEERING WITH WEIGHT TRANSFER ........................24
- FRONT-WHEEL DRIVE ...................................................24
- CORNERING FORCE .....................................................24
- FIGURE IT OUT ...............................................................25
- THE FRICTION CIRCLE ..................................................25

**CHAPTER 3 - TIRES** ........................................................28
- IDENTICALLY SIZED TIRES VS. TREAD WIDTH ..........28
- SPEED RATINGS FROM H-Z .........................................28
- PUTTING THE NUMBERS AND LETTERS TOGETHER ........28
- A TIRE HAS TO PERFORM IN ITS OWN ENVIRONMENT ........29
- HIGH PERFORMANCE TIRE SCIENCE .........................29
- THE FOUR FUNDAMENTALS OF GRIP .........................29
- AIR PRESSURE AND LOAD ..........................................30
- BODY ROLL AND CAMBER ...........................................30
- CENTRIPETAL FORCE AND SLIP ANGLES .................31
- VERTICAL LOAD .............................................................31
- HOW SIDE LOAD AFFECTS THE TIRE ........................32
- THE FRONT DRIVE DISADVANTAGE ...........................32
- WHAT THE TIRE TELLS US ...........................................32
- COMPOUND CHOICES ..................................................32
- HEAT CYCLING ..............................................................33
- TUNING WITH AIR PRESSURE .....................................33
- SHAVING TIRES CAN IMPROVE PERFORMANCE .....34
- THE EFFECT OF RIM WIDTH ON TIRE PERFORMANCE ........34
- TIRE SIZING TECH TIPS ...............................................35
- TIRE TECH TIPS .............................................................36
- TREAD WEAR GRADING ...............................................36
- TRACTION .......................................................................36
- TRACTION TEST PROCEDURE ....................................36
- TEMPERATURE GRADING ............................................36
- HOW TO CHOOSE THE RIGHT DRAG RACING TIRE ........36
- QUICK TRACTION TIPS .................................................38
- HOW TO INSTALL BEAD SCREWS ..............................38
- ROTATIONAL INERTIA ...................................................38

**CHAPTER 4 - SUSPENSION** ...........................................40
- SUSPENSION COMPONENTS ......................................40
- ISOLATED SUSPENSION MODEL ................................41
- TIRES ARE SPRINGS THAT BECOME STIFFER WITH INCREASING AIR PRESSURE .......................41
- SPRINGS .........................................................................42
- FUNDAMENTAL SUSPENSION CONCEPTS AND ADJUSTMENTS ......44
  - TOE .............................................................................44
  - BUMP AND ROLL STEER ..........................................47
  - CASTOR ......................................................................47
- SHOCKS AND TUNING YOUR SUSPENSION:
  - A CONVERSATION WITH TOIKO'S AFTERMARKET TECHNICAL DIRECTOR, RICHARD MEYER .............48
- DRAG RACING CHASSIS TUNING ................................53
- ROLL CAGE INSTALLATION FOR SAFETY AND HANDLING ........56

**CHAPTER 5 - BRAKES** .....................................................58
- TYPES OF BRAKES .......................................................59
- HOW DISC BRAKES WORK ...........................................59
- LARGE ROTORS REDUCE FADE .................................60
- TWO-PIECE ROTORS FOR ULTIMATE BRAKE PERFORMANCE ........61
- CALIPERS .......................................................................61
- BRAKE PADS ..................................................................61
- BRAKE FLUID ..................................................................61
- BRAKE SYSTEMS FROM BAER RACING AND STILLEN ........62
- BRAKE PROPORTIONING TUNING SECRETS ............63

**CHAPTER 6 - AERODYNAMIC PERFORMANCE** ..........66
- AERODYNAMIC DRAG ...................................................66
- EXTERNAL FLOW PATTERNS ......................................69
- INTERNAL FLOW DRAG .................................................69
- AERODYNAMIC NOISE ..................................................70
- THE DRAG EQUATION ...................................................71
- THE DRAG COEFFICIENT ..............................................71
- THE DRAG COEFFICIENT AND THE REAL WORLD ....71
- HOW TO PERFORM A COAST DOWN TEST ...............72
- AERO HP CALCULATION ...............................................72
- CALCULATING DRAG FORCE AND $C_d$ ....................72
- HOW TO CALCULATE AERO HP AND ROLLING RESISTANCE HP ........74
- WHAT YOU CAN DO WITH THIS INFORMATION .........74

**CHAPTER 7 - FUEL IS POWER** .......................................76
- FUEL MAKES POWER ...................................................76
- HOW TO MAKE POWER WITH GAS - VAPORIZE IT! ........77
- ENERGY DENSITY AND A/F RATIO ..............................79
- AIR/FUEL RATIO AND POWER OUTPUT ......................79
- BRAKE MEAN EFFECTIVE PRESSURE .......................79
- BRAKE SPECIFIC FUEL CONSUMPTION ....................80
- TIPS FOR TWEAKING YOUR FUEL SYSTEM ..............81
- TWO METHODS FOR CHOOSING THE CORRECT FUEL PUMP ........82
- FUEL SYSTEM DESIGN TACTICS .................................83
- CHOOSING THE CORRECT FUEL PRESSURE REGULATOR ........84
- DESIGNING YOUR FUEL SYSTEM ................................85
- THE ADVANTAGE OF HIGH-PRESSURE RETURN-STYLE FUEL SYSTEMS ON CARBURETED NITROUS OXIDE SYSTEMS ........85

**CHAPTER 8 - FUEL AND AIR MIXTURES** ......................86
- YOUR ENGINE IS A SELF-DRIVEN AIR PUMP .............87
- HUMIDITY AND AIR DENSITY .......................................89
- RELATIVE HUMIDITY .....................................................90
- COMPUTING RELATIVE HUMIDITY ..............................90
- BUILD A PSYCHROMETER TO FIND VAPOR PRESSURES ........90
- CALCULATE AIR DENSITY ............................................91
- HOW TO CALCULATE DENSITY ALTITUDE FOR HUMID AIR ........92
- HOW DOES THIS AFFECT YOUR ENGINE'S TUNING? ........92
- MANAGING FUEL DELIVERY ........................................94
- HOW TO BASELINE YOUR CARBURETOR JETTING ........94
- DETONATION CHECK LIST ...........................................95
- FUEL INJECTION TUNING .............................................95

**CHAPTER 9 - NITROUS TUNING** ....................................98
- A BASIC NITROUS SYSTEM .........................................98
- CONTROLLING THE SYSTEM .....................................100
- HOW NITROUS MAKES POWER ................................101
- FUEL BURNS FASTER WITH MORE OXYGEN ..........101
- THE IMPORTANCE OF TIMING MAX CYLINDER PRESSURE ........102
- TECHNIQUES TO TIME MAX CYLINDER PRESSURE ........103
- COMPRESSION RATIO .................................................103
- CAM CONSCIOUSNESS ...............................................103
- OCTANE RATING ..........................................................104
- AIR/FUEL RATIO ............................................................104
- CONTROLLING IGNITION TIMING ..............................104
- TUNING YOUR NITROUS SYSTEM .............................104
- UNEVEN AIR/FUEL DISTRIBUTION AND DETONATION ........105
- CHOOSE THE RIGHT SPARK PLUG ...........................105
- ELECTRONIC ACTIVATION AND CONTROL ..............105
- HOW THESE DEVICES WORK .....................................106
- THROTTLE POSITION ACTIVATED PROGRESSIVE NITROUS CONTROLS ........106
- RPM SWITCH .................................................................107
- TURBOS AND NITROUS ...............................................107
- HOW TO USE NITROUS TUNING TABLES .................109

**CHAPTER 10 - ENGINE BUILDING** ...............................112
- BLOCK PREP .................................................................112
- CHECKING MAIN BEARING CLEARANCE ................113
- BOTTOM END DESIGN TACTICS ................................113
- ROD AND PISTON PREP ..............................................115
- PISTON/RING DESIGN TIPS ........................................116
- SHOULD YOU USE HYPERUETECTIC PISTONS IN YOUR NITROUS ENGINE? ........117
- RING PACK AND CYLINDER WALL PREP ..................118
- ROD AND PISTON INSTALLATION ..............................118
- OIL PUMP AND WATER PUMP INSTALLATION .........119
- MILLING THE HEAD AND INSTALLING IT ..................122
- CAM AND VTEC MECHANISM INSTALLATION .........123
- ADJUSTING VALVES ....................................................125
- BUTTONING UP .............................................................126
- HOW TO DEGREE YOUR CAM ....................................127

# Honda Builder's HANDBOOK Vol. II
## INTRODUCTION

Writing a book about how to improve the performance of a Honda may seem presumptuous. After all, Honda Engineers totally dominated Formula One when the company was involved and currently they have a dominate position in the CART series. Furthermore, much of the technology, proved at the racetrack, actually made it to production cars in a big way. The VTEC system is an obvious example. You may ask, as most serious tuners have, how do you improve on an emission-legal naturally aspirated engine that makes 1.77 horsepower/cubic inch. That's what the '98 Type R 1.8 liter Integra makes: 195 horsepower at 8000 rpm with 130 lbs./ft. at 7500 rpm — on pump gas through the catalytic converter.

I believe the answer to my rhetorical question is that you don't "improve" on that kind of performance, you tune its potential to your specific purpose. The Honda Engineers designed the engine combination to get the most work possible from an engine designed to run on pump gas while remaining reliable and stable enough to drive on the street.

I put "improve" in quotes for a reason. I wanted to signal a different way to think of the problem. Since we can't really improve the power output of an engine that is state of the art, does that mean we should all just go buy a Type R and resign ourselves to being passive power consumers?

I don't believe so. Because, even though the Type R VTEC, the del Sol 1.6 L VTEC, and the GSR 1.8 L VTEC offer incredible specific power output from an efficient mass produced emission-legal performance engine, most of us don't have one of these killer combinations. The DOHC Integra motors without VTEC as well as the SOHC engines with VTEC on the intake have lots of potential. Even these mass-produced VTEC technology marvels are set to double their power output once you leave the limitation of one-atmosphere behind.

The point I'm trying to get to is the concept of tuning for specific performance goals. For example, as impressive as 195 horsepower from 1.8 liter is, the power curve is really too narrow for a serious drag racer. It's hard to launch a 2600 lb. car with 130 lbs./ft. of torque at 7500 rpm. The torque curve is pretty nonexistent below 6000 rpm, so if you have traction and get overly aggressive with the clutch release, you can easily pull the engine out of its power band bogging it off the line. Once you get going, the gear spacing on the Type R is just right and the car has a good tractive force curve, i.e. the gearing always keeps the engine in the power RPM. But this is something that can be improved upon. The Jackson Racing Supercharged Type R is an example of how one of the better Honda Tuners approached the issue.

So looking beyond peak power figures, we can see that ultimate power isn't necessarily the only goal. It depends on what you want to do with your Honda.

A street car and a good drag racing car loves torque. Torque is the twisting force generated by the engine that thrusts your car forward. Horsepower is a measure of how much work the torque force can do in a certain amount of time. Essentially,

4  Honda Builder's Handbook Vol. 2

horsepower is torque divided by time. The time line in this case is RPM, 5252 rpm to be precise.

A club road racer/autocross car needs peak power and since peak power tends to come from tuning the combination to work best at high RPM, the low end suffers so gear ratios and spacing become very important. Because gearing is a series of levers. The lower gears trade speed for torque multiplication while the reverse is true for high gears.

So broad torque versus peak power are the extremes of the tuning range. Of course your particular application may call for some combination of the two qualities.

How to get there from here? In naturally aspirated form, Honda has essentially optimized the engine for street driving. You won't see major gain in performance if you stay with a naturally aspirated combination. If you install headers and a free flow exhaust and a fresh air and/or ram air intake system, in addition to an adjustable fuel pressure regulator to feed the engine more fuel, you'll only realize a very minor power increase. And what additional power you do see is contingent on the additional fuel. Headers and free flow exhaust may help the engine breathe but you have to add fuel to the additional air flow to make more power.

The best bang for the buck, particularly with supremely optimized naturally aspirated combinations always comes from pressurizing the intake with a supercharger or turbo, with appropriate fuel management; or injecting nitrous oxide. Here you'll see incredible power increases. However you do need to consider installing rods and forged pistons to improve reliability once you add 50 or so more horsepower.

We haven't yet mentioned the rest of the car, such as suspension tuning, tire choice, and aero dynamics.

Most enthusiasts just want the slammed look, perhaps thinking they'll get featured in a magazine. Now there is nothing wrong with stylizing a car by slamming it on the ground. Just don't be disappointed when you discover it is undriveable and even the most wretchedly maintained commuter car would drive cir-

Jackson Racing Superchargers set a standard of craftsmanship and design we should all strive for. The supercharger is sized correctly for the volumetric efficiency of the engine, the fuel curve is managed artfully and precisely allowing the engine to make full use of the air going through it; and all the components are styled and fit appropriately to enhance appearance and durability.

Jackson Racing tuned a Tri-Y header design to their supercharger. If one has space enough a four-into-one design would produce more peak power, but since the stock accessories prohibit installing a true four-into-one design a tri-Y is the logical choice. When tuned properly the design gives broad torque curve without sacrificing too much peak power.

Excellence is in the details. One of the challenges was to give the driver a good feel for the throttle position. This machined bracket with Delrin roller was the perfect solution.

Most aftermarket air intakes are mounted on the shock tower. Because the engine rocks in the engine bay from torque reactions, Jackson Racing mounted their intake to the engine. The intake moves with the engine instead of at the joints.

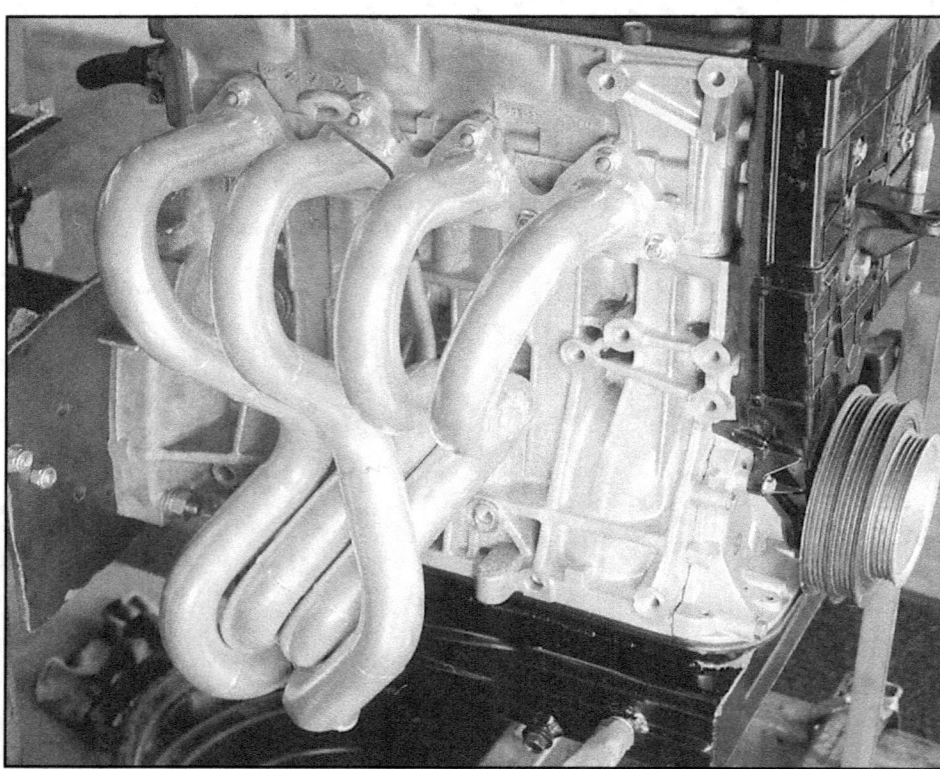

A properly designed collector uses the velocity of the exhaust gas to create low pressure which helps evacuate the cylinders. The oil pan is modified to clear the collector as well as having baffles installed to control the oil during hard cornering.

The most efficient headers have straight tubes that gradually blend into soft curves before the collector.

cles around you on a road course. There's more to suspension tuning than lowering the center of gravity.

Shocks and spring rates chosen to work in harmony with the tire and the suspension geometry make a car a pleasure to drive; or, if mismatched, can make driving a hellish nightmare.

The same can be said of aerodynamic modifications. However most of these are benign in terms of handling at average freeway speeds. In fact, aerodynamic road loads are less than the sum of mechanical rolling resistance until about 60 mph in most production cars. But aerodynamic force increases at the square of the speed so as you drive faster they stack up rather quickly. For example, a late 80s CRX takes around 11

A rollcage not only increases driver safety, properly designed and installed it reinforces the chassis making it resist flexing under cornering loads, which improves handling and grip.

*Honda Builder's Handbook Vol. 2*

horsepower to keep it going 50 mph. At 100 mph that becomes 60 horsepower. Need we say more?

All these areas offer potential performance enhancements for the smart enthusiast to put together a balanced package that puts the most area under the performance curve, or, if you like has the largest perfor-mance envelope. That, in essence, is what tuning is all about and as it happens that is what this second High Performance Honda Builders Handbook is all about — tuning the whole car.

My purpose is to give you the conceptual tools and knowledge to judge your performance needs and how to modify your car appropriately to meet them. I hope after you read this book and use it to develop your own car, you'll have an even greater appreciation of the engineering prowess of Honda. They are simply the best. And they gave you some of the best production car equipment on the planet to tune and enjoy. So don't abuse it, tune it correctly and you will be by far the fastest of the field.

— *Joe Pettitt*

As this radical RPS Performance Products built VTEC engine demonstrates, improving the performance of a Honda VTEC in naturally aspirated form means stepping into the realm of racing gas and critically tuned and matched components. The intake and exhaust, pistons, head work, and fuel system are tuned to work with each other. On the exhaust side, notice how the header pipes extend at an angle. This is to conserve exhaust gas velocity. The bends are very large again conserving momentum. The diameter grows larger in steps, which is why this design is called a "step header." The steps form a space analogous to a two-stroke engine's expansion chamber. The size of the intake manifold plenum and runners are tuned to create power within a specific RPM range. With naturally aspirated engines of limited size, the best way to make more power is to rev them up so you have more power strokes per minute.

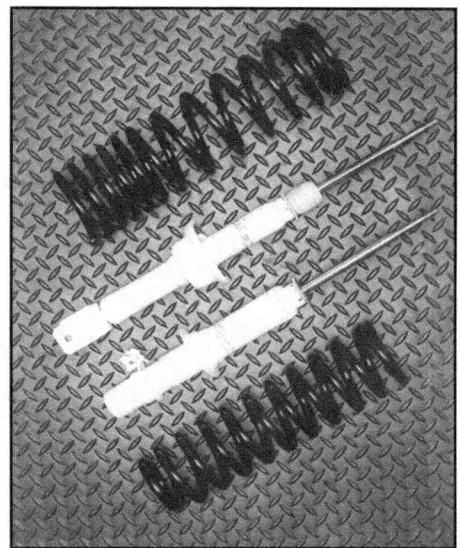

Installing shocks and springs is the quickest way to take advantage of the improved grip of the latest tire technology. Even if you aren't running a qualifying tire compound on the street, the right shocks and springs give you the right street stance. Don't slam your car, just drop the height slightly and give it a rake.

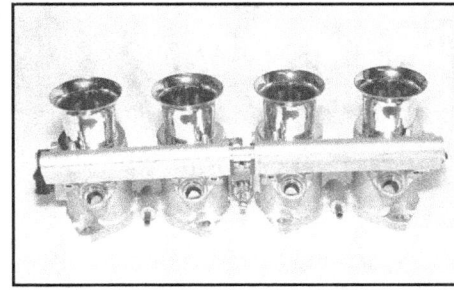

Advance Engine Management offers these fueling injector stacks. These are the perfect compliment to an aftermarket electronic fuel injection system.

Stillen aero kits give your car the aggressive lines of an ultra high performance machine. Aero kits don't usually reduce drag, but they do offer a means of managing airflow through intercoolers and other such equipment.

Transplanting a larger engine into a smaller chassis is a classic supertuner move. Here's how one Advanced Engine Management customer Civic looked with a 2.2 liter Prelude VTEC engine installed. Note the adjustable fuel pressure regulator with gauge.

# Honda Builder's HANDBOOK Vol. II
## HOW TO DRAG RACE

### TIPS FOR DRIVING A SMARTER, QUICKER RACE

Drag racing is not all horsepower and smoky burnouts. It's about reaching the finish line before the other car. That's how you win. Knowing your way around a drag strip and the subtleties of the timing equipment is the smart racer's way of getting quicker E.T.s. That's what this story is about.

However, reading about drag racing isn't enough. To get really good at it you have to do it. And while the import racing scene is expanding, you don't want to practice on race day. You need to do your tuning and practice long before that. Go to a drag strip and race. Most tracks have test and tune sessions in addition to hosting E.T. Bracket racing events. Bracket racing is an excellent arena to hone your skills, as the emphasis is on consistency and not on brutal leaves and insane trap speeds. Bracket racing is by far the most common format of grassroots drag racing, meaning you'll have plenty opportunity to race as often as you can and to apply the principles and techniques you'll be learning. You'll be a smarter, quicker racer and you just may find yourself taking home a trophy or two.

### PASSING TECH INSPECTION

Your first drag racing concern, after finding the event and getting to the track, is passing the technical inspection. The track officials want to make sure your car is in proper mechanical condition and that you have all the required safety equipment for your class. In general, most tracks require cars with 14.00-second E.T.s and slower to have seat belts, a neutral safety switch on automatics, and a radiator-overflow reservoir. The tech inspector will also check that you don't have more than 12 inches total of rubber fuel line on your car and that you didn't forget your helmet.

If your car is quicker than 13.99-seconds, then you'll have to have more safety gear. If you have nitrous or turbos, the tech guy will look at your car with a more critical eye. This is for your benefit because the quicker and faster you run, the more danger you are exposed to. And you don't want a minor failure to lead to a major one — such as a rollover. To do it right, you should order a copy of the NHRA rule book. This has safety requirements for most race car combinations and is a source that most tracks follow. You can order an NHRA rule book by contacting the National Hot Rod Association (NHRA) at 2035 Financial Way, Glendora, CA 91740, (818)914-4761.

### SELECTING A CLASS

If you're participating in a sanctioned E.T. Bracket race, your next step is to register in the proper class. Most tracks follow NHRA E.T. classes or some such grouping scheme. SuperPro 7.50- to 10.99-second E.T.s; Pro 11.00 to 11.99; Sportsman 12.00 to 13.99 and Street 14.00 and up E.T.s. Once you've decided on your E.T. bracket (we're assuming you have an idea of the E.T.s your car is capable of) and have registered,

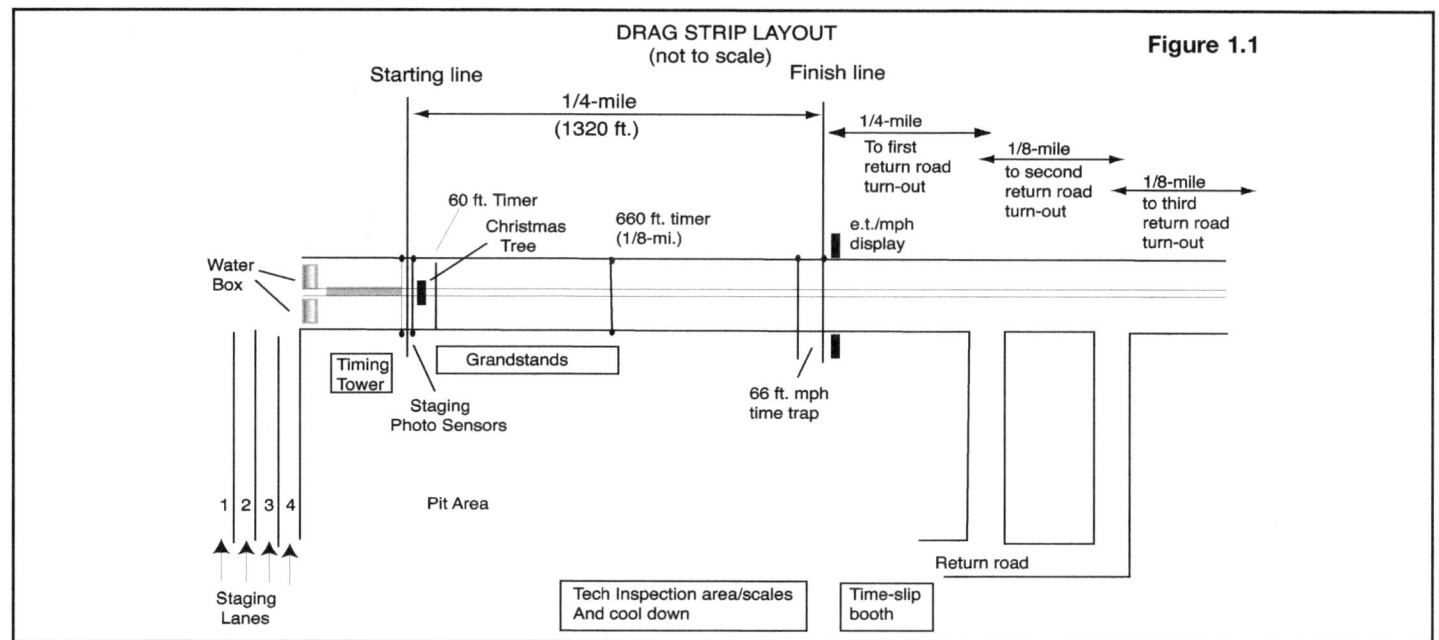

**Figure 1.1**

This is the layout of most drag strips. The starting line staging lights are designed to put your front axle at the beginning of the quarter-mile. Because your tires are round and the lights are close to the ground, they allow a few inches of play as to exactly where your axle is when staged. The 60 foot timer, 660 ft. timer and speed trap are valuable timing marks and you should track them to evaluate your tuning choices and driving tactics.

put the following information on your windows: car number (they give that to you at registration), dial-in (the E.T. you should get with a perfect run, 14.90 for example), and staging information if appropriate. Each track has a format for this info and on what windows you need to put it on. Ask the officials if this info isn't with the registration literature. Use shoe polish and make the letters big enough and on a side of the car that lets the traffic controller and scorer in the tower read it when you are staging.

The goal of bracket racing is to hit your dial-in E.T. on every run. This is virtually impossible, but a lot of racers get very, very close. If you click off an E.T. that's quicker than your dial-in, you lose the race, unless the other racer also runs quicker than his dial-in. In such cases, the racer who is closest to his dial-in wins. That's why most bracket racers register with a dial-in a few tenths of a second quicker than that which their car is capable. It keeps them from breaking out of their bracket — a smart move.

In bracket racing, when you race against a slower (or quicker) car, the Christmas Tree starting sequence will be different for each lane. If you're the quicker car, the other lane leaves first, then after the difference in your and your opponent's E.T., your lights come down and then you start. The idea here is the differential in start times should put you and your opponent at the finish line at exactly the same time. That's assuming both cars hit their dial-in E.T. and both drivers have perfect reaction times — an almost impossible scenario. Which ever racer gets across the finish line first without running quicker than his dial-in, wins.

### THE STAGING LANES

If you're at a test and tune session and you're car is ready, put on your helmet and pull into the staging lanes and wait for your turn at the starting line. If you're bracket racing you have to listen to the track announcer. The control voice will direct you to the staging lane for your class.

Once you're in the staging lanes the cars will move forward as the those in front of you make their passes. A lot of racers leave their hoods open and push the car forward in the staging lane to cool the engine. A cool engine has a cool intake track which can help make power. Finally, you get to the front of the line and (this is where the fun starts) you will be directed to the burnout box.

### THE BURNOUT

If you're in a rear drive car with street tires, the starter will most likely

**Staging lanes help organize racers into classes and run groups.**

have you drive around the water and then back into it. That avoids carrying water on the tires to the starting line. However, some officials will not allow you to drive around the water. If you're in a front drive car this doesn't really affect you. You won't be backing into the water box and you'll burn off the water anyway. Watch the track officials for signals and follow them explicitly. They'll signal you to begin your burnout and also to pull forward to stage for the race.

The purpose of a burnout is to heat the tire compound so that it will produce the maximum amount of stick. Tires with different compounds perform best at different temperatures. To get your tires to the proper temperature, you need to control the

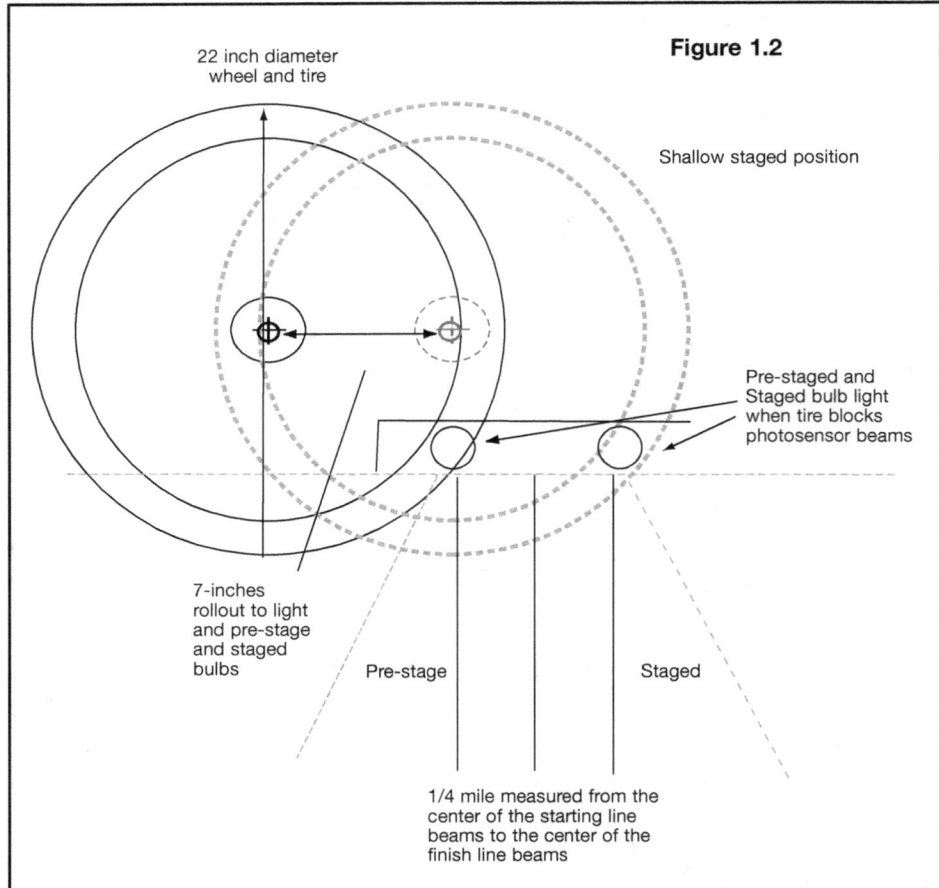

**Figure 1.2**

- 22 inch diameter wheel and tire
- Shallow staged position
- Pre-staged and Staged bulb light when tire blocks photosensor beams
- 7-inches rollout to light and pre-stage and staged bulbs
- Pre-stage
- Staged
- 1/4 mile measured from the center of the starting line beams to the center of the finish line beams

**Staging is vitally important. It affects your reaction times and influences your E.T.**

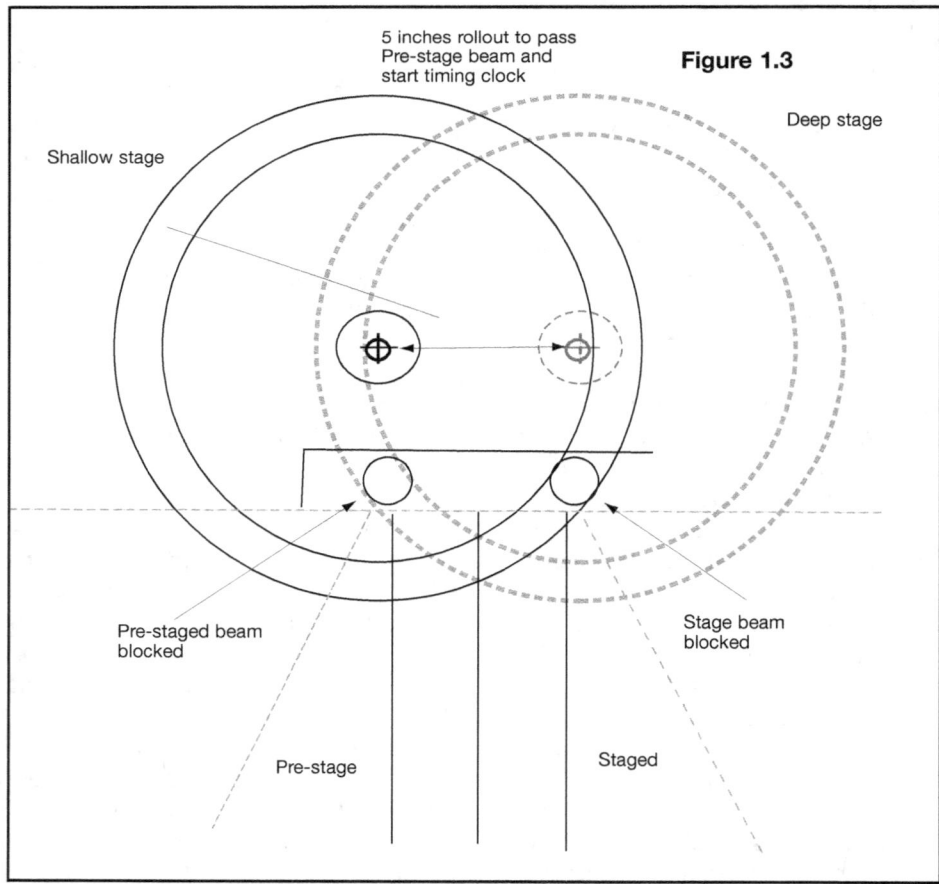

**Figure 1.3**

- 5 inches rollout to pass Pre-stage beam and start timing clock
- Deep stage
- Shallow stage
- Pre-staged beam blocked
- Stage beam blocked
- Pre-stage
- Staged

**The burnout is used to heat the tire compound to a temperature that produces the most traction. You don't have to burn the rubber off your tires, but it is a crowd pleaser. Pro racers control the time of the burnout as well as the RPM and gear used during the burnout.**

duration of the burnout as well as the RPM and gear that you perform it in and tire pressure. In addition, control the time it takes you to stage. This requires careful observation and testing to find the best combination.

For rear wheel drive cars, a line lock helps hold the car during the burnout. If you don't have one, just apply light pressure to the brake pedal as you feed in throttle. Front drivers use the parking brake to hold the car while doing the burnout. Don't burnout past the starting line. You don't need that much distance to get your tires to temperature and it just takes more time to back up and stage. So get the car stopped before the line.

### STAGING AND REACTION TIME

After you and your opponent finish your burnouts, the starting official will signal you to pull forward to begin the staging process. Most tracks use a "courtesy" rule stipulating that when one car lights the Pre-stage light, the

**Photosensitive cells at the start line staging system are protected by a housing from the sun and errant race cars.**

opponent has to light his Pre-stage and Stage lights, then the first car completes its staging.

Staging is vitally important in drag racing. It affects reaction times, and influences your E.T.s. When you stage your car, make sure it's pointed straight at the center of the lane of the finish line. That's where you want to go and if you're not pointed there, you'll have to make steering corrections and that adds time to your E.T., exactly opposite of what you want.

This doesn't apply as much to street cars as race cars, but it's a good drag racing technique so you should be aware of it. When you stage, look for the groove of rubber left by the other cars slicks and try to put your tires on these marks. The rubber compound left on the track can give you more traction, though sometimes it can hurt if it gets too thick. This is one of the reasons pro racers burnout past the lights. They're heating their tire compounds and putting a fresh groove of rubber on the track. When they back up and stage the crew chief always positions them so the drive wheels are in these grooves.

The staging line has two light beams that the front tires break, as you roll into the stage line, thus illuminating the Pre-stage and Stage bulbs at the top of the tree. A 22-inch diameter tire uses 7-inches of rollout to light the ambers and another 5 inches to break the beam. That gives you a total rollout of 12 inches. The distance from the center of the two stage beams to the center of the finish line is 1/4 mile. The starting line may also have a check beam to see if your car is lower than the 3-inch height minimum.

There are two staging strategies in drag racing. One is deep staging, the other is shallow staging. Both take advantage of the small rollout distance and how that affects the timing of your pass. Deep staging is when a racer rolls far enough forward to pass the prestage beam, making the prestage light go out, then creeping back until it just comes on again. Deep staging reduces rollout distance to start timing the run and so the reaction time and your chance for fouling out. Deep staging increases your E.T. because it breaks the beam and starts the clock when your car isn't traveling as fast as

**After your burn out, the starter will direct you to stage. You know you're staged when both the Pre-staged and the Staged lights on top of the tree are lit.**

it would if you shallow staged. Those extra five inches at the start really stack up at the finish line. Shallow staging is accomplished by stopping precisely when the staged light comes on. Shallow staging reduces E.T. and increases reaction time.

The lights on each side of the Christmas Tree control the lane they point at. When you're properly staged, both the Pre-Staged and Staged amber lights at the top of the tree in your lane will be shining. The larger lights are three ambers, one green, and one red. Most amateur drag racing is started with a Sportsman Tree. It begins the start by lighting each of the three ambers and then the green, all separated by .500 of a second. To get a good reaction time racing a street car, you should leave when you see the third amber shine. Reaction time consists of the time it takes you and your car to react and actually roll out of the staging beam. This time adds up, and is why you need to leave on the third amber bulb to get a decent reaction time. You'll learn more about reaction time in a moment.

When the track is running a Pro Tree program, all three ambers light simultaneously, then .400 of a second later the green light shines. If you don't leave when you see amber on a Pro Tree you'll lose. Some tracks measure reaction time from when the green light comes on until your tire breaks the stage beam. A perfect reaction time with a green-light system is .000 seconds. Other tracks base reaction time on the last amber, so a perfect reaction time would be .400 on a Pro Tree or .500 on a Sportsman Tree. Regardless of the type of starting format, the red light shines if you clear the beam before the green light comes on. This is how you "foul out" or "red light." It means you lose the race instantly.

Now obviously we're dealing with very short periods of time to react to the light, move your clutch and throttle feet and leave the starting line. So you have to focus on the job at hand but not get so intense you freeze up. This is supposed to be fun! But because there's a lot going on during the leave, you need to make a plan to be consistent. We'll assume the car will react to your input the same. There are ways to make it react quicker or slower and if it's not in good repair the car can be a source of inconsistent reaction times. But let's factor out the car and look at the most inconsistent component of the drag race — the driver.

You need to concentrate and be consistent to sort out a drag race. Concentrate on those things that affect your immediate race — lining up with the centerline of your lane, staging your car, doing your burn out. Don't think about the other guy, that can make you nervous and influence reaction times. (Usually you'll leave too quick and red light.) And keep a consistent technique for several runs before you change. For example, always shallow stage the car; leave

You know you're staged when you light up both staging lights at the top of the tree.

On a Sportsman Tree, a sequence of three amber lights, each .500-second apart, prepare you to launch your car.

When you see the last amber dump the clutch and power out, because .500 seconds later the green comes on and you can use up the rollout distance before breaking the beam and starting the clock. If your opponent is sleeping you'll have a few hundredths of a second head start. That'll add up at the end of the track. Remember, in drag racing, it's who gets to the finish line first, not who has the quickest E.T.

on the last amber bulb if you're on a Sportsman Tree; leave at the same RPM with the same amount of clutch.

A side note regarding reaction times: You can improve your reaction time and get very consistent by using a practice tree. Pro racers have a real tree set in front of their cars that they use with a practice tree. You don't have to go to such extremes, however as there are several compact practice tree devices. Portatree is one of the more popular units on the market. They have full-sized trees and also have a video explaining the nuances of reaction time and how to improve yours.

## THE LAUNCH

The launch is the most important and in many ways the most difficult aspect of drag racing. For the pros, mostly it's a matter of agonizing over the tune of the clutch. That's not to say the suspension tuning is not important or difficult, but the really difficult tuning decision is how aggressive to get with the clutch. For those of us driving production based cars, at least on the level I'm talking about, it comes down to the same decision. We're dealing with how fast we release the clutch, i.e. how much we let it slip, and the launch RPM. For an automatic transmissioned car it's a choice of stall speed of the torque converter.

When you chose a torque converter with a higher than stock stall speed, essentially this means the engine will rev higher before the resistance of the fluid moving through the converter equals the power output of the engine. At this point the engine's ability to rev higher is stopped or, stalled, which is why they call it stall speed.

Anyway, the idea of a higher stall speed converter is to let the engine rev up to an ideal engine RPM that's right at the torque peak. That way when you're at the starting line, you step on the brake, or activate the roll-control, step on the gas and the engine is pulling at the rear wheel with its maximum torque. Then when you release the brake— whoosh —the force shoots the car off the line down the track as quickly as possible.

A torque converter multiplies torque, in addition to letting you use a high-stall design, and a car so equipped has an advantage, providing the tire can grab hold of all the torque. But not all the advantage comes from having the engine at the torque peak and multiplying that force. A lot of the advantage comes from how the torque converter works to reduce the affects of rotational inertia of the engine and transmission.

Basically here's how it works. Since the engine is revved up to a certain RPM, say 4000 rpm, this is the stall speed. When you let off the brake and go full throttle, the car begins to move. But the engine doesn't start to increase RPM until the wheel speed, and hence vehicle speed, catches up with the engine and rotor of the torque converter. But since the engine isn't accelerating right off the line, the power that would have had to be used to accelerate the engine itself as well as some transmission parts is free to accelerate the car. This only happens briefly during the first few feet of that run. But these are the most critical. It is very difficult to overcome the inertia of the vehicle, let alone the inertia of the engine and other rotating parts. (See "Quarter Quandaries" sidebar for more information.)

For drivers using a manual transmission, this discussion of rotational inertia gives you a clue as to how to approach the launch. Ideally you need to balance the slip of the clutch with the available traction and the power of the engine. Not exactly an easy thing to do, especially with a front drive car.

We don't have the space to go into the detail necessary for a deep understanding of the physics of launching a front drive car. We'll get into that and driving tactics to take advantage of the physics in the chapter on suspension. The important thing to remember here, is that you should rev the engine fairly high and let the clutch slip, using clutch slip to bring the driveline and car up to engine speed on the launch. This reduces the affects of rotational inertia power loss, which are substantial. As for getting the feel for maximum grip on the launch, that takes lots of seat time. However, we will help you make the best use of that seat time in the chapters on suspension and on tires where we'll discuss the finer points of grip. (See "Quarter Quandaries" sidebar for more info.)

### DRIVING THE RACE

Now it's a matter of driving the car down the track and staying in the throttle through the speed trap and finish line. This is the really fun part of drag racing: Feeling the power and acceleration of your car. But don't get lost in the fun of it all. Well, at least not completely. You still have to concentrate on the run and try to drive as straight and true as you possibly can. This isn't nearly as easy as it sounds. You may have to correct the car while the tires are spinning moving you off course. Then again, you might be looking at the wrong thing as you drive your race.

That's why drag race schools such as Frank Hawley's video tape student racer runs. If you have a video camera you can mount in your car, do it. You'll be surprised at what you see. Over the years, Frank Hawley has taught many students and is a pro racer himself. It's interesting that he finds the same thing with student drivers.

For example, he's observed that most new drivers drive the strip in an arc. The groove angles toward the center of the track, then curves out toward the center of the lane in the lights. Hawley thinks the reason for this is fear of the wall. Pro drivers don't make an arc, they drive straight.

Another common mistake is driving way too close to the center line. This is mostly caused by the tendency you have of driving where you look. If you're looking at the center of the track while driving, instead of focusing on the center of the lane, you'll drive right next to it. There's a big difference in the length of the pass aside from the safety aspects of this driving style.

Another way smart racers improve their E.T. is by choosing the best shift points. The right way to do this is to have good dyno data. You'll need power at the wheel through the broadest part of the power band and a little past peak horsepower. Then you chart it out, calculating where your gear ratios put your motor in its power band when shifted at various RPM. The goal is to find the RPM at which you should shift that keeps your engine in its power band. When you start looking to shave hundredths off your E.T. you'll have to do this. But a traditional drag racing formula is to shift about 10 percent above your horsepower peak.

### SHIFTING

In addition to driving as straight as possible, a good drag racer chooses shift points that keep the car accelerating as quickly as possible. This sounds obvious, and, well it is. What isn't so obvious is how you do it. How do you choose the best shift points?

You've got two choices. You can dyno test your engine, or you can use one of the personal g-meters on the market to generate a force curve. The bottom line is you have to test your car or engine. There are other ways to derive a power curve for your car but the two mentioned seem to be the most convenient.

If you've dyno tested your engine and have a chart of its horsepower and torque through its speed range, then all you have to do is some simple math. What you're doing is discovering the RPM value where the torque multiplication of the transmission at the gear you will shift to is closest to that of the gear you are *in*.

The way this is done with a dyno sheet is to chart the torque at specific RPM values in the various gears. Then you see which shift RPM gives you the least difference between torque. When you generate a force curve with a g-meter it's essentially the same process since higher torque values will give you higher g-readings. Using the g-meter has the advantage of taking rotational inertia power loss into account, since the g-meter will display only the power that actually gets to the drive wheels. See the "How To Calculate Shift RPM" and "Quarter Quandaries" sidebars for more information.

### SHIFT RPM TELLS YOU HOW TO TUNE YOUR ENGINE COMBINATION

Since your gearing and tire size determine the RPM range in which your engine makes the highest average force, that RPM range is where you want to increase power. In other words, if you are shifting at 7000 rpm and in the following gear your RPM drops to 4000 rpm and that relationship holds true for all the gears, then your car will be much quicker if you make changes that improve power between 4000 and 7000 rpm.

### WHAT IF...

Another thing Hawley likes to talk about is "what ifs." You have to consider the possibilities of what can happen and what your response should be. For example, what happens if the throttle sticks open? Two options immediately come to mind: shut the ignition off or put it in neutral, says Hawley. Most people don't think about neutral because they don't want to hurt the engine. But what would you rather do, throw lots of rods or hurt your body or break your legs?

### SHUTTING DOWN AND TURNING OFF

You've also got to think safety when racing. Not only regarding use of the safety equipment on the car, but in your driving technique and manners. Right of way to turn offs is an area you don't really think about, but you should because many accidents happen in the shut off lanes from confusion on this point. Basically you have three choices of turn offs. Typically the first turn off is a 1/4-mile after the finish with two more at 1/8-mile intervals. Most street cars can slow and easily make the first turn off. But it's your choice. However, the guy closest to the turn off has the right of way. For example, right of way belongs to the

# HOW TO CALCULATE SHIFT RPM

To illustrate the concept of determining your optimum shift RPM, we're using the transmission ratios from a 1996 Integra RS/LS. Since we didn't dyno test this combination we relied on the factory torque curve and derived the torque values at the contact patch with the following formula: Drive Wheel tq =

$$\text{Drive Wheel Torque} = \frac{\text{Flywheel Trq} \times \text{Gear Ratio} \times \text{Final Drive} \times \text{Efficiency}}{\text{Tire Rolling Radius}}$$

flywheel tq x gear ratio x final drive x efficiency % / tire rolling radius. We had to estimate the rolling radius of the tire from the stock P195/60R14 tires. This tire has an approximate diameter of 23-inches and so a radius of 11.5 inches. We'll shorten the radius by .5 inch to simulate a loaded condition which is know as the rolling radius which is now 11 inches or 11 / 12 = .916 ft. (You need to convert the rolling radius into feet because torque is measured in ft./lbs.) Calculating drive torque at 6000 rpm, the formula takes the form (127 x 3.23 x 4.266 x 0.9)/0.916. The efficiency factor is estimated at .9 meaning the transmission is 90 % efficient or that 90 % of the torque gets to the drive axle. Of course this tactic doesn't take into account rotational inertia power losses, but it will give you a solid starting point from which to hone your shift points.

## RS & LS DRIVEWHEEL TORQUE @ RPM

| RPM | 2000 | 2500 | 3000 | 3500 | 4000 | 4500 | 5000 | 5500 | 6000 | 6500 | 7000 |
|---|---|---|---|---|---|---|---|---|---|---|---|
| FLYWHEEL TQ: | 105 | 110 | 118 | 118 | 118 | 120 | 123 | 127 | 127 | 120 | 117 |
| 3.230 | 1390 | 1456 | 1562 | 1562 | 1562 | 1588 | 1628 | 1681 | 1681 | 1588 | 1549 |
| 1.900 | 817 | 856 | 919 | 919 | 919 | 934 | 958 | 989 | 989 | 934 | 911 |
| 1.269 | 546 | 572 | 614 | 614 | 614 | 624 | 640 | 660 | 660 | 624 | 608 |
| 0.966 | 416 | 435 | 467 | 467 | 467 | 475 | 487 | 503 | 503 | 475 | 463 |
| 0.714 | 307 | 322 | 345 | 345 | 345 | 351 | 360 | 372 | 372 | 351 | 342 |

$$\text{RPM after shift} = \frac{\text{Ratio shifted to}}{\text{Ratio shifted from}} \times \text{RPM @ Shift}$$

After mapping out the torque curve in each gear with corresponding RPM points you're ready to calculate the RPM change between gears. Don't bother to do the math for the entire rev range of the engine. Just focus on the area near and above the power peak. With the broad torque curve of this engine you can see that even running the engine to 7000, 200 rpm past redline we still had shift points that lost substantial torque. But we lost the least amount, and that's one important step toward a quicker e.t. If the engine had a higher redline we'd get to a point where the shift could be made where torque in the gear you're shifting from equals torque in the gear you're shifting to. That's the ideal, but unless you can match the ratios to the power curve as racers do, you usually end up with a compromise. That's not bad, it's just the way it is with production cars. The trick is to sacrifice less power than your competitor.

| Shift RPM | 5500 | 6000 | 6500 | 7000 |
|---|---|---|---|---|
| RPM After shift: | | | | |
| 1st to 2nd | 3235 | 3529 | 3824 | 4118 |
|  | 1691 | 1681 | 1588 | 1549 |
| Torque in 1st | 919 | 919 | 919 | 919 |
| Torque in 2nd | 772 | 762 | 669 | 630 Difference |
| 2nd to 3rd | 3673 | 4007 | 4341 | 4675 |
|  | 989 | 989 | 934 | 911 |
| Torque in 2nd | 614 | 614 | 624 | 624 |
| Torque in 3rd | 375 | 375 | 310 | 287 Difference |
| 3rd to 4th | 4187 | 4567 | 4948 | 5329 |
|  | 660 | 660 | 624 | 608 |
| Torque in 3rd | 467 | 475 | 487 | 503 |
| Torque in 4th | 193 | 185 | 137 | 105 Difference |
| 4th to 5th | 4435 | 4804 | 5174 | 475 |
| Torque in 4th | 463 | 360 | 360 | |
| Torque in 5th | 115 | 103 Difference | | |

car in the lane on the side that the turn off is on. So if you are on the side away from the turn offs, you should wait until the other car passes you and then follow him off.

Sometimes, the driver may have had trouble, wasn't running as fast and was able to make the first turn off and you're waiting for him at the second or third turn off. What do you do?

You have to verify that the other car is not there. Each driver is entitled to his lane. So, if you are in the far lane, you don't ever assume that the other car is not there. Top fuelers have turn around crews that can guide the driver with hand signals. If you don't have a turn around crew, you can move your car to the far edge of the track and when you are almost stopped you can turn your car almost 90-degree and still be in your lane. Then you can look to see if the lane is clear before driving on to the return lane.

After you've moved safely onto the return road, stop at the time slip booth and pickup your time slip. If you're at all serious about your racing, save these. They contain great information on your run and help you tune your car and your technique. For example, the first line is usually your dial-in, which we've already discussed. Next is the reaction time. Then you have your 60-ft. times indicating how hard you left the line; 660-ft. times give you a measure of how quickly your car accelerated in the first half and your E.T. and MPH through the speed traps at the finish line. Your MPH is an average speed measured in the last 66 feet before the finish line.

Use the information on the time slip to evaluate the state of tune you've achieved. If your 60-ft. times are longer than usual you know you lost traction or power on the leave. Keeping track of all the times and atmospheric conditions and your car's combination, gives you an edge over your competition. If the weather changes, you'll have a database to guide you to the quickest combination.

Admittedly computer controlled fuel-injected cars "tune themselves" to a degree. But these cars still respond to small changes. All those small changes influence your run. So if you take good notes and keep track of your E.T.s, you'll find out quickly what works and what doesn't. That alone will put you in front of half of your opponents. You'll just have to be quicker than the other half. That's drag racing.

Most tracks have timing lights at various points along the strip. Typically these points are 60 ft., 660 ft., a speed trap beginning 66 ft. before the end of the quarter mile, and of course the finish line. These times are captured and printed on your time slip.

Here's an abstraction of a typical time slip. If you know how to read it, it'll tell you more than whether you've won or lost. Your 60 ft. times indicate how quickly your car accelerated off the line. E.T. is an indication of the quality of the acceleration over the 1/4-mile, i.e. good launch, no missed shifts, good shift points. MPH indicates the horsepower your car is making.

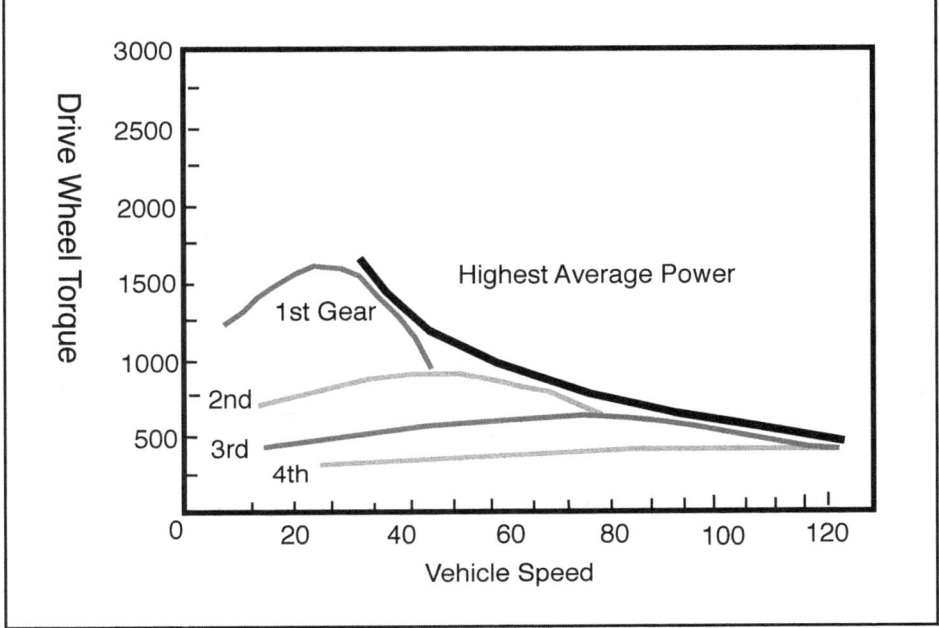

## TIME SLIP ABSTRACTION

| LEFT LANE | | RIGHT LANE | |
|---|---|---|---|
| DIAL-IN: | 14.80 | DIAL-IN: | 14.35 |
| REACTION: | .604 | REACTION: | .889 |
| 60FT: | 2.68 | 60FT: | 2.15 |
| 660FT: | | 660FT | |
| E.T.: | 15.74 | E.T.: | 14.29 |
| MPH: | 88.17 | MPH: | 97.44 |
| OVER/UNDER: | **WIN** | OVER/UNDER: | **FOUL** |

The drive force curve of each gear represents engine torque multiplied by the transmission ratios. The highest average power curve represents the combined torque curves of each gear. That's what you're after when choosing your shift RPM.

### QUARTER QUANDARIES
### Accelerating Rotating Parts Takes Power!

### by Patrick Hale
### Racing Systems Analysis

A lot of talk has been swirling around the racing community about lightweight rotating racecar parts — pistons, rods, cranks, flywheels, clutches, transmissions, driveshafts, ring gears, spools, axles, brake rotors, wheels, tires, etc. Drag racers clearly understand the importance of "static" weight and have several accurate methods to predict the effect of reducing "static" weight on their race car's performance including theoretical and empirical equations, power-speed calculators, and the QUARTER Jr. and QUARTER computer programs.

This article provides the equations and information for any racer who wants to determine the effects of "rotating" weight on the performance of an engine and/or race car.

First, a little background and a brief history lesson. Sir Issac Newton was the first person to correctly state the basic laws governing the motion of objects and to demonstrate their validity way back in 17th century England. Newton's second law forms the basis for most of the analysis in mechanics and can be stated as the familiar

$$F = m * a$$

where F is the force acting on the object, m is the mass of the object, and a is the resultant acceleration of the object. The correctness of this has been verified over and over again by accurate physical measurements in the laboratory, as well as by the empirical data and time slips from thousands of drag racers around the globe.

Just as the mass of an object (or race car) is a measure of its resistance to translational acceleration (i.e., down the dragstrip), the mass moment of inertia of any rotating object is a measure of its resistance to rotational acceleration (i.e., spinning faster). For an object of high inertia, the acceleration will be small for a given force or torque, and conversely, if the inertia is small, the acceleration will be large. For linear motion, the mass is used as a quantitative measure of inertia. For rotating motion, the mass moment of inertia is used as a measure of the resistance.

This inherent resistance to spinning faster that all the rotating parts in our race cars, have is constantly nibbling away at our engine's ability to accelerate our race car down the quarter mile. It also takes considerable horsepower to simply accelerate the engine! (See the Engine Dyno Testing sidebar.) Calculations suggest that up to 20 percent of an engine's power is used to accelerate all the rotating parts of the race car during low gear in high RPM, manual transmission equipped race cars and motorcycles. Other major losses of horsepower in the engine and drivetrain include friction of various types; sliding friction in the rings and bearings; windage losses in the engine, transmission, and differential oil sumps, etc. As racers, we are constantly chipping away at these losses so that more of the raw energy of the fuel we burn can be used to propel the race car ever quicker and faster down the track.

We all know how to determine the mass of our race car and parts. We simply put them on the scales and measure them! Determining mass moments of inertia (denoted by the letter "I") is not so easy. I is a function of the mass of the part and also how far the mass is located from the axis of rotation, actually, the square of the distance from the axis. In most cases, I must be calculated. Mass moments of inertia for simple shapes have been tabulated in engineering handbooks and this is where we'll start our analysis.

All the parts we are concerned with are generally shaped like disks or cylinders. A disk approximates the shape of a balancer and flywheel quite well, whereas a cylinder approximates the thin-wall tubular shape of a driveshaft, wheel rim, and tire tread. For a given weight, a thin-walled cylinder will always have the highest mass moment of inertia because all the mass is concentrated at the outer radius, the farthest distance from the axis of rotation.

The equation used to determine the mass moment of inertia of a thin-walled cylinder can be found in Mark's Mechanical Engineer's Handbook and is

$$I = m * r^2 / 386$$

where m is the weight of the part in lbs., and r is the outer radius of the part in inches (remember, the radius is equal to one-half of the diameter). The units of I when using this equation are in.-lbs.-sec$^2$. The other common units for mass moment of inertia you may see is lbs.-in.$^2$ and can be converted to in.-lbs.-sec$^2$ simply by dividing by the constant 386. For example; 386 lbs.-in.$^2$ = 1.0 in.-lbs.-sec$^2$.

The equation used to determine the mass moment inertia of a solid disk; that is a disk of uniform thickness, made of the same material throughout, without a hole in the center, is very similar to that for the thin-walled cylinder:

$$I = 0.5 * m * r^2 / 386$$

Notice that the only difference between the two equations is the constant 0.5 in front. This makes it very convenient for us to get accurate estimates of I for our parts.

In practice, the mass moment of inertia can never be greater than $1.0 * m\, r^2/386$, because the shape of a thin-walled cylinder has the highest value of I for a given weight. Depending on the actual shape of the part you're working with, the constant can vary between 0.5 and 1.0 determined by how closely the part resembles a flat, constant thickness disk on the one hand, and a thin-walled cylinder on the other! Some examples for this shape constant for various race car parts is included in the Shape Factor table below.

Now that we know how to calculate or estimate the values of I for the various rotating parts in our racecar, the next step is to estimate the amount of horsepower that we lose due to accelerating these parts. For this calculation we use the Inertia HP equation:

**Inertia HP = RPM * N-dot * I /601,848**

The Inertia HP equation can be used to calculate the HP required to accelerate any rotating object about its axis of rotation for a given level. As you can see, the Inertia HP is a linear function of only three variables:

**RPM = instantaneous RPM of the part (RPM)**
**N-dot = rate of acceleration of the part (RPM/sec)**
**I = mass moment of inertia of the part (in.-lbs.-sec$^2$)**

Each of these variables is just as important as the next. Doubling any one of them will double the Inertia HP, just as halving any one of them will reduce the Inertia HP by one-half. If N-dot is zero (i.e. constant RPM) the Inertia HP will always be zero. Inertia HP goes up with higher RPM, higher RPM/sec acceleration rates, and higher mass moments of inertia.

Let's take a look at a sample calculation just to put this all into perspective! Let's use the Inertia HP equation to estimate the power required to accelerate just the crankshaft in my 337 cid SBC and Powerglide equipped Super Comp dragster during low gear. The crankshaft weighs 55 lbs. and has a maximum radius of 3.5 inches. Using a 0.6 Shape Factor from the table below results in I = 1.05 in.-lbs.-sec$^2$. Typical values for the engine in low gear are 6600 rpm and N-dot = 1500 rpm/sec. Using the Inertia HP equation gives;

**Inertia HP = 6600 * 1500 * 1.05 / 601,848 = 17.3 HP**

This calculation tells us that 17.3 of the engine's roughly 450 hp are being used to accelerate the rotating mass of the crankshaft at this point in time on the racetrack. Other rotating parts are also consuming power. In high gear at the same 6600 rpm, the N-dot has dropped back to 400 rpm/sec. Hence, in high gear the HP loss is only 4.6 hp! Quite a difference! Now you should be beginning to realize where to focus your efforts in reducing rotating weight. Focus on those heavy components rotating at the highest RPM, namely the engine stuff and clutch/torque convertor. These are the same parts that also see the largest values of Ndot.

Any part in the drivetrain after a gear reduction in the transmission or rear end rotates much more slowly and has corresponding lower values of Ndot. For instance, let's do a similar calculation to that of the crankshaft above for a group of parts, including the Powerglide 1.82 low gear planetary assembly, output shaft, coupler, and 9-inch Ford pinion gear in my rear-engined S/C dragster. Let's assume that the combined mass moment of inertia for all these parts is the same as that of the crankshaft, i.e. 1.05 in.-lbs.-sec$^2$. (In reality, it's much lower!) At the same point in time that the engine is at 6600 rpm in low gear, these parts are rotating at about 3626 rpm (6600/1.82) and have an N-dot of 824 rpm/sec (1500/1.82). The Inertia HP can be calculated as only 5.2 hp! Parts after the rear gear ratio reduction have even lower RPM and N-dot values, and unless they have very high mass moments of inertia, will absorb little power when accelerated.

Look at the parts with the largest diameters — things like crankshafts, flywheels, clutches, torque convertors, and tires. Weigh each part and estimate the mass moments of inertia for each part using the Shape Factor table. Determine the values of RPM and N-dot from your on-board computer traces (maybe Racepak and others could start calculating these for you!) or use the QUARTER or QUARTER Jr. computer programs. Plug these values into the Inertia HP equation to estimate the power loss for each component. All it takes is the calculator you already use with your weather station to perform the math. You'll be in a much better position to determine if those new lightweight parts are worth the cost!

## SHAPE FACTOR TABLE

| Shape Factor | Typical Parts |
|---|---|
| 0.9 | all tubing, brake drums |
| 0.8 | hollow driveshafts |
| 0.7 | ring gear, wheels, tires |
| 0.6 | crankshaft, flexplate, pressure plate, torque convertor, disk brake rotor |
| 0.5 | balancer, flywheel, clutch disk, all solid shafts |
| 0.4 | camshaft, pinion gear, spool |

### ENGINE DYNO TESTING

Engine dyno testing is currently performed in a number of ways. Some engine builders prefer a step-test, where the engine is stepped from test RPM to test RPM to acquire steady-state, constant RPM data; whereas others perform transient engine testing, accelerating the engine at a controlled rate between 300 and 1000 rpm/sec. and recording data on the fly at the desired test RPMs.

Typically, higher torque and horsepower readings are obtained from the step-test than from the transient test technique. This result is fully explained by the Inertia HP equation. Some of the fuel's raw energy (pressure in the cylinders pushing on the pistons) is being used to accelerate the rotating masses of the engine, flywheel, coupler, mainshaft, and water brake pump during transient engine testing, thereby reducing the measured brake torque and horsepower readings.

Let's use a numerical example for a 500 cid Pro Stock engine to illustrate this point. Assume we are performing a 600 rpm/sec. transient test between 7000 and 9000 rpm. Assume the total mass moment of inertia of the engine, flywheel, coupler, mainshaft, and water brake pump equals 5.0 in.-lbs.-sec$^2$.

Thus, from the Inertia HP equation, the loss in horsepower at 7000 rpm due to accelerating the rotating mass at 600 rpm/sec. would be:

HP@7000
= 7000 * 600 * 5 / 601,848
= 34.9 hp

The loss at 8000 rpm would be different from that at 7000 rpm and is calculated as:

HP@8000
= 8000 * 600 * 5 / 601,848
= 39.9 hp

This explains how performing a 600 rpm/sec transient test would result in horsepower figures 34.9 and 39.9 hp lower than could be achieved using a constant RPM (N-dot = 0) step-test dyno procedure.

So what, who cares? What are you going to use the torque and horsepower figures for anyway? There are many answers to these questions depending on what you are trying to do.

First, if you're doing development work swapping out cams, changing timing, or valve lash, etc. — be consistent! Always use the same test procedure so that you can systematically compare your results. This includes both the acceleration rate (N-dot) and physical test hardware (I).

If you're buying an engine, comparing the results of two engine builders who use different dyno test techniques, do the math, use the Inertia HP equation, get the data back to the same basis, whichever one you like, but do the comparison on an equal basis. Remember, the highest horsepower and torque readings will be obtained from the step-test procedure using the lowest mass moment of inertia test hardware. The lowest reading will come from a 1000 rpm/sec transient test and a heavy flywheel, the difference may be significant! Until you get your calculator out and do the math, you won't know which engine is best.

— *Patrick Hale is the president of Racing Systems Analysis and the author of the popular QUARTER Jr. and ENGINE*

### QUARTER JR. 2.02
### CLUTCH SLIP 3000 RPM NO ROLLOUT

| Time | Distance | MPH | Accel | Gear | RPM |
|---|---|---|---|---|---|
| 0.00 | 0 | 0.0 | 0.36 | 1 | 3,000 |
| .201/0.00 | Rollout | 18.1 | 0.40 | 1 | 3,990 |
| 3.11 | 60 | 26.7 | 0.42 | 1 | 5,860 |
| 3.77 | 88 | 32.1 | 0.32 | 1 | 7,000 |
| 3.97 | 98 | 33.7 | 0.37 | 2 | 4,330 |
| 7.52 | 330 | 54.4 | 0.21 | 2 | 6,770 |
| 7.99 | 369 | 56.6 | 0.20 | 2 | 6,990 |
| 8.19 | 385 | 57.5 | 0.22 | 3 | 4,750 |
| 8.83 | 440 | 60.0 | 0.18 | 3 | 4,920 |
| 11.15 | 660 | 68.8 | 0.17 | 3 | 5,520 |
| 14.28 | 1,000 | 79.2 | 0.14 | 3 | 6,220 |
| 16.91 | 1,320 | 86.4 | 0.11 | 3 | 6,720 |

**ELAPSED TIME: 16.91 SEC    SPEED: 85.8 MPH**

### QUARTER JR. 2.02
### CLUTCH SLIP 4000 RPM NO ROLLOUT

| Time | Distance | MPH | Accel | Gear | RPM |
|---|---|---|---|---|---|
| 0.00 | 0 | 0.0 | 0.47 | 1 | 4,000 |
| .913/0.00 | Rollout | 20.6 | 0.43 | 1 | 4,560 |
| 2.74 | 60 | 28.5 | 0.40 | 1 | 6,250 |
| 3.19 | 80 | 32.0 | 0.32 | 1 | 7,000 |
| 3.39 | 90 | 33.6 | 0.37 | 2 | 4,330 |
| 7.05 | 330 | 54.9 | 0.23 | 2 | 6,820 |
| 7.44 | 362 | 56.6 | 0.19 | 2 | 7,000 |
| 7.64 | 379 | 57.6 | 0.22 | 3 | 4,760 |
| 8.27 | 433 | 60.0 | 0.18 | 3 | 4,930 |
| 10.67 | 660 | 69.0 | 0.18 | 3 | 5,540 |
| 13.79 | 1,000 | 79.4 | 0.14 | 3 | 6,240 |
| 16.41 | 1,320 | 86.5 | 0.11 | 3 | 6,730 |

**ELAPSED TIME: 16.41 SEC    SPEED: 85.9 MPH**

### QUARTER JR. 2.02
### CLUTCH SLIP 5000 RPM NO ROLLOUT

| Time | Distance | MPH | Accel | Gear | RPM |
|---|---|---|---|---|---|
| 0.00 | 0 | 0.0 | 0.53 | 1 | 5,000 |
| .811/0.00 | Rollout | 22.2 | 0.54 | 1 | 5,000 |
| 2.60 | 60 | 29.5 | 0.38 | 1 | 6,480 |
| 2.92 | 74 | 31.9 | 0.32 | 1 | 7,000 |
| 3.12 | 84 | 33.6 | 0.37 | 2 | 4,330 |
| 6.85 | 330 | 55.2 | 0.22 | 2 | 6,860 |
| 7.15 | 355 | 56.5 | 0.19 | 2 | 7,000 |
| 7.36 | 372 | 57.5 | 0.22 | 3 | 4,760 |
| 8.00 | 427 | 60.0 | 0.18 | 3 | 4,940 |
| 10.45 | 660 | 69.2 | 0.17 | 3 | 5,560 |
| 13.56 | 1,000 | 79.5 | 0.14 | 3 | 6,260 |
| 16.19 | 1,320 | 86.5 | 0.11 | 3 | 6,740 |

**ELAPSED TIME: 16.19 SEC    SPEED: 85.9 MPH**

### QUARTER JR. 2.02
### CLUTCH SLIP 6000 RPM NO ROLLOUT

| Time | Distance | MPH | Accel | Gear | RPM |
|---|---|---|---|---|---|
| 0.00 | 0 | 0.0 | 0.50 | 1 | 6,000 |
| .869/0.00 | Rollout | 21.5 | 0.51 | 1 | 6,000 |
| 2.66 | 60 | 29.6 | 0.37 | 1 | 6,520 |
| 2.96 | 74 | 31.9 | 0.32 | 1 | 7,000 |
| 3.16 | 83 | 33.6 | 0.37 | 2 | 4,330 |
| 6.90 | 330 | 55.2 | 0.22 | 2 | 6,870 |
| 7.15 | 350 | 56.2 | 0.19 | 2 | 7,000 |
| 7.35 | 367 | 57.2 | 0.22 | 3 | 4,750 |
| 8.07 | 429 | 60.0 | 0.18 | 3 | 4,940 |
| 10.51 | 660 | 69.2 | 0.17 | 3 | 5,570 |
| 13.62 | 1,000 | 79.5 | 0.14 | 3 | 6,260 |
| 16.25 | 1,320 | 86.5 | 0.11 | 3 | 6,750 |

**ELAPSED TIME: 16.25 SEC    SPEED: 85.9 MPH**

*Jr. computer programs for race car and engine performance analysis. He holds a Master's degree in Mechanical Engineering from Arizona State University. Hale can be contacted by writing to RSA, P.O. Box 7676, Phoenix, AZ 85011 or by calling (602) 241-1301.*

## QUARTER JR. SIMULATIONS SHOWING THE EFFECTS OF ENGINE/TRANSMISSION ROTATIONAL INERTIA LOSSES ON DRAG STRIP PERFORMANCE

As Pat Hale explained in detail above, most rotational inertia losses come from the parts that spin real fast and accelerate real fast. Most of these components are in the engine and transmission which are accelerated most quickly in first and second gears. Meaning that your car will accelerate less quickly as more of the engine's power is used to accelerate itself and driveline components like a flywheel and pressure plate. (Just to remind you an automatic transmission torque converter works to reduce low gear rotational inertia power losses, a big advantage for drag racers.) To demonstrate the effects of rotational inertia on quarter mile performance as well as demonstrating a driving tactic that reduces the effects of rotational inertia losses, we offer the above simulations.

We plugged in the specs for a '96 Integra LS with manual trans. Quarter Jr. requires the transmission gear ratios and final drive ratio, peak power at the RPM that occurs, the weight and frontal area of the car, tire diameter and tread width, whether the car has a clutch or converter, and the stall speed of the converter or the clutch slip during launch.

The only input we changed was the slip RPM. The rollout is 0 to better simulate the performance times found in magazine tests and the traction factor was set at the worst possible to simulate FWD. As you can see, if you pick your leave RPM right and slip the clutch, there's power, speed, and quicker E.T.s. That's assuming your tires have enough traction to make it worth slipping the clutch in the first place. If you don't, it may be quicker just to side-step the clutch at your launch RPM. You'll have to experiment to find out for sure.

## RPS PERFORMANCE PRODUCTS SUPER LIGHT-WEIGHT, HIGH-TECH CLUTCH

Controlling your clutch with the accuracy needed to achieve the performance gains talked about above is almost, if not all together, impossible. That's not to say you shouldn't try finessing your car off the line. You should.

However, be aware that this technique forces the clutch and pressure plate to work extraordinarily hard. Plus, the heat and energy generated by this technique only intensifies with greater traction at the drive wheels.

That's one of the reasons Rob Smith at RPS Performance Products spent his summer vacation mixing up and testing some really very nasty composite concoctions. He wanted to build his version of the ultimate clutch. A clutch that could take the abuse of side-step launching in second gear and not chatter, vibrate or fade. His clutch would also help upshift and downshift at high RPM because of its ultralight weight.

So easy to say; so hard to make happen. However, Rob is about the most focused mad-scientist on the import performance scene today and through sheer force of will it seems he formulated a friction material that performed to his high standards. We show you an early version of the clutch that, at press-time, is supposed to be installed in the first front drive car to score and back up a 9-second E.T. In fact, the clutch is an essential part of the strategy to put the car into the 9s.

We mentioned that Rob wanted to skip first gear. Why? Mostly because shifting takes time, but also because first gear amplifies the power at the wheel far above what you can hook to the track anyway, so it's wasteful. So if he can start the run in second gear, relying on the engine's torque multiplied through second gear and clutch slip to get the car moving, he saves the time of one shift, plus he saves one time of upsetting the chassis, spinning the wheels which adds to the time lost on the physical act of shifting.

Because the clutch is lighter, it also helps decrease the time between shifts and reduces the tendency of grinding gears at up/down shift. The reason a light-weight clutch helps in these areas comes directly from how your gear synchronizers work.

Essentially the synchronizer uses friction to grab the gear that you are shifting to and speed it up or slow it down to match the output shaft speed. When you disengage the clutch, what you're doing is releasing the pressure on the clutch disc that is sandwiched between the pressure plate and flywheel. But the clutch is still there with its rotational inertia, spinning at 7500 rpm if you shift at red line. Well the synchros have to overcome that inertia to match gear set speeds. So a lighter clutch, which has less inertia lets the synchros do their job a little easier and faster, which in turn lets you shift a little easier and faster.

Faster shifts plus more torque capacity. That's exactly what you want in a clutch.

**Rob Smith of RPS Performance Products, Inc. designed his firm's new composite clutch, "The Carbon Claw" to be one of the lightest weight units on the market yet give the highest torque capacity and fastest recovery rates. A racing clutch needs to stand up to intense heat while maintaining its torque capacity. RPS developed the Carbon Claw using a clutch dyno to measure each friction material's torque capacity at ultra high temperatures.**

# Honda Builder's HANDBOOK Vol. II
## CURVE CARVING ESSENTIALS

High Performance driving is really the art of managing weight transfer and thereby the amount of and distribution of traction at the wheels. The amount and distribution of traction at the wheels determines how the car handles. In other words, how the car responds, i.e. changes direction or acceleration, to driver steering, braking, and acceleration inputs. The ability to make the proper driving inputs to make the car go where you want it to, even when the car is near skidding and sliding, is what separates good drivers from average ones.

While many drivers learn how to drive aggressively, truly great drivers understand the finer reasoning behind the behavior of their cars. In short, that means understanding the physics behind your car's handling, or lack thereof.

In addition to developing your driving skills, this knowledge helps you decide what equipment to buy and install on your car and how to tune it so it does what you intend. Such is the goal of the present section.

Driving a car to its performance limits is done by controlling weight transfer using throttle, brakes, and steering. Applying the brakes shifts weight to the front of a car and can induce oversteer. (See diagrams illustrating oversteer, understeer, and neutral steer, and steady state cornering acceleration.) Likewise, accelerating shifts weight to the rear, inducing understeer. Cornering shifts weight to the opposite side, unloading the inside tires, causing a net loss of traction that limits the steady state of cornering acceleration.

What is meant by weight transfer? It is essentially the change in the distribution of the amount of weight that is on each of your four tires. The reason the distribution of weight can change is because the center of gravity (cg) of your car is above the road and the tractive forces of the tire on the road are at ground level. Your car's cg is a point that, were it suspended by a cable attached to the cg, it would balance perfectly. What's more, it would spin in any direction around the cg.

You can consider the distance from the road surface to the cg as a "lever arm" that inertia, acting on the cg of the car, uses to generate a torque or a twisting force. With a twisting force, known as a couple, the direction of that force is in opposite direction on each side of the "circle." See Figure 2.2. For example, if torque is generated in a counter-clockwise direction, the force will take an upward direction at 3 o'clock and a downward direction at 9 o'clock. The effects of weight transfer are proportional to the "lever arm" i.e., the height of the cg above the road. A car with a lower cg, can develop more cornering force because it limits weight transfer compared to a car with a higher cg. This is true, providing the tires maintain proper contact with the road. A lack of suspension travel or poor geometry can lose more adhesion than lowering your cg can gain.

What is at work here are the fundamental physical laws that apply to all large things in the universe, cars included. Sir Isaac Newton was first to put these observed behaviors of things

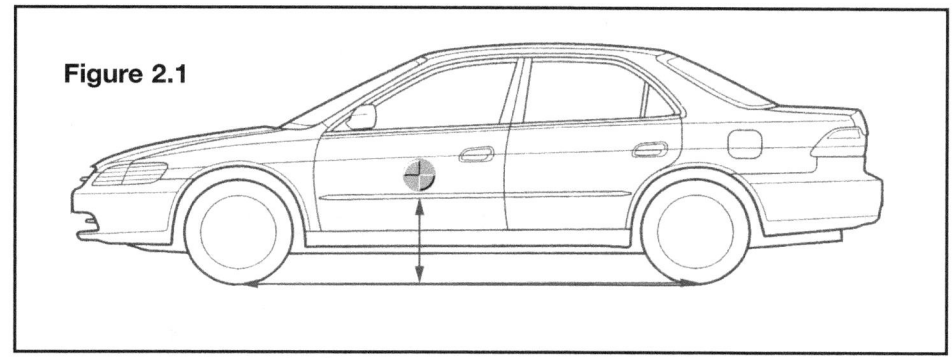

Figure 2.1

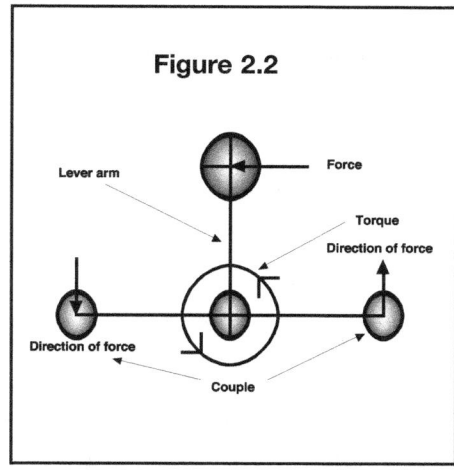

Figure 2.2

The mechanism of weight transfer is the mass of your car acting through the center of gravity (cg). The cg is above the ground and tractive forces are at ground level. This gives rise to a lever arm effect that moves weight from corner to corner and end to end depending on the direction of the tractive force. Roll stiffness (provided primarily by springs and bars) affects the rate or speed at which weight is transferred. In other words, stiffer springs and anti-sway bars do not change the amount of weight transferred. They simply get it there quicker so the car responds quicker in proportion to the stiffness of the springs and bars.

Torque couple and how it moves force, or, as you measure force at the wheel weight.

with mass in a written formula. His first Law states that an object at rest or in straight-line motion at a constant speed, will keep such rest or motion until acted on by an external force. The only reason a car will not coast forever is that the external force of friction, from the tires, air resistance, and driveline, gradually slows the car down. The tendency of your car to keep moving is its inertia, and this tendency is focused at the cg.

Newton's second Law describes the relationship between objects and the application of force. When a force is applied to your Honda, the change in motion is proportional to the force divided by the mass of the car. This Law is expressed by the famous equation $F = ma$, where F is a force, m is the mass of the car, and a is the acceleration, or change in motion, of the car. Newton's second Law explains why the world's quickest cars are powerful and lightweight. A bigger force, i.e. more torque acting on less mass such as vehicle weight, gives you more acceleration.

Newton's third Law says that every force acting on your car from another object, such as the road, is matched by an equal and opposite force on the object by the car. For example, braking causes the tires to push forward against the road with the road pushing back with equal force. As long as the tires stay on the car *and in contact with the road*, the road pushing back slows the car down. The weight transfer during braking comes about from the forces at the road surface because they are acting at a distance from the cg imparting a torque, and therefore force lifts the rear of the car as it pushes the front of the car down.

The additional force at the front can be measured, or more appropriately calculated, in pounds with this formula:

$$\text{Wt. Transfer} = \frac{\text{Vehicle Wt.} \times \text{cg height}}{\text{Wheel base}} \times g$$

Figure 2.3 diagrams the direction and magnitude of the forces as well as completing the algebra for a 3000 lb. Honda Accord braking at one full g or 32 feet per second per second. With the Accord's wheel base and an assumed cg height of 22 inches, the formula calculates that 617.39 lbs. of force will move from the rear of the car to the front during a full g deceleration. Figure 2.4 illustrates lateral weight transfer at one g lateral acceleration, so we just substitute track width for wheel base in the formula. While Figure 2.4 shows the total weight transfer per side, Figure 2.5 shows a top view to illustrate the distribution of the weight transfer between the front and rear tires. Your choice in springs, shocks, and antisway bar rates are the items that influence transferred weight

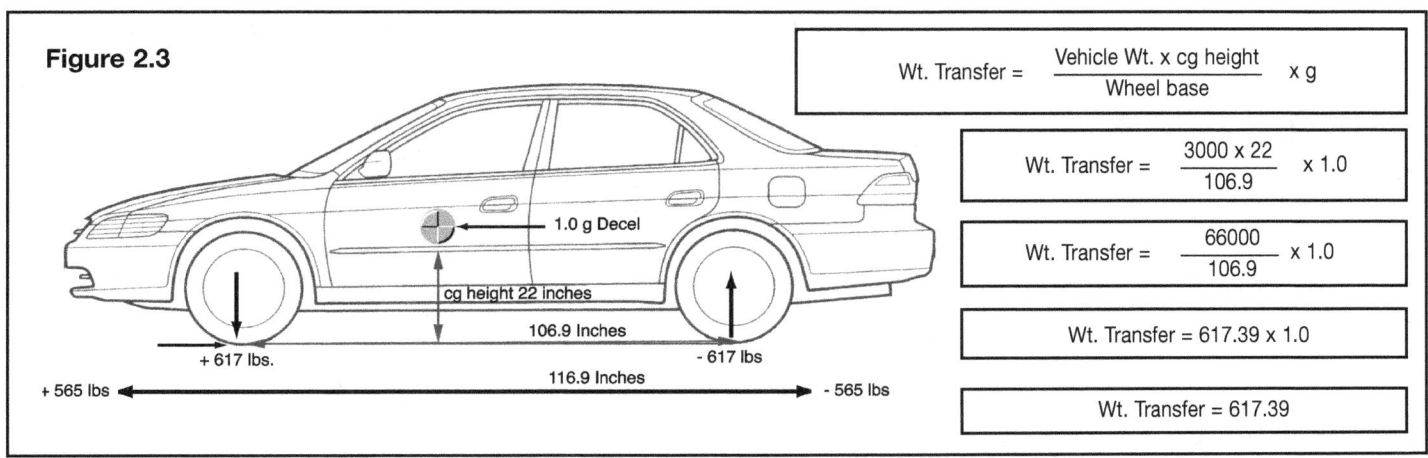

Figure 2.3

$$\text{Wt. Transfer} = \frac{\text{Vehicle Wt.} \times \text{cg height}}{\text{Wheel base}} \times g$$

$$\text{Wt. Transfer} = \frac{3000 \times 22}{106.9} \times 1.0$$

$$\text{Wt. Transfer} = \frac{66000}{106.9} \times 1.0$$

$$\text{Wt. Transfer} = 617.39 \times 1.0$$

$$\text{Wt. Transfer} = 617.39$$

**Breaking takes weight off the rear wheels and moves it to the front wheels.**

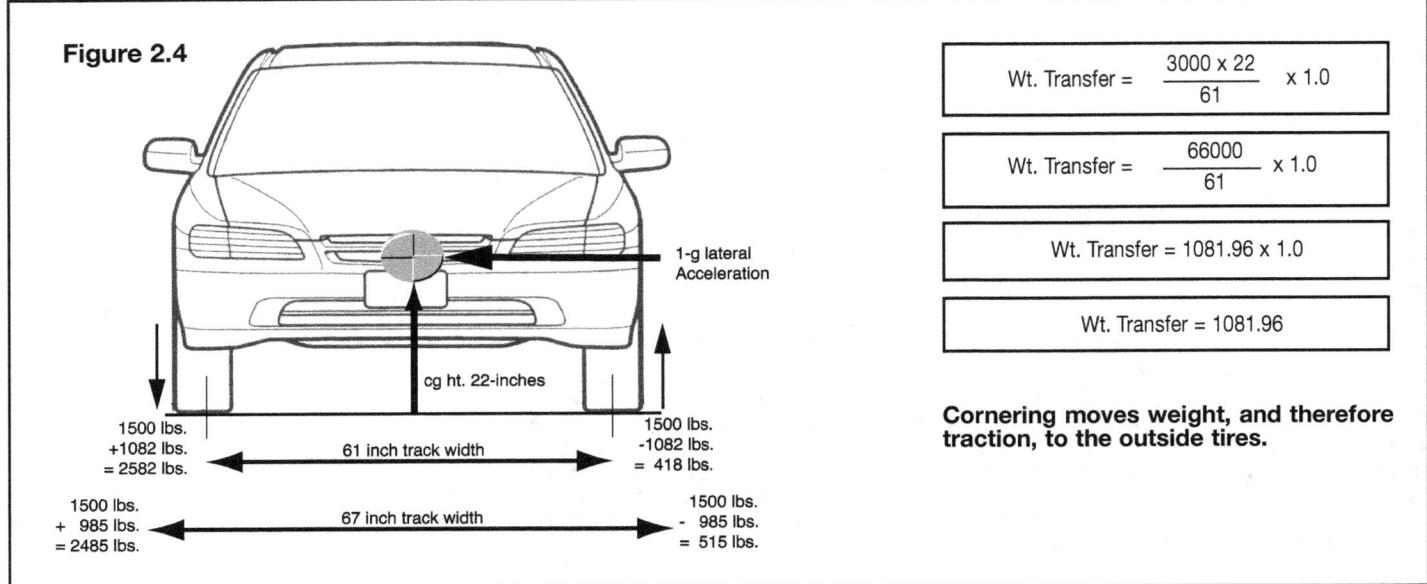

Figure 2.4

$$\text{Wt. Transfer} = \frac{3000 \times 22}{61} \times 1.0$$

$$\text{Wt. Transfer} = \frac{66000}{61} \times 1.0$$

$$\text{Wt. Transfer} = 1081.96 \times 1.0$$

$$\text{Wt. Transfer} = 1081.96$$

**Cornering moves weight, and therefore traction, to the outside tires.**

distribution, and therefore the handling of your vehicle.

The model presented is very simple. We intentionally left out factors such as roll center height, roll stiffness, spring rates, and such. We just want you to get the idea of the forces and principles behind weight transfer. In the real world a car with 61 inches of track with a cg height at 22 inches isn't likely to pull one g on the skid pad. It could, but it would require very wide and sticky racing tires.

### TIRES AND HOW THEY WORK

Why is it so difficult for our 61-inch-tracked car to pull one g lateral acceleration? To answer those questions, let's do a few experiments. If you don't have a spare wheel and tire around, get them off your car; or you can do the experiments with a heavy box or a shoe filled with lead shot. The values you get won't apply to tires, although the principles will.

Find the weight of the tire and wheel assembly. You can use a bathroom scale for this. Let's assume your combo weighs 50 pounds. Now put the wheel on the ground or on a table and push sideways against the tire until it slides. Be sure to push low near where the tire touches the ground. At this point you don't know how hard you had to push to get the tire (or whatever you rigged) to slide. But you can find out by putting the bathroom scale between your hand and the tire when you push. This isn't the most accurate method of measuring the force you needed to make the tire slide, still it gets us close. An average street performance radial that weights 50 lbs. should require around 70 to 80 lbs. of force on a dry street to get it to slide. On a wet street that'll drop down to 45 to 55 lbs. depending on the tire compound and inflation.

What this means is that on a dry road supporting only 50 lbs., the tire can generate 80 lbs. of sideways force. This tire, then can generate 1.6 g of lateral resistance before sliding because it holds 1.6 times it's weight in sideways force. We get our 1.6 figure by dividing the weight of the tire by the amount of traction, in this case it's resistance to sliding sideways measured in pounds. (This is also how we get what is called the coefficient of friction, which we'll discuss later in the chapter.) On a wet road at 55 lbs., that figure drops to 1.1 g. Truly phenomenal figures, really. This tire on a dry surface holds 1.6 times its weight from sliding sideways and just over its own weight in the wet. This is precisely what "grip" is all about. Grip is the tire's resistance to sliding.

A second experiment demonstrates why lightweight cars corner harder than heavy cars. This experiment involves weighing down your tire with ballast of some sort. We fastened 50 pounds to the wheel for a total weight of 100 pounds. With the additional weight it took 140 pounds of force to slide the tire sideways, giving us a potential of 1.4 g of lateral acceleration. This is the fundamental Law of adhesion: the force required to slide a tire is proportional to the weight supported by, or the vertical force on the tire. This is why, when your tire is weighed down with your car, you can't push hard enough to slide it sideways. The force required to slide a tire is its adhesive limit. You'll also hear the

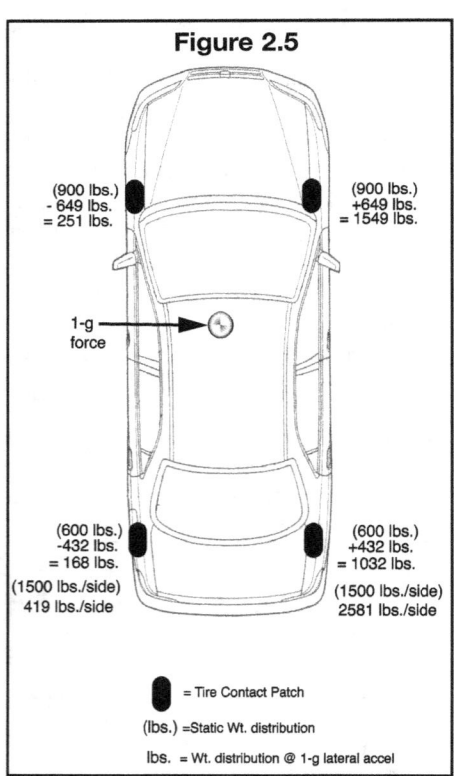

Figure 2.5

**Weight distribution change at 1-g lateral acceleration assuming a 60/40 front to rear static weight distribution and equal roll stiffness front to rear with a 61-inch track and 22-inch cg height.**

word "stiction," which is slang from combining "stick" and "friction."

But the meat of this experiment, the one that influences how much traction or grip a car has to work with is this: While the total force required to slide the tire increased with the vertical load, the coefficient of traction (or friction) declined. This means that even though the tire is generating more force, that force is proportionally less to the increasing vertical load or weight. This observation explains why you have a net loss of traction when braking, cornering, as well as explaining why acceleration is limited by the amount of weight transfer.

The coefficient of friction is found by dividing the traction force by the vertical load on the tire. Hence we get the formula cf = T/W; where T is the force with which the tire resists sliding, cf is the coefficient of static friction or coefficient of adhesion and W is the weight or vertical load on the tire contact patch. Both T and W have the units of force measured in pounds (weight is the force of gravity), meaning that "cf" is just a number, a proportionality constant. This equation states that the sideways force a tire can withstand before sliding is less than or equal to the ratio of vertical load to traction times the coefficient factor.

It's convenient to talk about the sideways or lateral acceleration of a car. Ignoring the net loss of grip from weight transfer, we can easily convert the force of grip phenomenon into lateral acceleration in g by dividing the tractive force of the tires by the weight of the car. So assuming a 3000 pound car with equal weight distribution and no weight transfer (impossible) with a cf of .9, we should see a maximum cornering force during steady state cornering of 2700 pounds.

**Outside tires 1500 lbs. x .9 = 1350**
**Inside tires 1500 lbs. x .9 = 1350**
                              **2700 lbs.**

We can state the pounds of force as g lateral acceleration by dividing the weight of the vehicle by the cornering force generated: 2700/3000 = .9 g.

The coefficient of friction is not exactly constant. Many effects come into play when driving that reduce the traction of a super sticky high performance tire to somewhere around .9 or so. Some of these effects are tire deflection, suspension movement, and roll stiffness of the front and rear suspension, temperature, inflation pressure, road surface, and on and on. Still the proportionality law holds reasonably true, though its effect on traction may seem dyslexic. For example, continuing with our 3000 pound car, this time with weight transfer and resultant changes in cf:

**Outside tires**
**2000 lbs. x .85 = 1700**
**Inside tires**
**1000 lbs. x .92 = 920**
                 **= 2620 lbs.**
**Again expressed as a force of g:**
**2620/3000 = .87 g**

This is why you have a net loss in traction when you are cornering. And why when cornering at the limit, i.e., at the adhesive limit of the tires, any weight transfer causes the unloaded tires to start sliding. This proportionality law is also why a rear wheel drive drag racing car doesn't achieve maximum acceleration unless all of the weight of the car is put on the rear wheels. And finally, this Law is why front drive cars have a serious disadvantage compared with cars with rear wheel, or all wheel drive for that matter.

A front drive car's drive tires have a lot of weight on them. Typical weight distribution is approximately 60/40, which is good for traction on the start, considering weight transfers to the rear, but on braking much more weight transfers forward. So essentially a front drive car's drive tires have to supply traction for accelerating out of the turn and for braking into the turn. It's easy to understand why they can get overheated and lose some grip or wear out quickly.

Back to the subject of reaching and even surpassing the adhesive limit of a tire. The transition should be very smooth in a well-designed tire. This is exactly what racers mean when referring to a "forgiving" tire. Such a tire gives the driver time to correct. Forgiving tires are much easier to control and much more fun to drive by the seat of your pants. "Driving by the seat of your pants" means sensing the slight

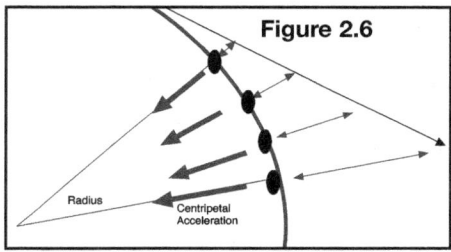

**The force your tires generate that bends the naturally straight path of your car into a circular path is known as centripetal force.**

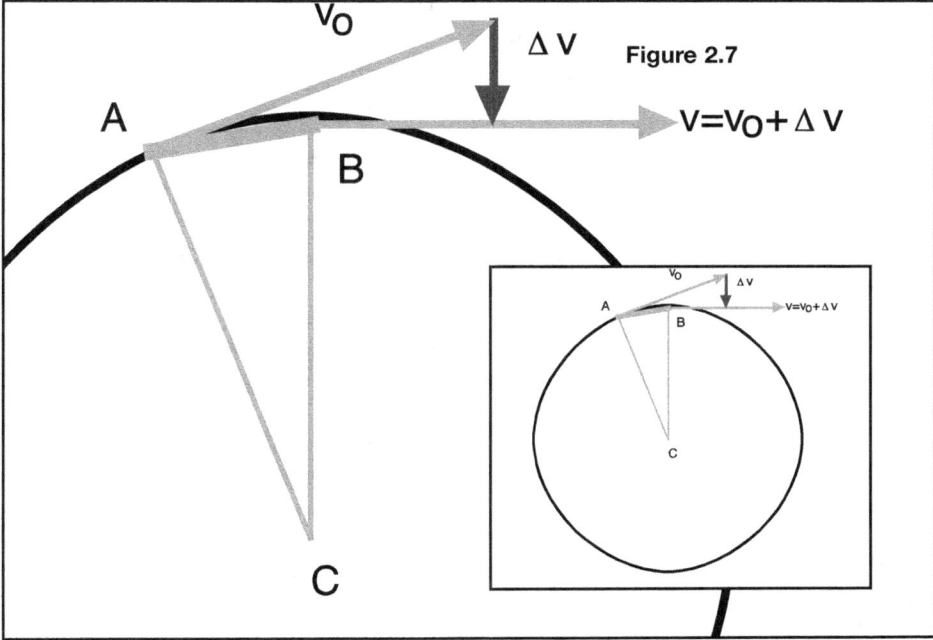

**As you drive forward on a circular path, you are also driving sideways. This sideways movement towards the the center of the circle generates centripetal force.**

*Honda Builder's Handbook Vol. 2* **23**

changes in cornering, braking, and acceleration forces that signal that one or more tires are about to slide. You can sense these changes literally in your seat, but you can also feel changes in steering resistance and in the sounds the tires make. The steering wheel feels lighter as you near and pass the limit; and the tires begin to squeal when nearing the limit which turns to a moan almost when you're at or slightly past maximum traction.

In sum then, the fundamental relationship between driver inputs and vehicle response are that accelerating gives the front tires less stiction and the rear tires more, that braking gives the front tire more stiction and the rear tires less, and that cornering gives the inside tires less stiction and the outside tires more. These facts are due to the combination of weight transfer and the grip phenomenon. Which means that to drive a road/slalom course fast, means to drive smoothly, translating your awareness of the effects of weight transfer into gentle control inputs that always keep the appropriate tires at max traction at the right times.

## STEERING WITH WEIGHT TRANSFER

The more load there is on a tire, the more cornering force it can generate even though its grip coefficient goes down.

A rear-wheel-drive on a dry sticky track, tends to create understeer. With a dry, sticky track, acceleration will tend to cause a higher level of load transfer making the tires grip better. This effect is greater than the loss of cornering due to the friction circle effect, especially in a lower horsepower vehicle. The result will tend to be more understeer.

Rear-wheel-drive on a wet, slippery track, tends to create oversteer. As you may know, accelerating on a slippery surface tends to cause the rear tires to slip, in this case resulting in oversteer. There will be very little load transfer to create understeer.

Note that our examples thus far show the same rear-wheel-drive car exhibiting totally different handling characteristics. On a dry track, we get understeer; in the wet, oversteer.

## FRONT-WHEEL-DRIVE

A car with front-wheel-drive racing on a dry, sticky track, tends to create understeer. With front-drive, the friction circle effect results in a loss of cornering in the front and the weight transfer results in an increase in cornering in the back. Both create understeer.

Front-wheel-drive on a wet, slippery track, tends to create understeer. It is probably not surprising to those of you who drive front-wheel-drive vehicles that wet and slippery conditions create understeer in this instance. The friction circle is predominant, generally resulting in more understeer than in the dry. The only way to get most front-wheel-drive vehicles to oversteer is to lift off the throttle or brake while cornering. To get a better feel for what this means, let's look at the effect of lifting during cornering.

With rear-wheel-drive, lifting off the throttle increases the cornering force at the rear by taking away the accelerating force creating understeer. At the same time, it increases the cornering on the front by transferring weight from the rear to the front. This creates oversteer. The two tend to cancel each other out and the result is that the vehicle attitude does not change much.

With front-wheel drive, lifting off the throttle increases the cornering force of the front tire by taking away the accelerating force and transferring weight to the front. Both actions result in oversteer.

## CORNERING FORCE. WHAT IS IT REALLY? AND HOW TO USE IT FOR THE QUICKEST LAP TIME

So how does this relate to driving through a series of turns quickly? Well the answer to that is complicated but we'll do our best to keep it simple.

What we're concerned with here are the forces causing your car to follow a circular path and how to manage them in order to drive as fast as our car is able. The forces that bend your car's travel along an arc have to act along the radius of the circle and cause your car to have a radial acceleration. In car-talk, it is accelerating toward the center of the circle. This doesn't sound accurate, does it? Well, it really is. Here's why.

To paraphrase Newton's First Law of Motion to meet our needs here, an object will travel in a straight line unless forced to do otherwise. So when your car is traveling around a turn, the tires are forcing it off its natural straight line path. The force your tires generate that bend the naturally straight path of your car into a circular path is known as the centripetal force. This is a force that pulls your car toward the center of the circular path, therefore it acts along the radius of the circle. (See figure 2.6)

Because we have a force being generated, we know, by using Newton's Second Law of Motion $F = ma$, which states that force equals mass times acceleration, that we have a mass (the car) that is accelerating. If you're driving in a circle, or any portion of a circle, you are accelerating toward the center, even if you maintain a constant speed.

This is exactly what you try to do on a skid pad. Inside your car, you feel the natural inertial tendency to continue moving in a straight line. You receive a centripetal force from the car through the seat and the belts. If you don't have a proper set of harnesses, you'll find yourself bracing against the door and holding too tight to the controls to get enough centripetal force to go in a circle with the car.

Figure 2.7 shows a vector diagram illustrating the reasoning that describes the force. Here you can see that as you drive forward on a circular path, you are also driving sideways relative to the naturally straight path you and your car would otherwise take in a world without friction. This sideways movement, toward the center of the circle is what causes, well actually is the acceleration that you feel as centripetal force.

As formal as we can get, the reasoning goes something like this. In figure 2.7 centripetal-2, we show the instantaneous velocity of two points, A and B on the triangle ABC. The distance traveled on the circumference of the circle A to B is where the acceleration occurred. We can write it as $X/R$. Further, we show the velocity of these two points as $V_o$ and V; with V equal to the sum of $V_o$ plus "delta" V, the change of velocity. We can write it $V_o / V$. These two terms are equivalent because we are describing a change in distance and a change in velocity of one object and therefore we can express it so:

$$\frac{x}{r} = \frac{V_o}{V}$$

Now the definition of acceleration is a change in velocity in time, or V = acceleration multiplied by time. Therefore this term can be replaced with *at*. During the time *t* our car moved from A to B a distance *x* which is equal to velocity multiplied by the amount of time or $x = v t$. Because we are dealing with small distances and amounts of time we can substitute the equivalent terms to get:

$$\frac{vt}{r} = \frac{at}{v}$$

We simplify this expression by cancelling *t* and transposing *v* and we arrive at the equation for centripetal acceleration or :

$$a = \frac{v^2}{r}$$

This equation simply says quantitatively that the acceleration (and so the force) needed to maintain a circular line increases with the velocity of the object on the arc and it increases as the radius gets smaller.

The equation for centripetal force comes directly from Newton's Second Law, giving us this equation:

$$F = M \frac{v^2}{r}$$

What is not obvious, but is of utmost importance to driving as fast as possible through a turn is, that *the necessary acceleration increases at the square of the velocity*. This means that the centripetal force your tires must give you for you to make it through a turn is highly sensitive to your speed. This explains why when you brake for a turn, your goal is to slow precisely to your car's maximum cornering speed to enter the turn. It also explains the wisdom of the racing cliche "slow in; fast out" of the turn.

One more aspect of driving with speed and precision that this equation explains is the need to use the whole road. That is to begin the turn from outside of the track and arc inside; then let it drift out to the edge as you exit. The reason is because the squared velocity is related by the radius, meaning the larger the radius, the faster you can go for a given amount of cornering force.

We've included a chart that shows the impact of speed and the radius of the turn, just to give you an idea of how important it is to not only stay on the road but drive through the turn as quickly as possible.

Now you're ready to know the secret to quick lap times. Unequivo-cally, the fastest way through a corner and to have the highest exit speed, is to be just over the adhesive limit of your tires near the exit. In other words, a controlled drift to the outside edge of the track. The controlled part is because you have to be pointed in the right direction so when the car slides to the exit you'll be traveling directly on the optimal racing line at the exit when the tires hook up again. If you properly time when you smoothly add throttle during this maneuver, you'll achieve the fastest exit speed and so the fastest and quickest time through the straight to the next turn where you repeat the maneuver. It sounds easy, but it is extraordinarily difficult to do with any regularity. But when you get it, it feels right and your lap times will show it.

## FIGURE IT OUT

In case your physics are a little rusty, here are three extremely useful equations. The first shows you how to get your lateral acceleration in g, if you know the radius of the turn or skid pad and the amount of time spent at that radius. The most common use of this equation is to figure g from a recorded E.T. of one lap around the skid pad. The value assumes a 100 ft. radius (200 ft. diameter) skid pad or corner.

The next equation shows you how to find MPH from a g level around a turn provided you know the radius. If you know the radius of the turn and the g you're pulling in it, you'll know if you're at the limit or overdriving your tires. Critical info with which to refine your technique or suspension tune.

**Lateral g from radius and time**

$$g = 1.227 \cdot r / t^2$$
$$g = 1.227 \cdot 100 \text{ft} / 11.5 \text{ sec}^2$$
$$g = 1.227 \cdot 100 \text{ft} / 132.25$$
$$g = 1.227 / 132.25$$
$$g = 0.927$$

This last equation shows you how to find the force required to achieve specific levels of lateral acceleration. You can use this to figure out how hard your tires have to work to make this happen. The trick to this is keeping your units of measure consistent. We use 1.4667 to convert MPH to ft./sec.; and 32.1 to convert weight to mass.

$$MPH = \sqrt{15 \cdot r \cdot g}$$
$$MPH = \sqrt{15 \cdot 100\text{ft} \cdot .927 \, g}$$
$$MPH = \sqrt{1500 \cdot .927}$$
$$MPH = \sqrt{1390.5}$$
$$MPH = \sqrt{37.28}$$

## THE FRICTION CIRCLE

The last concept we'll present is the friction circle. Understanding the friction circle and how it relates to your car's performance potential is fundamental to learning how to drive at the limit and click-off consistent lap times.

The limit of a car's forward accelerative performance is obvious. When its drive wheels spin, the tires can't put any more power to the ground, thus limiting acceleration. The limit in braking is also obvious. When the tires start sliding and lose their grip, they don't generate peak traction. It's the same with cornering.

Car magazines tend to list steady-state cornering power from a skid pad test as a decimal fraction of g, for example, 0.86 g. Steady state cornering is reaching the limit of adhesion of the tires at a steady speed while

$$F = ma$$

$$F = m \frac{V^2}{r}$$

$$F = 3000 \text{ lbs} / 32.1 \cdot \frac{(37.28 \cdot 1.4667)^2}{100 \text{ ft radius}}$$

$$F = 93.45 \text{ lbs} \cdot \frac{2989.75 \text{ ft} / \text{sec}^2}{100 \text{ ft radius}}$$

$$F = 93.45 \text{ lbs} \cdot 29.90 / \text{sec}^2$$

$$F = 2794.16 \text{ ft-lbs} / \text{sec}^2$$

following the arc of a circle. All the tires have to do is generate centripetal force. They aren't called upon to increase forward speed or slow the car. So cornering limits are a snapshot of one aspect of what we call handling.

Don't get the wrong idea — it is good to know the steady-state cornering limits of your car, but cars are not limited to such simple maneuvers. As we said above, cars can turn and brake at the same time, and turn and accelerate at the same time. And you can combine these accelerative demands with a little turning and a lot of braking, or a lot of turning and a little braking. But no matter how you combine these forces, you can be sure that each will have a limit: the limit of the tires and the suspension tuning managing the tires' friction, or grip.

The problem is how to define these limits. The Society of Automotive Engineers has established a convention for describing them. What they do is start with an X-Y axis. The vertical Y axis represents longitudinal acceleration i.e., up is forward acceleration; down deceleration or, in mathematical terms, negative acceleration. The horizontal X axis represents acceleration in pure cornering. The right side of the X axis represents the centripetal acceleration you'd feel when turning to the right, and the left side represents centripetal acceleration to the left.

If you measured your car's limit of adhesion in every possible combination of turning and braking, and turning and accelerating, the plot of those limits on an X-Y axis, the data points would tend to form a circle. That's a friction circle.

But why a circle? The reason is the way tires generate friction. You see they have a finite amount of friction. They only generate so much acceleration in any one direction. If you ask the tire to generate force in two directions at once, you have to divide the available friction to accomplish that. In simple terms, if you are cornering at the limit, all the tire's traction is used to generate centripetal acceleration toward the center of the arc you're traveling. If you try to either brake or accelerate, you are asking the tires for more traction than they have and they begin to slide. Once sliding they lose traction quickly and you'll probably spin off course.

The friction circle shows you the handling envelope of your car. It gives you the shape of the limits of your car's tires on a specific surface within a certain range of speed and accelerations. If you change these variables, the friction circle will change. The variables that have largest effect are the tire's rubber compound and design and the road surface. A racing tire has much more grip than an economy street tire and surely you've noticed a substantial reduction of traction in the rain.

For a particular car's suspension tune and tire combination on a particular surface, the friction circle tells you the fastest way through a series of turns or around a race track. Most credit Mark Donahue, the first racer to prove that staying at the limit of a car's handling envelope yielded the quickest lap times.

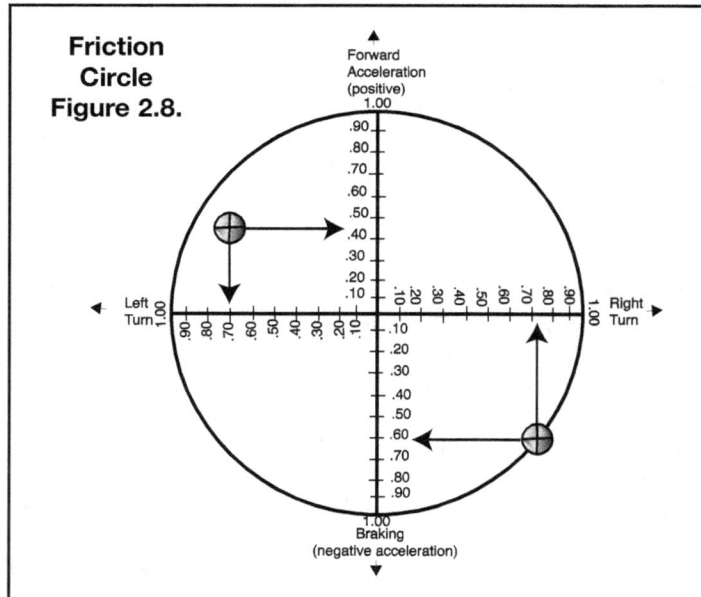

A friction circle plot shows you the magnitude of acceleration in g for all possible combinations of braking, accelerating, and cornering. The indicator in the lower right tells us that the car is generating just over .6 g braking acceleration and just over .7 g of centripetal acceleration to the right.

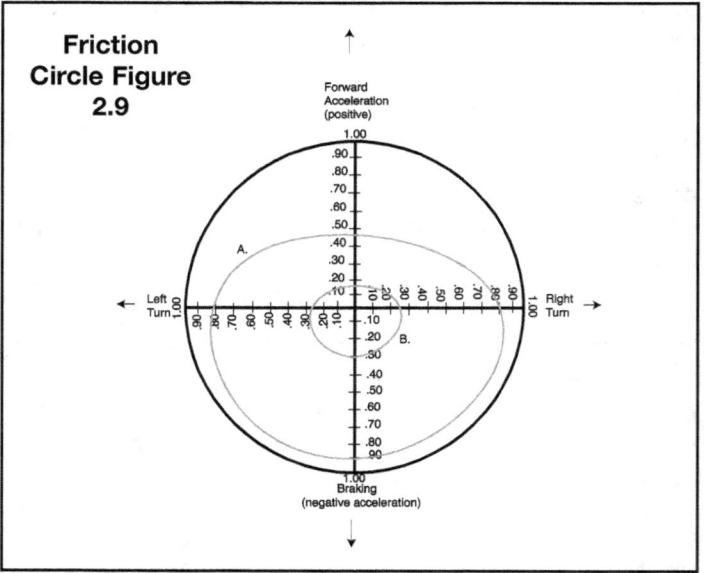

The handling envelope of a typical performance street car is shown as A. It shows that this car's forward accelerative ability is much less than its ability to slow quickly. Cornering acceleration is respectable for street tires. Trace B shows this same car on a slushy surface. Notice how the available friction of the road surface influences grip in all directions.

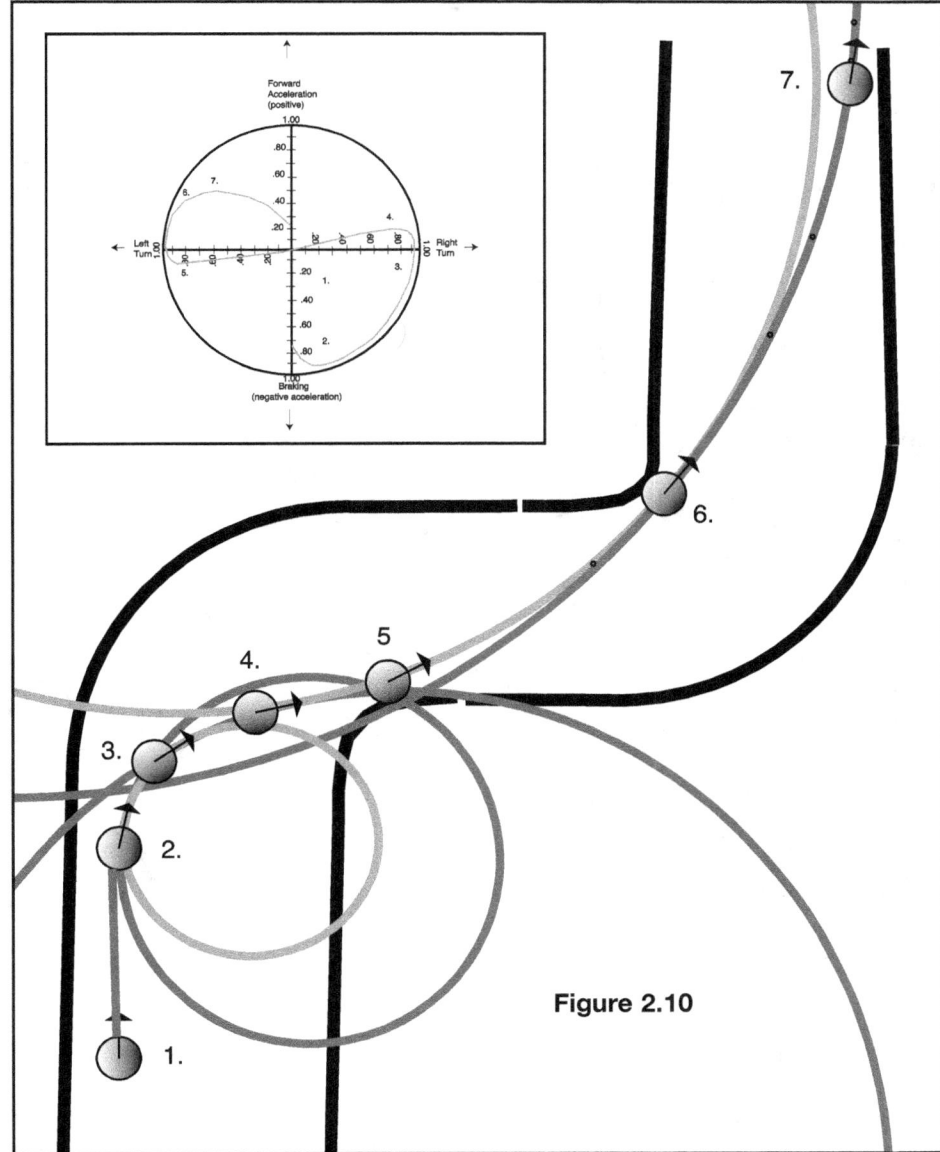

**Figure 2.10**

**The fast way through a turn.**

While we can't duplicate Mark Donahue's research, we can give you a reasonably in-depth analysis of why this would be true. If you follow along, using Friction Circle Figure 2.10 as a visual aid, it will hopefully become clear.

Before we start, however, we should mention that this figure uses circles of various radii to show the relationship of centripetal acceleration to braking, accelerating, and the tires' traction profile.

Point #1 is the braking zone. If you're running up on a turn at the end of a straight, you probably don't have enough cornering power to force your car to take the circular path necessary to make it. Notice that braking is initially all pure, that none of the available traction is used to turn the car. This gives you the ability to generate the highest level of braking, or negative accelerations.

At point #2, the driver begins to turn in towards the apex of the first corner. Since he's still braking hard, his cornering power is limited and so he must travel the fairly large radius arc #2.

Point #3 is where the driver, sensing that he has slowed to the point that he can travel a tighter arc, eases off the brake to free up traction to bend the car onto the tighter circular path of arc #3. Notice the strategy here. The driver makes all the short radius arcs before the first turn. This lets him use larger and therefore faster arcs exiting the turn. This maneuver transfers weight forward, giving the front tires more traction and the rear tires less. This helps the car rotate so it points at the first turn's apex.

You see a little forward acceleration at point #4. Since the car is pointing at the apex now, and he must change directions, he has for a brief moment a very large radius turn. He can squeeze the throttle, transferring weight back to the currently lightly loaded and partially sliding rear tires to get them to hook to stabilize the car and push it forward, and shave a few hundredths of a second off his lap time. But he has to make it quick because he's got to let off the gas and get the weight back on the nose and off the rear to help rotate the car so it now points at the apex of the second turn. This occurs very rapidly between points #4 and #5.

At point #5, the driver has the car rotated and pointed at the apex, which has also put him on an arc with a much larger radius than the one he used to hit the first turn's apex. Because he's on a larger arc, he can begin to apply throttle and accelerate forward, picking up speed. At point #6 he should be at full throttle accelerating as quickly as the car's tires will let him. As he gains acceleration, he unwinds the steering wheel putting him on a still larger arc, which again lets him accelerate quicker until he is running straight using all the traction of the drive wheels to accelerate the car forward to victory. At least that's the game plan.

Of course the fastest way out of a turn isn't necessarily the one that'll win races. You can get passed taking this line because you're driving on tighter arcs in the beginning of the series than someone on a passing line. He'd use larger arcs in the beginning of the series to get beside you and put you off the fast exit arc. One way to defend this is to let him in front, keeping to your line. He's going faster, so he'll have to take a larger arc at the entrance and his exit radius won't be as large as yours. Assuming you have the power, you'll be going faster as you enter the straight and be able to re-pass.

# TIRES

When you're shopping for performance tires, your range of choice is quite impressive though confusing. There are at least sixteen different tire companies from America, Europe, and Japan; each promising the ultimate performance tire. Yet these tires may vary wildly in tread design, construction, wet and dry performance, and price. The purpose of this chapter is to bring you a more complete understanding of performance tires; how they can improve or detract from your car's handling, braking, acceleration, and overall performance.

Let us begin with the information on the sidewall. There's a wealth of information to be found on every sidewall. Not every performance radial is a steel-belted radial. Some are still made with Fiberglass and Aramid and Rayon and this information is printed on the sidewall. The Goodyear tire here, for example, is constructed as follows: Tread, 6 plies: 2 polyester cord, 2 steel cord, 2 nylon cord. Sidewall: 2 polyester cord.

This is a popular type of construction for many, though not all, steel-belted performance tires. Also on the sidewall is federally mandated "grade labeling" with a number for tread wear and a letter following "Traction" and "Temperature." This is supposed to be of help to you when buying a tire. Though that is not always the case.

### IDENTICALLY SIZED TIRES DO NOT ALWAYS MEAN IDENTICAL TREAD WIDTH

Three tires with identical sizes on the sidewall (say, P225/70R15) may vary by as much as three-quarters of an inch in the width of tread they put on the road as well as in diameter. The variation occurs as a result of differences in shoulder design, construction, and mold shape.

Another area that affects how your car grips the road is tire compounding. Compound chemistry is a very complicated subject. However, an often correct rule is that a hard compound delivers long tread life at the expense of adhesion and wet weather performance and a soft compound delivers excellent "grip" but sacrifices long life.

### SPEED-RATINGS, FROM H-Z

A speed-rating tells you the speed capability of a specific tire. And in the United States, speed-ratings are normally reserved for performance tires certified to speeds of 130 mph or more. The most common speed ratings are H: up to 130 mph, V: up to 149 mph, and Z: over 149 mph.

### PUTTING THE NUMBERS AND THE LETTERS TOGETHER

The performance of your car should help in deciding whether or not you need a speed-rated performance tire. If your car came originally equipped with speed-rated tires, you should always install replacement tires having equal or greater speed capabilities.

In deciding on width and aspect ratio, it is usually advisable to get the help of a performance tire expert. A change to a shorter sidewall usually improves steering precision and response. But it may also affect your gear ratio, your speedometer reading, and your load-carrying capacity. It can also affect the sophisticated fuel metering system found in many of today's cars. A change to a wider tire can change the suspension geometry of your car, and may also result in clearance problems. So talk to a performance tire expert before making a change.

Also, look at the kinds of tires the performance car makers choose as O.E. for their top-level Performance cars. O.E. stands for original equipment, which means the tire has been used by a car manufacturer on one or more cars. To be O.E. approved, a tire has to pass a number of rigorous car manufacturer specified tests: wet and dry traction, tread life, rolling resistance, noise, durability, ride comfort, etc. And O.E. approval is a credential that is awarded only to tires that pass all of the tests. Not every performance tire has O.E. approval. And it is not stamped on the sidewall. So you should ask. Also ask what car it has been approved for. It should be similar in performance to your car.

## A TIRE HAS TO PERFORM IN ITS OWN ENVIRONMENT

As every enthusiast knows, a pure racing tire would make a very unsatisfactory, not to say dangerous, street tire. A pure racing tire has one purpose: to circumnavigate a racetrack as quickly and as safely as possible. To reduce heat build-up and unsprung weight, a racing tire is built to be as light as possible. Since there are no curbs, the sidewalls are very thin. In dry conditions, most racing tires have no tread at all — to give them maximum traction. If it rains, the race cars are parked, or changed to grooved racing rain tires, something that the everyday driver cannot do and would not do.

Since ultimate traction is the goal, long tread life does not rank high on the list of priorities. And tread compounds and tire construction are often tailored to match the speed and type of the racetrack. And/or the speed and type of the car.

An Indy Car on a road course uses a totally different kind of construction

**There is a wealth of information on your tire's sidewall.**

**Detailed on the sidewall is information on construction, traction values, temperature ratings and more.**

and tread compound than a NASCAR Winston Cup stock car on the high-banked oval at Talladega. Just as a Formula One car on the streets of Monaco uses a totally different kind of construction and compound than a 300 mph Top Fuel dragster. Each racing tire is purposely built for its own particular environment.

On the other hand, high performance street radials must deliver optimum performance under a wide variety of road and weather conditions. They must have sidewalls and construction strong enough to resist the road hazards of everyday driving. They need compounds capable of handling all kinds of road surfaces. Above all, they must deliver acceptable tread life, year in and year out, on a wide variety of differently designed performance cars.

## HIGH PERFORMANCE TIRE SCIENCE

With that brief introduction to performance tires, let's get into some serious tech. Here's where the proverbial rubber meets the road. And that is exactly it — the more rubber in contact with the road, the greater the grip, and the less stress exerted on the tread rubber.

As we high performance Honda enthusiasts place great emphasis on the grip of a performance tire, you should understand that this relates directly to the contact patch. If you look at Figure 3.1 it demonstrates how tire sizing determines the contact patch's size and shape.

## THE FOUR FUNDAMENTALS OF GRIP

First, longer patches provide more traction and braking grip than shorter patches. Second, wider patches provide more cornering grip than narrower patches. Third, larger patches (area) provide higher available grip, and reduce the work per unit area. And fourth, large, wide patches tend to aquaplane.

If you looked at the contact patch of a set of race tires, you would see how they tend to be much squarer in shape in order to give maximum tread width for a given rim or regulated limit. This optimizes grip because this design simply puts more rubber on the road. Stiff road race tire construction shortens the patch but still produces a patch approximately 10% larger than most road tires. But for drag racing, a much softer construction is better

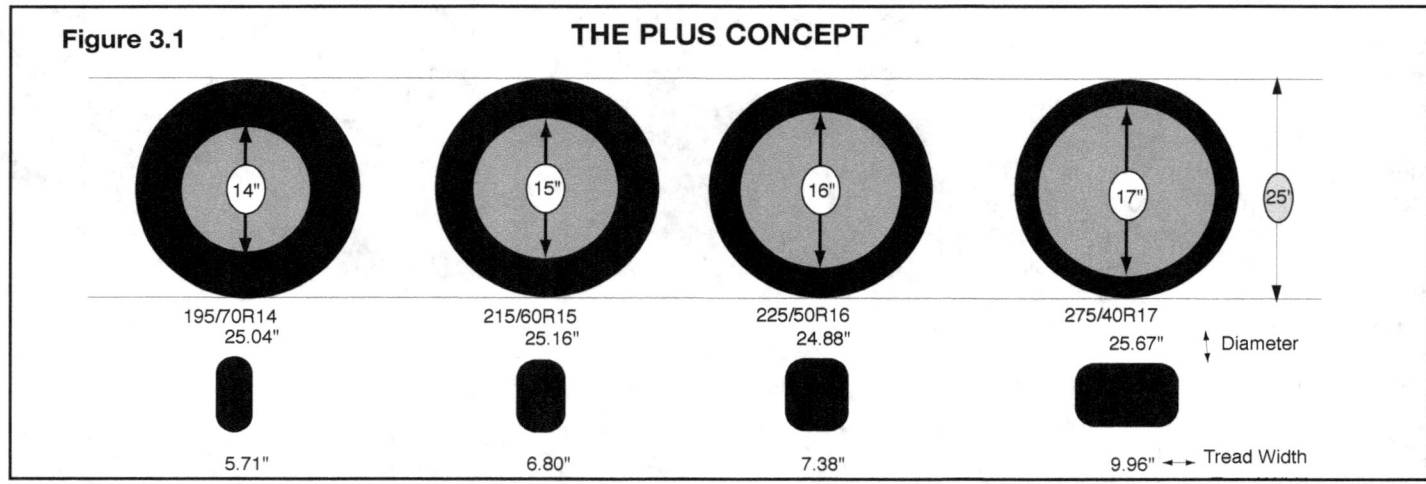

**Figure 3.1 THE PLUS CONCEPT**

Tire and wheel combinations change the contact path.

**Dunlop SP Sport W-10**

because it increases the length of the contact patch as well as absorbs some of the shock when the car launches.

### AIR PRESSURE AND LOAD CHANGE THE SHAPE OF THE CONTACT PATCH

As the vertical load increases, the contact patch area increases at the same rate. But if we study the shape of the patch with increasing loads we find no width increase above a fairly specific load; however the length increase doesn't show this limiting behavior. In other words, as you increase the load on a tire, the width of the contact patch reaches a limit but the length will increase until the wheel rim is flush against the tire tread. (See Figure 3.2.)

The effect of raising the tire pressure is that the contact patch grows shorter but the width remains stable. Recalling the fundamental rules of grip, it seems tires reach a load beyond which no more corner power is provided by a wider contact patch. This suggests that the tire may reach a limit of cornering speed related to load, and therefore to load transfer. Further, we can surmise that additional load will improve braking and traction, and that if you increase tire pressure you will reduce both without improving cornering power.

### BODY ROLL AND CAMBER

As a car's body rolls in response to weight transfer in a corner, the hard-working outside tire has the negative camber reduced. Savvy chassis tuners will normally configure around 3 deg of negative camber to keep the outside wheel vertical in a corner. With camber, the contact patch shape changes significantly taking on a conical shape which causes the outer shoulder of the tire to do most of the work. (See Figures 3.3 & 3.4.)

Negative camber does add to corner force generated by the tire but the effect is relatively small. Compared with the cornering force generated by slip angle, camber generates only 25% as much force per degree. The primary benefit of proper camber is preventing the contact patch from taking a conical shape which reduces the amount of rubber on the road and

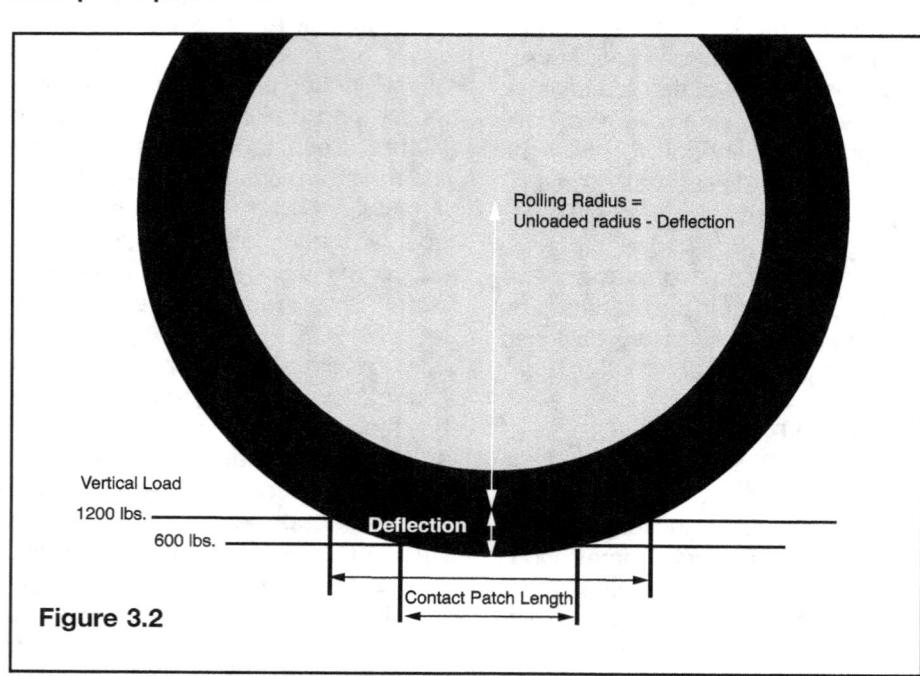

**Figure 3.2**

Air pressure and load influence the length of the contact patch more than width.

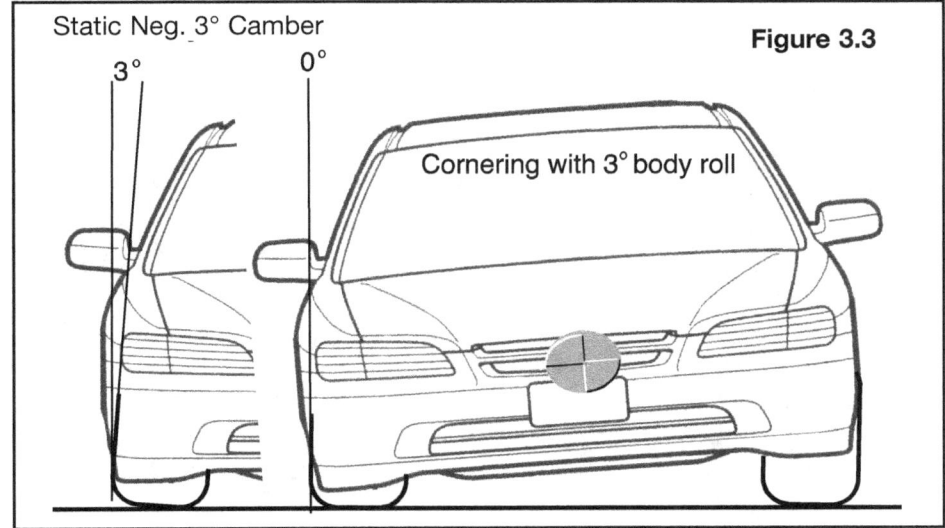

**Body roll changes camber settings**

**Pirelli P7000**

tends to overwork the outer shoulder. In addition, negative camber on the inside tire subtracts some degree of corner force since the geometry is working to pull the contact patch area off the road surface.

## CENTRIPETAL FORCE AND SLIP ANGLES

During lab testing, tires tend to show that peak lateral force almost always occurs at a 7 degree slip angle. However, in a real car on a real road in a real corner, the lateral loading placed on the tire and the resulting distortion of 7 degrees of slip isn't the magic number. After about 5 degrees slip angle you enter into a part of the grip curve where you see severely diminished returns. You can get more cornering force by feeding in more steering wheel angle, but you're working the tire so hard relative to the cornering force generated that you can't hold those slip angles for long. However, most drivers will push the tires into this area because they are operating in an area where the tires provide very little feedback through the steering wheel.

The reason the tires offer little feedback in this area comes from self-aligning torque. Self-aligning torque is a force generated by a moment arm between the castor intersect and the center of the contact patch. (See figure 4.21 in the chapter on Suspension.) This torque reaches a maximum at 4 degrees of steering angle, which is 3 degrees before the highest corner force is reached. So the driver, in turn-

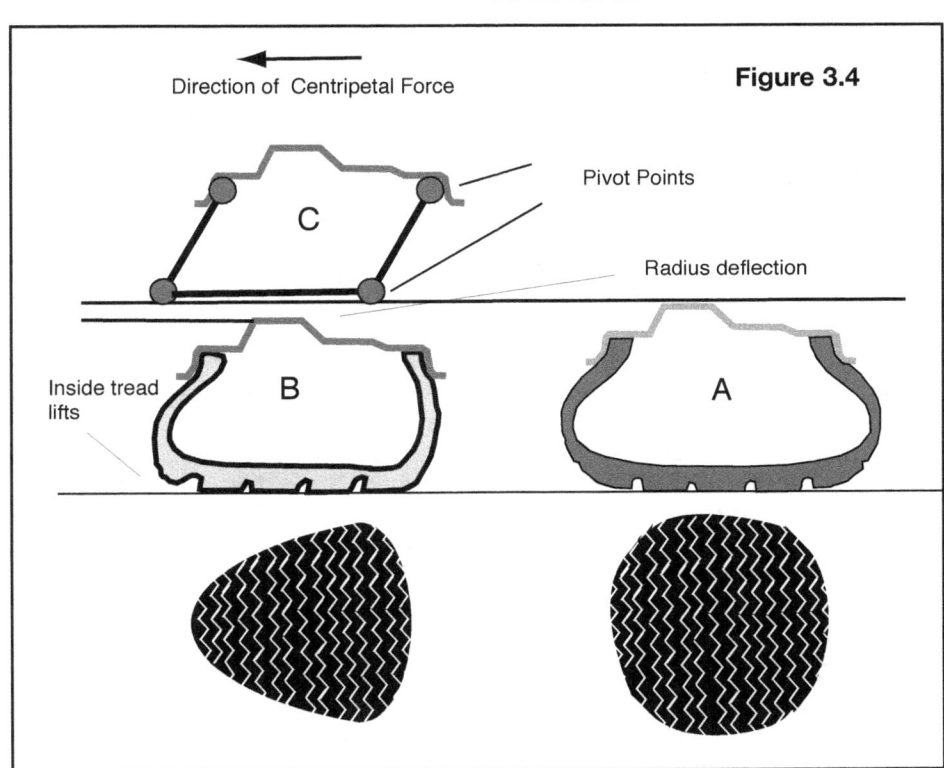

**Cornering force and camber changes alter the area and shape of the contact patch.**

ing the wheels beyond the point where the feedback hits a maximum to obtain better corner speed, may go beyond the best capability of the tires without being able to feel the effect. The best drivers can work in this area of reduced feedback.

## VERTICAL LOAD INCREASES CORNER FORCE BUT DECREASES FRICTION COEFFICIENT

A tire produces more lateral force with more load. This is why aerodynamic downforce improves cornering speeds by adding corner power to all the tires, neglecting for a moment the effect of weight transfer.

If you take into account the effects of weight transfer, you have a net loss of cornering force because the outside tires do not gain cornering force in proportion to the loss of load on the inside tires. Aerodynamic downforce works because you add vertical load on the tires but no extra mass to accelerate into the corner.

Yokohama A520

Yokohama A032R

Yokohama AVS S1

## HOW SIDE LOAD AFFECTS THE TIRE

When a car is cornering near its limit of adhesion, its tires are generating high levels of force which distorts the tire. The tread of most performance radial tires will move sideways relative to the wheel during cornering. At the same time, the rather stiff sidewalls nearest the wheel rotate around the beads as the relatively soft sidewalls nearest the tread act as hinges allowing the whole tread to move sideways. The belt under the tread tends to twist as the tire is distorted, reducing the size and effectiveness of the contact patch.

Recalling that maximum grip occurs with more rubber on the road, it is essential for makers of performance tires to control this distortion. For example, in the racing tire line, Dunlop designed a stiffer tire to keep maximum contact patch area. This approach gives a tire that distorts less and one that is not as affected by inflation pressure. The stiff tire has another benefit in that lower tire pressures can be used to improve traction and braking with less effect on cornering capability. (See Figure 3.4)

Of course the trade-off to this approach, at least for a street tire is a rougher ride. A tire, in this sense acts very much like a spring. In fact, tire engineers use a model of the tire as a series of radial springs. So if you increase the stiffness of the tire, you in effect increase the spring rate of the suspension.

## THE FRONT-DRIVE DISADVANTAGE

As we mentioned in the chapter describing basic driving skills, front-drive cars have a sizable disadvantage because of the disparity of work level demands from front to rear. As a general rule, the front tires have to do up to 70% of the work and with load transfer one tire may be saddled with generating more than 50% of the work in a corner. On the drag strip, weight transfer off the drive tires reduces the tractive force limiting acceleration.

The advantage of rear-drive cars is the design shares the work demands of the tires more evenly. In fact, the rear tires do more than 50% of the work. However, the advantage of rear drive isn't as great as it once was because tire makers, such as Dunlop, and their involvement with touring car racing have tuned tire designs for front-drive cars putting them back in contention.

Still, because of the inherent bias to the front-drive wheels of the work, it is essential to tune your chassis to distribute the work as evenly as possible to each of the tires.

Racers make careful recordings of all tire pressures and temperatures to help tire engineers understand the effect the car is having on the tires. Undue increases in tire pressure and temperature are both signs that any single tire or a single pair of tires is overworked, the result of which is increasing lap times due to progressive loss in grip.

## WHAT THE TIRE TELLS US

The information that is provided by the used race tire is invaluable. If overworked, the tire's surface looks very heavily grained. It exhibits deep rooting and wide spaces between peaks. The correct tire shows a fine grain pattern. Due to the width of race slicks, study of differing effects across the tire will reveal if a tire is rolling too much onto one shoulder, or if the toe-in or toe-out is incorrect. This information is discussed with the team engineers to help in optimizing the chassis settings to use tires more effectively.

## COMPOUND CHOICES

Tread compound selection is very important. A basic measure for selection is hardness at the working temperature. Once the tire reaches 100°C, the minimum hardness has been achieved, and grip has reached an optimum. This is why tires do not "come in" immediately. They must heat up before the compound can be fully effective. The rear tires on front-drive touring cars often do not reach this working temperature!

We are not concerned if a tire operates between 180-220°F (approximately 80-120°C) but, above or below these limits, either the compound will grain and tear, or it will overheat, becoming very soft and foamlike.

## HEAT CYCLING

Molecules are attracted to each other by a variety of chemical networks, or chemical bonds. When the tire tread is made, these chemical bonds are formed in a random manner; some are short and strong, some are long and weak, but most are somewhere in between.

When you first drive on a set of tires, it flexes around and makes heat while stretching and compressing the rubber compound molecules causing the weak bonds to break. Since these chemical bonds give the tread compound its strength and ability to grip the road surface, the process of breaking them down reduces the tread's effectiveness.

However, after the vehicle has stopped and the tires cool, the broken bonds begin to reform, doing so in a much more uniform manner that provides a consistency and strength that wasn't there before. To put it another way, once these bonds are reformed, the tire will not only be more predictable, but also longer wearing. That's why real racers always heat cycle their racing tires.

The technique is to drive on your tires until they reach their operating temperature range and then are allowed to cool for at least 24 hours. The compound reaches optimum strength after 48 hours, but 24 hours of cooling will work fine. Keep in mind that the cool-off rule applies only to the first heat cycle. After that, you should run your tires within their designated operating temperature range. For example, the BFG Comp T/A R1 used in road racing, should run at 160 to 230 degrees Fahrenheit. For autocrossing, you most likely will not get the tires that hot, but you want to maximize their temperatures as much as possible.

So, how do you know if you are overheating your tires? The answer is simple: take their temperature with a probe-type pyrometer. As we said earlier, a tire generates heat when it works. The harder it works, the more heat it generates. We'll discuss taking temperatures in the next section.

Each area has its own spring rate, or stiffness, with the outer and inner edges getting some of that from the tire's construction, while the center section depends almost solely on inflation pressure for its support. To maximize both performance and wear, you want to work toward consistent temperatures across the tread. In practical terms, the critical areas are the outer edge and the center section which should be within five degrees of each other.

## TUNING WITH AIR PRESSURE

Essentially, when you increase inflation pressure, you are increasing your tire's ability to carry a given load, and increasing its spring rate. In other words, at higher inflation pressure, the tire's sidewall deflects less than at a lower pressure. That's why higher inflation pressures tend to decrease the size of the contact patch. A tire with a higher inflation pressure also will demonstrate crisp "turn-in" characteristics. Additionally, even though a lower pressure may increase the contact patch, it can create "roll under." This is a condition found during hard cornering in which the dynamic forces on the tire pull the inside of the contact patch away from the road surface.

The best way to determine the correct tire pressure is by checking your tire temperatures with a pyrometer. This is done by checking the center of the tread, as well as the outer and inner shoulders. Ideally, the temperatures should be even across the tread. If the outer shoulder is substantially hotter than the center, then you should consider increasing the pressure. If the outer shoulder is a great deal cooler than the center, then you ought to consider lowering the pressure. Remember, though, that you should do this in increments of no more than two to three psi at a time.

Once the fronts are set, then you can adjust the rears to fit your driving style. You can dial in oversteer by increasing the rear tire pressures. Or, you may choose to go the other way, and increase the understeer by reducing the rear tire pressures. Ideally, you want to come out with a neutral handling vehicle.

The critical thing here is to get the front pressures correct first so that the tire temperatures are even across the tread area. As for what those temperatures ought to be, they will range anywhere from 100 degrees F, to around 220 degrees F, with the autocross tires coming in somewhere between 90 and 150 degrees F.

Finally, for wet weather conditions, you should consider increasing your pressures eight-to-ten psi to reduce the size of the contact patch. This increases the pressure on the contact patch, thus reducing the threat of hydroplaning. The extra pressure also helps keep the tread grooves open to evacuate the water and further help eliminate hydroplaning.

**Toyo Proxes FZ4**

**Toyo Proxes T1 Plus**

BF Goodrich Comp T/A ZR

BF Goodrich G-Force T/A R1

BF Goodrich Comp T/A ZR SSS

BF Goodrich Euro T/A

## SHAVING TIRES CAN IMPROVE PERFORMANCE IF TIRE TEMPS ARE TOO HIGH

Shaving reduces the amount of heat the tire generates and carries. It does this by reducing tread depth which reduces the tread mass available to store heat and reduces tread block flex.

You need to make the decision to shave or not before you use the tire. Shaving reduces tread squirm, flexing, and mass; which in turn allows the tire's tread surface to wear evenly for the life of the tire.

If your experience has been that your tires are running at their optimum operating temperatures, or even below them, then shaving isn't going to help. If your experience has been that they are running above the optimum temperature range, and there's nothing else you can do to correct the situation, then shaving is the way to go.

## THE EFFECT OF RIM WIDTH ON TIRE PERFORMANCE

First a basic rule: Under no circumstance should you mount a tire on a rim whose width does not fall within the recommended range.

With that out of the way you should know that within the recommended range, you will probably only see slight differences of performance and tire life with small changes in rim widths. It will take a large difference in rim width to produce a noticeable difference.

When a manufacturer designs a tire, they do so with a specific rim width in mind so the tire may be properly evaluated. This is the "measuring rim." A certain amount of latitude is built into the tire so that it can be mounted on rims somewhat narrower or wider than the measuring rim. From the narrowest to the widest constitutes the range of permissible rim widths for that tire. As an example of what we're talking about, let's take a Comp T/A R1 205/60R13. The measuring rim for this tire is 13x6 inches. However, the guidelines say rims from 5.5 inches to 8 inches are suitable.

In general, narrow rims hurt tire performance. The reason is that the beads are closer together, allowing the sidewalls to flex more easily slowing steering response and reducing overall cornering levels. In addition, narrower rim widths result in a slight "bowing" which could induce uneven tire wear. While tire pressure adjustments can partially offset this condition, the trade-off is that as you reduce tire pressures to neutralize the "bowing," you'll almost certainly decrease steering response as well. So, if there are all these disadvantages, why would you go to a rim narrower than the "measuring rim" in the first place?

One answer is circumstance. In some cases the rules under which you compete (where a wider rim might move you up into a less desirable class) will dictate a narrower rim that is less than ideal, but which will still get you the most tire on your car. In this case, you obviously will want to extract the maximum performance possible from that tire, despite the problems with the rim width.

A narrow rim can offer ride benefits. The narrower the rim, the less vertical the sidewall. This increases sidewall flex allowing the tire to curve or balloon out. This provides additional rim and sidewall protection from rocks or other objects that could cause air loss. Additionally, this greater sidewall flex allows the tire to absorb more road bumps and shock, thus resulting in a softer ride.

Moving to the issue of increasing rim width, the general trend is this: As the rim widens, steering response becomes quicker. This is critical not only in road racing, but also autocrossing. In most cases, what you've done by going to a wider rim is to make the sidewall more vertical in relation to the road surface. This decreases the deflection of the sidewall and thereby gives you improved steering response. Do note, however, that as with the use of narrower rims, you can induce abnormal tire wear, particularly in the shoulder area. More importantly, you've also reduced the sidewall's ability to absorb road shocks. Thus, more road shock is transmitted to your vehicle's rims and suspension.

**TIRE SIZING TECH TIPS**

Is bigger always better? Not always. Sometime it's best to go smaller.

Obviously, smaller can mean narrower width, such as switching to a 225/50ZR16 from a 245/45ZR16. The diameter of these two tires is very similar, only the width and aspect ratio change.

It can also mean smaller in diameter, such as changing to a 205/50ZR15 from a 205/60ZR15. In this case, the width stays the same and the diameter and aspect ratio change.

Other ways to change size might be to change rim diameter only, say a 225/50ZR16 to a 225/50ZR15, which in this case leads to a wheel/tire package that is one inch shorter. In any case, what we want to explore are those instances when going smaller can be an advantage. In racing classes where changes in final drive gearing are not permitted, but changes in tire or wheel size are allowed, you can substantially alter your gearing with a tire change. This also holds true for production cars, such as your Honda with front drive that makes it difficult if not impossible to change gear ratios.

In the previously mentioned conversion from a 225/50ZR16 to a 225/50ZR15 size, the change in diameter is about four percent, but you can gain a whopping seven percent reduction in gearing ratio.

This means that a 5580 rpm engine speed using the 60-series tire becomes 6000 rpm on the 50-series tire. The difference could help keep the engine in the power band coming out of a critical corner. On the other hand, using a 60-series tire might allow you to skip a shift or two. You may not have to shift into fifth at all on the straight.

Any of these changes could save you valuable tenths of a second. Obviously, there are handling differences between these combinations that need to be reviewed. But the gearing change is a factor many drivers overlook, and something one should consider.

Smaller tires also tend to generate less rolling and aerodynamic resistance. This is especially important for lower horsepower and smaller cars. It can be a big factor on high speed tracks, such as Road America, where top speed is critical, not only for better lap times, but also for setting someone up for passing at the end of straights.

Cornering drag is another aspect that must be taken into account. When you ask a tire to generate cornering force, it also generates a tremendous amount of "scrubbing" or cornering drag that slows the vehicle down.

Many of you have been in a situation where the brakes may have gone away. You have learned that a car can still be slowed enough to make the corner by throwing it into the corner and scrubbing off speed. This kind of cornering drag requires horsepower to overcome. By going to a smaller tire, low horsepower/lightweight cars may actually see higher cornering speeds resulting in quicker lap times.

The larger and heavier a tire is, the more torque required to accelerate the tire rotationally. Less weight results in a lower moment of inertia, meaning that less torque is needed to initiate rotation of the tire and wheel. That leaves more torque available to accelerate the car. It is the same concept as using a lightweight flywheel. Again, potentially quicker lap times are possible.

When racing in the rain, the narrower the tire, the less the tendency for hydroplaning to occur. Narrow tires are always better in downpours than wider ones, given the same tread pattern and tread depth. If you have a separate set of rain tires and the rules allow variation in tire size, you might want to

**Michelin Pilot XGT V4**

**Michelin Pilot HX MXM**

mount up the narrowest size allowed.

The only warning here is that if the track dries out during the race, you will be out there on smaller tires in dry conditions and tire life could be an issue. This is less a problem for small, light cars than heavier, higher horsepower ones. Lastly, there are never any guarantees in racing, but the more options you have, the more chances you have of gaining an advantage over the competition.

## TIRE TECH TIPS

Tires have many markings on the sidewall, but most people don't understand the technical meaning of them, especially UTQG.

What is UTQG? "Uniform Tire Quality Grading" is required by "FMVSS" (Federal Motor Vehicle Safety Standards) of the U.S. Department of Transportation. This standard requires motor vehicle and tire manufacturers and tire brand name owners to provide information indicating the relative performance of passenger car tires used in the U.S.A. in the area of tread wear, traction, and temperature resistance. This applies to all passenger car tires, except deep tread, winter-type snow tires, space-saver or temporary use spares, or tires with nominal rim diameters of twelve (12) inches or less. This is the standard with a history which had been judged as final in the Supreme Court of U.S.A. between the governments, vehicle manufacturers, and tire manufacturers.

## TREAD WEAR GRADING

The tread wear grade is a comparative rating based on the wear rate of the tire when tested under controlled conditions on a specified government test course. The test course consists of three loops of a total of 400 miles (644 kms) in the geographical vicinity of Goodfellow Air Force Base (AFB), San Angelo, Texas, U.S.A. The grading fixes 30,000 miles (48,279 kms) as 100% Index, and the grading shall be in multiplies of 20.

## TRACTION

The traction grades, from highest to lowest, are A, B and C. They represent the tire's ability to stop on wet pavement as measured under controlled conditions on specified government test surfaces of asphalt and concrete.

## TRACTION TEST PROCEDURE

The tire to be tested is inflated to 24 psi (165 KPa) and installed on the test apparatus (instrumented trailer). The tire is loaded to 1,085 pounds (492 kg). The trailer is towed over the wetted test area at 40 mph (65 km/h) and the rotating wheel is locked. The tire is dragged in this locked condition through the test area and the friction created is measured. From these measurements the friction efficiency index of a tire can be calculated using the following formula:

$U = T/F$

Where:
$U$ = Friction Efficiency Index
$T$ = Pulling Power
$F$ = Load

## TEMPERATURE GRADING

The temperature grades are A (highest), B, and C. These represent the tire's resistance to the generation of heat and its ability to dissipate heat when tested under controlled conditions on a specified indoor laboratory test wheel. Sustained high temperature can cause the material of a tire to degenerate and reduce tire life, and excessive temperature can lead to dangerous sudden failure.

The grade C corresponds to a level of performance which all passenger car tires must meet under the Federal Motor Vehicle Safety Standard No. 109.

Grades B and A represent higher levels of performance in the laboratory test than the minimum required by law in the U.S.A. The temperature grade is established for a tire that is properly inflated and not overloaded.

Recently, not only in the U.S.A. but in many countries, customers are anxious to check the UTQG as one of their decision making factors in the selection of passenger car radial tires. However, it is very important to know that the grades are obtained under controlled conditions, and are not completely applicable to actual usage.

## HOW TO CHOOSE THE RIGHT DRAG RACING TIRE

To begin with, racing tires are designed to fit the class structure of organized drag racing, most particularly the NHRA class structure. The most significant factors affecting tire construction are the weight of the vehicle and the amount of power it produces. This is essentially how sanctioning bodies determine drag racing classes anyway. The classes group cars of similar weight and horsepower together. The way Goodyear breaks this down is Top Fuel and Funny Car, Pro Stock, Super Gas, Competition, and Stock and Super Stock.

From a design standpoint, that means the construction of the carcass and the tread thickness and compound offerings vary from class to class. The general rule here is that the heavier the car, the stiffer the sidewall and tread area should be. For example, a pro stock or top fuel tire has a more flexible sidewall and tread area than does a comp class tire. These features are desirable on low-weight, high-powered, rear-drive cars because the flexible sidewall tends to wrap up and cushion the sudden force of acceleration and increasing load due to weight transfer. Plus, it has a slingshot effect that, though it increases reaction times, the car will E.T. quicker.

In addition, the sidewall works with the flexible tread area to make the tread elongate under sudden acceleration to provide a longer and bigger contact patch. If you freeze a top fuel tire in midflight, notice that the back of the tire is straighter than the front. The force of rotation as the car powers off the starting line throws the front of the tire forward, putting more rubber on the track. It also allows the tire to grow as it spins faster and faster as the car accelerates down the track. Tire growth provides an artificially high gear ratio and reduces frontal area to lower wind resistance; both help MPH and consequently the E.T.

Here's a subtlety that's often missed. Wrinkle-wall drag tires are designed to change the shape, size, and orientation to the contact patch shape relative to the direction of travel. When the tire is still, it presents a wide contact patch but not a very long one, relative to the direction of travel in order to put as much rubber on the track as possible, given the tire size. Grip is generated by the square area of rubber on the track plus the vertical load, as well as the shape of the contact area. A wide patch enhances lateral acceleration, while a long patch enhances acceleration on the longitudinal plane. You need lots of grip to get the car moving, so as large a contact patch as can be had is desirable. Once the tire starts rotating, centrifugal forces begin to change the shape into a narrow but long rectangle with the length of the rectangle being aligned with the direction of travel.

Production based FWD cars respond to tires with a stiffer sidewall and tread area. Getting the mass of a FWD moving at the start is of prime importance to a quick E.T. A soft sidewalled tire winds up and doesn't get the mass of the car moving as quickly as a stiffer sidewalled tire. The tire has to grab quickly with FWD cars because the weight and therefore the force the tire can generate is transferring off the drive tire.

Compounds aren't as varied as one would expect. In the Goodyear lineup there are seven. The R&D process regarding compounds is good old trial and error. The chemists play around and find something that works well with a car's weight and carcass design and power level. Then the racers have to tune the car to best use available grip (which changes with track conditions) with suspension and clutch adjustments, burnout, and leave technique.

In general, compounds are stickiest at around 180 to 220 degrees. However, you can get a tire too hot with an extended overpowering burnout and lose grip. Some teams are experimenting with infrared sensors that give the surface temperature, but what is most important is the temperature down by the cords of the tire carcass. That's why the quickest racers use a probe type pyrometer.

The recipe for a compound is one of the most highly guarded secrets in the industry. Cooking up compounds is a very fine art. Small differences in cure time and certain chemicals mixed in can change the characteristics of the compound. So even though all the manufacturers have access to the same materials, it is almost impossible for one manufacturer to duplicate another's compounds. That goes for the manufacture of the carcasses too, as compounds and tire carcasses are designed as a system.

While we're discussing compounds, it's as good a time as any to talk about durometer readings. Taking a durometer reading with the tire at room or ambient temperature will not give you a true value of the softness of the compound. Compounds vary in chemical makeup and some are pretty hard at ambient temperature yet some are so sensitive to heat, you can melt them rather quickly. The point is that to get an accurate durometer reading, you should measure the compound when it's in its operating temperature range.

One of the best uses of a durometer is to determine when your tire compound is too old or has heat-cycle hardened. To do so, you have to take the durometer readings of the tires at the same temperature and at the same time. For example, set your old tire and a new one outside for an equal amount of time and then take your durometer readings. This will give an indication of the degree of heat cycle hardening.

And that brings us to heat cycles and tire life. Every time you burn out

**BF Goodrich Comp T/A Drag Radial**

you begin a heat cycle. A heat cycle is when the tire is brought from ambient temperature up to its operating temperature of between 180 and 220 degrees. Every time the tire goes through this temperature cycle, the compound cures a little more. In general, this constant curing process is what limits tire life more than tread depth.

Most FWD bracket racers using a racing only tire can get about 40 to 50 passes, at least, before the compound goes away. It all depends on how competitive you need to be and how much power you're putting down. However, different tires have different life cycles. A whole season is a possibility, especially on a car that is way over-tired. Since the tire has an excessive reserve of grip, even when it begins to lose grip due to heat cycling and age, the car isn't

**Burning out brings the tire compound up to temperature. But notice the amount the tire is deflected. The parking brake is on keeping the car still, so no weight transfers off the front.**

**Right off the start, weight transfers off the front tires reducing potential traction. You can see this because the tires are far less deflected than during the burn out.**

**About 20 or 30 ft. out, the car isn't accelerating as quickly and some weight transfers forward, letting the tires grip better for more traction.**

You want the wheels to spin a certain amount. This is called a percent slip. Tires tend to have the best grip between 15 to 20 percent slip rate.

Applying a stripe of white shoe polish to the sidewall helps your crew chief to watch for tire spin as you leave the line.

putting out enough force to overload the tire.

Being aware of how heat cycling affects tire life can save you from going crazy at the track. It is easiest to visualize the life cycle of a tire as a curve. The traction remains flat for most of the life cycle then toward the end, as the compound starts to become very hard, the traction falls at a fairly rapid angle. Once you get to where the traction curve starts falling off, the tire becomes very inconsistent. And if you think it is the track instead of the tires and start making tuning changes, you can get real lost real fast and slow way down.

## QUICK TRACTION TIPS

Air pressure is one of your most important tuning tools. The air supports the sidewalls and the tread, so you can fine-tune sidewall wrap up for more consistent leaves. But ultimately the track conditions and your experience with the car will determine optimum tire pressure.

Keep in mind that you can go too low with your tire pressures. When the tire pressure is too low, sometimes the car will want to get loose and squirm around on the top end. Or you can force tire shake with too low air pressure in the tires. Tire shake occurs when you run over the distortions in the tire that occur under hard acceleration. Low air pressure is only one of many causes of tire shake. However, tire shake most often originates from the chassis tune and suspension geometry.

Tire and wheel compatibility is one more factor to consider. You should have appropriately matched wheels and tires. This puts you in the middle of the "tuning window," if you will, regarding air pressure. If you're running a mismatched combination, then you may have to use the air pressure to compensate for this. This doesn't cause a problem until you encounter less than ideal track conditions, and then you may not have the latitude to tune to the track.

While it isn't advisable to use a wheel that is narrower than the tread width by more than 2 inches, there are circumstances where a wider-than-tread-width wheel can help. If your RPM is too low through the lights, a wider wheel will restrict tire growth and the artificial raising of the gear ratio. Also, if you leave well but begin slipping in the middle of the track, a wider wheel keeps more tread on the track by restricting the crowning that occurs with tire growth.

One more thing — you should always measure the circumference of both tires at the pressure you intend to use them. If the difference is more than 1/2-inch per side, you'll have to stretch the smaller tire. Normally, to seat the bead you inflate the tire to about 25 psi. To stretch the tire you can take it up to 50 psi, then deflate back to the pressure you want and recheck circumference. This procedure is only good for bias-ply tires.

Perhaps the best tip of all regarding tire selection is to go to the track and see what the fast drivers are running. Check out a car similar to the one you have or intend to build. Because when it comes to getting the best out of your tires and your race car, it is experience that counts.

## HOW TO INSTALL BEAD SCREWS

Modern drag tires have a tremendous amount of grip — so much that the wheels sometimes spin within the tire. Screwing the tire bead to the wheel bead seat has proven effective in preventing this from occurring. Here's how to do it.

You'll need 24 screws per wheel and you'll install 12 screws on each side in the A, B, A, B pattern illustrated in the diagram. Use hex-headed sheet metal screws #14 x 3/4, grade eight or better. Dismount the tire and mark the wheel in the manner shown. Center punch the marks and drill out using a 5/32-inch bit. Be sure that the holes are aligned so that the screws will penetrate the center of the tire bead. Use one screw as a thread tap and tap each hole. Then inspect and deburr as needed.

Before mounting the tire, make sure there are no broken rim screws in the bead. If there are, remove them. Mount the tires so they will rotate in the direction specified by the manufacturer, then inflate to a maximum of 25 psi to seat the bead. With the bead seated, screw the bead to the rim. Make sure that the screw penetrates the bead and doesn't push it away from the seat.

## ROTATIONAL INERTIA

The weight of your wheel and tire combination has a direct influence on the performance of your car. Your wheel's heft or lack of it, tends to play-out in two main areas — unsprung weight, which mostly influence lateral acceleration and handling; and rotational inertia, discussed previously in the section by Patrick Hale.

The rotational inertia of a wheel and tire combo resists being accelerated. That means it takes engine power to get your wheels rolling in addition to all the other factors outlined in the drag racing section. That inertia also affects the braking performance of your car because what is hard to get rolling is hard to stop rolling. In other words, your brakes have to do more work to stop heavier wheels and tires than lighter ones.

We can't give you examples of every wheel and tire combination but we can give you the calculated effects on performance for a range of popular wheel and tires sizes and weights. This should help you in any future purchasing decision as well as help you evaluate and fine turn your own vehicle combination.

If you look at the Wheel & Tire Rotational Inertia Chart, you can see how much more your car weighs because of the effects of rotational inertia. Remember you must add the effective weight of your wheels to the vehicle weight which already has the weight of the wheels as part of its total. The effective weight is how much more weight is added to the vehicle as it accelerates, or brakes. For example, if you have a set of 225/50-15 tires and wheels you need to figure in 103 pounds to your vehicle weight to get a true idea of its accelerative potential.

This chart doesn't pretend to be accurate for every wheel and tire combo. We had to make a couple of assumptions to calculate the weights. We weighed a 16x8-inch aluminum wheel and made that the standard. We scaled the weight of smaller wheel sizes proportionally from that. Then we added the weight of the tires from the manufacturers' spec sheet. If you'd like to calculate the rotational inertia and effective weight values for your own tires and wheels, use the following formula:

$$I = 0.6 \cdot m \cdot r^2 / 386$$

We used the constant of 0.6 because as Patrick Hale states, the 0.5 constant is for a solid disk while 1.0 constant is for a thin-walled cylinder. We figure a tire and wheel isn't quite a solid disk nor is it a thin-walled cylinder.

## Wheel & Tire Rotational Inertia Chart

| Size | Diameter | Weight | Inertia (in.-lb./s/s)/Tire | Effective Wt. /tire | Effective Wt. *4 |
|---|---|---|---|---|---|
| 205/60-13 | 22.95 | 32.58 | 7.66 | 22.46 | 89.83 |
| 195/60-14 | 22.96 | 33.25 | 7.83 | 22.92 | 91.67 |
| 225/60-14 | 24.35 | 36.25 | 9.60 | 24.99 | 99.95 |
| 215/60-15 | 24.85 | 36.87 | 10.17 | 25.42 | 101.67 |
| 225/50-15 | 23.65 | 37.37 | 9.33 | 25.76 | 103.05 |
| 225/50-16 | 24.60 | 39.50 | 10.67 | 27.23 | 108.91 |
| 245/45-16 | 24.40 | 41.00 | 10.90 | 28.26 | 113.04 |
| 245/50-16 | 25.40 | 41.00 | 11.81 | 28.26 | 113.04 |
| 255/50-16 | 25.75 | 42.00 | 12.43 | 28.95 | 115.80 |
| 245/40-17 | 24.39 | 43.12 | 11.45 | 29.73 | 118.90 |
| 275/40-17 | 25.15 | 44.12 | 12.46 | 30.41 | 121.66 |
| 315/35-17 | 25.40 | 47.12 | 13.57 | 32.48 | 129.93 |

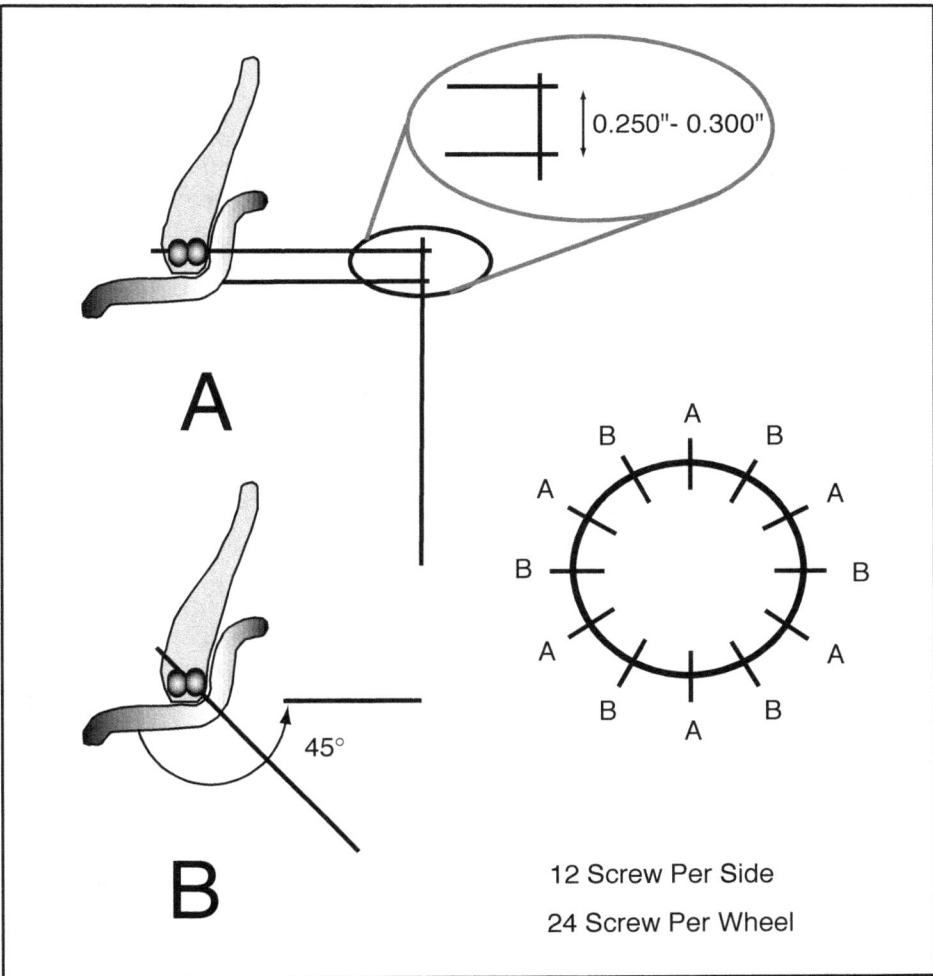

This diagram illustrates the proper method of fastening a race tire to a wheel.

# Honda Builder's HANDBOOK Vol. II
## SUSPENSION

In this chapter we build on the weight transfer concepts presented in the chapters on performance driving and tires to help you tune your suspension. The suspension generally consists of the components that, obviously enough, suspend your Honda's chassis. We won't go into the details of tuning every suspension component. There are several books on the subject already, and you'd need more pages than this entire volume to do it justice. So we'll just concentrate on the components you have control over that influence the handling of your Honda, and give you background info on the components that aren't easily adjusted but influence the components you can.

In other words, we'll focus on the components that influence weight transfer. That includes springs, shocks and antisway bars. We'll also address a few suspension alignment adjustments that significantly affect handling. Briefly, these are camber, which we discussed in the chapter on tires, castor and toe. In addition we'll cover geometry basics, just to give you a feel for it, but to be honest, changing suspension geometry is very difficult to do correctly. Besides the stock Honda geometry is very good anyway, so why mess it up?

### SUSPENSION COMPONENTS

To begin, let us state clearly why you need suspension.

The purpose of suspension is to allow your tires and wheels to move independently of the chassis in order to smooth out chassis movements and to keep the tires in proper contact with the road.

The usual components of the suspension are the shocks, springs, and control arms. The springs are load handling devices. They support the weight of the vehicle keeping it off the bump stops at an established ride height and yet are elastic enough to cushion the bumps we inevitably hit when driving. In keeping the car off its bump stops, it also keeps the tires on the road which gives us control. They also are the major determinate of ride rate. Ride rate is the frequency at which the sprung mass vibrates. It is a direct manifestation of the ratio of sprung weight, i.e. the body of your car and the spring rates. The shock absorbers are there, again obviously enough, to work with the springs to absorb the shocks of the bumps we inevitably hit when driving and to help calm the vibrations of the ride rate when the suspension is excited and absorbs a bump.

The control arms, or "links" as they are sometimes called, hold the wheel and tire as well as the brakes in such a way that the wheel and tire moves up and down to absorb the road shocks and bumps. In addition to locating the tires/wheels, the linkage should keep the tires flat on the road and keep them pointing in the right direction. Honda does this particularly well.

In the case of the wheels that steer the car, provisions are made to allow them to rotate about a vertical axis pointing them, hopefully, in the direction you wish to travel. The steering geometry also interacts with the suspension geometry and can take, if you'll excuse the pun, some surprising turns. Again, we'll discuss such concerns later in the chapter.

## ISOLATED SUSPENSION MODEL

Continuing with our discussion of suspensions, we'll simplify this complex problem with the help of Thomas D. Gillespie, who states in his *Fundamentals of Vehicle Dynamics* that, "At the most basic level, all highway vehicles share the 'ride isolation' at each wheel. The dynamic behavior of this system is the first level of isolation from the roughness of the road." By analyzing only one corner of a car's suspension you can get a better understanding of the working of the whole car's suspension since each corner works essentially the same way. This model is displayed in Figure 4.1.

### TIRES ARE SPRINGS THAT BECOME STIFFER WITH INCREASING AIR PRESSURE

We talked about tires in an earlier chapter, however we didn't mention this particular attribute. Tires as far as the suspension is concerned are springs. See Figure 4.3. Each tire has a spring rate and adds to the ride rate similarly to that of the suspension spring. From the isolated suspension model, the influence the tires have on ride rate is given in the formula:

$$RR = K_s K_t / K_s + K_t$$

Where:
RR = Ride Rate
Ks = Spring Rate
Kt = Tire stiffness

Most tire companies don't advertise or even list a tire stiffness rating. But that's okay since it's such a specialized parameter that you don't really need to know it exactly. You can consider tire stiffness similar to spring rate. Increase air pressure and you increase the tire stiffness. Now it's true that some tires have stiffer sidewalls than others; and that you can change the effective sidewall stiffness by changing the angle of the sidewall to the rim bead. (See the chapter on tires for more info.) But for the most part, air pressure and the aspect ratio are the primary factors.

In case you were wondering, those really low profile 18- and 19-inch wheel and tire combinations have seriously high tire rates. That's why these wheel and tire combos

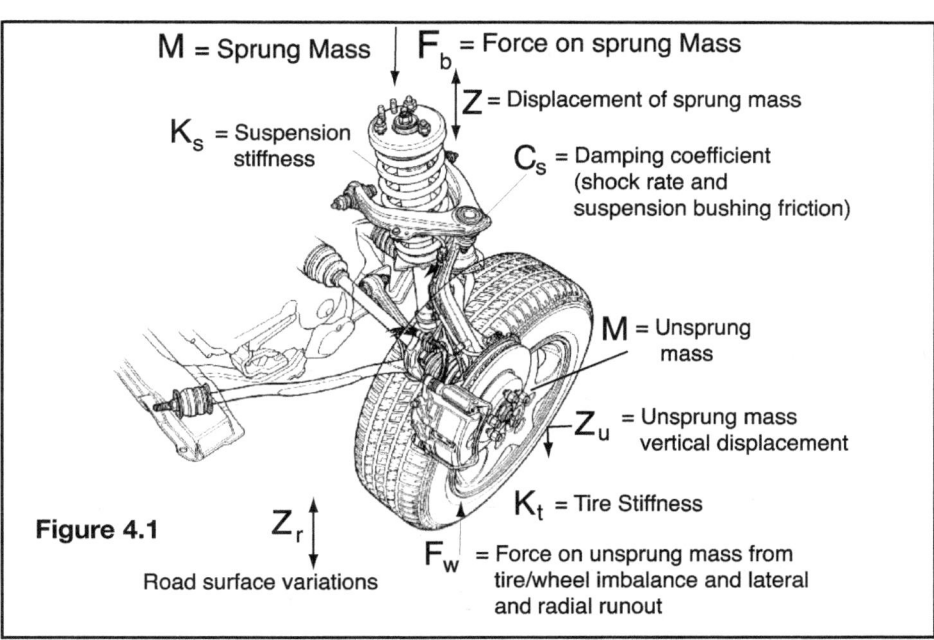

Figure 4.1 illustrates some of the forces at work in your suspension.

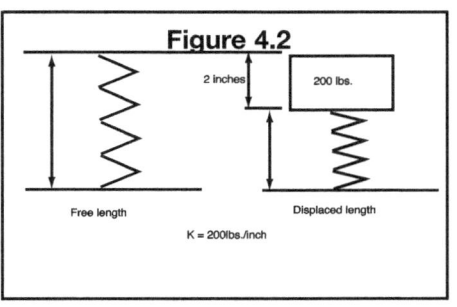

If a 100 lb. weight compresses a spring 1-inch and a second 100 lbs. compresses it another inch, we say the spring has a rate of 100 lbs. per inch.

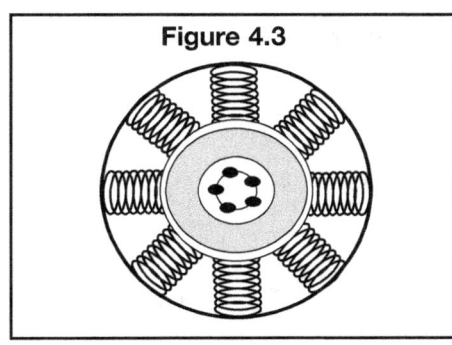

Pneumatic tires have a spring rate. In fact they are true progressive rate springs.

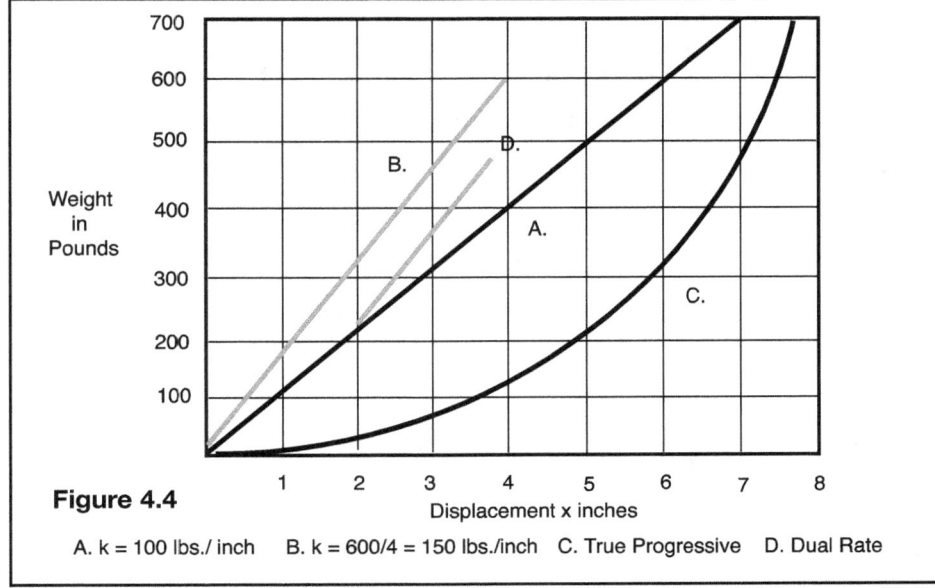

A. k = 100 lbs./ inch   B. k = 600/4 = 150 lbs./inch   C. True Progressive   D. Dual Rate

Spring rates tend to be linear. That is, as more weight is added to them they compress a certain amount for a specific amount of additional weight. There are progressive rate springs on the market, but they are better described as dual rate springs. After a certain amount of deflection, they take on a steeper curve. A truly progressive spring would have a geometric curve which is the curve you get from air lift style springs.

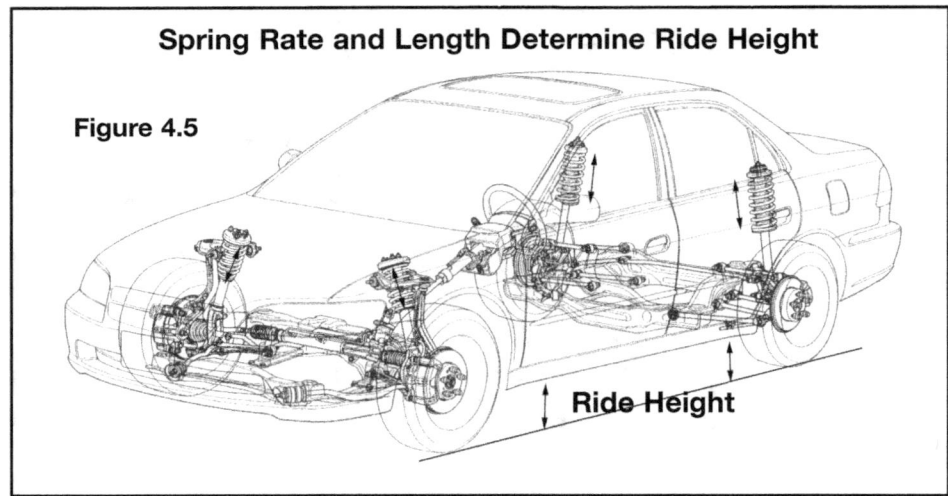

**Spring Rate and Length Determine Ride Height**

**Figure 4.5**

Ride Height

**The springs support your car's weight and will compress until the spring is pushing back on the body as much as the body is pushing on the spring. This is the static ride height. You can raise ride height by increasing spring rate keeping the same length. Do this by reducing the sprung weight or by relocating the upper spring mounts lower on the body. Lowering ride height can be accomplished by reducing spring rate, increasing sprung weight, raising spring mounting points, or shortening the spring. The advantage of lower ride height is a lower cg. The disadvantage in lowering ride height reduces the potential suspension travel within which to absorb road shocks.**

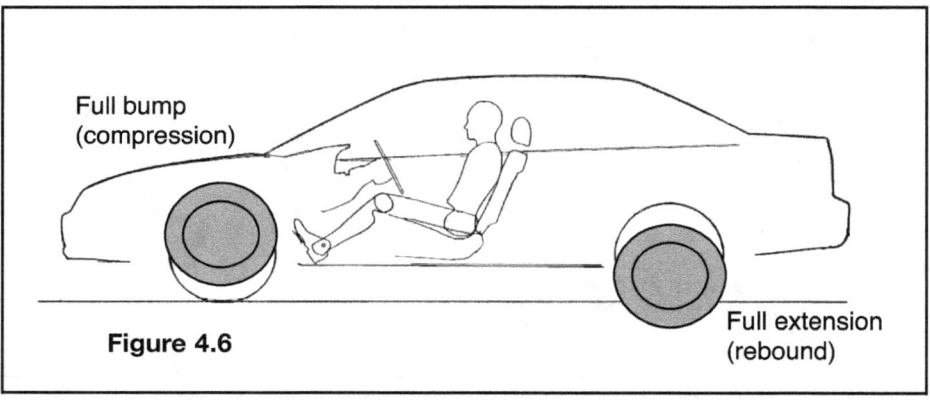

Full bump (compression)

Full extension (rebound)

**Figure 4.6**

**Your suspension has to move in order to absorb shocks from surface irregularities such as potholes, frost heaves, bridge seams and just rough pavement. When the tire and suspension moves up it's called compression or bump. As it extends, it goes into rebound. The distance the suspension and wheel can move is called suspension travel. A suspension with more travel is able to absorb larger shocks than one with less travel.**

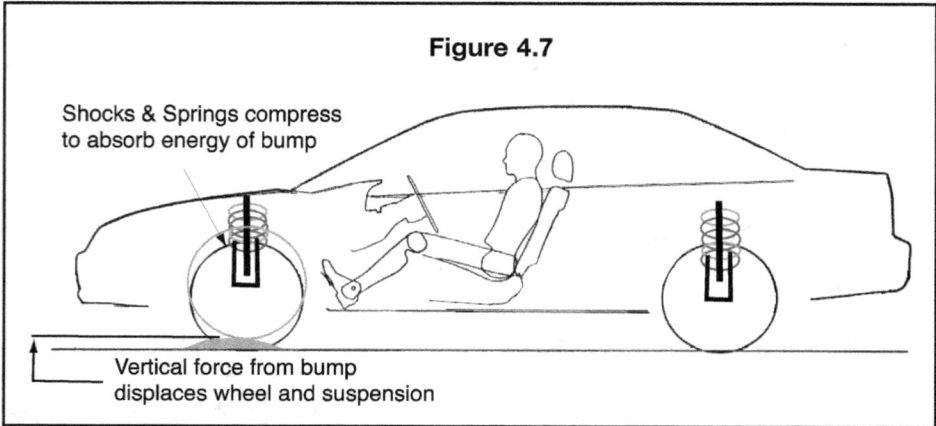

**Figure 4.7**

Shocks & Springs compress to absorb energy of bump

Vertical force from bump displaces wheel and suspension

**Shocks and springs work together. The springs are load sensitive devices which are totally insensitive to time. Shocks are speed sensitive devices which are very sensitive to the distance the shock valve is moving in time.**

installed with aggressive springs, which further raise the ride rate, have fairly harsh rides. They just vibrate at a higher frequency than most humans consider comfortable.

## SPRINGS

Speaking of vibrating, your Honda's suspension springs are of supreme importance to its ride and handling performance. The springs are the basic component of the suspension. Springs are really what suspends the chassis. Their primary function is to allow deflection or displacement in order to absorb bumps and irregularities in the road surface and to keep the tires in contact with the road. Springs do this by compressing and storing energy, then releasing that energy as they extend. When a car is still, the springs hold the car body at a specific distance off the ground, known as ride height. So while you are cruising down a smooth section of highway, your car should sort of float at a comfortable rate of oscillation as the springs, with the help of the shocks, do their job.

One of the more useful characteristics of a spring is that it stores and releases energy at a predictable rate. In fact, that's what a spring does as it vibrates, it is storing and releasing energy. The predictability of this process is what allows suspension tuners to, well, tune suspensions.

This property was first given mathematical expression by an english experimental physicist named Robert Hooke (1635-1703).

$W = kx$
Where:
W = weight (mass times gravity)
K = spring rate constant
x = distance of displacement

This equation, roughly stated in english, says that the spring rate, or constant k times the displaced distance equals the weight, or force required to cause x displacement. See Figure 4.4 to see it displayed graphically.

From this we see that the spring compresses as it carries more weight, or if more force is applied to it as occurs when absorbing a bump. Remember, weight is a measure of the force applied by a mass under the acceleration of gravity.

By selecting spring rates and calculating the mechanical leverage of the suspension you can determine how much force you put on the tire contact patch as weight transfers to the tires when the car is maneuvering.

In a previous chapter we discussed in length the physics of weight transfer and how such load shifting influences the grip of the tires at each of the car's corners. The useful part of knowing your spring rates, at each wheel, is then, knowing how to calculate weight transfer. You'll know how much force the suspension is exerting on the tire contact patch. And further, you can decide within limits how much weight you want each wheel to carry as the car transfers weight by choosing appropriate spring rates and lengths. This is fundamental property that allows you to tune your suspension. It's all about how much weight, or vertical force is on the tire contact patch that determines how much total grip the tires develop.

So if you change the distribution of weight transferred front to rear or side to side, by changing spring rates, you change the handling of the car. When you change rates side to side, you're changing what is called the roll stiffness of the suspension. And as you can see in Figure 4.10, roll stiffness can be different from the front to the rear. This is a key tuning tool and can be used to dilute the ill effects of poor weight distribution, though it cannot completely neutralize them.

Most tuners then use antiroll bars to fine tune roll stiffness to enhance the handling of a car under specific track and road conditions. We'll discuss antiroll bars more in depth in a moment. But first we need to step back to the concept of the spring rate constant.

That springs have a rate constant also means that they will vibrate at a certain frequency in a free state, or with a mass attached, it will vibrate at a slower rate proportional to the mass attached. This property allows you to tune what is known as ride rate.

Springs control so much of your car's suspension. Spring rates influence how much your car will pitch and bounce in response to road irregularities. Figure 4.9 shows several variations of pitch and bounce.

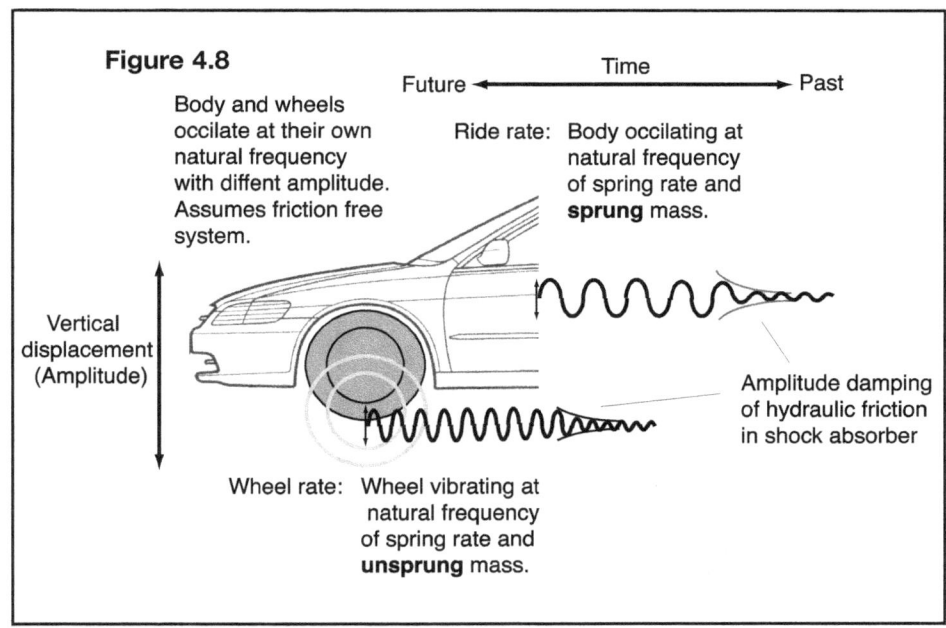

**Figure 4.8**

Body and wheels occilate at their own natural frequency with diffent amplitude. Assumes friction free system.

Ride rate: Body occilating at natural frequency of spring rate and **sprung** mass.

Vertical displacement (Amplitude)

Future ← Time → Past

Amplitude damping of hydraulic friction in shock absorber

Wheel rate: Wheel vibrating at natural frequency of spring rate and **unsprung** mass.

The body and wheels oscillate at different natural frequencies even though the same spring is involved. This is because the masses at each end of the spring are different. The body is much more massive than the wheels, consequently the body oscillates at a slower natural frequency than the wheels. This is advantageous because your insides would liquefy if you vibrated at that rate. However, for the tire this means that it can return to the road very quickly after absorbing a shock, and if the shock absorbers are tuned right, they keep the tire on the road.

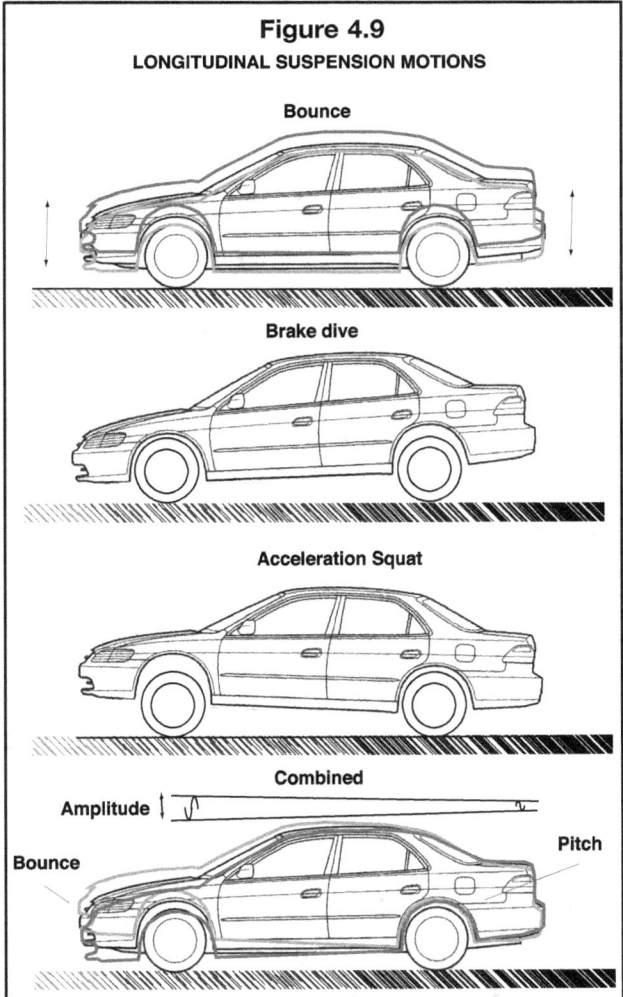

**Figure 4.9**
LONGITUDINAL SUSPENSION MOTIONS

Bounce

Brake dive

Acceleration Squat

Combined

Bounce is when the chassis moves up and down. Your car can bound at either or both ends separately or simultaneously.

Brake dive is when your car pitches forward, compressing the front suspension from forward weight transfer and the rear springs push the rear of the car up. The converse is true in acceleration squat.

Acceleration squat displays as the nose coming up and the rear squatting down. Again, weight transfer is causing the suspension to react.

Sometimes you get a combination of bounce and pitch. This can come from incorrectly matched springs and shock valving. It tends to occur on roads with bumps evenly spaced while you are traveling at a certain speed. You can also get corner to corner pitch — a corkscrew effect.

However, shocks, can reduce these effects. For example, proper shock rebound rates can reduce rear lift during brake dive as well as improving cornering transitions by keeping the inside of the car from lifting too much.

As discussed above, spring rates and lengths help determine ride height; but you can use these to alter the ride height for performance or styling preferences. For example, shorter springs on the front suspension lower the front of the car to give it a slant known as a rake. Lowering the nose relative to the rear can give you an aero dynamic advantage if the body "angle of attack" is tuned to produce less lift. Lift is a source of drag, but we'll discuss aerodynamic basics in a later chapter.

Before we leave this subject we need to talk about cutting springs.

Cutting springs is a time-honored way that performance enthusiasts tune ride height. There are two things you need to know about cutting springs. The first is that cutting springs obviously shortens the length, but it increases the spring rate. Unfortunately, the rate increase is not predictable so you'll get different rates for each spring. And since the rates are slightly different, the ride height at each corner will be slightly different. The differences we're talking about are extremely large, but if you're on the edge of a harmonic or resonance within the suspension, these subtle changes can sometimes make the handling of your car surprisingly quirky at the most inopportune time.

The second involves a right way and a wrong way of cutting springs. The right way is to use a cut-off wheel; the wrong way is to use a torch. Spring steel is heat-treated, and the heat from a cutting torch changes the heat-treating.

One more thing, springs do fatigue with age, so an old set of springs won't have the "spring" that a fresh set will.

## FUNDAMENTAL SUSPENSION CONCEPTS AND ADJUSTMENTS

### TOE

Toe is the difference in distance between the leading and trailing edges of opposite wheels. If the front of the wheels are farther apart than

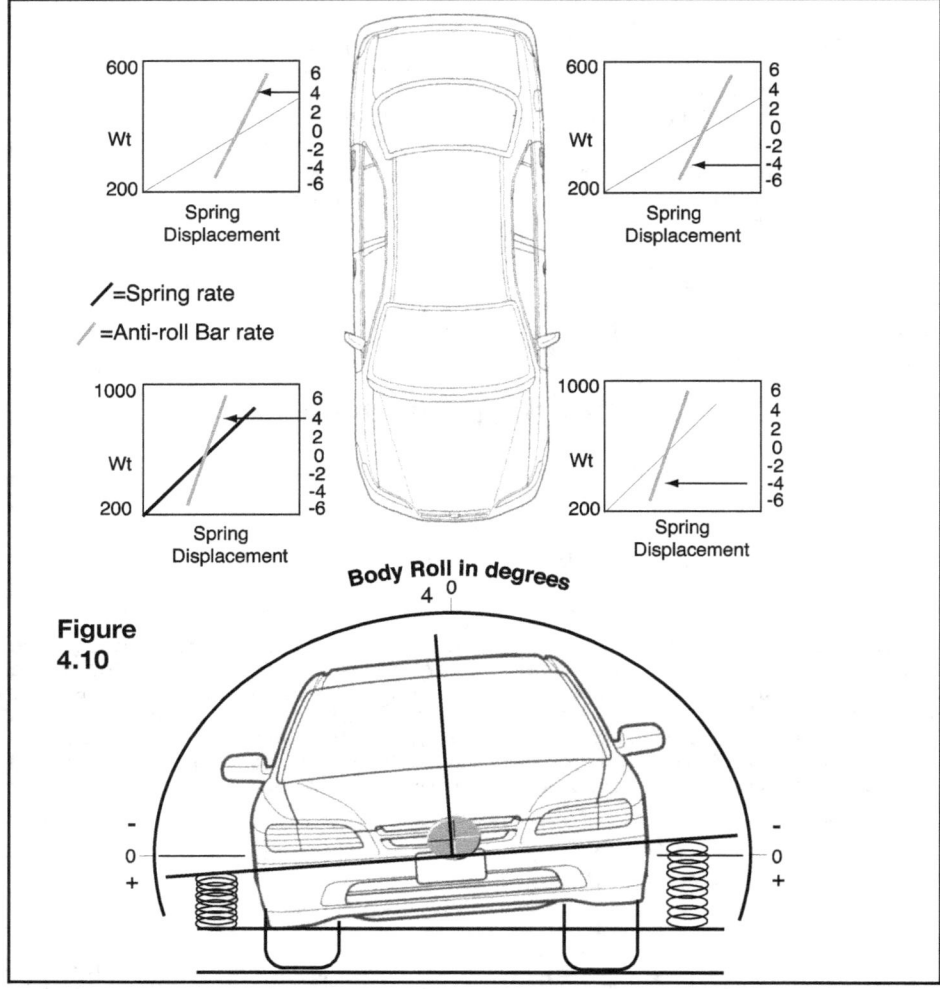

**Figure 4.10**

This diagram shows how spring rates help determine the wheel weights of a car in a turn. We included the rate curve for antiroll bars, which, after all, are just additional suspension springs that work only when the body is leaning. Notice how antiroll bars reduce wheel weight on the wheels toward the center of the turn. These spring rates are exaggerated to illustrate the concept, they aren't intended to be recommended for a particular car. In particular, the antiroll bar rates are very high, you'd probably see a curve closer to that of the spring rate.

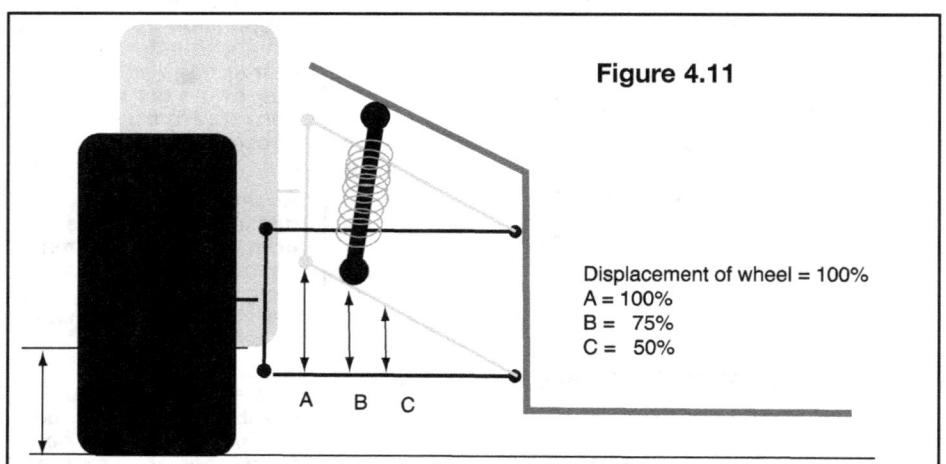

**Figure 4.11**

Displacement of wheel = 100%
A = 100%
B = 75%
C = 50%

There is a lot going on with the "simple" levers of the suspension links. One of the aspects of this system is motion ratio. As you can see, where you mount springs and shocks determines the component's motion ratio. This factors into the rate of springs and shock valving as well as determining the percentage sprung to unsprung weight of the suspension. You get better handling and ride as you reduce unsprung weight. This lets the suspension react faster since it has less inertia to overcome.

the rear, that is considered toe out. When the reverse is so, that is called toe in.

Toe is usually measured as a fraction of an inch or in millimeters. For example, you have 1/32-inch toe in. This is fine as long as you know that when you change the diameter of your tires, as in a plus 3 concept rolling stock upgrade, the linear measure is no longer accurate. That is why some alignment specialists prefer to use degrees of toe, which is not dependent on tire diameter for its accuracy.

If your suspension didn't have flexible bushings to absorb impact harshness and vibrations from the road, you could run zero toe, as race cars can with rod ends for pivot points. Zero toe reduces rolling resistance, tread wear as well as the tire temps.

Since your Honda does have flexible suspension bushings the toe setting cannot be zero. It has to be set to compensate for the forces of acceleration, braking, steady state cruising, and cornering which deflect the suspension causing a change in toe of the wheels. If you look at Figure 4.13 you'll see that toe applies to the front and the rear wheels.

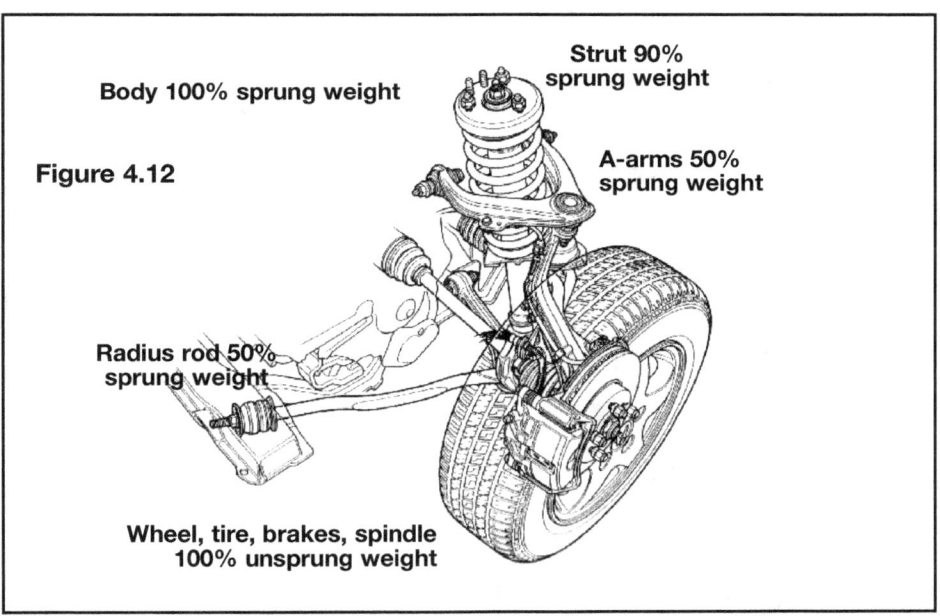

Figure 4.12

Not all suspension components are unsprung weight. Some are a combination, the proportion of each determined by its motion ratio. This figure illustrates some common values of various components. To be accurate however, you should measure the range of motion.

In Figure 4.14 you can see the relationship between the static setting, which is where you adjust it while the car is still. This is relative to the angle it takes while moving either in steady state or dynamic, i.e. braking, accelerating, etc.

Notice, that the desired settings are different for front wheel drive and rear wheel drive. Obviously the front drive pulls the wheels forward, thus requiring a static toe out setting.

Notice how under braking you get a toe out condition. This works in your favor as you enter a turn, however too much toe out makes the car feel twitchy when braking hard. The reason toe out helps when you enter a corner should be made clear after you understand "Ackerman" geometry. Basically Ackerman geometry is achieved using a trapezoidal arrangement of the tierods and steering link. When you steer the wheels in either direction, the geometry of the arms causes the inside wheel to take a greater angle than the outside wheel. This effect is exaggerated when you have a toe out condition. See Figure 4.15.

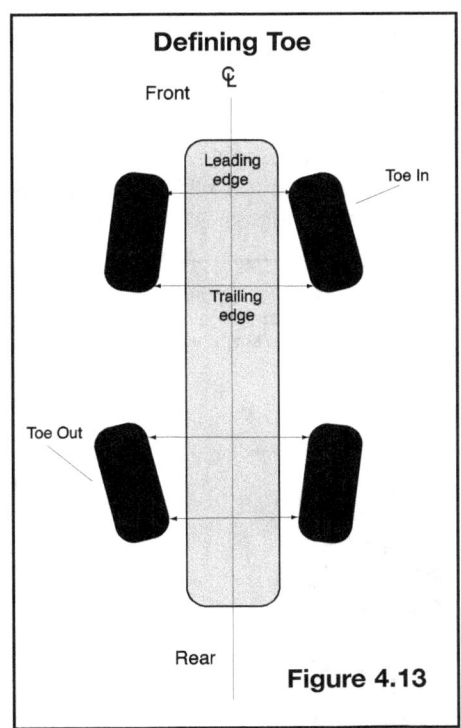

Figure 4.13

Toe is the difference of the distance between the front and rear edges of the tire. Both the front and rear suspensions also can have toe. Front toe affects handling very differently than rear toe.

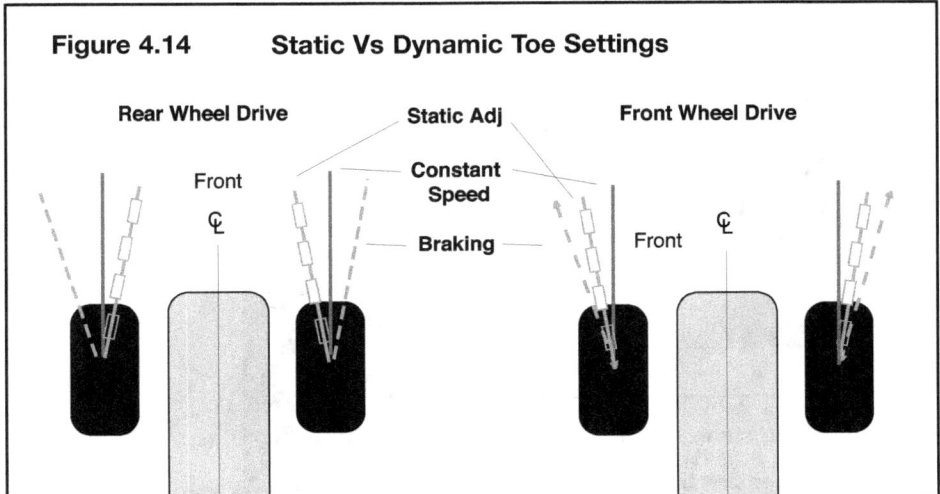

Figure 4.14  Static Vs Dynamic Toe Settings

Because your suspension has flexible bushings to absorb road shocks, noise, and vibrations, the toe is set at a value with the vehicle at rest, which will change once it is in motion. Rear drive cars and front wheel drive cars require different static settings because the suspension deflects differently if it is driving the car forward or being driven forward.

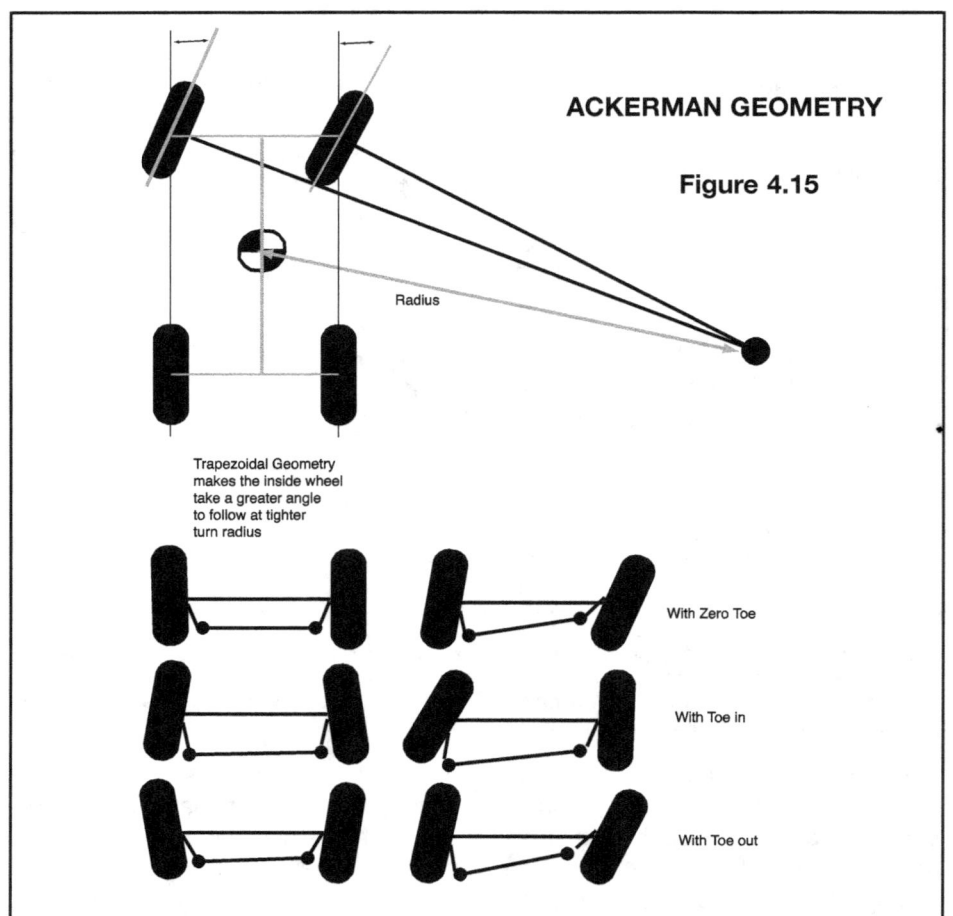

## ACKERMAN GEOMETRY

**Figure 4.15**

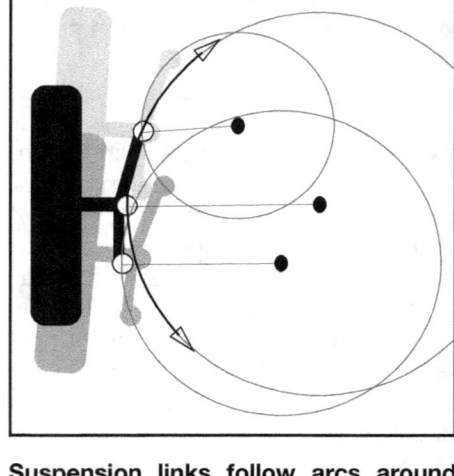

Suspension links follow arcs around their pivots. If the various arcs flow with each other, your steering is consistent. If not, you've got bump and roll steer.

set of tires like a torch. On the other side of the scale, toe in tends to produce understeer. If you haven't noticed, there is a trend here.

Essentially toe is a setting that fine tunes the gross handling characteristics determined by weight transfer distribution. If your car's understeering badly as you enter a corner, putting a .25 inch of toe out probably won't cause the car to oversteer. The most likely result is reduced understeer.

Several of the most common handling circumstances are displayed in a couple of figures. If you look at these carefully, you can see the slip angles of the wheels relative to the size of radius each wheel takes in a turn. These angles aren't exact, in

**Because Ackerman Geometry changes the amount of toe as you turn the wheels, it can be used to fine tune your handling. A little toe out can put the inside tire at a higher slip angle and therefore generate a bit more cornering force to help rotate the car into a turn. Toe in has the opposite effect, which may be what you want if your car is oversteering.**

Just as toe can be a help it can also hinder cornering and straightline performance. While a moderate amount of toe out will help your car turn in with precision, too much can make the car unstable at high speeds; cause excessive twitching when braking and will just burn through a

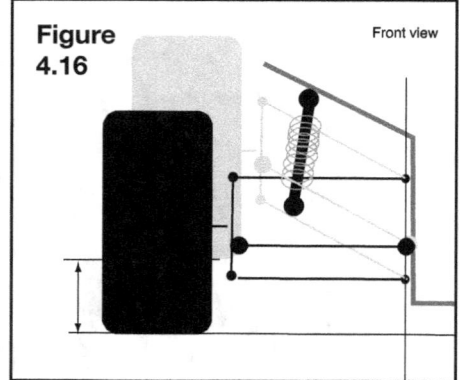

**Figure 4.16**

**Bump and roll steer is caused by a geometry error that forces a change of toe as the suspension travels through its normal range of motion. When the arcs of the various links don't "shadow" each other close enough, one of the components has to take a different path. If the component can rotate, this changes its attitude. If not, you get a bind.**

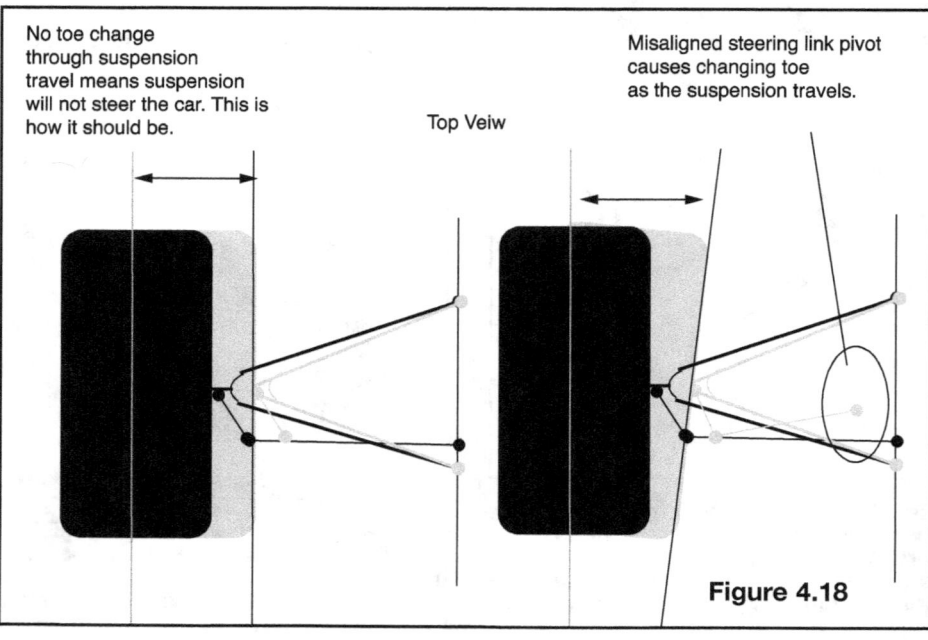

**Figure 4.18**

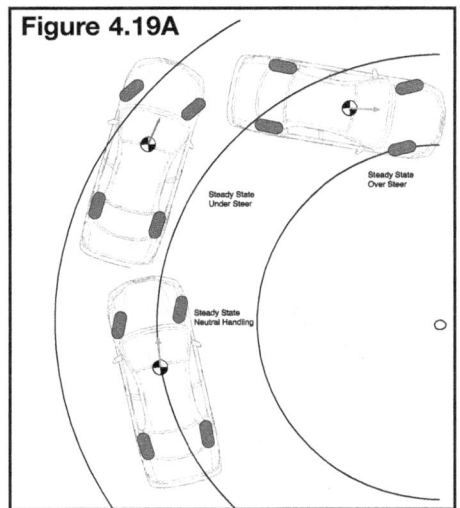
Figure 4.19A

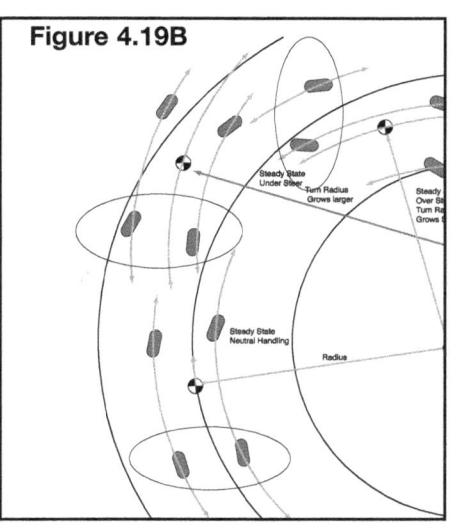
Figure 4.19B

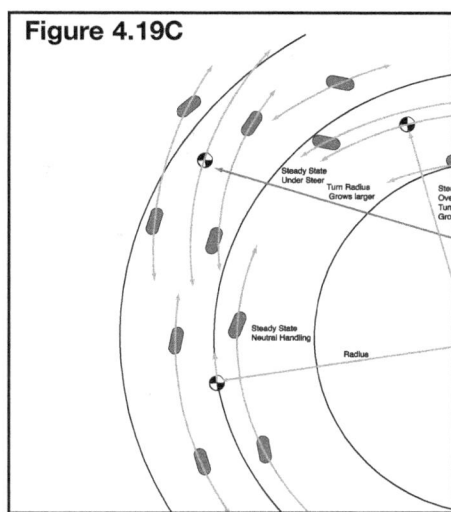
Figure 4.19C

Toe settings fine tune the inherent handling characteristics of your car. Changing the toe on the front tires affects turn-in response; changing it on the rear affects steady state cornering behavior and power-on corner exit behavior. Understeer is when you have to turn the wheel more to get it to make the turn; oversteer is when you have to take steering out to let the nose catch up to the rear. Neutral steer is when you get the tires at about a 7-degree slip angle and blast through the turn.

Rear toe setting influences steady state and corner exit behavior. This is because the front initiates the turn, the rear works very hard in the corner and the exit. Toe out tends to produce oversteer, particularly when powering out of a corner. Toe in produces understeer in the middle, steady state portion.

With a neutral steering car the ackerman angle lets the inside and outside tires take the appropriate radius, thus maximize the slip angles at each tire to create the most efficient cornering force. With too much toe in, the inside tire doesn't develop the optimum slip angle, and the outside tire develops too large of one. The result is understeer. Push. Oversteer is when the rearend comes around on you.

fact they are exaggerated to show the relationship more clearly.

When you're driving on the street, it's always better to keep all suspension adjustments within the range specified by the manufacturer. And when it comes time to set toe for an auto cross or race school, you really shouldn't have to vary the setting by more than .25 inch total or .125 per side.

## BUMP AND ROLL STEER

Bump steer is a change in toe of the front or rear suspension as it moves through its normal travel. The reason the toe changes is because the arc of the steering link is not the same as that of the suspension links. Therefore, as it travels on either the compression (bump, hence the name) or rebound stroke, the toe changes to varying degrees. See Figures 4.16, 4.17, 4.18, and 4.20.

Roll steer is a change in toe of the rear suspension which causes a steering input. It's related to bump steer in that they are both caused by toe changes, caused by suspension geometry. But it's called roll steer because it occurs as the body rolls during a turn. With roll steer, even if the car is on a glass-smooth track, the suspension will steer the car. Bump steer however also makes itself known on a bumpy section of road, even if you are going straight. So it's better to think of bump and roll steer as two separate entities, even though they are both caused by geometry errors.

## CASTOR

Castor is the angle of the steering axis as measured from a vertical line that intersects the center of the tire's contact patch. On the front wheels, castor determines the high speed stability, or lack of same. Generally the trend is more castor yields more stability, but at a price of increasing steering effort. The reason the steering effort increases, is because as the wheel turns on an inclined steering axis one of the two wheels wants to travel below the road surface. Since this is impossible it tries to lift the car up. This geometry is also where castor helps generate self centering force. That is, the steering naturally wants to resume a straight ahead ori-

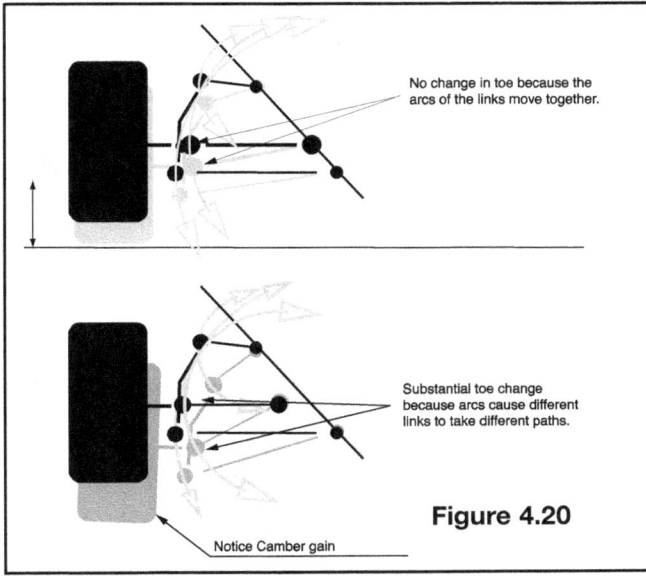
Figure 4.20

The position of the steering link joint is most critical in determining the amount of toe change relative to suspension travel. Not only in lateral plane shown, but its position fore and aft of the control arm link pivots and its height above the control arm pivots. As you can see this geometry gets complicated. Just something to think about before you go for the slammed look.

Honda Builder's Handbook Vol. 2

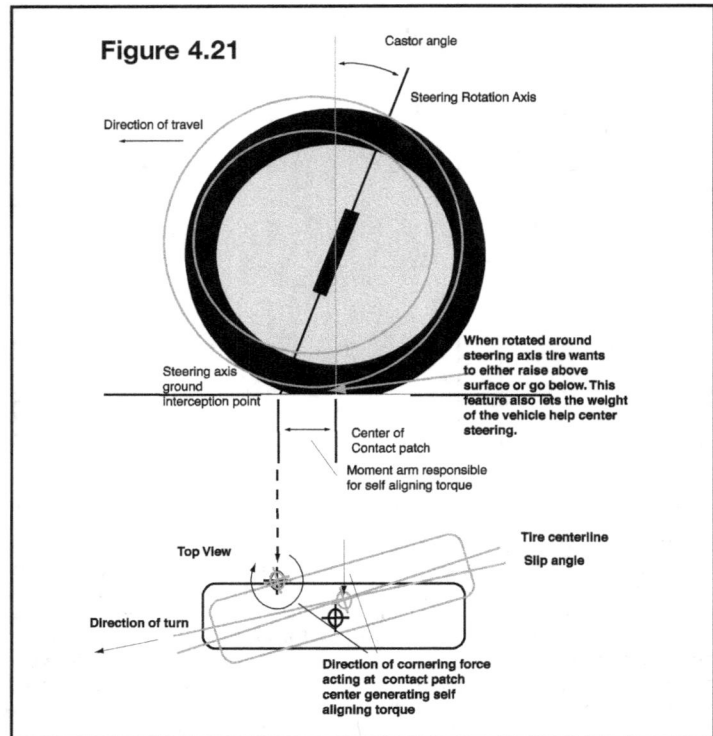

**Figure 4.21** Castor influences stability and handling.

**Figure 4.22** Scrub Radius

The tricky thing about suspension is that each component is influenced by the others. There are feedback loops within feedback loops. Castor angle and scrub radius are two more adjustments to consider. The castor angle, in addition to its role in high speed stability, influences camber gain adjustments. The scrub radius, which is determined by the lateral inclination and the longitudinal (castor) inclination of the steering axis, changes the way tires swing through the steering rotation.

entation. Driver's usually like this effect. Another source of self centering force is the lever arm established between the ground intersect of the steering axis and the center of the contact patch. See Figure 4.21.

### SHOCKS AND TUNING YOUR SUSPENSION:
#### A CONVERSATION WITH RICHARD MEYER, TOKICO'S AFTERMARKET TECHNICAL DIRECTOR

When you start enhancing the cornering and handling performance of your vehicle you're often going to get a stiffer ride. The idea then is to strike a balance.

Striking a balance in this sense is seeing how much grip you can generate and not totally destroy ride quality. Of course there is a point where you start to lose compliance (i.e. a very stiff ride) and you not only lose ride quality but you lose adhesion as well. That means you can have a situation where your car corners nice and flat but it's just dancing all over the road.

What happens to a car with either no travel or a spring that's so stiff it might as well be a bump stop, is the tires and wheels have to take up the slack, so to speak. We meet a lot of dissatisfied car owners with such suspensions.

If you look at a Formula 1 or an Indy Car, you'll notice it has very little suspension compliance. When a car generates enough aerodynamic down force to stick it to the ceiling, you need stiff, very stiff shocks and springs. But these cars use really tall sidewalled tires. There's got to be some give somewhere and these highly sprung race cars use the tire as an extension of the spring. This is true with all cars, really. So when you use springs that are too stiff with low aspect ratio tires, you've got no give in the suspension and you bend wheels or break something on the chassis. We've seen stress cracks in chassis with such combinations.

There are a few concepts you need to understand when you start tuning suspensions. First of all, don't screw it up. Don't do a lot of things wrong. Second, buy good components that'll give you the best combination for what you're trying to achieve. To do this, you need to understand how the various suspension components work and how changes made to these components affect handling and ride.

### The Purpose of Shocks

Shock absorbers have two important jobs. One is to control or damp out excess chassis motion such as roll, pitch, dive, and float. The other is to damp out excess motion at the tire/wheel. Springs and linkage allow necessary motion, but they cannot control excess motion. That is the job of the shock absorbers.

### How Shocks Work

Shocks work with the springs to control your tires and wheels. One way to think about this is springs are deflection or load sensitive devices. If you have a 100 lb./in. spring and put 200 lbs. on it, it will deflect (i.e. compress) 2 inches. It doesn't matter to the spring if you apply the weight over two weeks or within .25 second. It's only the total load that affects the spring. The shock on the other hand, within its normal range of operation doesn't care how far you move it, but it reacts to how quickly the force is applied. It's a velocity sensitive device.

Shocks use hydraulic friction which is the resistance of a fluid to flowing through some sort of conduit to resist motion. You've probably heard people talk about shock valving. That is the device shock manufacturers use to vary hydraulic resistance. Within the valve is a small opening that allows only a certain amount of oil to pass through it within a given time period. If you look at the cut-a-way diagram of a Tokico low-pressure gas charged shock, it shows some of the various passages we use with Tokico shocks. The fundamental equation that allows us to tune a shock is that for oil, or any fluid actually, the resistance to flow increases as a square of the velocity.

**Resistance = Velocity$^2$**

Essentially you've got a hole or port in a piston through which oil is passing. As the piston's speed or velocity increases, the resistance it encounters is not linear, it is geometric. So the resistance to flow is what allows us to tune shocks.

If we only had a low-speed hole, your car would ride fine until you hit a chuckhole. Then it'd feel like your suspension was welded solid. The solution to this problem is to use what is known as a blow-off valve. With a blow-off valve we have a device within the shock that responds to the geometric increase in pressure as piston velocity increases. At a specific pressure point, determined by the engineer's goal of resistance or for a combination of ride and control, he'll change spring tension. At some point there's enough pressure on the seat that it pops the valve open and lets more oil flow. Blow-off refers to the point where the pressure is high enough to open the valves. Displayed graphically it looks like the curves in Figure 4.24. The valves can be tuned to blow off with greater pressure or less. Curve A opens with less pressure, B needs more pressure.

Shock absorber performance is degraded by foaming (the result of cavitation). Foamy oil does not damp properly and so gas pressurized shocks were developed to eliminate the effects of oil foam.

Not all shocks use a low speed bleed (oil passage) like TOKICO's. The TOKICO design gives shock engineers an extra dimension in tuning. Correct low-speed tuning can have a large effect on both ride and adhesion. The ability to move the blow-off point combined with a range of low-speed bleed options allows engineers a wider range of damping curve shapes than that found in the less expensive shock designs. Since different driving situations (such as on vs off-road) have different damping needs, the more sophisticated the shock absorber, the wider the range of driving requirements that shock can meet.

Occasionally people ask TOKICO what valving is being used for a given application. This is not such an easy question to answer. For purposes of production tolerance, most companies use a target piston speed to

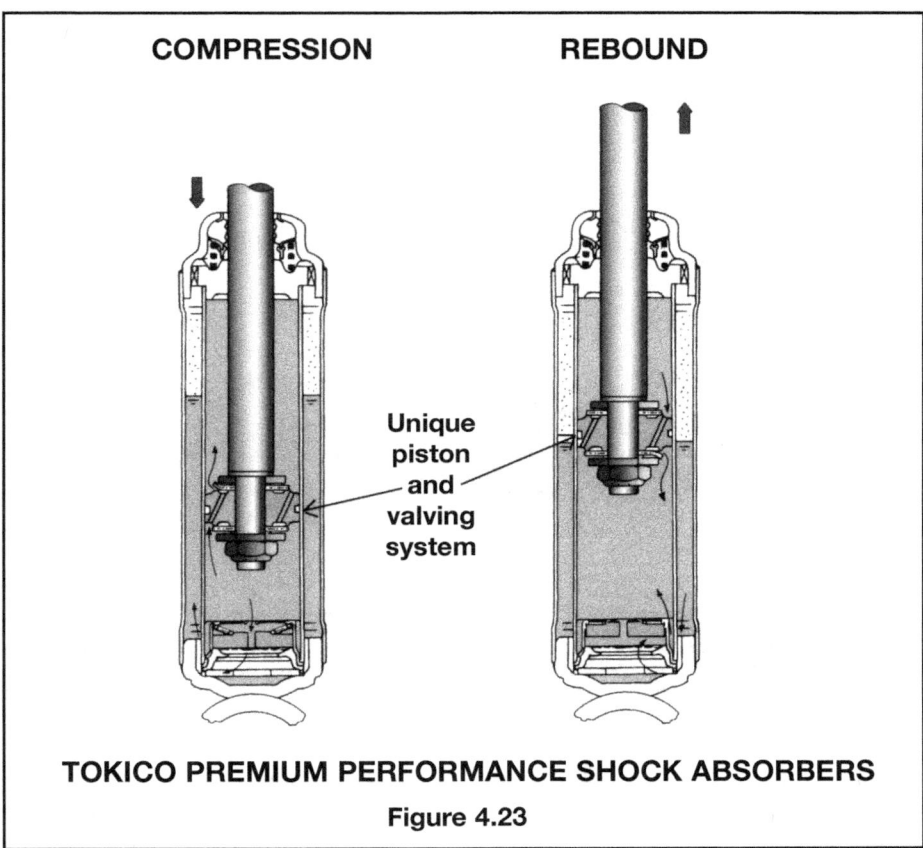

**TOKICO PREMIUM PERFORMANCE SHOCK ABSORBERS**
Figure 4.23

Tokico uses a Twin-tube low-pressure gas design. Since this design uses a bottom or base valve, Tokico feels it offers extra flexibility in valving. Mono-tube designs lack a base valve and must use high pressure to function correctly.

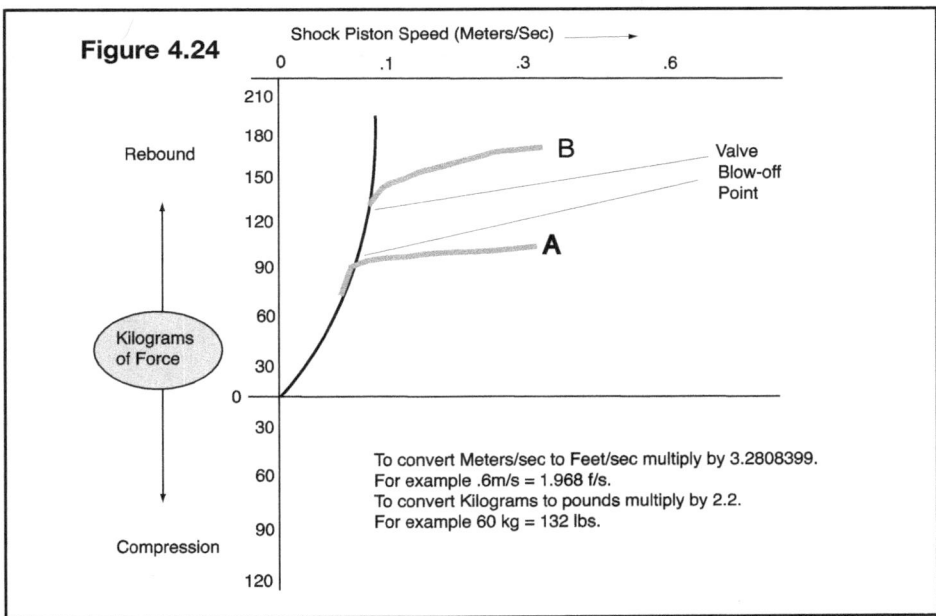

This chart displays the effect of shock valve blow-off.

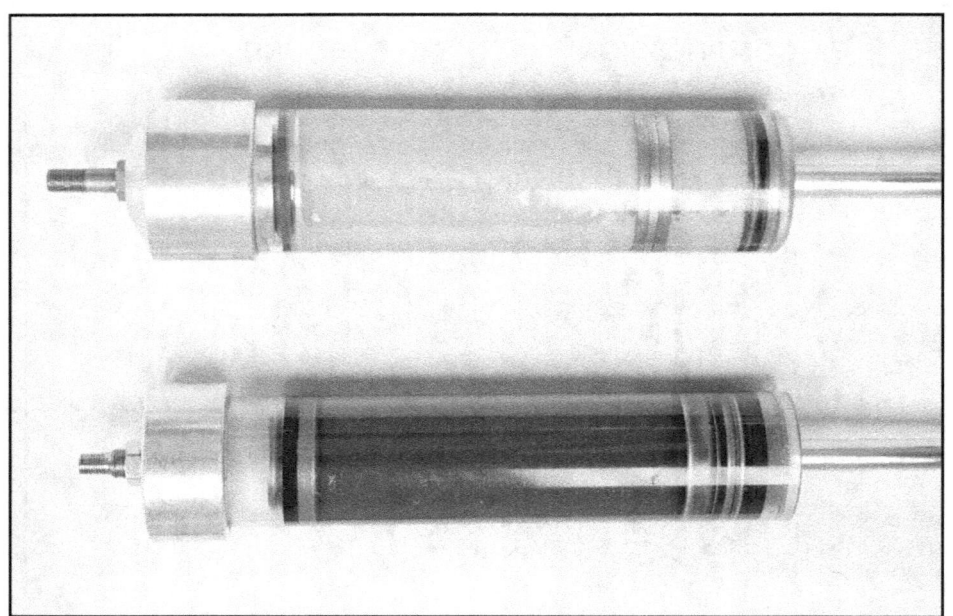

**No matter who makes the oil, there is a certain amount of air bound to the molecules of the oil. When you get the pressure drop behind the piston, it sucks the air out of the solution and you get foam. The problem is that foamed oil doesn't offer much resistance and you loose damping force as the oil foams or cavitates.**

measure a given level of resistance (damping force). To really compare different shocks, one needs to look at the whole curve. It is also important to know what units of measurement are being used. They can be lbs./sq. inch, kilograms of force, or even Newtons. Picking only one point or piston speed does not show the whole curve and as Fig. 4.25 shows, it is possible to have two shocks which look identical in terms of force. In this case, at .52 m/s (about 1.7 ft./sec.) these two units have the same force. But a look at the rest of the curve shows them to be very different. Curve A would probably ride fairly well, but it would not offer much control of either the chassis or the tires and wheels. Curve B would make the car feel pretty tight (minimal body roll) but the ride would be harsh and adhesion on rough or slick roads would probably be very poor. In the case of curve B, it has too much damping at low piston speeds in both compression and rebound. Too much low-speed compression damping would cause harshness and a lack of adhesion at the tire. The excessive low speed rebound damping would hamper the tires' ability to follow the road contours properly. It would also cause an abrupt ride that might feel like being yanked on the end of a bungee cord.

Even if you get a chance to see two complete damping force curves, it is critical that you know what they are telling you and what your car actually needs. Too much damping force can cause as many problems as too little damping force. Just saying you want a "stiffer" shock is not necessarily a solution.

### Approaches To Tuning Suspension

The first and most important question to answer is, what are you using the car for? Will it be a road racer, rally car, drag racer, everyday driver, or some combination? Where will you be driving it? Dry roads, wet roads, rough or snow-covered roads, or even off-road?

Remember, the objective is to get as much balanced adhesion from the four tire contact patches as possible.

The best setup to keep your tires on the road depends very much on the circumstances in which you will be driving. For example, a rally and a road race car would use very different suspension settings. Since rally cars run on a variety of surfaces, with many levels of potential grip, their suspensions must be set up to deal with a wide range of circumstances. As a result, rally cars tend to use suspensions with considerably more travel and considerably less roll stiffness than a road race car would use. The softer suspension lets a rally car maintain adhesion on very slick or

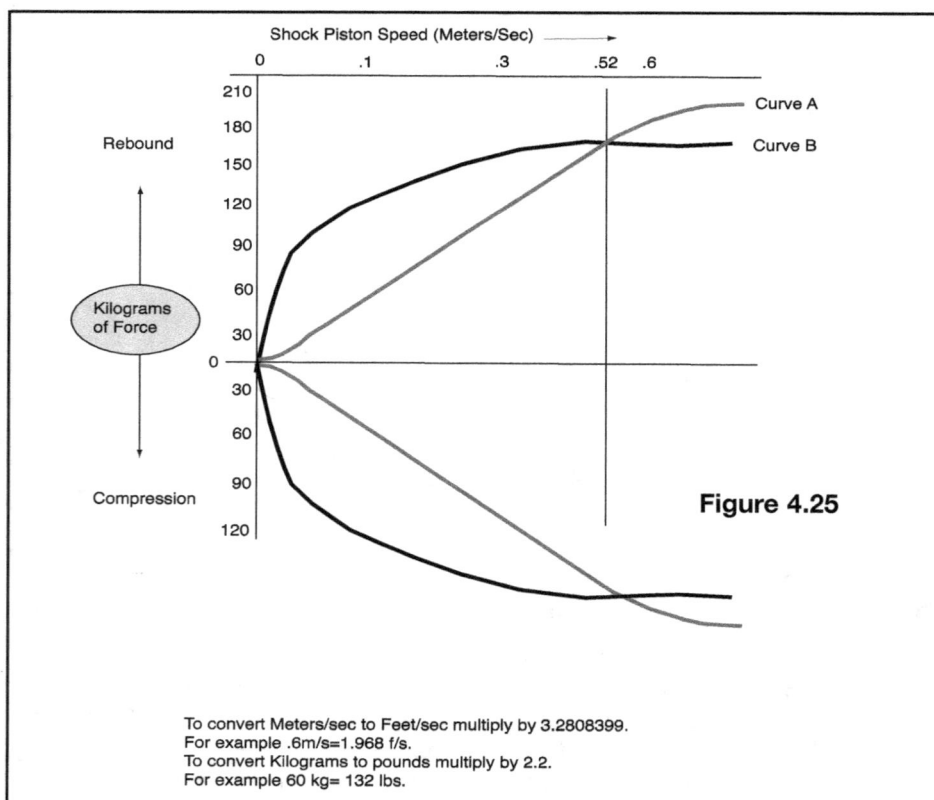

**It is possible to have two shocks with identical specs with different performances.**

rough surfaces. Less roll stiffness allows the car to load the tires more gradually in the turns or under braking. A stiff suspension would generate maximum load on the tires very quickly and break adhesion before the car could make it through a turn. The result would be a tree marker rather than a winning front marker.

While the softer suspension is necessary for a rally car, on a road racer it would be too loose. The chassis would tend to roll and wallow too much and due to the adhesion generated by racing tires, the extra body roll could cause problems with the suspension geometry.

Also, since road racers tend to minimize suspension travel, stiffer springs are necessary in order to prevent bottoming of the suspension or the chassis.

Shock absorbers for rally cars and road racers are also very different. Fig. 4.28 shows how different the requirements really are.

Since rally cars tend to use softer springs than road racers, it is important to avoid having too much low speed rebound control. Too much damping on the low speed rebound side could overpower the spring and slow the return of the tire to the pavement. At the same time, compression damping tends to be quite a bit higher than a road racer would use. However the lower spring rates increase the chance of bottoming the suspension on severe bumps or when a rally car lands hard after catching air on a big hairy jump. The higher compression works with the spring to reduce bottoming potential.

The use of stiff springs on road race cars means that we need enough rebound damping to control the springs and help minimize body roll. Compression on the other hand is much lower. Running very high compression in combination with a stiff spring would make the suspension very harsh and could hurt adhesion.

The next question may be how stiff can we go? There are various approaches to setting up race suspensions. Mark Donahue, the famous TransAm, CanAm, and Indy car driver and engineer, was an advocate of using just enough spring rate to avoid bottoming, and controlling the rest of the body roll with bars. This approach

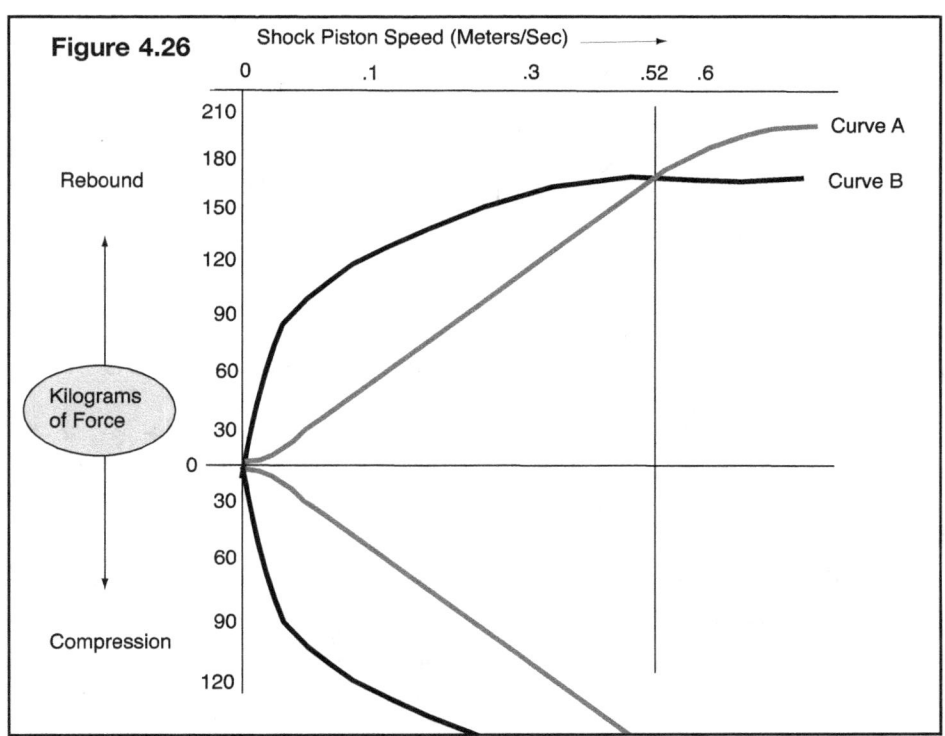

**Figure 4.26**

**If the curve charts confuse you, here's a quick explanation. The zero point is where there is no motion. One way to think about this is springs are deflection or load sensitive devices. If you have a 100 lb./in. spring and put 200 lbs. on it, it will deflect 2 inches. It doesn't matter to the spring if you apply the weight over two weeks or within .25 second. It's only the total load that affects the spring. The shock on the other hand, within its normal range of operation doesn't care how far you move it, but it reacts to how quickly the force is applied. It's a velocity sensitive device.**

has real advantages in terms of adhesion — especially on slick surfaces. Some people like to lower the car far enough that very stiff springs are necessary to avoid bottoming. Whichever method you use, it is important to keep in mind that suspension/tires should be viewed as a complete system. Matching the right combination of springs, bars, and shocks is critical for a car to perform up to its potential. This is true whether the car is a street car, rally car, drag racer, or road racer.

### Springs

When you want to lower a car, the most common method to reduce the ride height is to install shorter springs. It is also possible to simply relocate spring seats as mentioned in the caption with Fig. 4.5. Again, it depends upon whether you want to race the car, or use it on the street. Usually lowering a car means less travel. In this case it is important that the springs have a higher rate than stock. If you lower a car very far with stock rate springs, you will have bottoming problems.

If you are going to road race, linear springs are generally the best. Progressive, or variable rate springs, can generate negative handling characteristics when used on road race cars. Due to the short travel of most road race springs, locating a proper and smooth transition between the different rates is very difficult. If, as you enter a turn, the spring rate suddenly changes, it can upset the balance of the car. Variable rate coil springs can come in a variety of forms. The wire can be tapered, the coil spacing can be varied, and the coil diameter can vary (such as a cone shaped coil spring). The longer the travel, the better a variable rate spring works. That is why they have been used in rally cars and are often used by automobile manufacturers for OE applications. They can offer better ride quality in many instances.

Probably the single most common suspension mistake made by both professionals and amateurs is a lack of adequate suspension travel. While

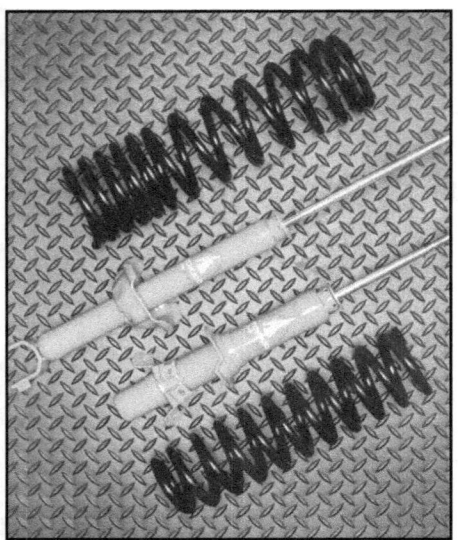

Tokico offers both linear and progressive rate springs. Progressive rates can offer a smoother ride.

lowering the center of gravity is desirable, too little suspension travel will not only hurt adhesion, but it can cause damage to the chassis and suspension of the car. A car that is too low can damage the shock absorbers by constantly rebounding off of the bumpstops. Most bumpstops are used to avoid metal to metal contact between suspension parts. As they are compressed they build up much higher forces than springs do. While shocks are designed to contain the energy of normal springs, they are not designed to contain the excess energy generated by constantly rebounding off of bumpstops (most shock absorber manufacturers will void any warranty for parts used on excessively lowered cars). Excess lowering can also generate stress cracks in the chassis. So remember, extreme lowering can not only slow you down, it can damage your car. (For street use, TOKICO offers matched spring and shock kits with correct lowering amounts).

### Caveat Racor

*WHILE WE ARE USING RACE CAR SUSPENSION TUNING FOR EXAMPLES, IT IS CRITICAL TO UNDERSTAND THAT TRUE RACE PARTS DO NOT BELONG ON STREET CARS. FOR EXAMPLE, AN UPGRADED PERFORMANCE SPRING FOR STREET PERFORMANCE MAY HAVE A RATE INCREASE OF 20% TO 60% DEPENDING UPON THE CAR. THAT SAME SPRING MAY HAVE TO BE INCREASED BY 100% TO 300% FOR ROAD RACE PURPOSES. JUST AS RACE PARTS FOR AN ENGINE CAN ACTUALLY SLOW A STREET CAR DOWN, RACE PARTS FOR THE SUSPENSION CAN MAKE A CAR UNSTABLE TO BE VIRTUALLY UNDRIVEABLE IN MANY STREET CONDITIONS.*

### Bushings

Another way to enhance handling performance is with stiffer bushings. By eliminating some of the flex of rubber, you can minimize things like camber and toe change. However, there is a price. The stiffer bushings can increase ride harshness and noise in the chassis. This is not a problem on a competition car, but for the street it is rarely desirable. Tires, shocks, springs, and bushings are all part of the suspension compliance zone. If you have already lowered the car, and put lower profile tires on the car, hard bushings may remove enough compliance to hurt not only ride and noise levels, but also adhesion on rough or slick surfaces. Factory rubber not only reduces harshness and noise, it also acts as a flexible pivot for any misalignment designed in the suspension. Putting hard bushings at too many points in some suspensions can cause binding.

*TIP: For competition purposes, hard bushings can be designed with an offset. This can give you the opportunity to gain camber where no factory adjustment was provided.*

### Shopping for Shocks

While shocks are critical to the handling of any vehicle, they are frequently the last part chosen. Even the auto manufacturers use shock absorber valving as a final tuning device. Shocks must have enough valving to control the springs and the tire/wheel mass. Using an OE or other inexpensive type of shock absorber or strut on a car with higher rate springs and altered travel will not give you the performance you need. Such parts may even make the car unstable.

There are three main factors to consider when looking for performance shock absorbers. One is the quality. Quality means materials used, tolerances maintained, and overall workmanship. Another is design. Design is important because it can limit the types of damping curves the shock manufacturer can provide. The third factor is total damping force. Even if you cannot find a shock with a sophisticated damping curve to fit your car, you need at least enough

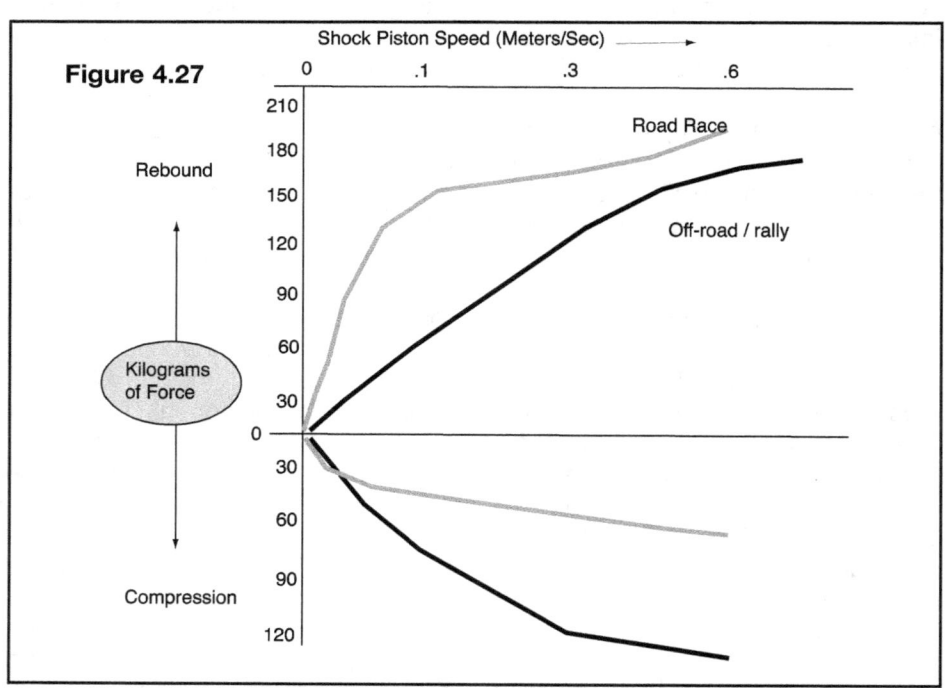

It is important to select appropriate spring pairs to compliment shock vavling tactics.

total damping force to control the higher rate springs you are using. Do not be confused by claims like 9, 10, or 14 stage valving. All shocks have 3 basic stages. Low speed, blow off (also called second stage), and high speed restriction. While it is possible with some designs to add a sub stage, the high numbers often quoted are marketing hype pure and simple.

Since you cannot really order up custom valving (except on very expensive race shock absorbers) you will have to try to find the best product for your needs in the aftermarket. There are a wide variety of shocks available. Their piston designs vary and their valving approaches vary. The photo on the next page shows a TOKICO piston design. In this case, the manufacturer uses deflected discs to control oil flow. To increase damping force, they increase the number or thickness of the discs. To decrease damping force, they do the opposite.

They can also vary the number or diameter of the holes in the piston. Small bleed orifices allow TOKICO engineers to alter the shape of the curve to a surprising degree. An example of this is shown in figure 4.29 which compares a TOKICO premium performance shock to an original shock for the front of a 1994 Honda Accord.

You will notice that compression is similar to the OE shock. Low speed rebound is actually less than the factory setting while rebound at the medium and high speed is considerably higher than OE. The result is a shock whose ride is almost identical to the factory shock but whose handling is substantially improved. By keeping the rebound damping force low at low piston speeds, TOKICO improves adhesion for both cornering and braking. Driving the car before and after the change improved adhesion so much, that it felt like 20 feet had been added to the width of the turn we were using.

Beyond just reduced performance in cornering, incorrect damping curves can actually reduce the efficiency of antilock brakes. Keeping the tire stuck to the road helps both performance and safety.

Recently, a number of what are called private brand or private label shocks have appeared in the market giving you more choices. There are a few primary manufacturers. Companies such as Bilstein, Gabriel, KYB, Koni, Sachs, Monroe, and TOKICO are primary manufacturers. Many brands, however, are made for packagers who are not the original manufacturer. This means they will be limited by what the original manufacturer can provide in design or quality. TOKICO does not sell to any private brand marketer in North America.

One other product which can increase the potential for chassis tuning is the adjustable shock absorber. There are four or five companies who offer some type of adjustable valving shock absorber. TOKICO offers an adjustable unit called the Illumina. It has 5 positions and can be adjusted with a small screwdriver. These units are ideal for someone who wants to autocross, drag race, or combine one or both with street driving. You will find a source list which shows many of the various manufacturers of suspension products for your Honda at the end of the chapter.

Adjustable spring perch shocks are also becoming more common in the street market. These shocks were originally designed for use on race cars. They offer a lot of flexibility for adjust ride height on race cars. They offer very little advantage for the street. In fact, if they are not properly adjusted, they can upset the handling balance of a car. They can also be lowered too far. In some cases, what looks like a really expensive adjustable spring perch shock may be a private brand part with inexpensive internal shock parts. A word to the wise — be careful.

*We consulted with Richard Meyer because he's a very sharp suspension tuner in his own right. Though he reps Tokico, most of what is presented here is purely the physics of suspension behavior and Tokico's tactics in dealing with them. He's also the first to say there are many good shocks on the market and he encourages you to learn as much as you can about all of them before your make your choice.*

## DRAG RACING CHASSIS TUNING TACTICS

Drag racing is an acceleration contest. The goal is not to be the fastest, but the quickest car through the measured quarter-mile. Of course speed is important. Presumably the faster one goes, the quicker one gets there, i.e. the finish line. But to get the speed you need to accelerate, which is defined as a change in speed. Once again we're back to the basic equation of $F = ma$.

To accelerate you've got to apply the force from your engine to the drive wheels, which grip the racing surface and accelerate the mass of your car. As we learned in the chapter on tires, a tire's grip is dependent, among

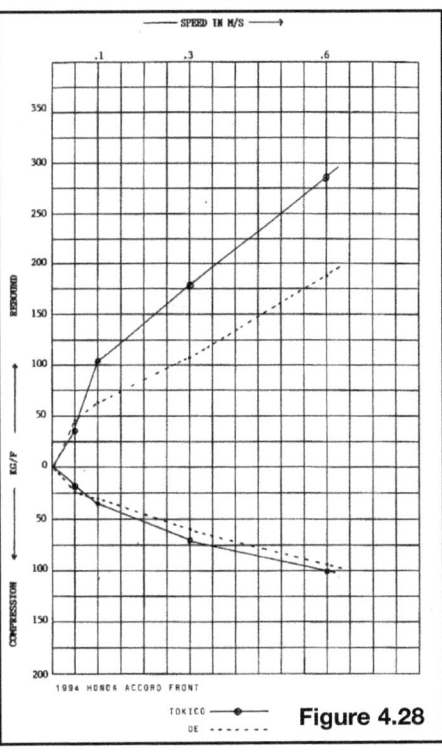

Figure 4.28

**Figure 4.28 compares OEM valving with Tokico valving.**

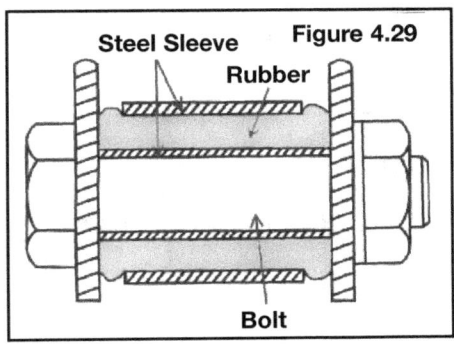

**This diagram shows bushing construction.**

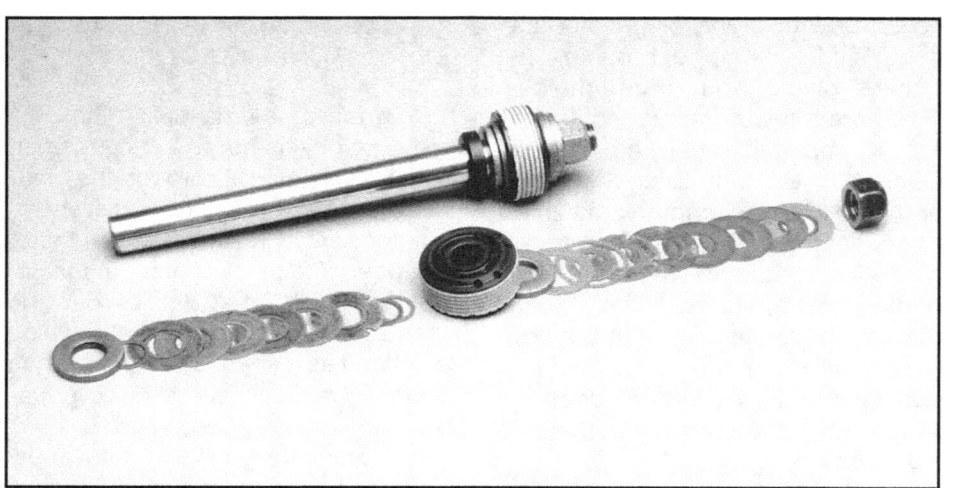

**Tokico tunes the blow-off point by putting more plates on the orifice. More plates cause it to blow-off at higher speeds and forces while less plates lower the blow-off point.**

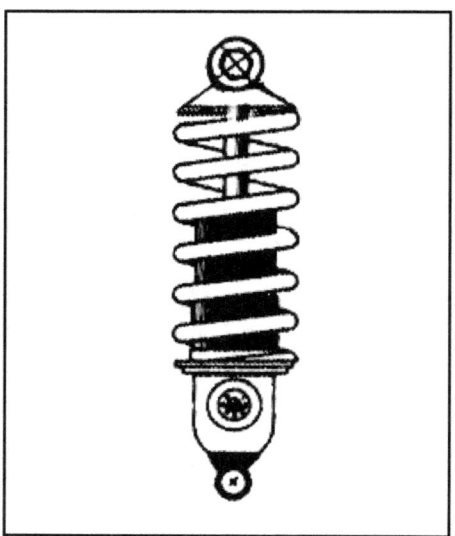

**Adjustable Coil-over shocks, such as the one shown, are primarily a racing component. They combine adjustable spring perches with the shock mount. This saves space and reduces weight. However OE shocks on most Hondas are a fixed coil-over design.**

Figure 4.30

$$F_{xmax} = \frac{\mu \dfrac{Wc}{L}}{1 + \dfrac{h}{L}\mu}$$

several other complex factors, on the vertical force exerted on the tire. We also learned in the chapter on performance driving about weight transfer. Those concepts apply to drag racing, but now we can get more specific in the dynamics of a front drive chassis at maximum acceleration.

Most Hondas have more power than the tires can hold, at least in first gear. As you modify your engine to make more power this gets extreme and where you only used to spin the tires in first gear, now you're spinning them in second and third. This is traction limited acceleration.

As we said, the ultimate limit to acceleration is the tire's coefficient of friction and the vertical force (weight) on the tire and the mass you are trying to accelerate with this force. But since the tire's vertical force changes as the chassis transfers weight, we know we have two basic systems we can manipulate to get more grip and therefore more acceleration. Getting the most from each is the way to quick E.T.s.

So the way to quicker E.T.s is twofold: First, generate more grip by using a stickier tire. In drag racing, drag slicks and various D.O.T. legal drag tires are designed for this very purpose. (See the section on drag tires in Chapter 3.) Second, manage the weight transfer in such a way as to optimize the vertical force on the drive tires while the car is accelerating. This is easier said than done, but that is the craft of chassis tuning.

The trick to tuning a chassis is to know the relationship and influences that the various components have on each other. See Figure 4.30 for an equation that describes the limits of traction for an independent front drive suspension.

Before we can calculate the max force, and from there calculate the acceleration rate, we need to fill in a couple of variables.

The weight of the vehicle is fairly easy, you just take it to a scale and measure it. The published figures from the factories are sometimes on the light side, but are a good place to start if you haven't physically weighed your car.

The length from cg to rear axle can be calculated if you know the front to rear weight distribution. Typical values for front drive cars is 60% front/ 40 % rear. If the car has an automatic transmission, a component that usually weighs more than a manual transmission, those values creep up to 65% front/ 35% rear.

For the following examples, we'll split the weight distribution difference and assume the car has a manual trans and so use a weight distribution of 62%/38% and that the car weighs around 3000lbs. with 1/2 tank of fuel and a driver. (To convert — lbs. x .0535924 = kg.) In addition, we'll assume the car has a 101-inch wheel base. Here's the equation that gives us the length to cg from the front wheel centers:

**cg distance =
rear wt. / total wt. x wheel base**

To find the weight on the rear use this equation:

**Wt. on rear axle =
Total Wt. x rear distribution %**

**3000 lbs. x .38 = 1140 lbs.**

Once we have that data then we substitute numbers for variables:

**cg dist = $\dfrac{1140 \times 101}{3000}$**

**cg dist = 38.38 inches behind front wheel centers**

With this dimension known, we just subtract to find the distance from cg to the rear axle center:

**c = 101.00 - 38.38 = 63.62**

The next variable we need is the height of the cg. This value is difficult to obtain. The difficulty lies not so much with the math, but with the

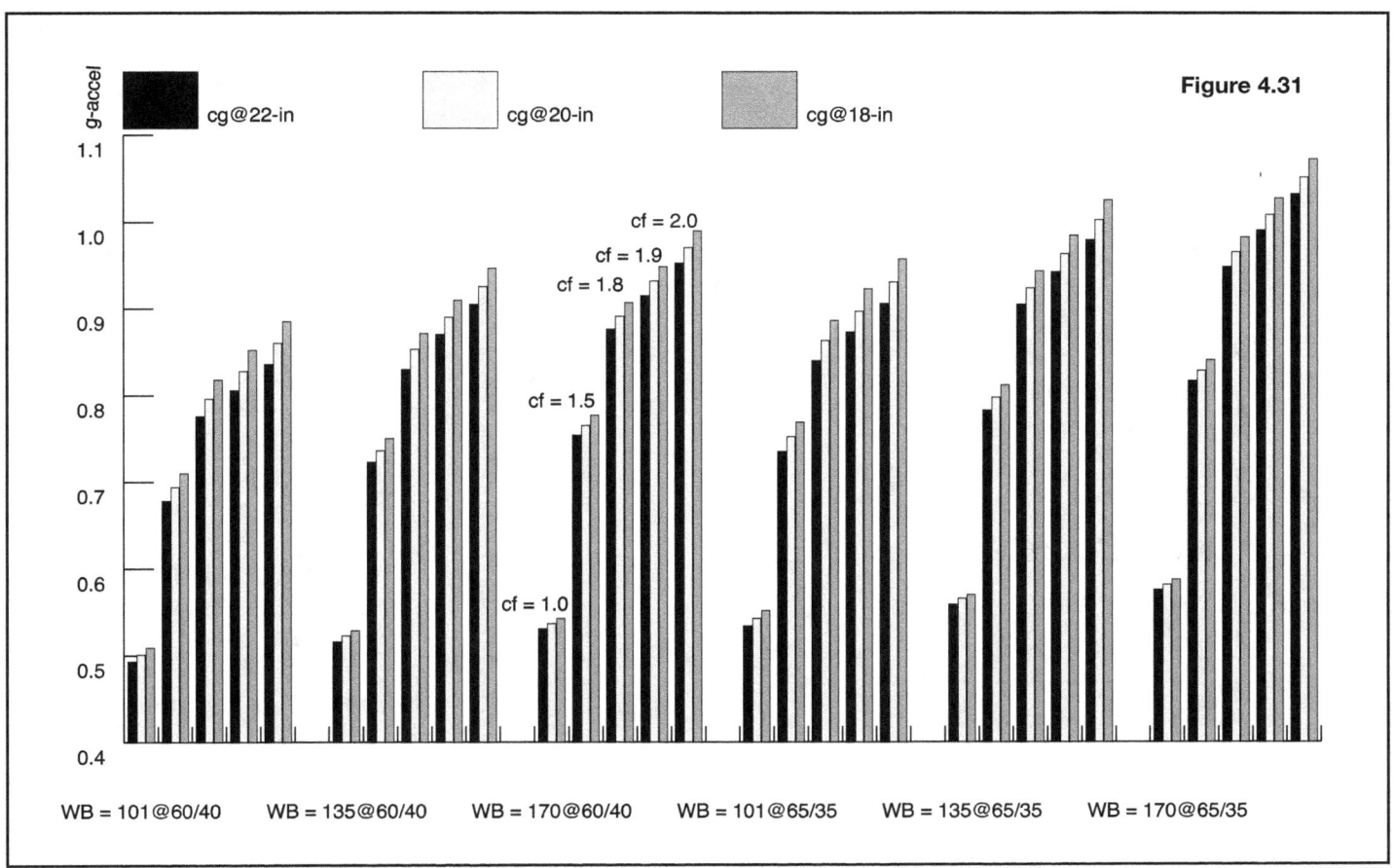

Figure 4.31

Changing cg height, wheel base, fore/aft weight distribution, and tire grip affect the accelerative powers of a front drive, independent front suspension car. To simplify analysis we displayed the extremes of the ranges we calculated. Essentially the chart shows the acceleration in g for a 101 inch, a 135 inch, and 170 inch wheel base car with 60/40 and 65/35 fore/aft weight distribution. Tire friction coefficients of 1.0 representing high performance street radials on a good racing surface and 1.5 representing a racing slick and 1.8 to represent super sticky drag slicks with a VHT on the track, and 1.9 and 2.0 to show an impossibly absurd extreme. You can see that the tire's grip is most responsible for acceleration. The wheel base change and static fore/aft weight distribution have somewhat equal influence which is displayed as the grouping of the acceleration curves. The change in cg height is represented by the 3-bar slope within each larger curve. What this indicates is that tires are most important. Lowering the cg height comes next, then putting as much weight as possible on the front axle. Extending wheel base by the use of a wheelie bar is an optimizing option after you've done everything else. The data below is the complete spread we calculated using the formula presented in the text.

| VEH WT. 2000 LBS 60/40 WT DISTRIBUTION = 1200 LBS FRT/800 LBS REAR | | | |
|---|---|---|---|
| Cg height: | 22/Est. 60ft. | 20/Est. 60ft. | 18/Est. 60ft. |
| Wheelbase = 101 | | | |
| Max g @ cf: | | | |
| 1 | 0.493/2.755 | 0.501/2.732 | 0.509/2.709 |
| 1.5 | 0.678/2.348 | 0.694/2.321 | 0.710/2.294 |
| 1.8 | 0.776/2.195 | 0.796/2.167 | 0.818/2.138 |
| 1.9 | 0.806/2.153 | 0.828/2.124 | 0.852/2.095 |
| 2 | 0.836/2.115 | 0.860/2.085 | 0.885/2.056 |
| Wheelbase = 135 | | | |
| Max g @ cf: | | | |
| 1 | 0.516/2.692 | 0.523/2.675 | 0.529/2.657 |
| 1.5 | 0.723/2.274 | 0.736/2.253 | 0.750/2.233 |
| 1.8 | 0.830/2.116 | 0.853/2.094 | 0.871/2.072 |
| 1.9 | 0.870/2.072 | 0.890/2.05 | 0.910/2.027 |
| 2 | 0.905/2.032 | 0.926/2.01 | 0.947/1.986 |
| Wheelbase = 170 | | | |
| Max g @ cf: | | | |
| 1 | 0.531/2.653 | 0.537/2.639 | 0.543/2.625 |
| 1.5 | 0.754/2.227 | 0.765/2.211 | 0.777/2.194 |
| 1.8 | 0.876/2.066 | 0.891/2.048 | 0.907/2.03 |
| 1.9 | 0.915/2.021 | 0.932/2.003 | 0.949/1.985 |
| 2 | 0.953/1.98 | 0.971/1.962 | 0.990/1.943 |

| VEH WT. 2000 LBS 65/35 WT DISTRIBUTION = 1300 LBS FRT/700 LBS REAR | | | |
|---|---|---|---|
| Cg height: | 22/Est. 60ft. | 20/Est. 60ft. | 18/Est. 60ft. |
| Wheelbase = 101 | | | |
| Max g @ cf: | | | |
| 1 | 0.534/2.647 | 0.543/2.625 | 0.552/2.603 |
| 1.5 | 0.735/2.255 | 0.752/2.23 | 0.769/2.204 |
| 1.8 | 0.840/2.109 | 0.863/2.082 | 0.886/2.054 |
| 1.9 | 0.873/2.069 | 0.897/2.041 | 0.923/2.013 |
| 2 | 0.906/2.032 | 0.931/2.004 | 0.958/1.975 |
| Wheelbase = 135 | | | |
| Max g @ cf: | | | |
| 1 | 0.559/2.586 | 0.566/2.57 | 0.570/2.553 |
| 1.5 | 0.783/2.184 | 0.798/2.165 | 0.812/2.145 |
| 1.8 | 0.905/2.033 | 0.924/2.012 | 0.944/1.99 |
| 1.9 | 0.943/1.991 | 0.964/1.97 | 0.985/1.948 |
| 2 | 0.980/1.953 | 1.003/1.931 | 1.026/1.909 |
| Wheelbase = 170 | | | |
| Max g @ cf: | | | |
| 1 | 0.576/2.549 | 0.582/2.535 | 0.588/2.522 |
| 1.5 | 0.817/2.14 | 0.829/2.124 | 0.841/2.108 |
| 1.8 | 0.949/1.985 | 0.966/1.968 | 0.983/1.95 |
| 1.9 | 0.991/1.942 | 1.009/1.924 | 1.028/1.907 |
| 2 | 1.033/1.903 | 1.052/1.885 | 1.073/1.867 |

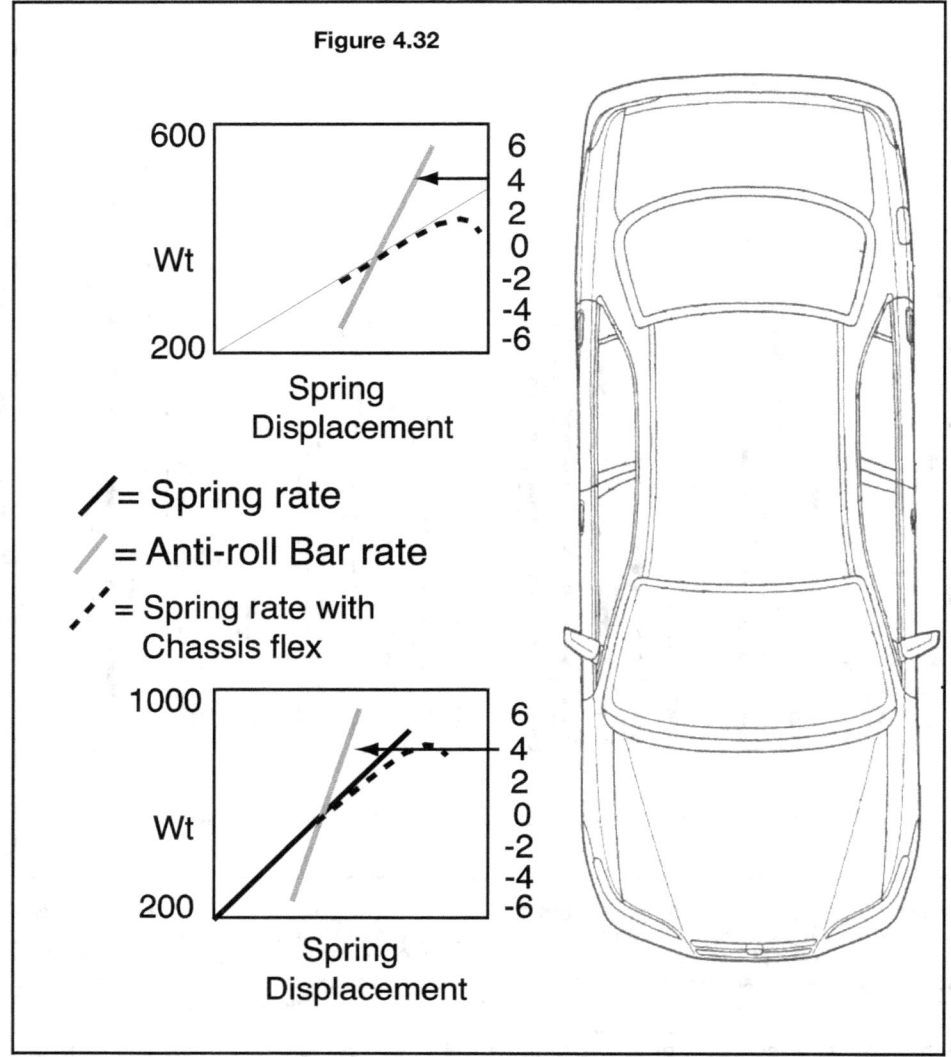

**Figure 4.32**

**Chassis flex alters effective spring rates, and therefore, how your car handles.**

physical aspects of weighing the vehicle. You'll see quickly the lengths you have to go to get this value.

Here's the equation, or at least one tactic to arrive at the cg's height. We take this equation from John Lawlor's *Auto Math Handbook*:

**cg height =**
**Wb x raised Wb x Wt. transfer**
**height raises x total weight**

Though if you're up for some trigonometry you can get a copy of Fred Puhn's classic *How to Make Your Car Handle* and just follow along. We'll assume that now we have accurate values to plug into our equation.

The traction equation is very useful because it shows you what changes make the most impact on the system. If you look at the chart comparing the effects of changes to wheel base, cg height and tire coefficient of friction, you see that the tire's grip is the most important part of the equation. We also provided the raw data for the chart for your analysis.

One of the more useful relationships exposed in the chart data is how little of both cg height and wheel base change acceleration potential. For example, the 101 inch wheel base is about that of an Integra, the slope of the acceleration curve shows that even if you put a wheelie bar on the car, giving it a theoretical wheel base of 156 inches, traction is barely increased with stock tire grip levels. Study this data, because it's real important. It'll tell you that it is much more important to get the stickiest tire possible on the drive wheels, than to worry about lowering cg height.

Following the logic of this equation, it seems obvious that raising the rear of the car and making it very stiff offers little if any improvement. In fact, if it does improve acceleration at the start, it's probably barely measurable and because raising the rear increases aero drag, the technique seems a net looser. Besides, most Hondas when you get the rear far enough up in the air to substantially change the position of the cg, are in very poor geometry and the roll steer can be severe. Our advice is don't do it unless you can prove with testing it's quicker.

## ROLL CAGE INSTALL FOR THE ULTIMATE IN SAFETY AND HANDLING

Usually when you mention a roll cage most assume you're speaking about safety. While that is true, a good roll cage pulls double duty making the chassis more rigid and therefore more tunable.

Figure 4.31 is a detail of the weight transfer Figure 4.10 used earlier in the chapter. It shows graphically an imaginary spring rate curve with chassis flex. If the chassis flexes, it deflects from the load much like a spring. We displayed it as a curve to exaggerate the change in spring rate at that corner. Also if the chassis is flexing here, it tends to influence damping rates as well.

This is why you need a rigid chassis if you want to tune your suspension. You can get your car to handle okay with a flexing chassis, but it will lack the precision required to be a great handling car that you can tune to changing racing surface conditions. The following photos illustrate a very good roll cage installation. Tomcat Fabrication installed the tubes in a later model Civic.

The key to a good cage is triangulation. A triangle is a strong structure. It keeps the chassis from flexing and caving in on the driver.

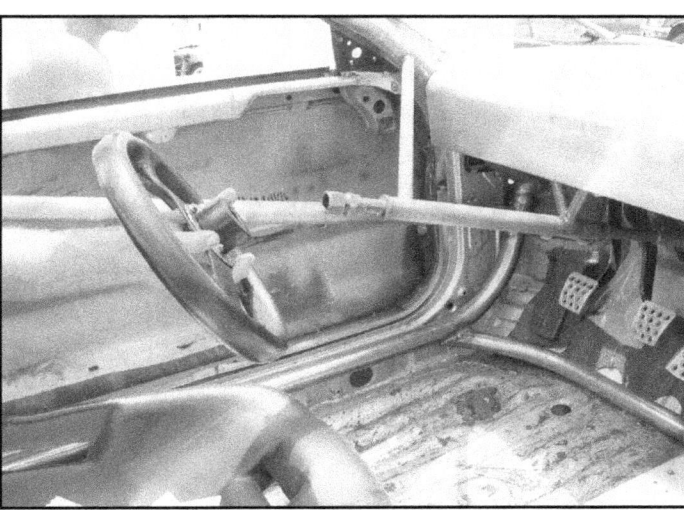

In this view of a quick release wheel, notice the tubes following the door sill and floor pan. There is a cross member supporting the sheetmetal dash.

Formed metal pads welded to tunnel spread the load to make the cage stronger, more rigid, and safer.

A complete cage wraps around the motor and ties into the shock towers and subframe. Doing this makes the structure stronger and more rigid. Is there a trend here? Tying the shock towers to the subframes reduces flex.

The pressure points are reinforced. You can weld the tubes to the body along the path of travel. Spreading the load as much as possible without addition of too much weight is the design goal. The joint where the main hoop and the door bars connect can have a lot of pressure put on it in a roll over. You don't want this joint to fail.

Bolt-on cross braces work well as long as there is a structure to triangulate. Otherwise, these bolt-on shock tower braces, look better than they perform.

# Honda Builder's HANDBOOK Vol. II

## BRAKES

Brake performance is fundamental to vehicle performance. Negative acceleration is part of the perfomance envelope of your car. It can generate x-amount g lateral acceleration, x-amount g forward acceleration and x-amount g in braking or negative acceleration.

Braking or negative acceleration is governed just like positive or lateral accelerations, by Newton's Second Law. To put the braking forces at work in a variant of the f=ma equation automotive engineers use the following:

```
Max = - WD x g
Where:
Dx = -Fxf - Fxr - DA - Wsin 0
Fxf = front axle braking force
Fxr = rear axle braking force
DA = aerodynamic drag
0 = uphill grade
```

The front and rear braking forces include the torque of the brakes as well as rolling resistance of tires and bearings, driveline, etc. In addition, aerodynamic drag helps slow the car as does uphill grades. To keep this discussion simple, we'll neglect rolling resistance and aerodynamic drag. So most of the calculated results here will be lower than what you'd experience in an actual test. (See Baer Racing Test Sidebar near the end of this chapter for more information.)

The basic concept to get here is that you have a mass, you and your car, that's accelerating in this case negatively. How quickly you negatively accelerate the mass is equal to the amount of force your brakes generate, at least up to the limit of the adhesion of your tires. Perhaps a good model to work with is that of an all-wheel-drive car at maximum acceleration. But in this case, the brakes provide torque at each wheel, with the limits of traction governed by weight transfer. That means that the amount of force the front tires generate depends on the amount of weight transferred, which depends on the force generated by the rear tires, which again depends on weight transfer. We'll try to clarify this circular relationship a bit later in the chapter.

A rather surprising relationship with respect to braking distances and time to stop from a particular velocity appears when you do the math. Assuming a brake system in good working order on a level road, time to stop doubles with a doubling of velocity; but the distance to stop is squared, so it takes four-times the distance. Just something to think about the next time you're "drafting" on the freeway at 80 mph.

To calculate the forces generated by .5 g stop in a 3000 lb. car:

$F = w*D$
$F = 3000*.5$
$F = 1500$ lbs. of force

To calculate the stopping distance for the same car from 60 mph:

**Stopping Distance =**
**Original velocity**
**2 X deceleration rate**

Here we have:

60 mph = 88 ft./sec.
.5 g = 16.2 ft./sec.

88 ft./sec. 2
2 x 16.1 ft./sec./sec.

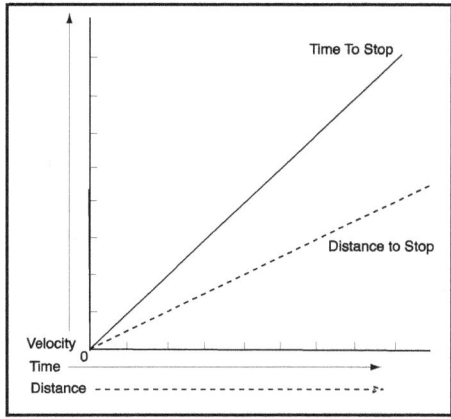

The time it takes to stop is directly proportional to the speed. The distance, however, is squared. Twice the velocity requires four times the distance to stop.

**Distance = 240.5 feet**

To calculate the time to stop just plug in the acceleration rates into this formula:

**Time to Stop = Original velocity decel force *Mass of car**

88 ft./sec.
16.1 ft./sec./sec.

**Time = 5.47 seconds**

### TYPES OF BRAKES

Essentially there are two types of brakes installed on your Honda: disc brakes and drum brakes. The disc brakes are mounted on the front and the drum will be mounted on the rear axle unless your model has four-wheel disc brakes.

Each type has its own performance profile, which is essentially a torque curve. Drum brakes typically experience a drop in torque force during the mid portion of the stop. However the torque seems to come back up as the vehicle slows.

Disc brakes have a flatter torque curve, and so are more predictable. As you can imagine, this is why performance models and higher line models come with four-wheel disc brakes. Since the torque curve of disc brakes are flatter it is easier for a driver to stay at maximum brake force, or at least close to it.

## How To Get The Most From Your Brakes

Ultimately braking force occurs, if you'll excuse the cliche, where the rubber meets the road. The tire works essentially the same way when it's braking, cornering or accelerating. It has to have a certain percentage of slip to generate maximum force.

As a general rule, on dry roads, tires make the most force with about an 18% slip rate. Slip is the relative speed of the circumference of the tire compared to the road surface. For example, if your vehicle speed is 100 mph and tread of your tire is traveling at 90 mph it has a 10% slip rate. Total lockup, that is the tread is stopped but the car is moving, is 100% slip. When the tire is rolling freely with the tread matched with road speed, that is 0% slip.

An interesting observation about slip percentage and braking performance is the optimum slip is about the same in wet or dry conditions. The differences are essentially two. First, in the wet your tires can't generate the level of force they can on dry roads, so you don't stop as quickly. Second, the curve near peak friction is much more abrupt than the dry friction curve and has a much steeper slope to 100% slip than the dry curve. The upshot of this is that it is very easy to lock up your tires and skid when the road is wet. But it does give you a clue as to how the brakes should feel when nearing impending lockup in both wet and dry conditions. However the wet condition is more difficult to manage. This is why racing drivers like to practice in the rain.

## Velocity Reduces Traction

As you increase speed, be aware that your tires lose a certain amount of grip. Both peak and slide friction are reduced with speed on dry as well as wet roads. However the effect is very dramatic on wet roads because tire tread has to move water. At sufficient speed, the tire can't move the water fast enough and it builds a wedge underneath the tire and you are hydroplaning.

You can improve wet weather performance by using higher inflation pressures. This seems to help the tire move water from under the tread. Higher inflation pressure doesn't seem to help very much with dry road braking performance. Yet it is a handling tuning aid and shouldn't be ignored. Just don't over or under inflate your tires. See the chapter on tire performance for more info.

## Weight Reduces Traction

Increasing the weight of the vehicle does not improve braking traction. The relationship is the same as that discussed in the chapter on handling.

### HOW DISC BRAKES WORK

To conjure up a mental map of how brakes work, and fail, or fade, for that matter, let us consider the worst case scenario. The harshest conditions a set of brakes ever faces, doesn't necessarily come from a high horse powered sport car hurtling down the road then braking late into a turn. The harshest conditions occur when you're coming down a steep, long grade that forces you to keep the brakes applied for a long period of time. The only way to make this harder on the brakes is to overload your vehicle, such as might occur when you're vacationing, or hauling a bunch of gear to the race track.

The very act of being prudent means you're going to be on the brakes over a long period of time to keep the speed down. That means the brakes aren't going to get much air flow because of the slow speed. Which means the brakes are literally cooking from the inside out.

From this condition the brakes can suffer from a number of potential failures that reduce or eliminate braking efficiency entirely.

First, the brake rotors reach heat soak capacity. It can absorb only so much energy, and that's what brakes do, convert kinetic energy into heat energy. Since in this hypothetical situation we don't have sufficient airflow to expend the heat back to the ambient air, we reach the limit of the rotor. This causes an almost total loss of friction because the temperature at the surface of the pad is beyond its operational limit. In comparison, a racing pad operates up to around 1150 to 1200°F and still sustains high friction though it's optimal friction occurs in the 700 to 800°F range. An overloaded car braking almost continuously down a long grade, or driving with spirit down the same grade, braking at your fear threshold, can generate enough heat in the brakes to raise the temperature of the pads to 1300 to 1500 degrees. That's why you see pads sometimes literally crumble from the backing plates. Racing pads have addressed that problem but most stock brake pads aren't usually tested at those levels. When the rotor reaches its capacity to absorb heat, it's almost certain the caliper has reached its thermal limit as well. At this point the brake fluid resident in the caliper will boil, if it hasn't already. These two conditions converge and your brakes...just fade away.

The saving grace in all of this is that most of the time we aren't sustaining such a condition over a long enough duration to cause catastrophic brake failure. But add a few more pounds and the need to reduce speed even further down a slightly longer grade and you can have an unintentionally exciting ride down the mountain. As a rule, by the time you find you don't have enough brake, it's too late. That's not to say that the factory brakes are poorly designed. They aren't. The factory engineers design a brake system to work within a performance window that assumes a load limit commensurate with the vehicle's specifications.

At Baer Racing and Stillen, brakes are designed to perform to a far higher limit. These braking systems are designed so that, from the moment you touch your brake pedal, you know that this is the way brakes should feel. Perhaps more importantly, these systems deliver the finest braking performance available in terms of the shortest stopping distances and repeatability of those stopping distances, which is the measure of fade resistance of the system. This is a performance stat you shouldn't ignore, particularly if you've already improved the accelerative performance of your machine. If you can get to speed quicker you need also to stop proportionally as quick to achieve balance in your vehicle combination.

## LARGE ROTORS REDUCE FADE

If you'll recall from the hypothetical circumstances with which we opened, overheating is the crisis leading to brake fade; then to complete failure. The critical agent a brake system must manage therefore is heat. The preferred strategy of high performance brake system engineers to manage heat is to use large rotors. The rotor is a heat sink. True, a larger rotor offers more area for the pads to create friction in addition to a slight advantage in leverage. However, the greater mass of a larger rotor is the dominant advantage sought by brake engineers because it can contain more heat than a less massive rotor. If you can't, or aren't willing, to step up to bigger rotors, then your next best option is to step up to high performance brake pads. We'll talk more about this option later.

Brake system engineers don't rely exclusively on the rotor mass to absorb heat though. They also use air flow to carry braking heat to the atmosphere. But they do so in ways not always obvious.

Everybody thinks that wheels pump air. They don't. If you want to demonstrate to yourself how little air a wheel moves, put some vegetable oil on a wheel and go for a drive. The oil will work its way toward the outside of the wheel but not inside. So there is very little air flow hitting the outside surfaces of the rotor, making that channel of convection heat exchange almost totally ineffective, though some heat is transferred to the atmosphere from these rotor surfaces.

So the engineer designs a method to more effectively convect heat to the air. The solution brake engineers devised is to use the rotor as a rudimentary centrifugal air pump. So rotors are cooled primarily from the air coming into the center of the hub which then passes through the internal vents which also provides cooling to the caliper. As an aside, the reasoning behind curved vaned rotors isn't, as most would assume, to improve air flow. The curved vane is simply a means to get more vane, i.e. more mass with which to absorb heat and provide strength, in the rotor. It also works to stop stress cracks from migrating to the edge of the rotor, particularly with cross-drilled rotors.

The uneven cooling of rotor combines at times with the uneven retention of heat due to the unequal distribution of mass, of brake rotors. This leads to performance and durability problems of one-piece rotor designs. One of the problems is some rotors suffer more outer cheek failures than others.

Another problem, less ominous than the former but more common, is the rotor surface angle change in relation to the caliper pads. This causes a change in the friction and thus changes the braking force, which you'll feel as inconsistent and basically uncontrollable braking near or at the threshold of traction. There are several reasons but one of the most common is what is known as bell effect. As the rotor heats, the shape of the rotor changes. If it has more or less material in certain areas, i.e., the hat, it will grow unevenly and "bell" out. This is accentuated by the fact that the outer surface, the side facing the wheel doesn't get any air flow.

The reason a one-piece rotor tends to "bell" is it expands more on the side with the hat. There is more mass on this side to expand as well as absorb heat because the hat's on the outer side. But there is less tendency for the rotor to bell on the back side because there is less material to expand. So as the rotor grows, it grows more on the outer side. A shallower hat, it turns out, aggravates the "bell effect" and engineers are doing some pretty wicked things to alleviate this problem in future production cars. They're designing rotors with expansion ribs to let the outer surface expand without stressing the rotor so it doesn't crack.

## TWO-PIECE ROTORS FOR ULTIMATE BRAKE PERFORMANCE

One solution to this problem that works very well and is used on race car brake systems is to use a two-piece rotor and hat. The rotor is symmetrical and fastens to the hat. The fastening points are natural expansion paths, keeping the rotor true even when glowing cherry red, giving you excellent torque management and modulation at the extremes of traction.

Before leaving the topic of rotors, we should address the issue of slotting and cross drilling the rotor. Both Stillen and Baer Racing offer crossdrilled and slotted rotors, but each firm differs slightly on their reasons for doing so. Baer Racing systems come standard with slotted rotors. According to Baer Racing's Marketing Manager, Todd Gartshore, this gives the surface something of a finish but is less invasive than cross drilling. "Any time you slot or cross drill a rotor," says Gartshore, "you're creating a stress riser. The benefit of slotting in contrast to cross drilling is that slotting works the same way as cross drilling." It provides a gas relief path and cleans the surface of the pad for best performance. "However," says Gartshore, "you should be cautious because most slotted rotors are slotted in the wrong direction." Slotting technically only works if it's reversed to the rotation. The slot has to drive into the pad to provide the best effect. Baer Racing cuts a reverse slot as well as offering cross drilling to customers who so desire.

At Stillen, the prevailing opinion is that proper cross drilling increases the initial pad bite giving a quicker braking response. In addition, Stillen's Marketing Manager, John Butler, said the cross drill also sweeps and cleans the brake pad allowing the pad to breathe properly (out gassing) which helps maximize the friction capabilities of the pad. Cross drilling also adds air surface to the rotor which maximizes the rotor's ability to dissipate heat.

## CALIPERS

The role the calipers play in a brake system is both obvious and subtle. Obviously, the caliper's principle function is to force the brake pads onto the surface of the rotor. That is fundamentally how friction is created in the brake system to transform the kinetic energy of vehicle motion to heat. Regarding the more subtle aspects, one needs to ask, how much force can a particular caliper generate? Or, more importantly, how much force can it contain before it begins to distort? When a caliper begins to distort, or deflect, the pressure at the pad decreases and so its braking effort. Plus, the angle at which the force is directed changes such that more pressure is usually directed to the outer edge of the rotor while reducing pressure to the inside edge. The net result is loss of braking performance at the limit because the pads aren't producing equal friction across the swept area of the rotor, and the calipers' instability make controlling braking force haphazard.

A proper caliper also manages the torque of the rotor/wheel/tire assembly correctly. By this we mean the force behind the rotation of the rotor. Basically when the caliper squeezes down on the rotor, it encounters forces greater on the trailing side of the caliper (downstream in the direction of rotation) that it must overcome to produce equal pressure across the pad surface. Usually multi-piston caliper designs use various piston diameters to manage what is called pad taper. A larger diameter piston produces less pressure for a given pedal pressure. By positioning the pistons of appropriate diameter precisely within the caliper, the torque is neutralized and equal pressure is exerted across the pad face. Furthermore, a street caliper needs to have capabilities not required of a strictly racing caliper. For example, dust shields and antirattle/squeal devices and parking brake mechanisms on the rear brakes are such capabilities.

## BRAKE PADS

"On pad choice," says Todd Gartshore, "we're always searching for the best compromise between cold friction, linearity, hot friction, and noise. We have a lot of choices. For example, Performance Friction, one of our suppliers, has pads that produce higher friction, but at that level you compromise a tremendous amount in terms of added noise, a bit in cold friction, some in linearity." But the noise associated with these pads just isn't acceptable to some people on their street car. On a race car it's a different matter.

Most racing pads are preburnished. Essentially, that means they aren't prone to out-gas. When a pad outgases, it releases gases from the pad material and adhesive when extremely hot. These gases tend to form a layer between the pad and the rotor resulting in severe loss of friction. Most modern pads do not have this problem. Some stock pads still suffer from this phenomenon, but they do it over time because you don't run them to the limit right from the start.

## BRAKE FLUID

The most overlooked element of your brake system is the brake fluid. "Most owners never think about the brake fluid unless they're topping it off," says Stillen's John Butler. "Brake fluid is easily contaminated by moisture. It can also boil as mentioned before. Both can introduce air into the brake lines and jeopardize the efficiency of the hydraulic system. Air in the lines will cause a soft spongy pedal feel. The air will compress in the lines, instead of a normal firm feel of uncontaminated brake fluid. The remedy is to change fluid every 15,000 miles. The brake fluid can be upgraded also. Stillen recommends Motul Dot 5 synthetic brake fluid which has a higher boiling point and doesn't attract water as easily as the petroleum based brake fluid."

On the subject of brake fluid, Baer Racing has three recommendations. For serious street performance, Baer suggests Ford HD DOT 3 which has a boiling point of 326° F. The next higher level of performance, which they label "Track," calls for Performance Friction Z-Rated DOT 3 fluid with a boiling point of 385°F. For full race application, they sell Castrol SRF DOT4 with a boiling point of 518°F.

Baer Racing's Sport and Track PBR-based brake system uses one-piece 12-inch x 1.1-inch rotors (sport) and 13-inch front rotors (Track) clamped by 4-piston PBR calipers. All Baer Racing brake systems come complete and ready to hang and feature subtle embellishments like NAS stainless fasteners and ARP hardware. You also have finish options such as slot and cross-drill patterns, metal finish of rotors and calipers.

Pro level and Extreme+ packages feature Alcon calipers. The Pro package uses 13-inch x 1.1-inch one-piece vented rotors and 4-piston Alcon caliper. Pro+ steps up to a two-piece 13.5-inch x 1.25-inch vented Alcon rotor and 4-piston Alcon caliper. The Extreme+ package takes up to a 6-piston Alcon caliper grabbing a 13.5-inch x 1.25-inch two-piece vented rotor.

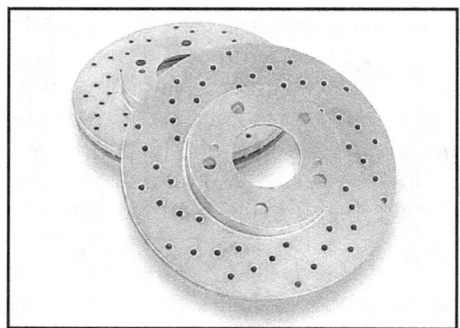

Stillen's Sport rotors feature a computer generated cross-drill pattern on the rotor they say increases the initial pad bite giving a quicker braking response. Use with Stillen brake pads and lines to get great performance without breaking the bank.

## BRAKE SYSTEMS FROM BAER RACING AND STILLEN

### Stillen

Steve Millen, President of Stillen, and crew use a computer generated cross drill pattern on the rotor that they say increases the initial pad bite giving a quicker braking response. The cross drill pattern also sweeps and cleans the brake pad allowing the pad to breath properly (out gassing) which helps maximizes the friction capabilities of the pad. The cross drilling also adds air surface to the rotor which maximizes the rotor's ability to dissipate heat.

Using these rotors in conjunction with Stillen's choice of high performance brake pad is the most effective brake package available without changing to bigger components. Stillen chose a carbon pad material that, according to engineers, holds friction at higher heat ranges. They call the pad material 3Metal-Matrix2. The pad material works by slightly coating the rotor with carbon which tends to reflect heat from the rotor and reduces the rotor wear rate. As with all of Stillen's brake systems, the pad choice is intended for street performance with the best compromise between friction and high and low speed stopping ability and quietness.

### BAER RACING Pro, Pro+ and Extreme+ SYSTEMS

The Alcon calipers Baer Racing uses in these systems are essentially race car calipers that Baer Racing orders specially machined in order to make them roadworthy. These Alcon calipers have dust and weather seals surrounding the pistons and feature anti-rattle and squeal components. These features make Baer Racing Alcon calipers the ideal dual purpose caliper. Alcon, in case you aren't familiar, is one of only three brands found in IndyCar competition. You'll find Alcon brakes on the fastest racing cars in the world in venues from SCCA Trans Am to German Touring Car, even on Penske's NASCAR machines.

### Baer Racing Sport & Track Systems

Front PBR calipers are aluminum two piston units employing pad guided caliper technology (PGC). The term "pad guided" refers to the way the caliper and pad work together to clamp the rotor. An iron anchor bracket saddles the rotor on both sides and is rigidly mounted to the spindle. Machined notches then locate the pad backing plate so that it maintains precise alignment, i.e. runs parallel, with the rotor at all times. This virtually eliminates pad taper problems. The caliper itself is then retained by the brake pads via button clips built into the backing plate. A retaining pin locks the assembly in place, allowing the caliper to float freely with the pads. In turn this allows the caliper to be built from a single piece of lightweight aluminum, the pistons being the only moving parts. These calipers produce performance that exceeds most lowcost four-piston "racing only" calipers, yet features proper street seals, is DOT approved, and fits moderatesized wheels.

Since both front and rear PBR calipers have seen extensive use as original equipment, from Corvette and 1LE Camaros, to Ford Mustang Cobra and Aston Martin, service components are readily available. Pads and seal kits are as close as your first parts store or GM or Ford dealership.

Baer Racing offers a variety of pad compound choices. They chose street pads with exceptionally good cold friction for quick acting initial torque, in addition to being extremely linear; letting the driver modulate the brakes in a controlled fashion with superior fade resistance. "But," as Baer Racing's Todd Gartshore says, "it's really the first elements that make a dynamic pad. You would have to go to a racing pad to exceed the friction level this pad will produce. However, the noise such pads create would be unacceptable."

Baer Racing brake systems are impeccably designed. They feature subtle embellishments like NAS stainless fasteners and ARP hardware that strictly speaking isn't necessary. However, the chief engineer thinks they are necessary because of the

# STILLEN TECH TIPS: HOW TO BREAK-IN YOUR BRAKES

Did you know you get the absolute worst performance from your brakes when they are brand new? The pads and rotors perform better when they are changed out of sequence. The rotors should be seasoned and you should change pads before or after the rotors. There is nothing wrong with having a complete brake job, but you don't get best performance until the components have a chance to wear.

**INITIAL BREAK IN:** Avoid excessive or high speed braking for the first 160-200 miles. Harsh breaking can cause heat spots with consequent reduction of braking efficiency.

**GENERAL CARE:** It is important to understand the basics of the brake system and how it works to understand how proper care will help increase longevity of the components. A moving car develops energy. The faster it moves the more energy it develops. This is kinetic energy. The amount of kinetic energy developed is a function of speed (MPH) and vehicle weight. The brake system converts this kinetic energy into heat. The brake component capability of dissipating heat is a function of rotor size and design, caliper pressure, and friction material. If you have experienced brake fade you have a basic understanding of generating heat beyond the limits of your brake system.For example, the heat level does not change by using a Brembo Performance Brake System, or a Baer Racing Alcon based system. But by using larger rotors, aluminum hats, more efficient calipers with greater piston pressure and aggressive brake pads these brake systems can handle extremely high levels of heat.

Because we're dealing with a much broader "thermal window" if you will, it is important to warm up the brakes slowly and to let them cool down slowly as well. Doing so slows the heat expansion and contraction rate of the metal, especially the rotors,as they heat up and cool down helping to reduce the probability of warping the rotors. This is especially important for rally or race events because of the higher temperatures developed. Be careful not to stop suddenly from high speeds, and once stopped, continue to press firmly on the brake pedal. This will cause uneven rotor cooling because of the brake pads being pressed against the rotor allowing the rotor not to cool where the pads are. The same is true by setting the parking brake after aggressive braking.

**IMPORTANT!** Because of the heat build up in the brake system during extreme use, you need to let the brakes cool down by driving normally for a short distance before stopping. This cool down period not only helps the longevity of the brake system, but also the entire vehicle.

**WHEELS:** When mounting the wheels, it is extremely important to hand tighten the lug nuts and then progressively tighten them in a crisscross pattern to 85 ft./lbs.

duty cycle and the fact you need proper torque and friction management. Perhaps these subtleties go beyond what most people will accept but Baer Racing is primarily an engineering firm. Marketing is what they do so they can do what they like to do — race.

## BRAKE PROPORTIONING: THE TUNING SECRET THAT GIVES MAXIMUM PERFORMANCE

To achieve maximum braking force, ideally you'd want both the front and rear brakes to reach lock-up together. In practice, this is very difficult, if not impossible to do, particularly for road cars that encounter a host of road friction levels, vehicle loading and weight distribution, etc.

If you recall the topic of weight transfer discussed in the first couple of chapters and how it affects traction, then you'll understand why brake proportioning is required. When you brake hard a lot of weight is transferred forward. This takes vertical force off the rear tires, reducing the amount of force the rear tires can generate. However, the weight transferred forward increases the amount of force the front brakes can generate. Hence, we need to manage the amount of pressure we deliver to the brakes as we squeeze down on the brake pedal.

That's exactly what a proportioning valve does. It proportions pressure. Usually it delivers less pressure to the rear brakes after a threshold pressure level. For example, it might distribute equal pressure front and rear until 450 psi. From that point up it delivers 35% less pressure to the rear brakes.

The same concept applies to adjustable proportioning valves, only they are driver adjustable, if you put them in the cockpit. If not, you just set them for particular combinations of vehicle and conditions and let it alone.

Since it's virtually impossible to get all the wheels to reach lockup simultaneously, you go for the next best. And that is having the fronts lock up just before the rears.

The reason you want the front wheels to lock first is that you have more control. If the rears lock first you tend to yaw or oversteer. As the rear comes around the front wheels keep the same angle, and unless you provide some counter steer, they will generate cornering force that will snap the car around on you. If the front locks up, you'll lose steering, but you'll just slide in one direction until you get the wheels rolling again.

To better understand the importance of proportioning as well as the difficulty of optimizing proportioning, let's analyze a maximum braking effort with weight transfer.

If you recall from the chapter on tires we talked about the tire adhesion, or grip. Remember that the amount of force a tire can generate is dependent on the load it is carrying. The proportion of side force to vertical load is called a static friction coefficient. If a tire with a vertical load of 1000 lbs. generates 900 lbs. of side force, it has a coefficient of .9 (900/1000 = .9) The coefficient is not constant. As a general rule it will decrease by .01 for each

## BRAKE FORCE EQUATIONS:

### Front Max Braking Force

$$= \frac{\text{Tire grip CoEff (front wt+(cg height/wheelbase) * Rear Max Braking Force}}{1 - \text{CoEff} * (\text{cg height/wheelbase})}$$

### Rear Max Braking Force

$$= \frac{\text{Tire grip CoEff (rear wt+(cg height/wheelbase) * Front Max Braking Force}}{1 + \text{CoEff} * (\text{cg height/wheelbase})}$$

---

**Model #1 without weight transfer**

**cg height** = 21 inches,
.9 coefficient, 101 inch wheelbase;
60/40 Wt. Distribution
**lbs. of force front/lbs. of force rear:**
1620 lbs./1080 lbs.
**Decel in g:** .9
**Stopping time:** 5.06 seconds
**Stopping distance:** 371.13 feet

**Model #2 with weight transfer**

**cg height** = 21 inches,
.9 coefficient, 101 inch wheelbase;
60/40 Wt. Distribution
**lbs. of force front/lbs. of force rear:**
1751.53 lbs./706.65 lbs.
**Decel in g:** .82
**Stopping time:** 5.56 seconds
**Stopping distance:** 407.64 feet

**Model #3 with weight transfer**

**cg height** = 16.8 inches,
.9 coefficient, 101 inch wheelbase;
60/40 Wt. Distribution
**lbs. of force front/lbs. of force rear:**
1738.83 lbs./794.94 lbs.
**Decel in g:** .84
**Stopping time:** 5.39 seconds
**Stopping distance:** 395.45 feet

**Model #4 with weight transfer**

**cg height** = 21 inches,
.9 coefficient, 101 inch wheelbase;
42/58 Wt. Distribution
**lbs. of force front/lbs. of force rear:**
1378.01 lbs./1305.13 lbs.
**Decel in g:** .894
**Stopping time:** 5.09 seconds
**Stopping distance:** 373.44 feet

---

.10 increase in vertical load. So with 1100 lbs. on the wheel its coefficient will be .89 or 979 lbs. of side force instead of 990 lbs. But even with a smaller coefficient, the total force is greater. That's why the front tires do most of the work in braking, a rear drive car can accelerate quicker, and why the tires on the outboard side of a turn do most of the cornering.

A 3000 lb. vehicle with a 60/40 weight distribution has 1800 lbs. on the front tires and 1200 on the rear. Let's assume this car has high performance street tires with a friction coefficient of .9. Without weight transfer, the front tires can generate 1620 lbs. of force; the rear 1080, for a total of 2700 lbs. of force. (See Model #1.) This means that the max braking effort of this car expressed in g would be .9 or 28.98 ft./sec./sec. Put racing slicks with a coefficient of 1.2 on the car and it generates 2160 lbs. at the front and 1440 lbs. at the rear. This gives it a total force of 3600 lbs., allowing it to generate a max negative acceleration of 1.2 g or 38.48.

Understand, these are phenomenal braking efforts. The example with a .9 coefficient could stop from 100 mph in just 371.13 feet in 5.06 seconds. With racing slicks the distance to stop from 100 mph drops to 278.35 feet in just 3.80 seconds. You can't get that kind of performance in the real world, at least not without adding aerodynamic down force, because weight transfers off the rear tires and onto the front during braking. How much weight transfers depends on how quickly you are decelerating, and how quickly you can decelerate depends on how much weight transfers.

Because of the dependency between the front and rear tires for total braking effort, and because weight transfers off the rear reducing the maximum possible braking, proportioning the rear brakes to exert the proper amount of force is essentially impossible to achieve with a mechanical proportioning valve, though you can get close. The chief advantage of electronic Antilock Braking Systems (ABS), in addition to the obvious safety advantages when applied properly, is that it can achieve almost ideal proportioning, thus increasing the maximum braking force over purely mechanical means. To illustrate this let's look at the four models shown, only this time we'll include the effects of weight transfer and the effects of friction coefficient.

For model #2, our car again has 1800 lbs. on the front tires and 1200 lbs. on the rear tires and all have .9 coefficient. So the first instant of application there is 2700 lbs. of force possible. But as the weight transfers forward, the rear tires generate less force. How much less depends on how quickly the car stops. The equation describing maximum braking effort is very similar to the equation that describes maximum forward acceleration, with the exception that you have to solve for the front maximum force using an assumed rear force because they are dependent on each other and vice versa. (See Brake Force Equations chart.)

Applying these formulas to our present example we find that now we need to know the height of the cg and the wheelbase length because just as in handling these determine weight transfer. So let's say the cg is 21 inches above the ground and the wheel base is 101 inches. When we work through the math we find that the front tires generate 1751.53 lbs. of force and the rear tires contribute 706.65 lbs. toward the total of 2458.18 lbs. of braking force. Divide that by the weight of the car which gives you a decel rate of .82-g instead of .9-g. So in terms of stopping distance and time, we arrive at 0 mph from 100 mph in 407.64 feet in 5.56 seconds compared with 371.13 feet in 5.06 seconds. With racing slicks we find the front tires making 2339.75 lbs. of force; the rears making 722.03 lbs. of force for 1.02 g maximum deceleration. Now our trip from 100 mph to 0 mph takes 4.46 seconds and we travel 327.28 feet compared with 278.35 feet in just 3.80 seconds when no weight transfers — an increase of 48.9 feet and .66 seconds.

With these simulations we can see the effect weight transfer has on the maximum braking force possible. Essentially the same process occurs when cornering. Weight transfers off the inside tires to outside tires raising the inside tires coefficient of friction slightly and reducing the outside tire coefficient (.01/.10 increase or decrease in vertical load when near load rating). However, there is always a net loss in friction force, so there is a net loss in cornering force and braking force.

It doesn't take a rocket scientist to figure out that lowering the cg is going to increase max possible braking force since it reduces weight transfer, and that a longer wheelbase will reduce weight transfer too, therefore increasing braking force. What may not be so obvious though is the static weight distribution. Obviously certain static weight ratios front to rear yield better braking performance than other ratios. Before checking in to the effects of static weight distribution, let's look at the effects of lowering the cg on our model.

If we lower the cg 20 percent, from 21 inches to (- 4.2 =) 16.8 we find in model #3, that the forces generated at each axle has changed. With the lower cg and tires with a .9 coefficient of friction, the front tires now generate 12.7 lbs. less force (1751.53 lbs. - 1738.83 lbs.); and the rear tires generate 88.29 more force (794.94 lbs. - 706.65 lbs.) increasing overall braking force by 75.59 lbs. This increase is good for .02-g, increasing the max braking acceleration to .84-g, which stops us in 395.45 feet and 5.39 seconds. That's 12.19 feet shorter and .17 second quicker than with the cg 4.2 inches higher.

If lowering the cg has that kind of effect, what does arranging static weight distribution do? It helps a lot.

For model #4, we'll run the numbers with a 21 inch cg height but we'll change the static weight distribution to 42/58, a ratio shared by the Acura NSX. This arrangement yields 373.52 lbs. less maximum force (1751.53 lbs. - 1378.01 lbs.) from the front, but 598.48 lbs. more (1305.13 - 706.65 lbs.) maximum force from the rear tires for a total force of 2683.14 or 224.96 lbs. (2683.14 - 2458.18 lbs.) more braking force than with a 60/40 front to rear weight ratio. This combination can generate .894-g of braking force, right at the .9 coefficient limit of the tires, so it's very efficient and it brings us to a stop in 373.44 feet in 5.09 seconds.

For our last exercise, let's see what happens when we reduce the overall weight of the model, but keep the 42/58 weight distribution. Let's take 500 lbs. off the car leaving us with a curb weight of 2500 lbs. and giving us a 1050 lbs./1450 lbs. front/rear static weight distribution. The front tires give 1148.31 lbs. of force max effort and from the rear, 1087.64 lbs. of force, for a total of 2235.95 lbs. of max braking force. That's less than we had previously because we have less vertical load on the tires. What does this do to stopping distance and time?

Surprisingly, we don't see any improvement. We get the same .894-g from the total tire braking forces putting us at 0 mph in 373.44 feet in 5.09 seconds as when the car weighed 3000 lbs. What's going on?

The answer lies at the contact patch. In both of the last two models we were very near the .9 coefficient of friction of the tires. Ultimately that is the limit of how much force the tire can generate and so the limit of how quickly the car accelerates (negative acceleration for braking). So even though we removed 500 lbs. (125 lbs./wheel) from the car, that just meant less vertical force and so less side force. That's doesn't mean there aren't advantages to having a lightweight car. When you are braking less weight, you can have less massive rotors, which reduces rotational inertia and overall vehicle weight as well as unsprung weight. Accelerating up to speed generally uses two drive wheels, front or rear, so a lighter car will use less force from the tires to accelerate it at an equal rate as that of a heavier car. In addition, you have to factor in wear rates of the tread. So even if you get to a point so optimized that you can't improve braking force, there are still compelling reasons to take weight from the vehicle. It just helps to know were to take it from and where to reposition it.

## BAER RACING BRAKE TEST DATA: 1996 INTEGRA GSR 100-0 MPH

| Stock: Stop# | feet | time | mph | Baer Claw: feet | time | mph |
|---|---|---|---|---|---|---|
| 1 | 438 | 6.20 | 100.0 | 381 | 5.40 | 101.6 |
| 2 | 403 | 5.90 | 99.6 | 368 | 5.00 | 98.7 |
| 3 | 444 | 6.40 | 100.5 | 408 | 5.50 | 100.4 |
| 4 | 466 | 6.60 | 97.8 | 425 | 5.60 | 99.5 |
| 5 | 625 | 8.90 | 101.0 | 416 | 5.40 | 102.1 |

Comparing the test data from Baer Racing with our results shows the forces acting on the car that we ignored for simplicity's sake. The real car stops shorter than our model predicts but takes more time. Two separate mechanisms are responsible for the differences. As mentioned, we ignored aerodynamic and rolling resistance forces, which help stop the car and would therefore display as shorter stopping distances. The increase in time to stop is a function of the accelerometer triggered test equipment and the fact that the brakes do not generate a totally linear deceleration rate. Still, the results are close enough to let you predict general performance trends in response to changes made to the vehicle combination.

You'll notice how the stock system doesn't have the thermal capacity to handle the 100-0 mph stops nearly as well as the Baer Racing system. However, in the 60-0 mph stop tests (not shown), the stock system was almost the equal of the Baer Claw system. But again, its performance began to fade after four stop tests. From high speeds, the Baer Racing system is clearly superior. From highway speeds, the stock system is adequate until you over power it with heat from repeated panic stops.

# Honda Builder's HANDBOOK Vol. II
## AERODYNAMIC PERFORMANCE

The aerodynamic characteristics of your Honda affect its performance and passenger comfort to such a degree that if you go for the lowest amount of drag, at least on a production car, other areas of vehicle performance will suffer. Certainly you don't want to degrade your interior environment at the expense of the absolutely lowest drag force. However, you do want to increase its performance and operational economy by reducing air resistance.

The aerodynamic elements within your control allowing you to release the aero-horsepower your Honda now stealthily consumes are aerodynamic drag, external flow patterns, internal air flow and aerodynamic noise.

### AERODYNAMIC DRAG

The total power required to maintain a constant vehicle speed, called road load horsepower, is the sum of all resistances or losses the vehicle experiences at a fixed speed. You can divide road load horsepower into two general parts for discussion: aerodynamic horsepower, which includes all aerodynamic losses both internal and external to the vehicle; and mechanical horsepower or rolling resistance horsepower, which includes drive train power losses from the clutch to the drive wheels, the wheel bearing losses of front and rear wheels, and the power losses in all tires.

The aerodynamic portion of road load power increases as a function of the cube of the car speed. The mechanical portion increases at a slower rate with car speed. This demonstrates how important aero drag is. At 55 mph and up, any percentage reduction of the vehicle's aerodynamic drag makes a decrease in fuel consumption of one-half or more of that same percentage possible. What that means from a performance perspective is less power was used to keep the vehicle at a steady speed; so more power is available to accelerate it quicker than before.

Aero drag comes in five flavors: form drag, lift drag, surface drag, interference drag, and internal flow drag.

Form drag comes directly from the basic shape of your car. Its specific contours determine how smoothly air passes over it and to what extent the air flow breaks away or separates from the body by abrupt changes in the surface. The body shape, then, determines the distribution of aerodynamic forces perpendicular to its, or the wind's, direction of travel. And if you added all such forces, that would be the form drag.

Lift drag, or what some call induced drag, comes from any lift force, either positive or negative (down force), generated by the moving vehicle. The magnitude of the force is mostly a function of the basic body shape. Generation of lift forces, either down force (usually a good thing) or up force (usually not a good thing) requires energy and the cost of using that energy is lift drag.

Surface drag is frictional resistance resulting from air passing over your car's body. This friction is due to the viscosity of air and occurs in a thin layer of slow moving air, called the boundary layer. Surface drag increas-

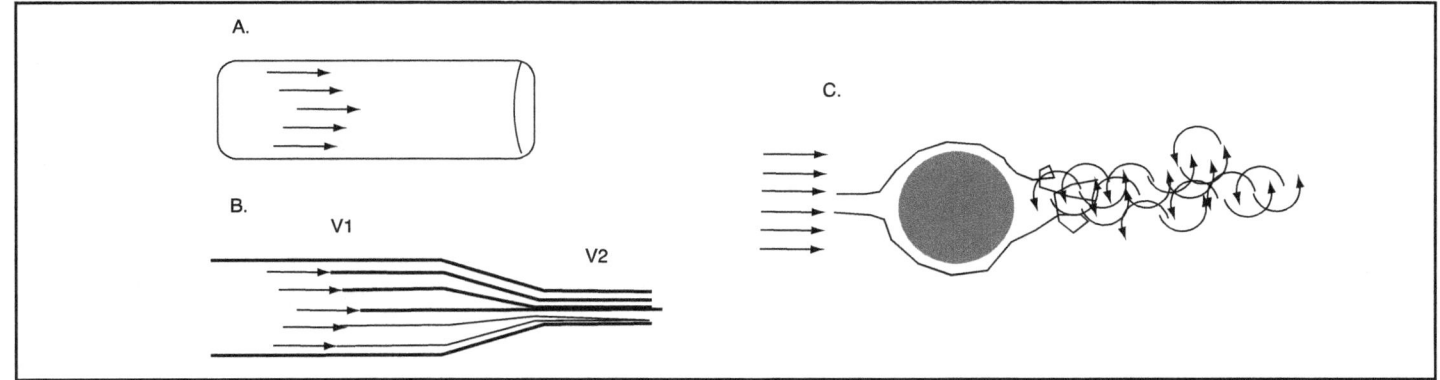

Figure A shows that fluid next to a surface has less velocity than that near the center. The molecules next to the surface do not move at all, but those farther away move increasingly faster. So the faster moving molecules rub on the slower ones causing frictional losses. Viscosity measures the force required as layers of fluid molecules to slide over one another. Figure B illustrates simple laminar flow. The flow lines represent the path a molecule of the fluid would take. Laminar flow is desirable because it generates the least friction thus flowing more with less energy. Note that laminar flow obeys Bernoulli's Equation within certain limits of velocity. The limits are defined by a relationship called the Reynolds number. The Reynolds number is a ratio between the dynamic inertia of air and its viscosity. Figure C shows turbulent flow. The path a molecule takes is not smooth and predictable. It's very erratic and more friction is generated with this kind of flow.

es as the exterior car body area touched by the air flow increases.

Interference drag is caused by the projection of styling elements as well as functional equipment and hardware that sometimes occur on the car's body. These elements interfere with air flow and cause serious flow disturbances, thereby contributing drag losses far in excess of what they would produce alone.

Internal flow drag is the sum of all energy losses produced when air passes into, through, and out of all systems requiring or permitting air flow.

Form drag and lift drag (which are both primarily a function of basic body shape) amount to 65% of total drag, so unless you're prepared to redesign your car, you won't find huge increases in performance here. However, you can make improvements, so don't give up on this area. Since the force increases at the cube of the speed, if you're planning to travel rapidly, small gains at highway speed pay off big at racing speeds. The remaining 35% of aerodynamic drag lies with: internal flow — cooling and ventilation — each of which contributes about 6%; interference drag on modern cars produces about 15% of the total drag; and skin friction losses accounting for the remaining 8%.

The best way to reduce form drag is to have, or design, a body shape that minimizes pressure on the front of the vehicle and minimizes suction on the rear of the vehicle. The classic tear drop shape is the ideal, but it isn't the most stylish or functional shape for a car. One of the easiest ways to reduce form drag is to reduce frontal area by lowering your car.

The current trend to a simpler, more flush design has helped to reduce form drag. Design elements such as smooth, fastback bodies and relatively blunt rear end shapes offer lower form drag.

Lift Drag develops from the fact that car bodies accelerate air flow causing low pressure on its upper surface, especially in such areas as the leading edge of the hood, the windshield corners, and the leading edge of the roof. Aerodynamic lift results from lower average pressures developed on the upper surface than on the underbody. The magnitude of the lift force and its distribution to the front and rear wheels is decided by the ground clearance, the contours of the body and underbody, and the angle of attack of the body to the air. Lift by itself is not a serious problem at highway speeds. At much higher racing speeds lift can be a real problem. In general, the strategy to reduce aero lift is to make modifications to your body that reduce areas of accelerated flow (low pressures) on the upper surface and areas of decelerated flow (high pressures) on the underbody.

## BERNOULLI'S EQUATION

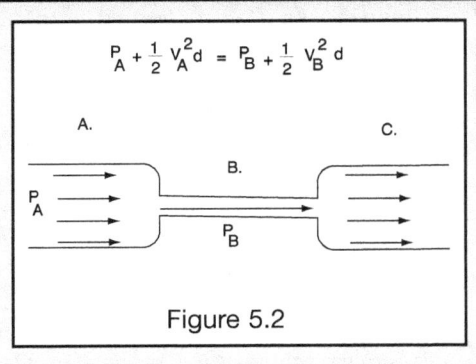

Figure 5.2

Bernoulli's equation tells us that as a fluid's speed increases, it exerts less pressure. Using the illustration to the left, here's an example. Assume the flow speed A is 5 ft./s; of B 20 ft./s; with density d at .0763 lbs. per square foot with 14.7 psi. (Atmosphere pressures are standard conditions.) This gives us:

(14.7 *144 to convert psi to pound per square foot)
$2116.8 + 1/2 * 5^2 * .0763 = P_B + 1/2 * 20^2 * .0763$
$2116.8 + .954 = P_B + 15.26$
$2117.75 = P_B + 15.26$
$2117.75 - 15.26 = P_B + 15.26 - 15.26$
$2102.49 \text{ lbs./ft.}^2 = P_B = 2102.49/144 = 14.6 \text{ psi}$

So with a 15 ft./s velocity increase the air lost approximately .1 psi.

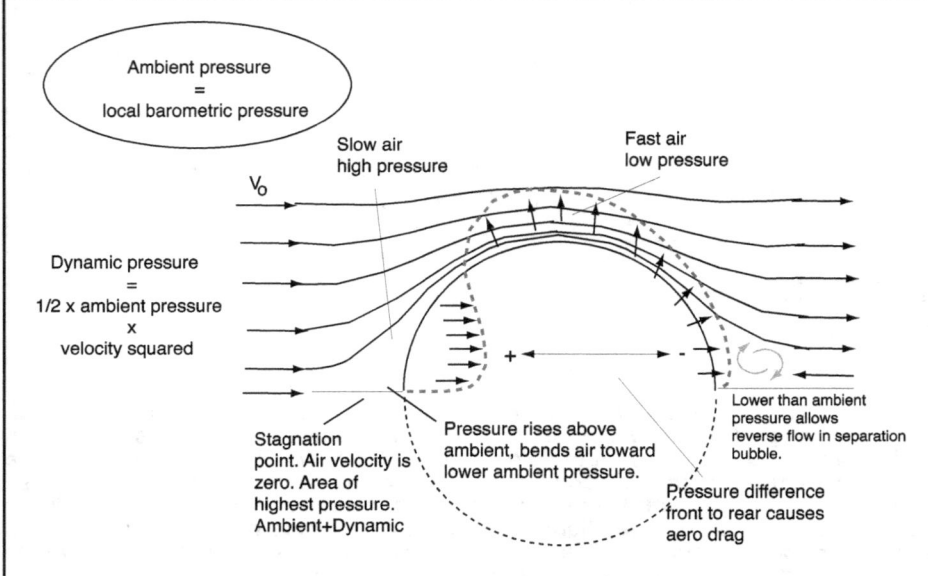

**Bernoulli's Equation**, as it is applied to aerodynamics, describes the behavior of air as it flows over the body of a car. In essence, it states an inverse relationship to pressure and velocity in a fluid. In other words, as a fluid speeds up, the pressure it exerts on its surroundings is less. As it slows, the reverse is true. In free air, this also explains why air streams bend in response to pressure changes. Air tends to flow from high pressure to low pressure. That fluid can be water flowing through pipes, or air flowing over, around and through a vehicle's body.

Surface Drag occurs when the viscosity of air produces a thin layer (the boundary layer) next to the vehicle body, which is slowed by friction. The viscosity friction losses in the boundary layer and the drag of small surface imperfections within this layer are considered surface drag. You may have heard bench racers talking about reducing surface drag or skin friction by waxing their cars. It doesn't make any difference at the speeds most racing is done, let alone freeway driving.

Although surface drag is a small part of total aerodynamic drag, there are large differences in relative surface drag for typical body fasteners. In general hexagonal fasteners, such as sheet metal screws, have the most drag. Hex-key fasteners reduce that by 90%, round head fasteners come in with a 250% reduction, a flat oval head makes 400% less drag than a sheet metal screw, and a flush rivet barely makes a ripple. These values are for highway speeds. Remember, aerodynamic forces increase at the cube of the speed.

Another area to consider is the trim items and body panel joint lines. These are engulfed in the boundary layer and can be thought of as surface imperfections. The surface drag of these elements in longitudinal flow is insignificant. It's apparent that a flat upstream edge and a slightly turned-in downstream edge will minimize the surface drag for these structures.

Interference Drag is when you hang things on your car like side mirrors and big rear spoilers and cosmetic enhancements. You're increasing the aerodynamic drag of your car significantly and it has a cumulative effect. These items when subjected to the same air speed individually create much more drag when they are on your car. Exterior vehicle body projections, such as windshield wipers, radio aerial, rear view mirrors, accessory bug deflectors, license plates, door handles, air scoops, roof pillars, rain gutters, large bezels or bright work strips, exposed door hinges and roof luggage rack, all contribute to the total interference drag. So do the various mechanical components projecting from under the vehicle, such as an engine pan, suspension arms, exhaust system, frame rail, and rear suspension.

Here's how interference drag works. We'll illustrate using the interaction between a rear view mirror near the windshield pillar. Assume the drag of a mirror by itself is 1.0. The area at the base of the windshield of a passenger vehicle has air flow velocities 25-30% higher than vehicle speed in the air escaping laterally from the blunt shape at the base of the windshield. The drag of the mirror in this area of accelerated flow is now as high as 1.66 because of the square function of the velocity. Mirrors tend to have an abruptly terminated shape (they're sort of flat on the mirror side). This will spread a wake of turbulence behind it, disturbing the airflow on the basic body side behind it. Because the mirror's wake increases in size

**Air flow over the centerline shows the basic behavior of air as it obeys Bernoulli's Equation.** As air encounters the front of the car, some of it stops completely before being deflected. This is the stagnation point. The stagnation point registers the highest pressure because the sum of the ambient pressure and the dynamic pressure act on this point. The air bends over the top of the nose because the pressure below it is less than that above it. In compliance with Bernoulli's Equation, it moves faster. The concave shape between the hood top and the windshield lets the air slow down and thus a pressure rise occurs in this area.

downstream, the increase of drag by the mirror may be 40 to 60%. (You've seen how wakes behave behind boats...it's almost the same thing.) This is how the mirror or any other similarly placed and shaped object may contribute to the total vehicle drag some 2.5 to 3.0 times greater than its individual drag in free flow.

So what does that tell us about placing hardware on your Honda's body? The obvious conclusion is you should install these in areas with the lowest possible velocity. Doing so minimizes interference drag.

**Here are a few more tips:**

High drag items such as mirrors etc., should be kept as close together as possible to minimize the size of their total wake. You should also place these elements in line with each other and the air flow and as close together as you can get them.

Low drag hardware, such as good air scoops and smooth door handles, should be separated as much as possible to permit each element to develop its own efficient flow pattern without drag inducing interaction.

A high drag body is less affected by interference drag than a low drag body. This is because the high drag body shape has a lot of separated flow so all the hardware and their wakes tend to become hidden in the already turbulent flow pattern. Low drag body shapes are greatly increased in drag by the application of small projections. Knowing where the fast air is, and not putting things in its way, can give you more top end speed and a quicker E.T. too.

## EXTERNAL FLOW PATTERNS

The direction and velocity of air flow as it passes over a vehicle body and the resultant high and low pressure areas that develop on the body surface is a function of the vehicle shape. The longitudinal path of the air streamlines over the vehicle and is altered by the tendency of air to flow from high pressure to low pressure areas. This introduces lateral and occasionally reverse flow components on the body, i.e. separation bubbles and turbulence.

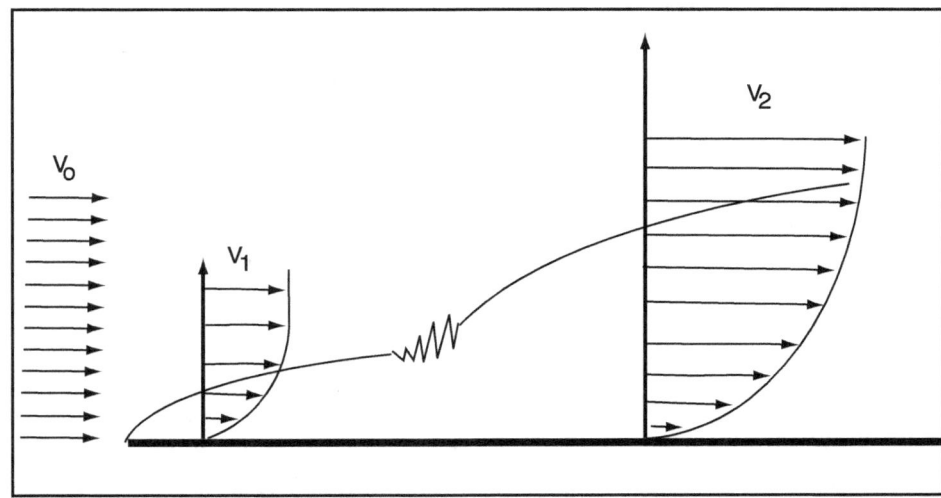

The boundary layer is the slow moving air molecules, relative to the main air flow velocity, near the surface of your car. It starts with zero thickness and grows deeper as air travels over the body. It also starts out with laminar flow, but as it grows, it reaches a critical point defined by the Reynolds number, and begins to tumble and breaks into turbulent flow. Once in turbulent flow, the boundary layer increases its depth. Friction drag increases with the growth of the boundary layer.

## INTERNAL FLOW DRAG

For your Honda to function properly, you need air to flow through it as well as around it. The engine cooling flow plus passenger ventilation flow and any internal flow required to cool brakes or other mechanical components, such as oil coolers and turbocharger intercoolers, all contribute to internal flow drag. Internal flow drag isn't often talked about regarding passenger cars because it is so hard to make changes to the basic layout of the car to improve internal flow. This drag component results

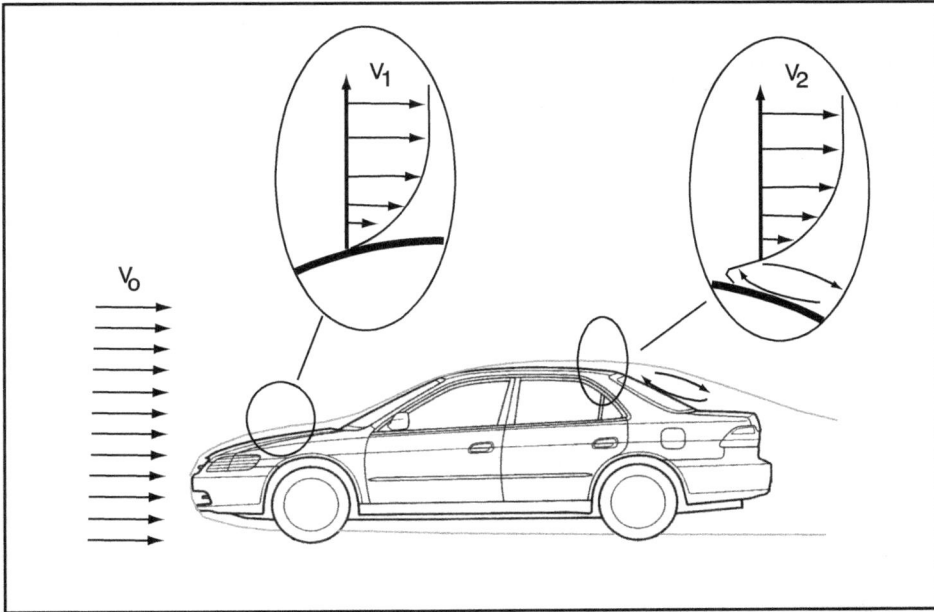

Areas of increasing velocity and decreasing pressure ($V_1$) help to push the air along the surface and inhibit the growth of the boundary layer. Aerodynamicists call this a favorable pressure gradient or slope. Areas of decreasing velocity and increasing pressure let the boundary layer grow until ultimately degrading to turbulence. At some point as air flows along the back of the car, the boundary layer will begin flowing in the opposite direction($V_2$). At this point the main flow is detached from the body and flows off the body in about the direction it was going when it detached. The reverse flow is caused by the below ambient pressure in this area which allows air behind the car to be forced into the "separation bubble."

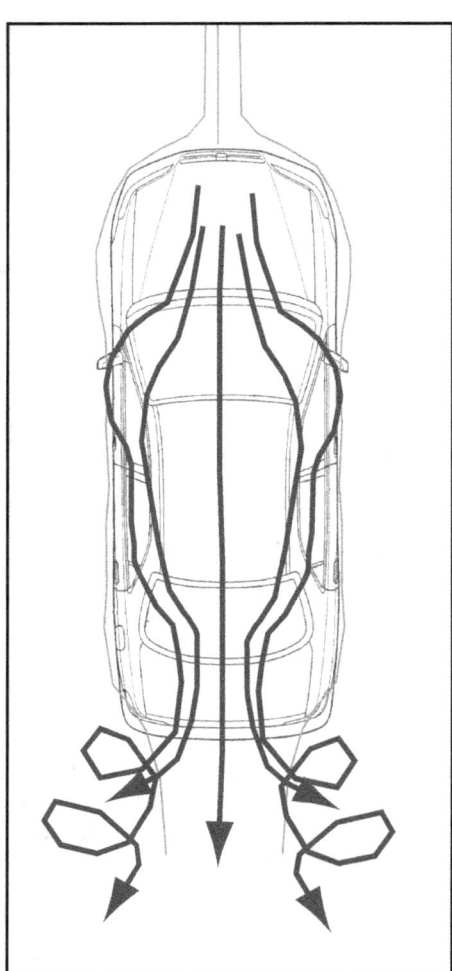

**Vortex formation in the wake of a car comes from the higher pressure air from the sides rushing into the low pressure of the separation area. The collision of the air coming in from the side with that from the roof sets both flow streams spinning.**

from momentum or energy losses of the air as it flows through either the engine compartment, under the car, or through the passenger compartment. One of the ways to conceptualize internal flow is its flow circuit configuration. In other words, the channel that the air takes on its journey as it enters the car body, travels through it, and then exits.

For example, the ideal circuit for an engine-radiator internal flow system requires a smoothly-edged, clean intake opening that leads to a completely enclosed diffusing duct, converting velocity energy to pressure energy with low losses. This arrangement minimizes air flow energy loss by changing velocity into a pressure drop across the radiator core which is then directed into a contracting duct that exits the air at a convenient low pressure area. It's just about impossible to get this design on a production sedan because of grill style constraints, duct volume and cost and mechanical fan drive.

In a way, you can consider a heat exchanger (radiator, intercooler, etc.) air flow circuit as a rudimentary jet engine. If you balance the energy losses of the circuit's intake, duct, radiator core, and exit against the energy addition of the fan and radiator heat rejection, it is possible to accomplish the engine cooling job with little or no net loss in an efficient system. That's exactly what you see on the front hoods of some GT category racing cars. If you improve on any one of the cooling air flow elements, you will minimize the mechanical requirements of the engine fan. This can be done by placing the intake and exit for both water-cooled or air-cooled engine cooling systems in the highest and lowest pressure areas possible on the body surface.

To choose the most advantageous locations for these duct entrances and exits, you have to know about the distribution of static pressure developed on the car body as a result of air flow. As we've said, body shape affects the flow velocities and so it affects the static pressure distribution. In addition, side winds alter the flow pattern changing the static pressure distribution in certain areas.

Still, in general, it is possible to take in air for internal flow in either a high pressure/low velocity area such as the base of the windshield, or at a low pressure and high velocity area such as the corner of the windshield or the windshield header. But you need to use specific techniques for each. You can use a flush opening to intake air in an area with high static pressure. Scoops are best used in high velocity/low pressure areas, but must project far enough from the surface to get the forward facing opening outside the decelerated boundary layer. You can engineer an air exit on a flush surface by using rear facing projecting outlets of correct design. Keep in mind that projecting intake and exit shapes tend to increase aerodynamic drag over that of flush intake and exit areas.

### AERODYNAMIC NOISE

Most of the total vehicle interior noise at highway speeds is attributable to aerodynamic noise. But since that's more a concern for the automaker's engineers, we'll only talk briefly on the subject.

Any noise from a body-mounted part indicates interference drag on the vehicle. Repositioning or detuning the part for the disturbing frequency is necessary. How's that for brevity?

**The separation of the boundary layer causes the pressure behind the car to go below ambient. This is the mechanism of the element of form drag that resists forward motion. Lift losses come from the fact that work is being done and therefore energy must be expended. The stagnation point has the highest pressure and force. The separation area has the lowest. This difference in pressure is what resists your forward motion and is form drag. Lift comes from the pressure difference below the car and above.**

## AND NOW THE EQUATIONS...

The above covers the basics pretty well, but to really understand what aerodynamicists are talking about, you have to savvy the math. So here are the primary aerodynamic or fluid dynamic equations. We're skipping the Reynold's number and Bernoulli's equation because the former only applies if you have a wind tunnel and are very into this field; the latter is discussed in *High Performance Honda Builder's Handbook, Volume One*.

### THE DRAG EQUATION

$$D_A = 1/2p \ V^2 \ C_d A$$

Where:
$C_d$ = Aero drag coefficient
A = Frontal Area of Vehicle
P = Air density

("D" is the SAE symbol for drag, the subscripted A distinguishes the notation to avoid confusion.)

The term $1/2p \ V^2$ describes the dynamic pressure of air. That is the pressure that is exerted on a surface as it, or the air moves at a specified velocity. The coefficient of drag $C_d$ is determined by testing and the frontal area A is the scaling factor which takes into account the surface area on which the dynamic pressure of air acts upon. Frontal area is most critical for the total drag.

As we discuss in the chapter on engine management, air density is variable depending on temperature, pressure, and humidity. Dry air at standard conditions (59°F and 29.92 InHg) has an air density of .0763 lb./ft.$^3$. However, these drag equations use mass density, so you must divide the weight density by the acceleration of gravity. Hence:

.0763 lb./ft.$^3$ / 32.2 ft./sec.$^2$ = 0.00236 lb.-sec.$^2$/ft.$^4$.

To estimate *p* using the mass density of standard air use the following equation:

$$p = 0.00236 \left(\frac{P_r}{29.92}\right)\left(\frac{519}{460+T_r}\right)$$

Where:
$P_r$ = Atm pressure in Inches Hg
$T_r$ = Air Temp in °F

For those on the SI (metric) system the equation takes the same form, but with these values:

The wheel grabs air which is pulled into the wheel well. This flow pattern obviously causes turbulence. You can reduce the wheel's drag by having the body and wheel fit as flush and as close as possible. Check out NASCAR racers, they do aero very well.

$$P = 1.255 \left(\frac{P_r}{101.325}\right)\left(\frac{288.16}{273.16+T_r}\right)$$

Where:
$P_r$ = Atm pressure in kilopascals
$T_r$ = Air Temp in °C

If you're hard core, you can calculate the actual air density of local conditions, by using the virtual temperature equation. You can find it in the chapter on air/fuel tuning.

### THE DRAG COEFFICIENT

$$C_d = \frac{D_A}{1/2p \ V^2 \ A}$$

The above equation divides the drag force by the dynamic pressure multiplied by the frontal area. The drag force is determined by wind tunnel tests, or coast down tests, which are more accessible to the average performance enthusiast. (We'll show you how to do that later in the chapter.) What the $C_d$ means is that drag force is X times as large as the dynamic pressure acting over the frontal area. For example, a flat plate has a $C_d$ of 1.95, meaning that the drag force is almost twice that of the dynamic air pressure acting on the plate's surface area. High drag results from the separation area much larger than the plate itself. That's one of the reasons separation of the flow from the body is not in harmony with going faster, unless you want to slow down.

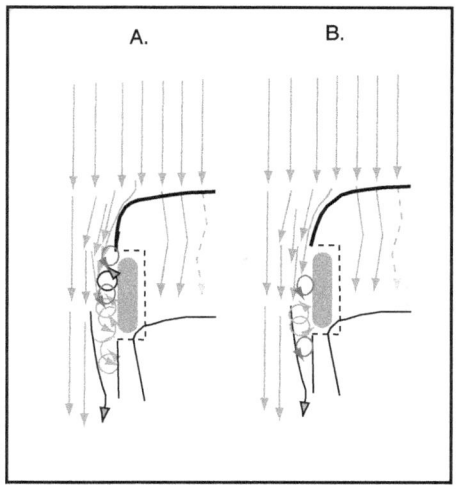

From the top angle we can see the interaction of the wheel and the turbulent flow down the side of the car. If you can blend the curve of the body gradually into the wheel well area, you can reduce drag and turbulence.

### THE DRAG COEFFICIENT AND THE REAL WORLD

The $C_d$ is a good number to know, but how does it work in the real world? You should know that $C_d$ calculations assume no side winds. Just totally straight flow across the longitudinal line of the car. We all know this isn't what we drive in, so it's good to know how crosswinds affect your car's handling.

Let's talk about the affects of head winds first. Because the velocity of the air is squared in the equation, a head wind causes much more drag than a tail wind of equal magnitude. So assuming you're traveling at the same speed in both instances, a head wind costs you more power than an equally speedy tail wind.

When it comes to side winds, we all know that most modern cars are very stable, at least at highway speeds and slightly above. But when you're blasting down the drag strip tripping the lights at 135 mph (217Km/h), a nasty gust of wind gets your attention rather quickly. What's going on?

Well, a lot. The whole shape of the car and the steering system interacts with the wind. When your Honda hits a gust of side wind, the side force acts first on the nose and generally pushes the car in the direction of the gust. The side force acts on the body at the center of pressure, usually located ahead of the center of gravity. Because of the distance between

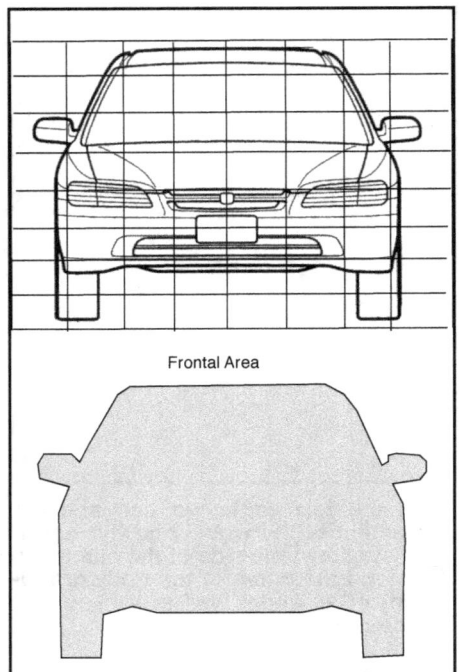

Frontal Area

**When measuring frontal area, don't include the space beneath the car and between the wheels. Notice how large the side mirrors look in silhouette. For maximum top end, it's reasonably easy to remove these appendages. Another popular method to reduce frontal area is just lowering the car. Reducing frontal area is one of the most efficient ways to lower drag.**

these two points, the forces generate a torque that steers the car. If the center of pressure is in front of the Cg, the car wants to go with the wind; if behind, it tends to turn against it.

While on the subject of side winds, we need to talk about their effect on lift. In general, if there is no side wind, a Honda passenger car (and most of today's passenger cars) will have a coefficient of lift in a lower range of .3 to .5. This can change quickly in a swift side wind at a steep angle.

Lift can be determined for each of the axles, which if you recall the discussion on tires will reduce the grip available for cornering and control. Front lift reduces steering control and rear lift reduces stability in the manner of oversteer. A general principle that determines rear lift generation is: any design that releases the air at a downward angle creates lift. This is most often the case for the rear of the car. However, modern designs employ a flat horizontal structure to release the air in a manner that reduces lift and drag. A side wind can increase the lift generated if it is strong enough to redirect the air flow off that flat structure where the body terminates, forcing it to release off the side of the vehicle which tends to have a soft radius that can direct the air downward. This is one of the reasons why a side wind can disturb the car more than you'd think and is why fastback designs tend to be a little more sensitive to side winds than even station wagons or sedans.

You can minimize lift by judicious use of belly pans, spoilers, and angle of attack. Just a three-degree rake on the body can reduce lift by some 40%.

## HOW TO PERFORM A COAST DOWN TEST

You can measure aero drag force and convert it to lbs. of force or horsepower. All it takes is a level road with a speed limit at least 5 mph faster than the speed at which you wish to calculate drag horsepower, a stop watch and a calculator.

First establish the MPH at which you want to know the power loss. Let's say it's 60 mph. If you do a 10 mph coast down with 60 mph as the average, that means you'll time how long it takes for your car to coast from 65 mph down to 55 mph. The easiest way to do that is to reach a speed a little faster than the test window, put the gearbox in neutral and time how long it takes to coast from 65mph down to 55 mph. You should perform this timing in both directions to cancel any grade of the road. You should also be aware of any wind in the test area. Remember a head wind takes away more power than a tail wind gives back.

## QUICK AERO HP CALCULATION

Once you have your coast down times, you can use the following equation to calculate the horsepower required to maintain 60 mph.

$$HP @ MPH = \frac{V \times Wt.}{775 \times t}$$

**Where:**
**V = average mph (target speed)**
**Wt. = scale weight of car plus effective weights of wheel and driveshaft. (See drag racing section for more information on rotating inertia and effective weight.)**
**t = seconds required to coast down**

Calculate the horsepower value for each coast down time, then average them to get the aero horsepower value for that speed. You can then refer to the chart at the end of this chapter that lists various aero horsepower categories, starting at 50 mph. These tables will tell you how much power it will take to push your car through the air at various speeds all the way up to 300 mph!

One final point to this testing scheme. For the most part we are measuring aero horsepower, but hidden in this is the rolling resistance. So it's not purely aero drag. But it's very close, and it gives you some usable values to make tuning and gearing decisions. A more complete method is given later in the chapter, but it requires, measuring the barometric pressure and humidity.

## CALCULATING DRAG FORCE AND $C_d$

While it's good to know the horsepower it takes to drive your car through the air, sometimes knowing the force in lbs. or Newtons let's you make more informed tuning choices. Therefore we'll demonstrate the use of the aerodynamic equations given above.

First, you have to perform a coast down as outlined above. You can get the raw force of drag in lbs. or Newtons without taking a barometer and wet bulb reading, but you won't be able to establish your $C_d$. (Reference the Engine Management section for details on how to generate that information.) Also, the back of the book has some good formulas and conversion factors to help you.

Before you can use the drag equations, you need to find the force. This is done with a version of f = ma:

**D force = Mass times the change in velocity/time for that change.**

**Or: $D = -m \frac{\text{delta } V}{\text{delta } T}$**

As in the coast down procedure given above, the mass is the weight of the vehicle including the effective weight of all four of it's wheels. We don't have to calculate for the driveshaft since we don't have one.

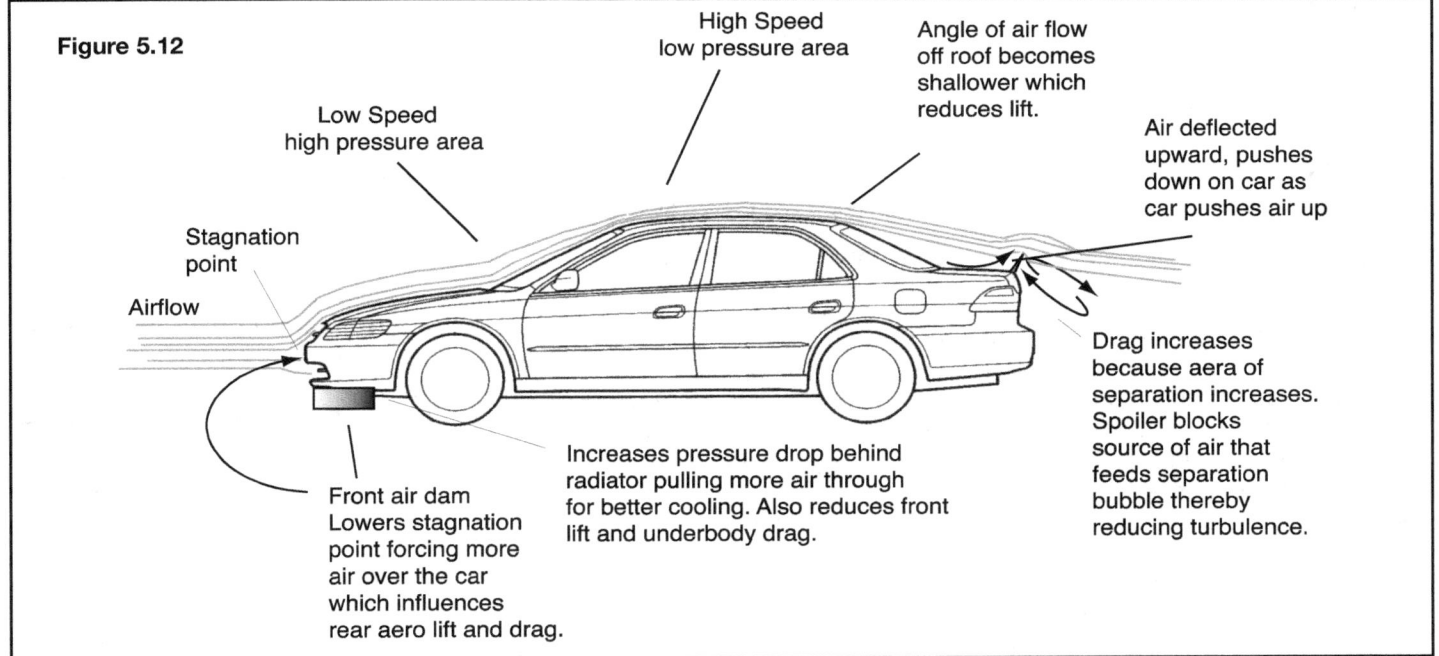

**Figure 5.12**

Installing an air dam changes the way air flows over the entire car. This chart details how two popular bolt-on devices influence aerodynamic performance.

To use this formula you have to know a few tricks of the physics trade that have to do with the acceleration of gravity.

Essentially you have to convert the weight of the vehicle to mass by dividing its weight by gravity or 32.2 ft./sec.². There are a couple of ways of doing this but it tends to be less confusing if you divide the acceleration ratio (V/T) by 32.2 ft./sec.².

For example:

We've got a 2951 lb. car with fuel and driver. The effective weight of all four 35 lb. wheels is 73.5 lbs. which when added to the weight of the car brings it to 3024.50 lbs.

We coast it from 65 mph down to 55 mph in order to average 60 mph which is 88 ft./sec. Acceleration is a change in velocity, which is denoted by the delta V. So the change in velocity, again measured in ft./sec., is 65 mph (95.329 ft./sec.) minus 55 mph (80.663 ft./sec.) = 14.69 ft./sec. The time it takes to coast down is 18 secs.

$$D = -3024.5 \text{ lb.} \cdot \frac{95.329 - 80.663 \text{ ft./sec.}}{18 \text{ sec.}}$$

By dividing the change in velocity by the time we get ft./sec./sec. or ft./sec.², which is an acceleration. In this case we get .816 ft./sec.².

$$D = -3024.5 \text{ lb.} * .816 \text{ ft./sec.}^2$$

When we divide that figure by the ft./sec.² value of gravity 32.2 ft./sec.², we get the coast down deceleration in percent of g, which turns out to be .025 g.

$$D = -3024.5 \text{ lb.} \cdot \frac{.816 \text{ ft./sec.}^2}{32.2 \text{ ft./sec.}^2}$$

$$D = -3024.5 \text{ lb.} * .025$$

When you multiply the weight of the car by the %g, you get the lbs. of force exerted on the car that cause the deceleration. For this example, we arrive at -76.53 lbs.

$$D = -76.53 \text{ lbs}$$

Before you can calculate the $C_d$, you need to subtract the rolling resistance from the measured drag force. But before you can do that you need to calculate the rolling resistance.

Rolling resistance force is difficult to quantify exactly. It's the result of many different processes and forces taking place within the tire and acting on it. The design of the tire, it's inflation pressure, the road surface, speed, aerodynamic drag are just a few of the mechanisms at work to produce rolling resistance.

However, there are several methods to derive a coefficient from known operation conditions which work very well. The Institute of Technology in Stuttgart developed a method that takes into account the increase in rolling resistance that occurs with increasing speed. So we'll use that one to calculate rolling resistance.

The formula the Institute developed is:

$$f_r = f_o + 2.34 * f_s (V/100)^{2.5}$$

**Where:**
**V = speed in MPH**
**$f_o$ = Basic Coefficient**
**$f_s$ = Speed Effect Coefficient**

These two coefficients are tire inflation pressure sensitive. Their respective values are determined by the chart below:

| Infl psi | $f_o$ | $f_s$ |
|---|---|---|
| 10 | 0.0175 | 0.014 |
| 15 | 0.015 | 0.012 |
| 20 | 0.014 | 0.01 |
| 25 | 0.0125 | 0.0075 |
| 30 | 0.01 | 0.005 |
| 35 | 0.0095 | 0.0045 |
| 40 | 0.008 | 0.004 |
| 45 | 0.007 | 0.003 |

Rolling resistance only applies to straight line performance, because it will increase as the tires generate cornering force and slip angles. There are other factors involved but cornering force friction is the largest.

For our model the following is assumed to be so:

Tire inflation is set at 35 psi.

**Thus:**

$f_r = .0095 + 2.34 * .0045(60/100)^{2.5}$
$f_r = .014$

**Multiply by the weight of the car:**

$R_x = .014 * 2951 = 40.032$ lbs.

With this information we can establish a reasonably accurate coefficient of drag $C_d$. If you want the actual drag and $C_d$ values under the conditions you test or race, you need to have a barometer reading and wet bulb reading from which to calculate the local test atmospheric density. If you are more interested in comparing information with manufacturers, you can use the equation with the standard values given above. To adjust for dry air density at various barometer pressures, use the equations above.

The equation to find the $C_d$ is:

$$C_d = \frac{D_A - R_x}{1/2 p\, V^2\, A}$$

**Where:**
$D = 1/2 p\, V^2\, C_d A$

**Where:**
D = measured drag force
$R_x$ = rolling resistance
$C_d$ = Aero drag coefficient
A = Frontal Area of Vehicle
P = Air density

Since we know rolling resistance, now we can calculate the $C_d$.
Substituting the values:

$$C_d = \frac{76.53 - 40.032}{1/2 * .00236 * 88\,\text{ft./sec.}^2 * 18.5\,\text{ft.}^2}$$

$$C_d = \frac{39.498}{169.16}$$

$C_d = .22$

Obviously our calculated $C_d$ is very low and doesn't reflect what would happen in the real world to a production car with 18.5 square feet of frontal area. The normal range would be in the .36 $C_d$ which would see a coast down time of 13.5 seconds from 65 mph to 55 mph.

## HOW TO CALCULATE AERO HP AND ROLLING RESISTANCE HP

Calculating the horsepower consumed by aero drag and rolling resistance is now straight forward. You simply multiply the pounds of force by the speed of the vehicle in ft./sec., then divide by 1 horsepower which is equal to one pound at 550 ft./sec.:

**aero drag =**
39.498 lbs. * 88 ft./sec./555 ft./lbs./sec.

**aero drag = 6.31 horsepower**

So at 60 mph (88 ft./sec.), 39.498 lbs. of aero drag takes 6.31 horsepower to overcome.

The rolling resistance component is interesting because at this speed it is about equal to the aero drag:

**Rolling Resistance HP =**
40.032 * 88 ft./sec./550 ft./lbs./sec. = 6.41

Of course, this relationship diverges as speeds increase because of the geometric rise in aero drag with higher speeds. This is true because tire rolling resistance increases much slower than aero drag.

At 60 mph at sea level under standard atmospheric conditions (dry air, 59°F, 29.92 inHg), it takes 12.72 horsepower to drive this car.

## WHAT YOU CAN DO WITH THIS INFORMATION

Now you know how to figure out aero drag and its associated power consumption, as well as rolling resistance and its power absorbing qualities. The question then is, what to do with it?

This information lets you make correct tuning choices. If you make a body change, how does it affect the top end speed of your car, or the speed through the lights at a drag strip? This is very important as speeds rise. The relationship as we've said is geometric, so more efficient air management releases engine power to accelerate your car.

With this information you can calculate the best gearing for maximum top speed of your car. You need to know the RPM of peak power, from a dyno test for example or other means, such as the use of an g meter and timing or observing peak g. And you need to know the gear ratios of your car and tire diameter. With these numbers, you can put these values in an equation and figure out your car's top speed.

Simply calculate the speed that would occur mechanically by virtue of the engine RPM at peak power and the gearing and tire diameter:

**MPH =**
**RPM * Dw / final ratio * gear ratio * 336**

For example, consider a car with an engine making 170 horsepower at 7600 rpm with 195/55-15 tires that are about 23-inch in diameter. Final drive is 4.40 and 5th gear is .787.

Taking .5-inch off the tire diameter for deflection, that gives us:

**MPH = 7600 * 22.5 / 4.40 * .787 * 336**
**MPH = 147**

Where would aero horsepower equal drive wheel power? If you check the aero horsepower chart to find how much horsepower it takes to go 147 mph, you see it depends a lot on the aerodynamic efficiency of the car and the efficiency of the transmission. Say you tested the car and it took 11 horsepower to drive it at 50 mph. Since there are power losses in the driveline and accessory drives, say 15%, that means we're losing around 25.5 hp, meaning we've got 144.5 ponies to work with. Reference the column for 11 drive HP and you find that 153 horsepower is good for 140 mph. We know the gear is such that 140 mph doesn't let the engine make peak power, right? So it's not going 140 mph. What will happen is the aero horsepower will balance with the drive wheel horsepower and the car will "top out" at some speed less than the maximum potential indicated by the gearing and tire size.

This combination is pretty close and probably should be left alone. But if you wanted a little more speed from this package, what should you change?

Since tire diameter influences final drive and is relatively easy to change compared with transmission gears, installing a tire of less diameter may let you nudge the car's top speed up a few MPH.

To solve for tire diameter at that MPH, use this form of the equation:

**$D_w = F_{dr} * T_{gr} * 336 * $ MPH / RPM**

| MPH | \ | \ | \ | HORSEPOWER @ 50 MPH | \ | \ | \ |
|---|---|---|---|---|---|---|---|
| 50 | 11 | 12 | 13 | 14 | 15 | 16 | 17 |
| 51 | 11 | 12 | 13 | 15 | 16 | 17 | 18 |
| 52 | 12 | 13 | 14 | 15 | 16 | 18 | 19 |
| 53 | 12 | 14 | 15 | 16 | 17 | 18 | 20 |
| 54 | 13 | 14 | 15 | 17 | 18 | 19 | 21 |
| 55 | 13 | 15 | 16 | 18 | 19 | 20 | 22 |
| 56 | 14 | 16 | 17 | 18 | 20 | 21 | 23 |
| 57 | 15 | 16 | 18 | 19 | 21 | 22 | 24 |
| 58 | 15 | 17 | 18 | 20 | 22 | 23 | 25 |
| 59 | 16 | 18 | 19 | 21 | 22 | 24 | 26 |
| 60 | 17 | 18 | 20 | 22 | 23 | 25 | 27 |
| 61 | 17 | 19 | 21 | 23 | 24 | 26 | 28 |
| 62 | 18 | 20 | 22 | 24 | 25 | 27 | 29 |
| 63 | 19 | 21 | 23 | 25 | 27 | 28 | 30 |
| 64 | 20 | 22 | 24 | 26 | 28 | 30 | 32 |
| 65 | 20 | 23 | 25 | 27 | 29 | 31 | 33 |
| 66 | 21 | 23 | 26 | 28 | 30 | 32 | 34 |
| 67 | 22 | 24 | 26 | 29 | 31 | 33 | 35 |
| 68 | 23 | 25 | 27 | 30 | 32 | 34 | 37 |
| 69 | 24 | 26 | 29 | 31 | 33 | 36 | 38 |
| 70 | 25 | 27 | 30 | 32 | 34 | 37 | 39 |
| 71 | 26 | 28 | 31 | 33 | 36 | 38 | 41 |
| 72 | 26 | 29 | 32 | 34 | 37 | 40 | 42 |
| 73 | 27 | 30 | 33 | 36 | 38 | 41 | 44 |
| 74 | 28 | 31 | 34 | 37 | 40 | 42 | 45 |
| 75 | 29 | 32 | 35 | 38 | 41 | 44 | 47 |
| 76 | 30 | 33 | 36 | 39 | 42 | 45 | 48 |
| 77 | 31 | 34 | 38 | 41 | 44 | 47 | 50 |
| 78 | 32 | 36 | 39 | 42 | 45 | 48 | 52 |
| 79 | 33 | 37 | 40 | 43 | 47 | 50 | 53 |
| 80 | 34 | 38 | 41 | 45 | 48 | 52 | 55 |
| 81 | 35 | 39 | 43 | 46 | 50 | 53 | 57 |
| 82 | 37 | 40 | 44 | 48 | 51 | 55 | 59 |
| 83 | 38 | 41 | 45 | 49 | 53 | 57 | 60 |
| 84 | 39 | 43 | 47 | 51 | 54 | 58 | 62 |
| 85 | 40 | 44 | 48 | 52 | 56 | 60 | 66 |
| 86 | 41 | 45 | 49 | 54 | 58 | 62 | 66 |
| 87 | 42 | 47 | 51 | 55 | 59 | 66 | 68 |
| 88 | 44 | 48 | 52 | 57 | 61 | 65 | 70 |
| 89 | 45 | 49 | 54 | 58 | 63 | 67 | 72 |
| 90 | 46 | 51 | 55 | 60 | 65 | 69 | 74 |
| 91 | 47 | 52 | 57 | 62 | 66 | 71 | 76 |
| 92 | 49 | 54 | 59 | 63 | 68 | 73 | 78 |
| 93 | 50 | 55 | 60 | 65 | 70 | 75 | 80 |
| 94 | 51 | 57 | 62 | 67 | 72 | 77 | 82 |
| 95 | 53 | 58 | 63 | 69 | 74 | 79 | 85 |
| 96 | 54 | 60 | 65 | 71 | 76 | 81 | 87 |
| 97 | 56 | 61 | 67 | 72 | 78 | 84 | 89 |
| 98 | 57 | 63 | 69 | 74 | 80 | 86 | 91 |
| 99 | 59 | 64 | 70 | 76 | 82 | 88 | 94 |
| 100 | 60 | 66 | 72 | 78 | 84 | 90 | 96 |
| 102 | 63 | 69 | 76 | 82 | 88 | 95 | 101 |
| 104 | 66 | 73 | 80 | 86 | 93 | 99 | 106 |
| 106 | 70 | 76 | 83 | 90 | 97 | 104 | 111 |
| 108 | 73 | 80 | 87 | 95 | 102 | 109 | 117 |
| 110 | 76 | 84 | 92 | 99 | 107 | 114 | 122 |
| 112 | 80 | 88 | 96 | 104 | 112 | 120 | 128 |
| 114 | 82 | 92 | 100 | 108 | 117 | 125 | 133 |
| 116 | 87 | 96 | 105 | 113 | 122 | 131 | 139 |
| 118 | 91 | 100 | 109 | 118 | 127 | 136 | 145 |
| 120 | 95 | 104 | 114 | 123 | 133 | 142 | 152 |
| 122 | 99 | 109 | 119 | 128 | 138 | 148 | 158 |
| 124 | 103 | 113 | 123 | 134 | 144 | 154 | 165 |
| 126 | 107 | 118 | 129 | 139 | 150 | 161 | 171 |
| 128 | 111 | 123 | 134 | 145 | 156 | 167 | 178 |
| 130 | 116 | 127 | 139 | 151 | 162 | 174 | 185 |
| 132 | 120 | 132 | 144 | 156 | 168 | 180 | 192 |
| 134 | 125 | 137 | 150 | 162 | 175 | 187 | 200 |
| 136 | 130 | 143 | 156 | 169 | 181 | 194 | 207 |
| 138 | 134 | 148 | 161 | 175 | 188 | 202 | 215 |
| 140 | 139 | 153 | 167 | 181 | 195 | 209 | 223 |
| 142 | 144 | 159 | 173 | 188 | 202 | 217 | 231 |
| 144 | 150 | 164 | 179 | 194 | 209 | 224 | 239 |
| 146 | 155 | 170 | 186 | 201 | 217 | 232 | 248 |
| 148 | 160 | 176 | 192 | 208 | 224 | 240 | 256 |
| 150 | 166 | 182 | 199 | 215 | 232 | 248 | 265 |
| 152 | 171 | 188 | 205 | 223 | 240 | 257 | 274 |
| 154 | 177 | 195 | 212 | 230 | 248 | 265 | 283 |
| 156 | 183 | 201 | 219 | 237 | 256 | 274 | 292 |
| 158 | 189 | 207 | 226 | 245 | 264 | 283 | 302 |
| 160 | 195 | 214 | 234 | 253 | 272 | 292 | 311 |

**Use this chart with data you generate from coast down tests.**

In this case we know the MPH, the RPM, the final drive and transmission gear:

**4.4 * .787 * 336 * 140/7600 = 21.43**

Technically, if we could reduce the tire diameter a few tenths we could see a few more MPH. In reality, the combination of gearing, tire diameter, engine power curve, and aerodynamic drag is so closely matched, you'd really have to work with the drag on the body or make more power before you'd see a benefit from changing gears or tire diameter.

That's a fairly quick way to do it. You could also use the aero drag and rolling resistance equations to fine tune your top speed combination, or for drag racing maximize gearing and aerodynamics to improve trap speed and thus your E.T.s.

# Honda Builder's HANDBOOK Vol. II
## FUEL IS POWER

### FUEL MAKES POWER

Because fuel makes power, you should know as much as possible about it and how it behaves. Turbos don't make power. Nitrous systems don't make power. The fuel, reacting with oxygen in the charged air, makes the heat that creates cylinder pressure to make horsepower. If you want to know how to tune your Honda to the ultimate, you have to get this concept.

A proper engine fuel provides quick starts, fast warmup, rapid acceleration, smooth performance, good mileage in various driving conditions and climates, and minimizes engine maintenance. That's a hefty shopping list but for the most part, pump gas provides all these benefits. Yet for high performance applications, you need to use a racing gasoline. Specially blended to resist detonation, racing gasoline allows you to run higher compression ratios than what is possible with pump gas. Racing gasoline also has more British Thermal Units (BTU) per unit of measure, about 1200 BTU more on average, than pump gas. The BTU content of a fuel is a measure of the potential heat a given unit of fuel can produce. Heat is what makes the pressure in the cylinder and that's where you get more power from racing gasoline.

We won't be able to tell you everything about pump and racing gasolines here. The purpose is really to get you acquainted with some of the basic concepts which will let you educate yourself more quickly and accurately as you start tuning your Honda's engine to take advantage of racing gasolines.

Let's start with the engine factors that shape the properties needed in a good gasoline. The first is compression ratio. All the compression ratio does is heat things up. In effect, compressing the air/fuel mix heats it, thereby making it ready for the spark jumping across the electrodes to ignite.

So what is the advantage of a higher compression ratio? That's your control over the heat in the combustion chamber before you ignite it, which influences burn rate. With lower compression you can run more timing advance. This is because at lower compression ratio when you start the mixture burning, it takes longer to heat and raise the pressure in the chamber. Basically it's a tuning tool. Instead of lighting it off way early, as with a low compression combination, you can fire the cylinder closer to the dead center with a higher compression combination. Ultimately you have to get peak cylinder pressure at the same crankshaft degree for peak performance. So whether you use the pistons to heat the mix or burn it early to make heat is of little consequence. The real limitation is the fuel's resistance to detonation, called its octane rating.

The rule of thumb that raising compression makes horsepower is only partly true. The average engine is compromised in a lot of ways. It has to do a lot of different things in a variety of situations, particularly street engines. So if you ran your engine at the highest compression the fuel would support, the number of situations in which the engine would function properly would be very few. About the only time you could drive such an engine would be on the coldest winter days. On hot summer days, forget it. You'd rattle the heads off the block.

So you can optimize an engine for track conditions, for the type of racing, or sometimes for the rules. For example, you may have cubic-inch limitations, such as in some of the touring car classes. If you have a cubic inch limitation, you know you can't get power by making the engine bigger. The only way you can make more power is by doing more work in the same period of time. That means the engine will have to rev higher and make peak power at higher RPM.

For example, consider a 2-liter engine revving to 10,000 rpm. The problem with running at 10,000 rpm is that pump gas won't burn that fast and remain stable because it's not that good of a fuel. If you use a good racing fuel that has the appropriate energy content and octane rating, you still have the problem of burning it at a rate that makes power at 10,000 rpm. So to get racing fuel to burn fast you have to get it real close to its auto- ignition point, then light it off with a spark plug.

With an engine combination designed to make power at very high RPM, there just isn't any other sound way to put a predictable amount of heat in the chamber before igniting the mix. The heat goes up in direct proportion to how much the gas is compressed. So compression ratio is simply part of the overall combination.

If you're burning alcohol, which takes a different temperature curve, and has a slower burn rate compared to gasoline, then the compression ratio of that engine will be higher for most combinations. Most enthusiasts get excited by the thought that they can make all sorts of power with alcohol. But it's not all that simple. On one hand alcohol stays stable, it doesn't self-ignite in conditions that gasoline does. The advantage of alcohol is that for the same amount of air flow, more energy is released.

There is a limit, both mechanically and chemically, as to how much you can raise compression ratios to get more efficiency from an engine. First of all, you have to have some clearance between the piston and the head. That's the mechanical limit. But more relevant to our topic is the limitation of the fuel. At some level of compression, an air and gasoline mixture will self-ignite. That's the chemical limit. When that happens you've got detonation and we've talked in depth about that subject earlier.

In the broadest terms you can get into detonation in two ways. One we've just discussed: a compression ratio that raises the pressure in the combustion chamber beyond the fuel's ability to resist self-ignition. The other occurs when the pressure in the combustion chamber rises to that point after the spark plug fires the charge. In this case as the main flame front travels across the combustion chamber and pressure begins to rise in the cylinder, a second flame front is generated by an area in the combustion chamber with raised temperature and pressures high enough where it self-ignites in little pockets within the combustion chamber. The rattle you hear in severe detonation is the flame fronts colliding.

The most common causes of, let's call it dynamic detonation, are too much ignition advance and/or a hot spot in the combustion chamber. Obviously, if you light off the fuel too early, the piston isn't going to be heading down the bore soon enough to keep the pressure in the chamber from reaching self-ignition levels. A hot spot can cause this condition to occur in the chamber even if the timing is set properly for the fuel.

A gasoline's resistance to detonation is known as its antiknock rating or it's Octane value. The Octane rating on most pump and racing gas is an average of two laboratory tests using a single cylinder engine with sensors to detect detonation. Research Octane Number (RON) is decided at 600 rpm and determines the fuel's resistance to detonation from compression. Motor Octane Number (MON) is determined at 900 rpm with the intake air heated and ignition advanced to get the fuel to detonate. A mixture of reference fuels, isooctane and heptane are used and get a relative value from which to rate the test fuel. Add the motor octane value to the research octane value and divide the sum by two (R+M/2) gives you the average value. This is the octane rating you see on pump and racing gas, although racing fuel usually has both listed in the literature.

A high octane number does not indicate a more powerful fuel. It indicates that, for example, your 10:1 compression ratio aluminum headed engine won't detonate on (R+M/2=) 92 octane premium fuel. That's assuming you haven't advanced the timing to get the two or three horsepower you can find at the expense of significantly higher cylinder pressures and a high risk of detonation.

Most modern fuel-injected stock engines have sensors that allow you to use middle grade fuel, such as 89 octane or lower. The sensors detect detonation and the computer retards the timing or adds fuel or a combination of both. Since the timing is retarded, the power stroke is shortened and therefore the engine loses some power.

What a high octane fuel does then, is let the engine operate the way it was designed in so far as compression ratio and efficiency is concerned. For example, Unocal 100 octane unleaded racing gas is advertised for use in engines with up to 11:1 compression ratios. That means an engine in good operating condition and tuned, i.e. timed correctly with proper fuel curves, shouldn't start detonating with this fuel. Therefore you won't have to back off the timing or fatten up the mixture to compensate for a problem. The engine takes advantage of the high compression, has a powerful air/fuel mixture, and is timed for a long power stroke. That's really what an appropriate octane number is all about.

## HOW TO MAKE POWER WITH GAS — VAPORIZE IT!

For gasoline to burn, for it to react with oxygen, it has to be a vapor. We'll repeat that to make sure you get this point: Gasoline has to be suspended in the charged air to burn. Technically, this is known as atomization or vaporization. Vaporization occurs when liquid fuel turns into a vapor or gaseous state. (For more info on vapor as a gas, see the chapter on engine management.) If the fuel is still in a liquid form in the combustion chamber, all it does is take up space and raises the dynamic compression ratio. If you get enough fuel remaining in liquid form in your engine you can raise the dynamic compression ratio enough to force detonation. This is an extreme case and is given purely to drive home the point that liquid fuel does not burn.

Fuel tends to do some very weird things if you put too much in the engine. It tends to recombine. It goes from little droplets at the carburetors and as it travels down the runner it starts forming bigger droplets; it is the same with injectors that are too large. So when it gets to the actual cylinder, it's a river and it is so heavy it just falls to one side. It doesn't burn in this form, only the surface of it burns. You may have a ton of fuel going through the engine, but very little of it is burning when it needs to burn to make power. It gets spit out the pipe, where it absorbs heat from the exhaust tract, vaporizes, and then burns with a big flame out the tail pipe like a top fuel engine.

The trick to making big horsepower with an internal combustion engine, particularly with nitrous or turbos or both, is getting the fuel vaporized. That is the job of the carburetor or the fuel injectors. These devices take liquid fuel and disperse it into the intake air in small droplets. Droplet size is critical to the rate at which fuel will then vaporize. Fuel can only vaporize from the surface area of the droplet.

The rate fuel vaporizes is key to how much power you can create. The intake charge is moving very quickly and is in the engine a very short time before it is ignited. For a carbureted engine, all you have is the distance from the venturi to the chamber and the time it takes for the charge to travel that distance. On a port-injected engine there's even less distance and time for vaporization.

Looking for more efficient ways to vaporize fuel and keeping it suspended in the charged air keeps engine tuners and the petroleum company's chemists up late at night. Manifold, carburetor, and fuel injector designs are all the product of this pursuit. As simple a process as evaporation can become a serious challenge when you have only a scant few fractions of a second to work with.

Most of this work is done by the chemists that refine pump gasoline and racing gasoline. Their job is to blend several petrochemicals to produce gasoline that performs as stated at the beginning of this section. The way they do this is to blend certain elements that vaporize easily at low temperatures. These are usually called the front ends or light ends or volatiles. The petroleum companies actually blend various ratio of these volatile compounds into pump gas to compensate for seasonal changes in average temperature. For example, they put more volatiles in gasoline in the winter, when it's cold to help cars start in the morning.

Most pump gas runs around 10 to 15 psi on the Reid Vapor Pressure test. This indicates how much of the gas is made of these light compounds. Racing gas on the other hand has a much lower RVP, around 6 psi and isn't seasonally adjusted so you don't have to go chasing jet sizes or pulse widths to compensate for the fuel. That's why it's hard to start engines using racing gas in cool weather. But the pay-off to hard starting is that since the gas has less light ends or volatiles, it has more of the dense, high BTU content compounds.

Of course, these dense high BTU content compounds have to vaporize to burn too, so they can't be too dense. A compound can have enormous amounts of BTUs, but if it doesn't vaporize in the cylinder it won't turn them into heat. It also has to vaporize enough to give you good throttle response. And that is perhaps the trickiest trick the chemists perform: blending compound to have a certain rate of vaporization for a given temperature rise.

This is known as the distillation curve. Most racing gasolines have an advertised distillation curve in the product literature. When it comes to choosing a racing gas for your combination this is one of your most valuable guides. You might think the BTU content should be, but most racing gasolines are so close in BTU content it doesn't really matter. What matters is how quickly and at what temperatures the gasoline turns to vapor.

Here's how it works. Trick 108 (R+M/2) octane racing fuel has an advertised distillation curve beginning with an initial boiling point (IBP) of 97°F. At 137°F, 10 percent of the gas has turned to vapor; at 202°F, 50 percent has turned to vapor; at 243°F, 90 percent has vaporized; and when it hits 295°F, all of the fuel is vaporized. This indicates how quickly the heat in the engine will help turn the fuel to vapor so it can burn to make power. While you want as cool and as dense an intake charge as possible, as the distillation curve indicates, a little heat doesn't hurt. As the intake air travels through the manifold it picks up heat. Then the fuel uses the heat to vaporize, cooling the air back down. Then the charge gets compressed and heat from friction of the compression as well as from the engine surfaces raise the temperature of the charge and the fuel hopefully vaporizes completely to make some heat of its own.

Most people think that octane is an indication of how quickly or slowly the fuel burns. That is not correct. According to the chemists at Phillips Petroleum, the hydrocarbons used to make gasoline will oxidize, or burn, at virtually the same rate, given the same conditions. The rate of burn, or the speed of the flame front, is basically the same for all gasolines as long as it's not detonating. The controlling mechanism of burn rate or flame front travel is the amount of oxygen in the combustion chamber available to react with the fuel. More oxygen means a faster flame front, at least to the natural limits of the fuel, and vice versa.

Another confusing concept about making power with gasoline is its energy or heat content. We've already talked about the BTU content of gasolines so we won't rehash it here. What we need to talk about is releasing all the energy in a specific amount of gas. Actually we're already talking about this concept, since the primary method of releasing the BTU content of gasoline is to vaporize it first.

But here's a key tuning concept: Use a gasoline with the highest calorie, or BTU content per unit of measure that will vaporize in your engine in the ambient temperatures on race day.

You don't necessarily want the most dense gas or fuel with the highest BTU content. Straight toluene is loaded with BTUs, but getting it to vaporize and react with oxygen is another story.

## ENERGY DENSITY AND A/F RATIO

A tuning aid you'll hear about around the pits is jetting, or setting injector pulse widths in accordance with the specific gravity of the fuel. Specific gravity is the ratio of the density of a material to the density of water at a specified temperature. In the metric system this is usually 3.98°C where water has a density of 1000 kg/cm$^3$. In the United States, we use the weight of a gallon of water at 60°F where it weighs 8.373 pounds.

As the temperature of the fuel rises, it becomes less dense. If it's less dense, then for given pulse width or jet size, you're introducing less BTUs and assuming the air density is unchanged, the engine will run lean. This is a valid tuning concept with very subtle gains in power. Still it will show power increases however slight, so if you need that last fraction of a horsepower, here's one place to find it.

An invalid tuning concept is using the most dense fuel, thinking that fuel will have the highest BTU content. The specific gravity of a fuel and it's energy density do not have a direct correlation. When choosing a fuel to tune your engine to, you need to look at its BTU content per pound or gallon. Most of this information comes with the fuel's literature. In addition, as we've said earlier, select a fuel with a realistic distillation curve. Once again, if the fuel will not vaporize, it will not oxidize; it will not burn to make heat.

Still it is very important to compensate for the energy density and the weight density, i.e., specific gravity of a fuel. If you're running a finely tuned engine just on the edge of detonation and you get a substantial decrease in the specific gravity of your fuel, you'll go lean and quickly get detonation. On the other hand if the specific gravity increases, you'll run rich. A slightly rich condition does not result in a substantial loss of power, so almost always this is not concern. Essentially the same relationship holds true for the energy density or BTU/lb. of gasoline. Also you should know that fuel, like most things, grows less dense as it heats up. This is because the molecules vibrate more and push each other farther away.

## AIR/FUEL RATIO AND POWER OUTPUT

Now let's learn a little about fuel mixture and its effect on performance. Figure 7.1 illustrates a fuel mixture curve for horsepower. As you can see, the slope on the left, or rich side, is closer to horizontal than the right, or lean, side of the curve. This shows horsepower drops off more rapidly when slightly lean than when slightly rich. In addition, engine damage is most likely to occur when running lean.

Most stock or mild engines are set on the rich side, so they can run all year round and travel from a higher altitude to a lower altitude without running too lean. Even electronically controlled fuel injection is calibrated in such a way. This is why during a race, performance will usually pick up as the air gets cooler at night. Cooler air has higher density than warmer air, so the air/fuel ratio is affected. If the fuel remains the same, the mixture will be lean. As the mixture gets leaner, the engine will develop more power because it is approaching the maximum horsepower point from the rich side of the curve. It is desirable to stay slightly on the rich side for two reasons. First, there is only a minimal loss of power, second, you can hurt your engine if the air to fuel ratio is just slightly on the lean side. If you are already operating on the lean side, and the air gets better, your vehicle will slow way down and the probability of hurting your engine goes way up. If this happens immediately, go up four jet sizes or increase the duty cycle of the injectors to improve performance and get a safety margin.

## BRAKE MEAN EFFECTIVE PRESSURE

When you combine gasoline with air in the proper proportions discussed above, the gas reacts with the oxygen in the air and creates heat. The hotter the fire, the greater the pressure which then forces the piston down the cylinder forcing the rod to spin the crankshaft to generate torque. This is why we say fuel makes the power.

Horsepower comes from the pressure in the cylinders. In fact, there are only four variables that contribute to power generation in an internal combustion engine. They are the mean effective pressure in the cylinder, the stroke length of the crankshaft, the square area of the piston top, and the number of power strokes per minute.

We'll write this as an equation:

$$HP = \frac{MEP \times CID \times RPM}{33,000 \times 12 \times 2}$$

This equation says that horsepower is the result of several relationships: First is the theoretical average pressure (MEP) acting on the piston

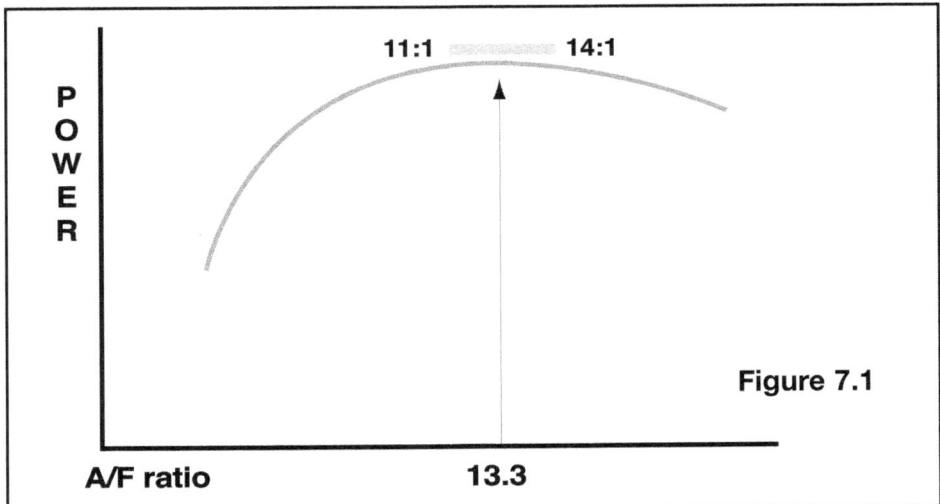

Figure 7.1

This curve shows the relationship between air/fuel ratio and power. The curve is shallower on the rich side indicating minor power loss from rich ratios.

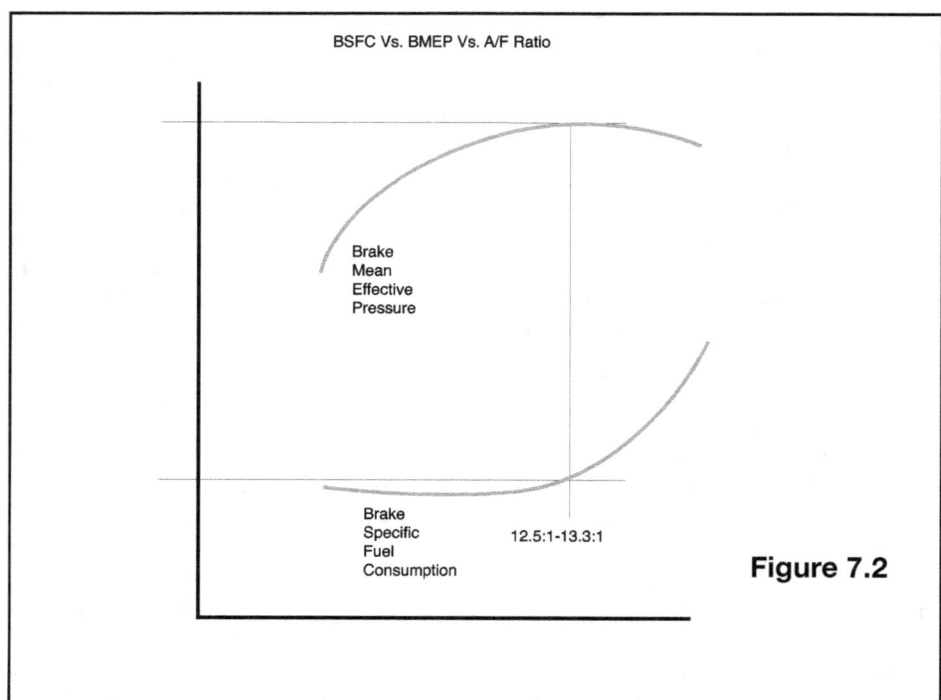

This Brake Mean Effective Pressure curve is the same as the power curve in figure 7.1. It shows that power comes from cylinder pressure which comes from mixing fuel with air and reacting to it. The Brake Specific Fuel Consumption curve shows the relationship between air/fuel ratios, power output, and fuel efficiency.

through its stroke. Second, the number of power strokes per minute, which is the RPM/2; third, the CID gives us the piston top area and the stroke length/12 to convert the ratio to feet. Finally, the numbers are divided by 33,000 pounds-feet/minute which is the value of one horsepower.

This is the theoretical power the engine produces, it is not brake power, i.e. the power measured at the flywheel. Brake horsepower is the net power the engine makes, that is minus the power lost to friction.

The reason we went through this mathematical exercise is to show you where the power from your engine comes from. For your engine to increase power, you have to increase at least one of these variables. That means you either have to increase the MEP, the stroke, the size of your engine, or the RPM at which peak power occurs. Of course you can reduce the friction horsepower, but this area is hard to get consistent gains compared to the others.

The easiest approach to making more power is to increase the MEP. The way you do this is to stuff more fuel and an appropriate amount of additional oxygen to make more heat, which makes more pressure.

This is the mechanism that makes cool air intakes work. Cooler air is denser than hot air, so it has more oxygen to react with the gasoline, which makes power.

This is also the mechanism behind supercharging, turbocharging, and nitrous. More fuel, combined with more oxygen, creates more pressure for a longer duration in the cylinder and that raises MEP.

Of course, since we're talking about pressure, we should mention the limits of the fuel. Once you've reached the compression limit of the fuel, it will detonate and you will lose power instantly. That's one of the ways you can tell you're engine is detonating. If the acceleration falls off unexpectedly, get off the throttle and check your plugs.

## BRAKE SPECIFIC FUEL CONSUMPTION

In case you haven't noticed, fuel is very important. It's so important, engineers have devised ways of measuring its use in very specific terms. Brake specific to be exact. Any time you see "brake" before a unit of measure it means a dynamometer was used to determine the value or magnitude. A Brake Specific Fuel Consumption rate (BSFC) of 1/2 pound of fuel per hour for each horsepower is expressed in decimal form as .5, i.e. 5/10ths; 50/100ths which are simply other ways of expressing 1/2. To make 100 hp at a .5 BSFC means that the engine uses 50 lbs. of fuel per hour to generate 100 horsepower.

Why do we use .5 BSFC? This value has been found to be a good average number of fuel consumption in gasoline fueled internal combustion engines at full throttle high load. An engine doesn't really operate at .5 BSFC all the time. t will vary how much power it produces per unit of fuel consumed as it sweeps through its engine speed, or RPM range. This observation is displayed graphically in the BSFC Map graphic (Fig. 7.2). As you can see in the figure, the BSFC varies a great deal, but the average consumption is right near .5 lbs. of gasoline per hour per horsepower. It's just a convenient number that lets you calculate safe fuel needs for a given power output.

It may not be obvious, but you need a dynamometer to get BSFC numbers. Engine tuners use them out of convenience, since one has to assume a power output level.

So even though an engine doesn't always operate at a single BSFC value, you can establish an average. And this average will tell you how much fuel you have to deliver to the engine in order to make a certain amount of power. This is very handy when you are designing your fuel system.

The fuel system is what delivers the fuel to either the carburetor(s) or the fuel injectors. If the fuel system can't deliver the required amount of fuel to these components, it doesn't matter which expert did your heads, chose your cam, and fabricated your headers — the engine will only make as much power as the fuel will support.

We're not trying to say that simply delivering a certain amount of fuel guarantees that you'll see X-amount of power at the flywheel. For example, your fuel system and engine management system can deliver just the right amount of fuel to make 500 hp and if the timing's not right, or the cams not right, or...you get the picture.

So you have to have a properly designed fuel system. We've heard from a lot of tuners that probably 80% of performance problems are directly related to inadequate fuel delivery. No matter if your engine is naturally aspirated, ingesting nitrous, super charged, turbocharged or both, or all three, the fuel system is the back-bone that supports all these systems' effectiveness.

## TIPS FOR TWEAKING YOUR FUEL SYSTEM

Developing your Honda is a process that involves chasing down and correcting "weak links" in the performance chain. A car is a collection of systems that work together to produce power and motion. If one of these systems fails to deliver a required function, the performance of the whole machine suffers.

As you increase displacement and RPM, or add airflow enhancing components and agents such as turbos and nitrous, the engine's need for fuel increases. If the fuel system on your Honda fails to deliver an adequate fuel supply to the carburetor or fuel injectors, then the air-to-fuel ratios will be affected. This occurs usually toward the lean side. However, it is possible to have too much pressure leading to an overly rich condition.

Though a faulty fuel delivery system is not the only cause for lean or rich air/fuel ratios, it is a primary system that must function properly. If the fuel system doesn't deliver enough fuel to your carburetor and nitrous system, then no amount of tuning will achieve optimum engine performance.

There are three basic concepts regarding fuel delivery. One is the rated volume of the pump, the second is the inside diameter of the fuel line and third is the pressure, measured in pounds per square inch. Pressure and volume are related in that a higher pressure, for a given diameter of fuel line, will yield more volume, at least up to a point. And obviously a larger diameter line will have a higher volume capacity.

Delivering an adequate supply of fuel, requires that the system overcomes accelerative forces. Fuel must be pumped up to the carburetor, or fuel injectors, against earth's gravity, against the acceleration of the car and the friction within the fuel line. As a general rule, a fuel line with a horizontal length of 13 feet between the tank and pressure regulator will lose 4 psi per g of acceleration. Losing pressure means you are also losing mass flow and that means you might be losing performance.

The solution to this performance problem is to design a system that has an adequate reserve of pressure to overcome the effects of gravity (earth's and the gs during launch) and to install a fuel line that is of adequate diameter and is as free of needless bends as possible. Bends in the fuel lines and connections are a source of turbulence and friction and reduce flow.

The trend in fuel system design has been toward high pressure systems to overcome the obstacles stated above. In drag racing, Warren Johnson is credited with starting this move in the early '80s. His crew designed a high-torque fuel pump which revolutionized the way racers thought about fuel systems. Since then, using a high torque, high pressure, and high flow pump has been refined with the concept of using return lines, which offer advantages in fuel pressure stability, cooling and bleeding off air that may be trapped in the fuel.

The old way with a big Holley pump and regulators near the carbs was very hard on the electric motors. With this kind of system, you have a long column of fuel that would constantly stop and start as the regulator opened and closed to maintain its pressure setting. At the same time, the fuel pump's motor, being part of a hydraulic system, would stop and start with the fuel. Stopping an electric pump motor is very hard on the unit. Depending on where in its cycle it stopped, it could create a closed circuit and burn out, which in fact was a big problem with these early systems. By using a return line, the pump is allowed to stay in constant motion, thus delivering consistent pressure in the fuel line.

If you want a state-of-the-art fuel system, the following ideas will help you achieve it. Of course, you'll still have to do the testing and tuning, preferably at the race track.

**1. Delivering a consistent supply of fuel begins with choosing a proper fuel tank.** A proper fuel system has a tank with baffles to keep the fuel from sloshing away from the outlet during acceleration. It should also have fuel outlet bungs that are positioned such that the force of acceleration feeds fuel into the fuel line before the pump.

**2. Electric fuel pumps do not pull fuel well, they're better at pushing it.** The less restriction you have before the pump, the more efficient and stable your fuel supply will be. Low pressure, high volume systems are more sensitive to restrictions than high pressure, low volume systems. Since the system is gravity fed at this end by accelerating off the line restrictions, then this can really impede the flow of fuel.

**3. You can reduce the turbulence in the fuel line exiting the fuel tank by massaging the insides of the fitting to improve flow.** It's similar to porting the heads. Drill out the I.D. of the fitting, then hand blend the angles of the male and female fittings. You have to be careful not to enlarge the I.D. too much or you'll compromise the integrity of the seal. But if you have a fuel delivery problem this can help some.

**4. You want to filter debris from the fuel before the pump.** That way it can't lodge in an unknown position and cause a restriction or perhaps hurt the pump. It's best to position the filter so it is easy to inspect and clean. Be sure to use a filter with lots of capacity reserve so it doesn't offer much restriction to the system before the pump.

**5. Pros use high torque motors to generate reliable high pressure.** A weak motor tends to stop at lower pressure and when it does it will draw more current from the battery and wear out quickly. Pump pressures are related to the amount of voltage available. If you need more pressure, run a 16-volt battery, but balance that against the heavier weight of a 16-volt battery. Another tact is to use a 12-volt because of weight and then use 10-gauge wire from the kill switch, directly to the pump to deliver the max amount of voltage offered by the battery. The wiring can act as a restriction and reduce fuel pressure and flow.

There is also good aftermarket support for regulated power supplies that keep the pump's voltage constant, within a range of battery voltage. So within that window, the fuel pump should deliver consistent fuel volume and pressure.

**6. A spring actuated valve sets fuel pressure after the pump.** The valve releases excess pressure by returning high pressure fuel to the fuel tank. It's common to run 30-35 psi between the pump and a second pressure regulator just before the carburetors. This arrangement keeps the pump from stopping, which keeps the pressure and volume more consistent, since the column of fuel isn't starting and stopping, and it saves the electric pump. Plus, it keeps the fuel cool and bleeds off air.

**7. You need a second pressure regulator to reduce pressure to the carburetors.** Too much pressure to the carburetor will blow past the needle valve and raise the level in the fuel bowl, causing a rich fuel mixture. Run a return line off the regulator block to a "T" fitting just before the fuel pump. The amount of fuel returned is controlled by a jet and this further bleeds off air and also cools the fuel as the fuel line is very close to the engine at this point.

**8. Here's another pro racer trick. Use a plug in the regulator block to install a fuel pressure gauge.** Since you can't really run it in the cockpit, why have it on the car? Check pressure between rounds to verify. Use a second plug to let you check the low pressure side (near carbs, if you're running them.) We know one very successful bracket racer that likes to run pressure to the carb at approximately 9.5 psi — as high as he can without fuel pressure blowing off the needle valves and upsetting fuel bowl levels. This racer has found that fuel pressure only varies by .2 to .3 psi when he runs it this high. He used to run 8 to 8.5 psi and pressure would fluctuate about 1 psi when the car left then slowly recovered. The racer is not sure if dropping a pound hurts that much, but eliminating a variable can't hurt when tuning the car for track conditions.

9. If you can't science out a starting line bog, try this. Run -10 lines to the carbs. Most racers use -8, but we've heard reports that after installing a high pressure fuel system, a -10 line seemed to help. Basically, you get a reserve in the lines to feed the carbs during the initial launch g-shock. The reason you need that is with the g-shock adding to the psi in the lines, the regulator, which is set at 9 psi, will shut fuel flow off and momentarily starve the carb. The preceding scenario assumes the lines are laid so the force of the launch pushes the fuel in the lines toward the carb and regulator. You can also drill out the opening in the carb by .050 inch and blend the angles. Don't use a larger diameter drill bit or you won't get a secure seal.

## TWO METHODS FOR CHOOSING THE CORRECT FUEL PUMP

### Method #1

When purchasing a fuel pump there are two factors to consider: performance and cost. By correctly matching a fuel pump to your requirements, you can fill your needs without spending money needlessly. Using the tips below you should be able to choose the correct pump for your vehicle.

**1) Determine the horsepower the pump will have to support.** Be realistic, no inflated values.

**2) Estimate the number of gallons of fuel per hour required to support the horsepower from 1).** Note: these figures are for gasoline, double them for alcohol. For four cycle engines: multiply horsepower by .08 to .095. For two cycle engines: multiply horsepower by .095 to .11. The result is the number of gallons of fuel per hour (gph) required.

At this point in the design process you should over-engineer the fuel delivery capacity. By multiplying the target horsepower by .08 to .095, you're getting a gallons per hour requirement. This is related to BSFC, though instead of gallons/hr., BSFC uses lbs./hr. The gallons/hr. is more convenient since it's easier to measure the fuel flow volume instead of its mass. (See Fuel Flow To Horsepower charts.)

**3) Determine the fuel pressure at which the pump will operate.** For carbureted engines this should be 6 to 10 psi. For fuel-injected applications you will have to estimate the required pressure.

**4) Examine the flow versus pressure curve for the pump you are considering.** Your flow requirements should be on or below the pump's plotted performance.

Note: In some instances it is impractical to use a single fuel pump. It is possible to run two pumps in parallel, resulting in an approximate doubling of flow rate if done correctly.

In high pressure applications, two pumps may be run in series. This occurs when trying to increase the fuel flow rate in a late model fuel-injected vehicle. The resulting flow of this arrangement is not equal to the sum of the two pumps' flow rates (it will be less).

### Method #2
### Pressure and Flow

I like to refer to pressure and flow as night and day. How many times have you heard someone say, "It can't be a fuel problem, because I had good fuel pressure"? Consider this, if you put a small valve just before the carburetor and closed it down creating a restriction, wouldn't you still have good pressure before the valve? In this instance though you would have depreciated flow to the carburetor.

Now let's look at the other scenario. How often have you seen someone at the dragstrip run a hose from the fuel pump to a 1 gallon container and measure the time to fill the can? When the calculations are all done, the announcement is made, "It can't be the fuel pump because I am pumping so many gallons per minute."

Now let's look at the proper way to check fuel flow. First, all reputable pump manufacturers rate their fuel pumps at gallons per hour @ some pressure. What you should do first is estimate the horsepower of the engine you are trying to feed. Divide the estimated horsepower by 2 to get a fuel flow rate required to support that maximum horsepower at a BSFC of .50. Once you have your theoretical fuel requirement in lbs./hr., convert it to

### FUEL FLOW / HORSEPOWER @ BSFC = .70

| HP | lbs./hr. | Gals./hr. | Gals./min. | Mins. to flow 1-gal | Secs. to flow 1-gal |
|---|---|---|---|---|---|
| 500 | 350 | 56.45 | 0.94 | 1.06 | 63.77 |
| 480 | 336 | 54.19 | 0.9 | 1.10 | 66.42 |
| 460 | 322 | 51.93 | 0.86 | 1.15 | 69.31 |
| 440 | 308 | 49.67 | 0.82 | 1.20 | 72.46 |
| 420 | 294 | 47.41 | 0.79 | 1.26 | 75.91 |
| 400 | 280 | 45.16 | 0.75 | 1.32 | 79.71 |
| 380 | 266 | 42.90 | 0.71 | 1.39 | 83.90 |
| 360 | 252 | 40.64 | 0.67 | 1.47 | 88.57 |
| 340 | 238 | 38.38 | 0.63 | 1.56 | 93.78 |
| 320 | 224 | 36.12 | 0.60 | 1.66 | 99.64 |
| 300 | 210 | 33.87 | 0.56 | 1.77 | 106.28 |
| 280 | 196 | 31.61 | 0.52 | 1.89 | 113.87 |
| 260 | 182 | 29.35 | 0.48 | 2.04 | 122.63 |
| 240 | 168 | 27.09 | 0.45 | 2.21 | 132.85 |
| 220 | 154 | 24.83 | 0.41 | 2.41 | 144.93 |
| 200 | 140 | 22.58 | 0.37 | 2.65 | 159.42 |
| 180 | 126 | 20.32 | 0.33 | 2.95 | 177.14 |
| 160 | 112 | 18.06 | 0.30 | 3.32 | 199.28 |
| 140 | 98 | 15.80 | 0.26 | 3.79 | 227.75 |
| 120 | 84 | 13.54 | 0.22 | 4.42 | 265.71 |
| 100 | 70 | 11.29 | 0.18 | 5.31 | 318.85 |

### FUEL FLOW / HORSEPOWER @ BSFC = .50

| HP | lbs./hr. | Gals./hr. | Gals./min. | Mins. to flow 1-gal | Secs. to flow 1-gal |
|---|---|---|---|---|---|
| 500 | 250 | 37.93 | 0.63 | 1.58 | 94.90 |
| 480 | 240 | 36.41 | 0.60 | 1.64 | 98.85 |
| 460 | 230 | 34.90 | 0.58 | 1.71 | 103.15 |
| 440 | 220 | 33.38 | 0.55 | 1.79 | 107.84 |
| 420 | 210 | 31.86 | 0.53 | 1.88 | 112.97 |
| 400 | 200 | 30.34 | 0.50 | 1.97 | 118.62 |
| 380 | 190 | 28.83 | 0.48 | 2.08 | 124.86 |
| 360 | 180 | 27.31 | 0.45 | 2.19 | 131.80 |
| 340 | 170 | 25.79 | 0.42 | 2.32 | 139.55 |
| 320 | 160 | 24.27 | 0.40 | 2.47 | 148.28 |
| 300 | 150 | 22.76 | 0.37 | 2.63 | 158.16 |
| 280 | 140 | 21.24 | 0.35 | 2.82 | 169.46 |
| 260 | 130 | 19.726 | 0.32 | 3.04 | 182.49 |
| 240 | 120 | 18.20 | 0.30 | 3.29 | 197.70 |
| 220 | 110 | 16.69 | 0.27 | 3.59 | 215.67 |
| 200 | 100 | 15.17 | 0.25 | 3.95 | 237.24 |
| 180 | 90 | 13.657 | 0.22 | 4.39 | 263.60 |
| 160 | 80 | 12.13 | 0.20 | 4.94 | 296.55 |
| 140 | 70 | 10.62 | 0.17 | 5.64 | 338.91 |
| 120 | 60 | 9.10 | 0.15 | 6.59 | 395.40 |
| 100 | 50 | 7.58 | 0.12 | 7.90 | 474.48 |

gallons per hour by dividing pounds of fuel by 6.2-6.8 lb./gal. depending on the density of the fuel. Now we take this number (let's use 100 gal./hr.) and divide it by 60 to get our required flow in one minute. (In this case it would work out to be 1.66 gal./minute.) If we take the reciprocal of this (1 divided by 1.66), we would get the fraction of a minute required to flow 1 gallon. This would be .6 minutes or 36 seconds.

Now we get practical. Plumb a pressure gauge into a fuel line just before the carburetor or injectors, followed by a small petcock or needle valve. Once you have safely attached the fuel line to a sealed, vented measuring container of at least two gallons, turn on the pump and adjust the petcock valve until the pressure reads whatever pressure that the pump is rated at. At this point, stop the pump, drain the container and then get ready to measure the time required to fill one gallon in the container with flow at rated pressure! This method will ensure accurate results and cut through all the claims and counterclaims.

**TIP: If this is an electric pump, make sure that you monitor voltage to the pump and make sure that the hot wire feeding the pump and ground wire will carry the amperage necessary to achieve full rated flow. Once you qualify your entire fuel delivery system using this method you will be amazed at how many "gremlins" disappear.**
— From Uncommon Sense In Engine Development presented at the 1997 SuperFlow Advance Engine Technology Conference.

## FUEL SYSTEM DESIGN TACTICS

There are two types of fuel pumps produced for gasoline engines: low pressure (4 - 10 psi) and high pressure (30 - 90 psi).

### Low Pressure Pumps

Low pressure pumps are intended for carbureted engines. Common examples are the 110 and 140 gallon per hour (gph) units marketed by a number of manufacturers. These pumps are rated under free flow exit conditions (no outlet restriction). When the outlet of the pump is restricted (real world conditions), the flow capacity is usually significantly less than the rated performance.

Low pressure pumps are the most economical to produce. In most carbureted applications, a low pressure pump will provide adequate performance and enjoy a cost advantage.

### High Pressure Pumps

Flow capabilities of high pressure pumps are specified at typical real world pressure levels. This results in pumps performing much closer to the manufacturer's claim than most low pressure units.

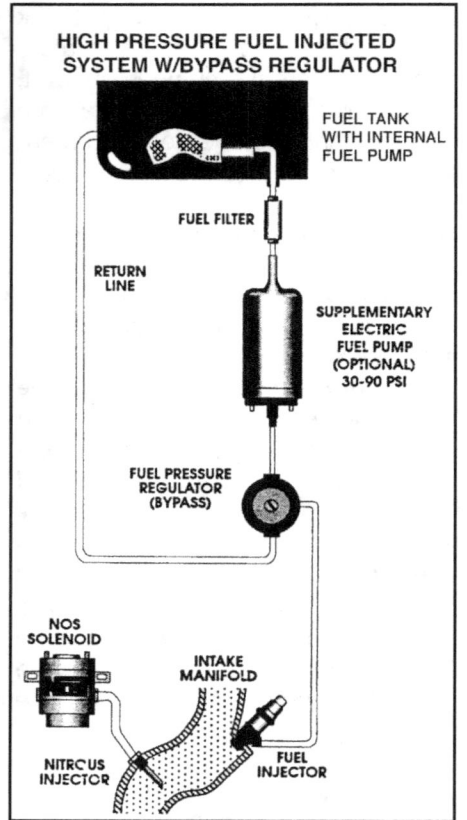

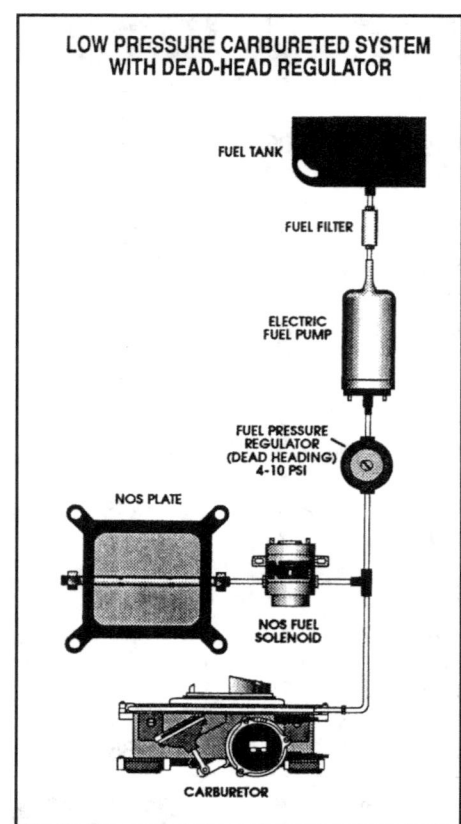

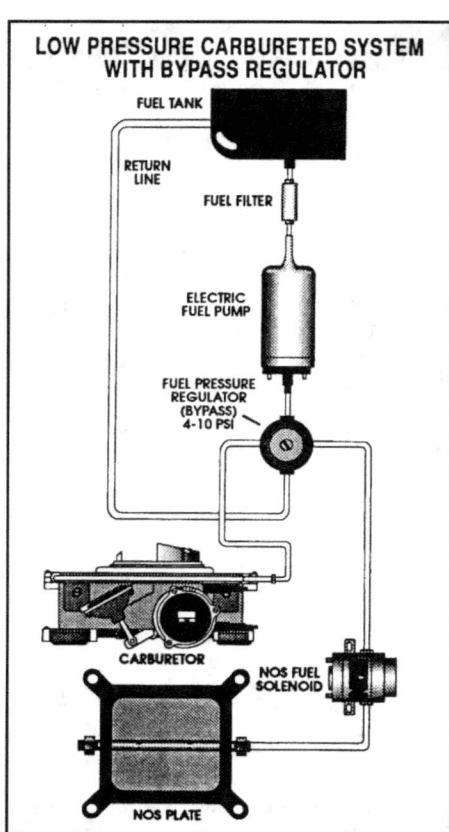

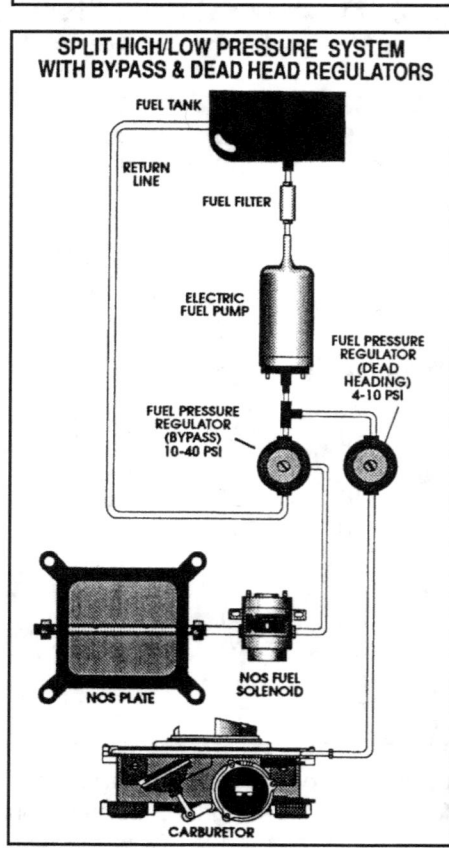

High pressure pumps will work well in carbureted applications when matched with the correct bypassing fuel pressure regulator. Never attempt to use a high pressure pump with a dead-heading fuel pressure regulator.

High pressure pumps are constructed with closer tolerances and more costly production techniques. High pressure pumps will tolerate more severe operating conditions and, last longer than low pressure units.

## CHOOSING THE CORRECT FUEL PRESSURE REGULATOR

There are two types of fuel pressure regulators available: Dead-heading and Bypassing. When working with a low pressure pump, either type can be used successfully. When using a high pressure pump a bypassing regulator must be used.

NOTE: Attempting to use a dead-heading regulator with a high pressure pump will result in premature pump failure and/or burst fuel lines.

Regardless of which type of regulator you choose, it is important that the regulator be matched to the flow capabilities your fuel pump. Listed below are the characteristics of the two types of regulators available.

### Dead-Heading

Fuel is regulated down to a set value using a diaphragm/spring arrangement. The only fuel which passes through the regulator is that which will pass into the engine.

If fuel requirement goes to zero, such as when the engine stops, fuel flow through the regulator ceases. If the fuel pump remains on, the fuel pressure in the line upstream of the regulator will climb to the value at which the pump stalls.

Dead-heading regulators are relatively inexpensive, yet provide acceptable performance in most applications.

### Bypassing

A bypassing regulator controls fuel pressure by returning excess fuel to the fuel tank or the fuel line upstream of the fuel pump. This offers several advantages over the dead-heading type unit: Stress on the fuel pump is reduced by lowering the fuel pressure at which the pump operates.

(The fuel pump will not see pressures above that of the regulator setting.) Fuel pressure is more constant with a bypassing regulator (diaphragm type units pulse). However, in most carbureted applications this is not critical. When using nitrous oxide injection, turbos, or a supercharger, it is desirable to eliminate fuel pressure pulsing (air/fuel ratio will fluctuate when the regulator pulses).

## DESIGNING YOUR FUEL SYSTEM

For satisfactory performance the entire fuel system must be matched to the fuel flow requirements. Following the guidelines listed below should provide acceptable performance.

### Pump Location

When mounting a fuel pump, it is desirable to locate the pump as near the fuel tank as possible. This will minimize the chance of vapor lock on hot days.

### Fuel Line Size and Length

The inner diameter of the fuel line should be as big as the inner diameter of the fuel pump fittings.

If two lines need to be split or joined in a "Y" or "T" arrangement, the cross sectional area of the two lines should be equivalent to the cross sectional area of the single line.

Fuel Lines should be kept as short and free of tight bends as practical.

### Fuel Filters

Fuel filters should provide adequate filtration, without being excessively restrictive. Several different types of filters are available. When choosing a filter make sure that the flow capability is matched to your pump.

## THE ADVANTAGE OF HIGH PRESSURE RETURN-STYLE FUEL SYSTEMS ON CARBURETED NITROUS OXIDE SYSTEMS

If you're running a nitrous oxide injection system, these are usually configured to operate with 4 to 10 psi fuel pressure. NOS kits are set up to operate at these levels to be compatible with typical carbureted fuel systems. In most low-to-moderate output applications, this works fine.

In high output and competition environments, there are performance and tuning advantages to be had from using elevated fuel pressure for the NOS injection system.

Here's how it works. The fuel injection side of an NOS injection kit is a fixed orifice/constant flow device. When the NOS system is activated, the fuel solenoid opens fully; variations in fuel flow will only result from changes in fuel pressure.

The relationship between fuel pressure and fuel flow follows a fundamental law of fluid mechanics. This relationship is stated as **Flow is proportional to the Square Root of fuel pressure.**

At carbureted fuel pressure levels, small changes in fuel pressure produce significant changes in fuel flow rate. At fuel injection type fuel pressure levels, the same size pressure fluctuations produce much smaller changes in flow rate. Examples one and two provide a comparison of the effects of typical fuel pressure fluctuations.

### Example One

Fuel Pressure = 5 psi
Fuel Pressure Fluctuation: +/- 1 psi

This can produce flow deviations of:
1) Sq. rt. of 4/5 = .89 or 89 percent of baseline
2) Sq. rt. of 5/6 = 1.09 or 109 percent of baseline.

This means that just a +/- 1 psi fluctuation in fuel pressure can change fuel flow up to 20 percent.

### Example Two

Fuel Pressure = 30 psi
Fuel Pressure Fluctuation -/+ 1 psi

This can produce flow changes of:
1) Sq. rt. of 29/30 = .983 or 98.3 percent of baseline
2) Sq. rt. of 30/31 = 101.6 or 101.6 percent of baseline

So, a +/- 1 psi change in fuel pressure only changes actual fuel flow about 3.5 percent with the higher pressure.

The advantage this gives you is reducing the potential variation in fuel flow rate to the NOS injection system, keeping the nitrous/fuel ratio much more constant. This in turn minimizes lost horsepower due to overly rich conditions and prevents engine damage from excessively lean mixtures. Then you can make much finer adjustments to the nitrous/fuel ratio, so you can walk right to the edge and not fall off.

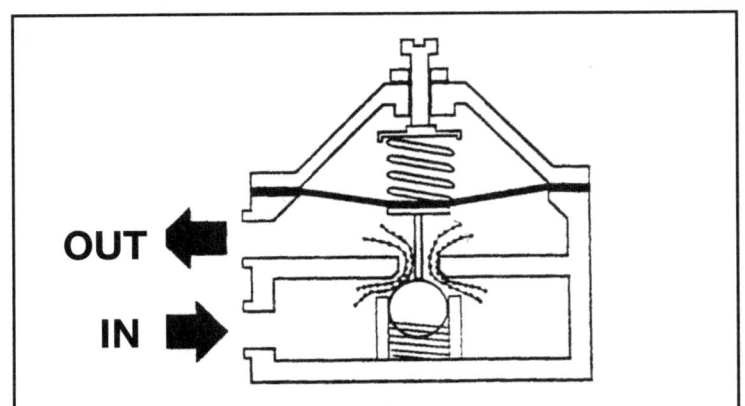

With a deadhead fuel regulator, fuel is regulated down to a set value using a diaphragm/spring arrangement. Only the fuel passing through the regulator passes into the engine.

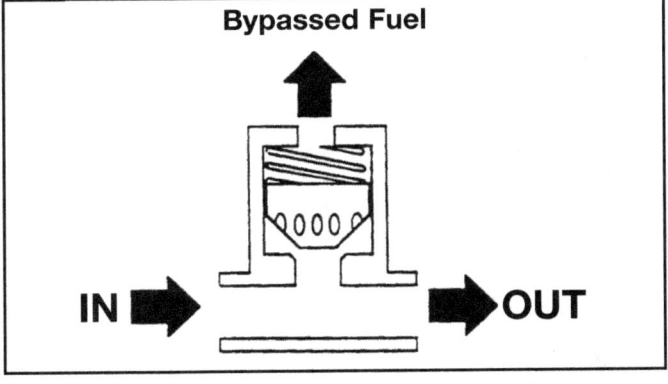

A bypassing regulator controls fuel pressure by returning excess fuel to the fuel tank or the fuel line upstream of the fuel pump. This offers several advantages over the deadhead regulator. One of the more important advantages is that it keeps fuel pressure more constant than a deadhead regulator.

# Honda Builder's HANDBOOK Vol. II
## FUEL AND AIR MIXTURES

In this section we're going to give you the information you need to science out the art of mixing fuel with air to make power. Basically we'll talk about air flow rates and the appropriate fuel flow to get specific air to fuel ratios.

As we showed you in the previous chapter that while the power comes from the fuel, it has to be mixed with appropriate amounts of oxygen to make good power.

If you've read what Russ Collins has to say about fuel injector behavior at duty cycles over 85 percent in the *Honda Performance Handbook Volume One*, then we're sure you'll be interested in the series of charts given in the chapter on fuel — especially if you're running nitrous, a turbo or supercharger.

To use a dry manifold nitrous system, turbo, or supercharger successfully, you have to tune the ratio of nitrous to fuel. The only way to do that with a fuel-injected engine is to know how much fuel your injectors are able to deliver in addition to being aware of how much additional oxygen the nitrous system, turbo, or supercharger is delivering.

In this volume, we've included several helpful charts to make it easier for you to mix fuel with air for power. The Flow rates, Power Potential and Idle Requirements chart on page 97 shows a breakdown of the stats on several Lucas injectors with typical flow rates. We give the max horsepower ratings for each injector, the amount of air flow each will support, as well as the minimum air flow required to keep an air/fuel ratio that will keep an engine idling. That should give you a feel for how the injector's fuel flow rating influences air/fuel ratios at max power and idle RPM.

There are also two charts on page 96 that display the time schedules of batch-fire and sequential injectors. The batch-fire schedule presents the time relationship between engine speed and injector firing frequency for a batch fire injection system. Batch fire systems fire the injectors every revolution so the time between injector pulses is much shorter than sequential systems that fire only on the intake cycle. Be sure to read Russ Collin's thoughts on injectors in the *Honda Performance Handbook, Volume One*.

We've also crunched the numbers to generate a volumetric efficiency table for each of the popular Honda engine sizes. On page 93, there are charts for each: 1.6 liter engine, 1.7 liter engine, 1.8 liter engine and 2.2 liter engine. These show the air flow at a couple of percentages of volumetric efficiency so you can see how they'll influence injector sizing.

Because dry manifold nitrous systems, turbos, and superchargers pump up the fuel pressure to the injector to increase fuel delivery, we've included a chart that plots the flow increase from higher fuel pressures. We also give you the correct formula to predict the flow rate change.

Before we discuss mixing fuel with air, let's have a look at air flow.

## YOUR ENGINE IS A SELF-DRIVEN AIR PUMP

Properly tuned it should make 125 hp at peak torque and 140 hp at peak power for every 100 Standard Cubic Foot per Minute (SCFM) put through the engine. A SCFM is defined as cfm X air density (lbs./ft.$^3$)/.0763 lbs./ft.$^3$.

The statement above is an observed generality of 4-cycle internal combustion engines. Our source for this generality is from some of Super-Flow's technical literature, which states, "As a rule, an engine consumes approximately 1.25 SCFM of air per horsepower at peak torque and 1.4 SCFM at peak power." This is a pretty good rule of thumb, according to the engineers at SuperFlow. Not gospel, just a good yardstick by which to measure and compare the state of tune of your engine with other parameters, such as Brake Specific fuel Consumption (BSFC), Brake Specific Air Consumption (BSAC), and Volumetric Efficiency (VE).

We begin this section with that observation to express the importance of air flow through an engine. Since an internal combustion engine is a self-driven air pump, it has to move air and fuel through it, in order to make power.

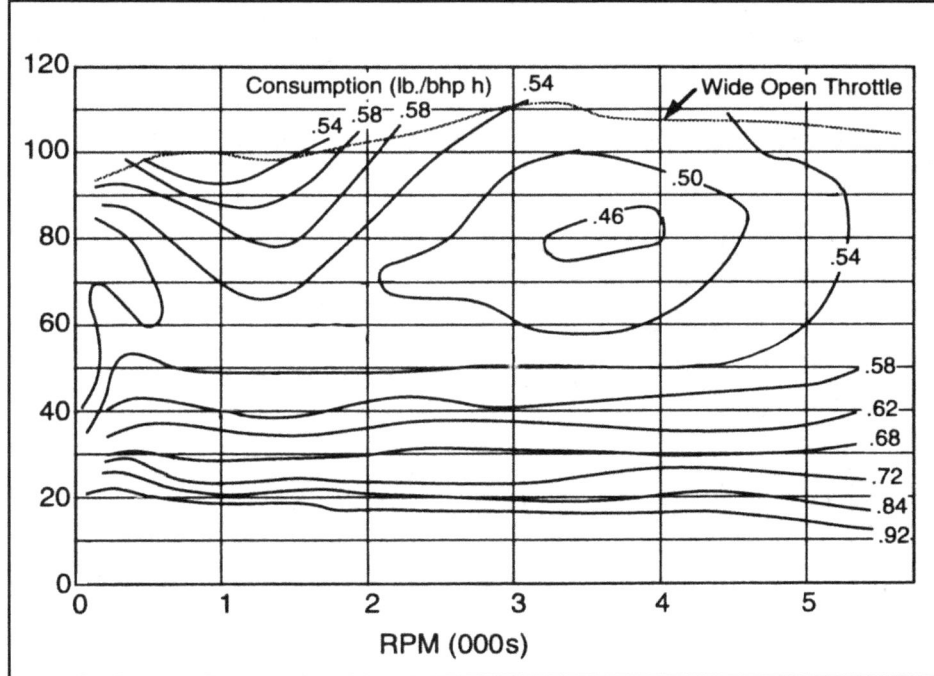

**Brake specific fuel consumption isn't a static value. As the engine sweeps through its rev range under various loads and throttle openings, it comes in and out of efficiency islands. Most engines make best use of fuel at peak torque, that is they make the most power for the fuel used at that point.**

Air flow is an indication of the rate of work being done which is what horsepower measures. Of course an engine also requires fuel, but air flow is of such basic importance to the power output of an engine, that we thought it logical to begin our discussion of basic engine theory with, well, the basic ingredient, which is the oxygen content of air.

The air we breathe, at least on a global average, is two-thirds nitrogen and just less than one-third oxygen. Oxygen molecules are the ones that

### PEAK POWER AND PEAK TORQUE AIR FLOW AND FUEL FLOW RATES AT BSFC .50

| Horse power | scfm Peak Pwr | scfm Peak Trq | lbs./min Peak Pwr scfm*.0763 | lbs./min Peak Trq scfm*.0763 | Oxygen lbs./min @Peak Pwr | Gasoline lbs./hr HP*.5 | Gasoline lbs./min BSFC/60 | A/F ratio @Peak Pwr lbs./min | A/F ratio @Peak Trq lbs./min | Oxygen/Fuel @Peak Pwr lbs./min |
|---|---|---|---|---|---|---|---|---|---|---|
| 100 | 140 | 125.00 | 10.67 | 9.53 | 2.03 | 50.00 | 0.83 | 12.8 | 11.43 | 2.43 |
| 95 | 133 | 118.75 | 10.13 | 9.05 | 1.93 | 47.50 | 0.79 | 12.8 | 11.43 | 2.43 |
| 90 | 126 | 112.50 | 9.60 | 8.57 | 1.82 | 45.00 | 0.75 | 12.8 | 11.43 | 2.43 |
| 85 | 119 | 106.25 | 9.07 | 8.10 | 1.72 | 42.50 | 0.71 | 12.8 | 11.43 | 2.43 |
| 80 | 112 | 100.00 | 8.53 | 7.62 | 1.62 | 40.00 | 0.67 | 12.8 | 11.43 | 2.43 |
| 75 | 105 | 93.75 | 8.00 | 7.14 | 1.52 | 37.50 | 0.62 | 12.8 | 11.43 | 2.43 |
| 70 | 98 | 87.50 | 7.47 | 6.67 | 1.42 | 35.00 | 0.58 | 12.8 | 11.43 | 2.43 |
| 65 | 91 | 81.25 | 6.93 | 6.19 | 1.32 | 32.50 | 0.54 | 12.8 | 11.43 | 2.43 |
| 60 | 84 | 75.00 | 6.40 | 5.71 | 1.22 | 30.00 | 0.5 | 12.8 | 11.43 | 2.43 |
| 55 | 77 | 68.75 | 5.87 | 5.24 | 1.11 | 27.50 | 0.46 | 12.8 | 11.43 | 2.43 |
| 50 | 70 | 62.50 | 5.33 | 4.76 | 1.01 | 25.00 | 0.42 | 12.8 | 11.43 | 2.43 |
| 45 | 63 | 56.25 | 4.80 | 4.29 | 0.91 | 22.50 | 0.38 | 12.8 | 11.43 | 2.43 |
| 40 | 56 | 50.00 | 4.27 | 3.81 | 0.81 | 20.00 | 0.33 | 12.8 | 11.43 | 2.43 |
| 35 | 49 | 43.75 | 3.73 | 3.33 | 0.71 | 17.50 | 0.29 | 12.8 | 11.43 | 2.43 |
| 30 | 42 | 37.50 | 3.20 | 2.86 | 0.61 | 15.00 | 0.25 | 12.8 | 11.43 | 2.43 |
| 25 | 35 | 31.25 | 2.67 | 2.38 | 0.51 | 12.50 | 0.21 | 12.8 | 11.43 | 2.43 |
| 20 | 28 | 25.00 | 2.13 | 1.91 | 0.41 | 10.00 | 0.17 | 12.8 | 11.43 | 2.43 |
| 15 | 21 | 18.75 | 1.60 | 1.43 | 0.3 | 7.50 | 0.12 | 12.8 | 11.43 | 2.43 |
| 10 | 14 | 12.50 | 1.07 | 0.95 | 0.2 | 5.00 | 0.08 | 12.8 | 11.43 | 2.43 |
| 5 | 7 | 6.25 | 0.53 | 0.48 | 0.1 | 2.50 | 0.04 | 12.8 | 11.43 | 2.43 |

## PEAKPOWER & TORQUE AIR AND FUEL MASS FLOW RATES AT BSFC .45

| Gasoline lbs./hr @ HP*.45 | Gasoline lbs./min @ BSFC/60 | A/F ratio @PeakPwr lbs./min | A/F ratio @PeakTrq lbs./min | Oxygen/Fuel @PeakPwr lbs./min |
|---|---|---|---|---|
| 45.00 | 0.75 | 14.22 | 12.70 | 2.7 |
| 42.75 | 0.71 | 14.22 | 12.70 | 2.7 |
| 40.50 | 0.68 | 14.22 | 12.70 | 2.7 |
| 38.25 | 0.64 | 14.22 | 12.70 | 2.7 |
| 36.00 | 0.60 | 14.22 | 12.70 | 2.7 |
| 33.75 | 0.56 | 14.22 | 12.70 | 2.7 |
| 31.50 | 0.53 | 14.22 | 12.70 | 2.7 |
| 29.25 | 0.49 | 14.22 | 12.70 | 2.7 |
| 27.00 | 0.45 | 14.22 | 12.70 | 2.7 |
| 24.75 | 0.41 | 14.22 | 12.70 | 2.7 |
| 22.50 | 0.38 | 14.22 | 12.70 | 2.7 |
| 20.25 | 0.34 | 14.22 | 12.70 | 2.7 |
| 18.00 | 0.30 | 14.22 | 12.70 | 2.7 |
| 15.75 | 0.26 | 14.22 | 12.70 | 2.7 |
| 13.50 | 0.23 | 14.22 | 12.70 | 2.7 |
| 11.25 | 0.19 | 14.22 | 12.70 | 2.7 |
| 9.00 | 0.15 | 14.22 | 12.70 | 2.7 |
| 6.75 | 0.11 | 14.22 | 12.70 | 2.7 |
| 4.50 | 0.07 | 14.22 | 12.70 | 2.7 |
| 2.25 | 0.04 | 14.22 | 12.70 | 2.7 |

combine rapidly with the molecules of the fuel to create heat and raise the pressure in the combustion chamber to make power. Nitrogen doesn't burn, but it sure takes up a lot of space in the intake manifold and combustion chambers. So does water vapor, i.e, humidity, suspended in the intake air. Adding fuel to this mix changes the temperature and therefore the pressure and density of the intake charge as well as taking up its own space. All these factors affect flow. The idea we're trying to highlight is "air" is not just "air." It's not a static value and it depends on how you want to look at the atmosphere. Check this out. Measured by volume, air is about 20.95% oxygen and 78.06% nitrogen with the remaining .99% taken up with trace elements like helium, hydrogen, carbon dioxide, etc. By weight, nitrogen makes up 75.5% of the atmosphere's mass with oxygen contributing 23% of the mass; the remaining 1.5%, I suspect, is contributed by the aforementioned trace elements.

So there's a difference between volume and the weight or mass of the atmosphere. That difference affects how much oxygen is available under various temperatures, atmospheric pressures, and altitude. The oxygen content of the atmosphere varies under different conditions.

What we're really interested in is the oxygen content of the air. Because increasing the oxygen content of the charge and mixing it with more fuel is how you make an engine more powerful. That's what you're doing with healthy doses of nitrous or high boost pressures, you're really only increasing the oxygen content of the charge.

In a conversation with Ken Dutwieller at the '97 NHRA Winston World Finals, I mentioned these percentages and he said those may be accurate for a global average, but in the environment from which engines draw air, oxygen usually accounts for around 19% of the mass of the intake charge. It does fluctuate, but he said 19% is a good working number.

Here's why air doesn't usually contain nearly 21% oxygen. The primary factors that determine air density and its oxygen content are air temperature and the barometric pressure.

Air density (i.e., the ratio of mass to volume) of a cubic foot of air decreases as the volume increases, if the increase in volume was accomplished by raising the temperature of the cubic foot of air. This is a good way to think of the ideal gas law. If you think of it in terms of density rather than mass and volume separately, you can see that increasing the temperature and keeping the pressure constant requires a proportional decrease in density.

This is why altitude density is very important to pilots and why air density is important to you if you want to tune your engine properly. We'll discuss this further, since air density most directly affects the power output of your engine. The relative humidity is also

## PARTIAL PRESSURES OF GASES

To explain the concept of vapor pressure, we need to go back to Dalton's studies which led him to the atomic-molecular theory of matter, but which also included studies of the behavior of gases. These led him to propose, in 1803, what is now called Dalton's law of partial pressures :

For a mixture of gases in a container, the total pressure exerted is the sum of the pressures that each gas would exert if it were alone.

This law can be expressed in equation form as: $p = p_1 + p_2 + p_3 + ...$

Where p is the total or measured pressure and $p_1, p_2, ...$ are the partial pressures of the individual gases.
For air, an appropriate form of Dalton's law would be: $p(air) = p(N_2) + p(O_2) + p(CO_2) + ...$

At temperatures near ordinary room temperature, the partial pressures of each of the components of air is directly proportional to the number of moles of that component in any volume of air. (Air behaves very much as an ideal gas). When the total pressure of air is 100 kPa, or one bar, the partial pressures of each of its components (in kPa) are numerically equal to the mole percent of that component. Thus the partial pressures of the major components of dry air at 100 kPa are nitrogen, 78 kPa; oxygen, 21 kPa; argon, 0.9 kPa; and carbon dioxide, 0.03 kPa.

# DENSITY ALTITUDE

If you're a pilot, you've probably seen this chart. It shows the relationship between pressure altitude and density altitude. This is a subject that's confusing for pilots as well as performance enthusiasts, so pay attention. It'll help you fine tune your combination so you'll go quicker when your uninformed opponents slow down or hurt their engines. The crucial thing to understand, however, is that density altitude is just one way of looking at the air. It doesn't take into consideration the water vapor content. The water vapor content is important to you because it, along with the temperature and barometer tell you how much oxygen is available to your engine with which to make power.

There are three important factors that affect air density: ALTITUDE, TEMPERATURE and HUMIDITY. As you increase altitude, air density decreases. The warmer the air, again, the less dense it is. Humidity is also important because it influences engine power output and aerodynamic lift. At high ambient temperatures, the atmosphere can retain a high water vapor content. For example, at 96°F, the water vapor content of the air can be eight (8) times as great as at 42°F. However, high density altitude and high humidity do not often go hand-in-hand.

As density altitude increases, the molecules of air decrease which means there will be less air flowing over your car and into the engine. The further effects of high temperature and high humidity are cumulative, resulting in an increasingly high density altitude which reduces all performance parameters. Don't confuse density altitude with pressure altitude, indicated altitude, true altitude, or absolute altitude.

The published performance criteria in the Pilot's Operating Handbook is generally based on standard atmospheric conditions at sea level (59°F and 29.92 InHg, dry air). When the temperature rises above the standard temperature for the locality, the density of the air in that locality is reduced and the density altitude increases. This decreases aerodynamic drag and downforce as well as decreasing horsepower output of the engine.

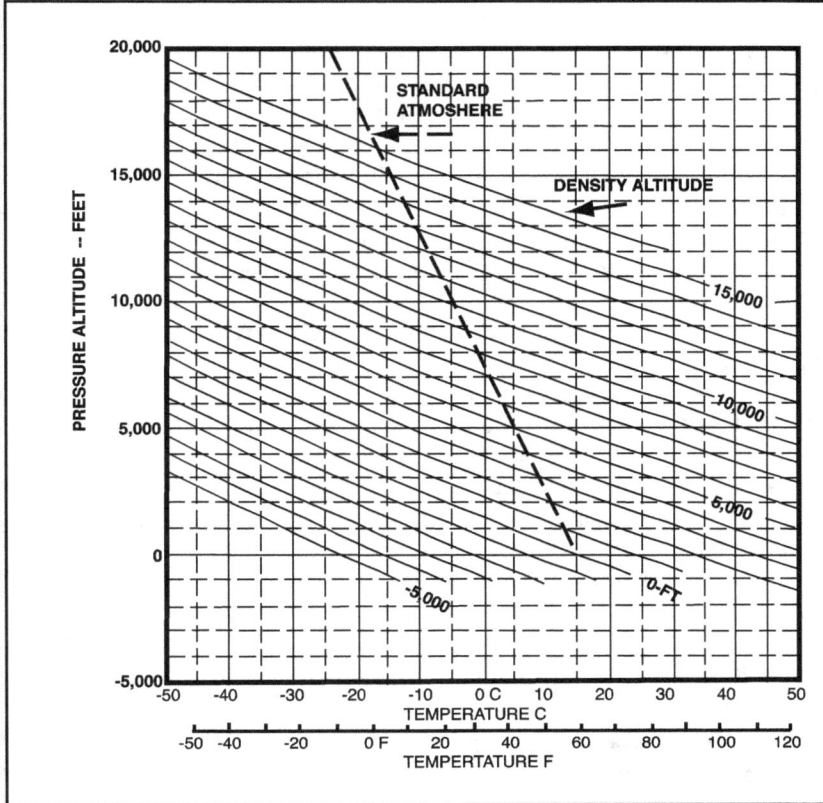

The graph shows density altitude for most temperature/barometric pressure combinations. If you're using an aircraft altimeter, set it at 29.92 inches; it now indicates pressure altitude. Read outside air temperature. Enter the graph at your pressure altitude and move horizontally to the temperature. Read density altitude from the sloping lines.

Example: Pressure altitude is 4,950 feet; and temperature, 97°F. Enter the graph at 4,950 feet and move across to 97°F. Density altitude is 8,200 feet. Note that in the warm air, density altitude is considerably higher, indicating less dense air, than pressure altitude. As you can see, this gets you close to knowing how much oxygen is available to your engine, but doesn't factor in the increasingly important effects of humidity as the temperature rises.

important but less so, since the moisture content of air, reduces its density less than altitude and temperature.

## HUMIDITY AND AIR DENSITY

In the strictest sense, changing the temperature of air doesn't affect its mass because as the air molecules heat and need more space to vibrate, there are simply less of them in a given volume, a cubic meter, or cubic foot, for example. This is what happens when a gas, such as the atmosphere expands. Its density, the mass/volume, changes, but not necessarily the mass. Mass is simply weight/gravity. Cubic volume doesn't necessarily affect this measure. However, adding water vapor to the air certainly does affect its mass, because water vapor has less mass than the average molecular mix of air. Now while that's a fine thing to know, in order to use that information in a tuning sense, we have to answer a question. To what degree is the mass changed? Then we can calculate the density of air with and without its water content. By doing this, you can determine the amount of oxygen available to react with fuel, enabling you to tune to the ragged edge.

To answer that question we need to go back to the composition of the atmosphere. The proportions of the gases that normally compose "dry" air are essentially stable. In terms of the number of molecules, 78.08% of the atmosphere is nitrogen, excluding water vapor. Oxygen accounts for 20.95%, and the rest comes from other trace ingredients including 0.03% of carbon dioxide.

Water vapor evaporates into and condenses out of the atmosphere so easily that its proportions, by volume, can range from near 0% to as much as 4% of the air. According to Avogadro's Law, equal volumes of gases at the same temperature and pressure contain an equal number of molecules. Thus we can expect that the number of molecules in a given volume of air before the addition of the water vapor will be the same as the number of molecules in the same volume after the water vapor is introduced.

However, since the proportion of molecules that are water molecules will be higher and since a molecule of water has less mass than a molecule of any of the other major constituents of air, it follows that as the proportion of water vapor in the air *increases*, the average mass of the molecules composing that portion of air will *decrease*, which in turn lowers the density. Of course, decreasing the amount of water vapor in the air will raise the density. The mass ratios for molecules of water, nitrogen, oxygen, and carbon dioxide, for example, are roughly 9:14:16:22.

That's why, perhaps contrary to your intuition, high relative humidity conditions have less oxygen and higher barometric pressures than colder low pressure conditions. We performance enthusiasts seem to equate high pressure with good, powerful air. As we'll see, that isn't always the case.

### RELATIVE HUMIDITY

*What is relative humidity? And does it affect your engine's power output?*

You hear a lot of talk about relative humidity and the density of air. Well, to be honest, relative humidity is better at telling you what you probably already know — that it's hot and sticky. How this atmospheric condition affects your engine is not an easy correlation to make, since it changes so much. That's why they call it relative humidity. But since you have to go through the same steps to find the water vapor content of the air, we might as well start with good ol' RH.

The definition of relative humidity is the ratio of the amount of water vapor actually in the air compared to the amount of water vapor the air can actually hold at that particular temperature and pressure. This is expressed in mathematical terms as follows:

**Relative Humidity =**

<u>Water Vapor Content</u>
**Water Vapor Capacity**

If we speak in terms of water vapor pressure, the formula for relative humidity can be modified as below:

**Relative Humidity =**

<u>Actual Vapor Pressure</u>
**Saturation Vapor Pressure**

**Actual Vapor Pressure** is the measure of the air's actual water vapor content.

**Saturation Vapor Pressure** is a measure of the air's TOTAL capacity for water vapor.

Since relative humidity is given in terms of percent, 75% relative humidity means that the air contains three-quarters the amount of water vapor required for saturation. For example, in the desert, where the air is hot and dry, the relative humidity would be much lower than in a tropical rainforest, where the air is very moist.

### COMPUTING RELATIVE HUMIDITY

The table on this page shows how we can use the reported values of temperature and dew point temperature to determine relative humidity.

By using this chart, a temperature of 86 degrees Fahrenheit (F), would give us a saturation vapor pressure of 42.455 mb. The dew point temperature of 64.4 degrees F would yield an actual vapor pressure of 20.644 mb.

Plug these values into the formula above and you get:

**Relative Humidity =**

**(20.644 mb / 42.455 mb) X 100%
= 48.6%**

A 48.6% relative humidity at 86°F would begin to feel a little uncomfortable and sticky. But what would it tell us about the oxygen content of the air? It doesn't tell us anything directly. But the vapor pressures do, courtesy of Dalton's Law of partial pressures and Avogadros Law.

### BUILD A PSYCHROMETER TO FIND VAPOR PRESSURES

Here's how you do it. First you piece together a psychrometer. Find the following:

Tape, water, 2 identical thermometers, gauze (2" X 2"), rubberband and a piece of cardboard (8" X 11").

Then:
1. Wrap the gauze around one of the bulbs and tie it firmly in place with a rubber band.
2. Wet the gauze.
3. Place the thermometers side by side with the two bulbs just hanging over the edge of a desk or table.
4. Use the cardboard to fan the thermometers.
5. Fan vigorously until the temperature of the thermometer with the wet bulb stops going down.

| COMPUTING RELATIVE HUMIDITY | | | |
|---|---|---|---|
| AirTemp | | Pressure | |
| °C | °F | (mb) | (kPa) |
| .01 | 32.0 | 6.120 | .612 |
| 2 | 35.6 | 7.060 | .706 |
| 4 | 39.2 | 8.140 | .814 |
| 6 | 42.8 | 9.354 | .935 |
| 8 | 46.4 | 10.730 | 1.073 |
| 10 | 50.0 | 12.300 | 1.230 |
| 12 | 53.6 | 14.027 | 1.402 |
| 14 | 57.2 | 15.988 | 1.599 |
| 16 | 60.8 | 18.185 | 1.815 |
| 18 | 64.4 | 20.644 | 2.064 |
| 20 | 68.0 | 23.388 | 2.388 |
| 22 | 71.6 | 26.447 | 2.644 |
| 24 | 75.2 | 29.850 | 2.985 |
| 26 | 78.8 | 33.629 | 3.362 |
| 28 | 82.4 | 37.818 | 3.781 |
| 30 | 86.0 | 42.455 | 4.245 |
| 32 | 89.6 | 47.578 | 4.757 |
| 34 | 93.2 | 53.229 | 5.322 |
| 36 | 96.8 | 59.453 | 5.945 |
| 38 | 100.4 | 66.298 | 6.629 |
| 40 | 104.0 | 73.814 | 7.381 |
| 42 | 107.6 | 82.054 | 8.205 |
| 44 | 111.2 | 91.075 | 9.107 |
| 46 | 114.8 | 100.94 | 10.094 |
| 48 | 118.4 | 111.71 | 11.171 |
| 50 | 122.0 | 123.44 | 12.344 |

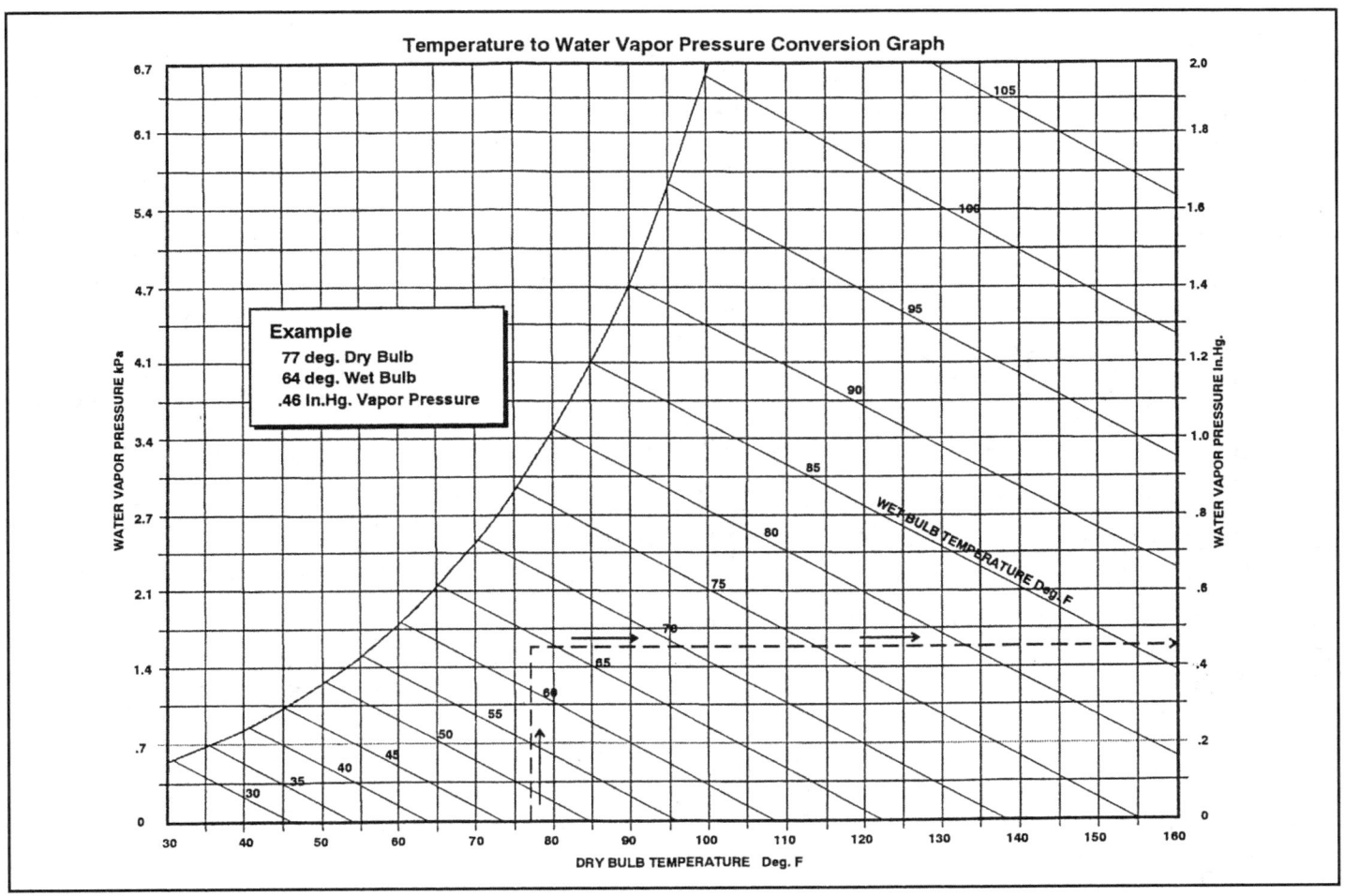

Use this chart, courtesy of Harold Bettes and the SuperFlow dyno crew, to quickly reference relative humidity and its affect on local barometric pressure. The graduations on the right show inches of Mercury. Using it is easy, though you need a barometer to read local (i.e. race track) vapor pressure. Then, get local wet-bulb and dry-bulb temps. Coordinate the temps and follow the graph lines to the info you want to know. Example: 85°F dry; 70°F wet temps is just shy of 60% RH with a loss of over .5-inch of barometric pressure.

6. Record the temperature readings on both thermometers.

The thermometer with the dry bulb gives you the saturation vapor pressure, the wet bulb gives you the actual vapor pressure. The wet bulb simulates the dew point. It is essentially the same vapor pressure.

If you want to know the relative humidity, just plug in the numbers and do the math.

**CALCULATE AIR DENSITY**

If you want to know the density of the air to make a tuning decision, you need a barometer reading for the race track. An altimeter isn't what you need, you need a barometer. Fortunately they aren't that expensive and you can get by with a relatively inexpensive one, but you'll have to take good notes and calibrate your tuning factors to that barometer. Then, once again, just plug in the numbers and do the math. Here's the equation and the tables you need to find your way.

1. Take a barometer reading and note the atmospheric pressure at the race track. This will be $P_t$. So, $P_t$ = barometric pressure, which is the total pressures of all the gases' vapor pressures.
2. Get a wet-bulb temperature. Refer to the chart to get the appropriate vapor pressure for water at that temperature reading. This will be $P_{H_2O}$.
3. Subtract $P_{H_2O}$ from $P_t$: $P_t - P_{H_2O} = P$ (dry atmospheric pressure in millibars) This is how much pressure is exerted by dry air.
4. Convert the dry air pressure from mb to Pascals (Pa), by multiplying by 100: Pa = mb x 100.
5. Use the Ideal Gas Law to find the density of the air: $D = P/(T*R)$

6. To convert your temperature readings to the appropriate scale, use the following formulas:

**From °F to °C**
**Tc = (.556)*(Tf-32);**
**Tc = temperature in °Celsius,**
**Tf = temperature in °Fahrenheit**

For example, you read a Fahrenheit temperature of 100 degrees. Using the above formula, you first subtract 32 from the Fahrenheit temperature and get 68. Then you multiply 68 by .556 giving you 37.8 degrees Celsius.

**From °C to °F**
**Tf = (1.8)*Tc+32;**
**Tc = temperature in °Celsius,**
**Tf = temperature in °Fahrenheit**

To give an example, suppose you record a temperature of 100°C and need to convert it to °F. First multiply 100 by 1.8. to get 180. Then add 32 to 180 to get 212°F.

**From °C to °K**
**(Tk = Tc+273)**

Simply add 273 to the °C temperature to get °Kelvin. Kelvin is the metric absolute temperature scale.

7. Substitute your observed data into the equation.

Let's say your data indicate a local air temp of 21.11°C = 294.11°K (70°F), local pressure is 94277 Pa (942.77 mb, 27.84 InHg). The equation should take the form:

$$D = (94277/(294.11 \times 287))$$

Use 287 for R, the gas constant

$$D = 92477/84409.57$$
$$D = 1.117 \text{ Kg/m}^3$$

In the metric system, this is both the mass density and the weight of the dry air. In the U.S. system, pounds are a unit of force, but we can still convert $Kg/m^3$ to $lbs./ft.^3$ by multiplying $Kg/m^3$ by .062428.

## WHY PARTIAL ATMOSPHERIC PRESSURE TELLS YOU ITS OXYGEN DENSITY

To get this you have to understand that the pressure you measure with a barometer is the *vapor pressure* of all the atmosphere's component gases and water vapor.

The partial pressure of an individual gas is then defined as:

$$P_i = n_i / n_t * P_t$$

Where:
$P_i$ = partial pressure of gas i
$n_i$ = number of moles of gas i
$P_t$ = total pressure of all gasses
$n_t$ = total number of moles all gasses

## HOW TO CALCULATE DENSITY ALTITUDE FOR HUMID AIR

The last handy set of calculations is how to find density altitude for humid air. This is a trick of meteorology. The way the scientists do this is they find the virtual temperature. Virtual temperature is an imaginary temperature that accounts for water vapor. The formal definition of virtual temperature is the temperature that dry air would have if its pressure and specific volume were equal to those of a given sample of moist air. Virtual temperature is how meteorologists use the ideal gas law equation for dry air and compensate for the humidity level. We'll present the formula and a sample calculation to show you how it's done.

You need to find your local air temp (actual temp) in °C, barometric pressure in mb, saturation pressure in mb, and the actual pressure in mb. (See above for definitions and how to get these values.)

$Tv = Tk/[1-(E/P) \times (1-0.622)]$
$Tv$ = virtual temperature
$E$ = actual vapor pressure
    24.99 (mb)
$Tk$ = actual temperature in °Kelvin,
70°F = (21.11°C+273.15) = 249.26
$P$ = barometric pressure
    942.77 (mb)

Substituting 12.50 for E, 24.99 for P, and 294.26 (21.11+273.15) degrees for Tk, you get:

$Tv = 294.26/[1-(12.50/924.77) \times (1-0.622)]$
  $= 294.26/[1-(0.0136) \times (0.378)]$
  $= 294.26/[1-(0.0051)]$
  $= 294.26/0.9949$
  $= 295.77$ °Kelvin
  $= 295.77-273.15$
  $= 22.39$ °Celsius

To use the virtual temperature, substitute that value in the density equation using the Ideal Gas Law. This then tells you your density altitude for the local humidity conditions. Use this as a frame of reference, i.e. it's easier to visualize decreasing air density with increasing altitude. In addition, you should use density altitude to make aerodynamic calculations for actual local conditions.

## HOW DOES THIS AFFECT YOUR ENGINE'S TUNING?

Most obvious is that the density of the air determines how much oxygen each parcel of air ($kg/m^3$ or $lbs./ft.^3$) contains.

In the example above, we arrived at a dry air density of 1.117 $Kg/m^3$.

To Convert to $lbs./ft.^3$:

$$1.117 \times 0.062428 = .0697 \text{ lbs./ft.}^3$$

Of that weight, only .23% is good old $O_2$. ( By volume the atmosphere is 20.9% oxygen, by mass it's 23%.) Multiplying our measured dry air density by .23 we get:

$$.016 \text{ lbs./ft.}^3 O_2$$

To compare this with a standard condition of $.0763 \text{ lbs./ft.}^3$ of air, let's multiply it by 23% and we get:

$$.017 \text{ lbs./ft.}^3 O_2$$

Not a huge difference, right? Well, yes and no. Since tuning slightly to the rich side doesn't tend to lose that much power, it isn't a big deal unless your competitor is tuning just a little better. Or, if the air gets denser and you've tuned to the edge, your engine won't be able to use the additional oxygen to create more power.

Remember, for each 100 peak horsepower, your engine is flowing about 140 standard CFM (140 x .0763) or 10.67 lbs. of air per minute. Now that's .18 lbs. per second (10.67/60 = .18). To make 300 horsepower you need to flow .18 x 3 = .54 lbs./sec. of air. (We're talking standard $.0763 \text{ lbs./ft.}^3$ air.)

Adding fuel to the air complicates the analysis, and our 300 horsepower under standard conditions at BSFC average of .5 requires .042 lbs./sec. of fuel. [ (300 hp x .5)/3600 sec.; 3600 is the number of seconds in an hour.] This gives you an air/fuel ratio (.54/.042) of 12.86:1. That's pretty crisp tuning, right? But what happens when the air density changes, even slightly?

For this analysis we need to look at the mass flow of $O_2$ and get an oxygen to fuel ratio because air/fuel ratios are based on 23% of dry air weight being oxygen.

$$.54 \text{ lbs./sec}*.23 = .124 \text{ lbs./sec.}O_2$$

To get the oxygen to fuel ratio, that's equivalent to 12/85:1 air/fuel ratio: .124/.042 = 2.95:1.

So with standard density air, that's approximately how much oxygen and fuel you will need to flow through your engine each second to make 300 horsepower.

What happens when the air becomes less dense?

Again, for each 100 peak horsepower, your engine is flowing about 140 standard CFM (140 x .0697) or 9.76 lbs. of air per minute. Now that's .16 lbs. per second (9.75/60 = .16). To make 300 horsepower with standard air, you need to flow .54 lbs./sec. of

## 1.6 LITER ENGINE

| RPM | AIR FLOW @ 100% VOL. EFF. CFM | lb./min. | AIR FLOW @ 85% VOL. EFF. CFM | lb./min. |
|---|---|---|---|---|
| 11000 | 311.92 | 22.77 | 265.13 | 19.35 |
| 10000 | 283.56 | 20.70 | 241.03 | 17.60 |
| 9000 | 255.21 | 18.63 | 216.93 | 15.84 |
| 8000 | 226.85 | 16.56 | 192.82 | 14.08 |
| 7000 | 198.50 | 14.49 | 168.72 | 12.32 |
| 6000 | 170.14 | 12.42 | 144.62 | 10.56 |
| 5000 | 141.78 | 10.35 | 120.52 | 8.80 |
| 4000 | 113.43 | 8.28 | 96.41 | 7.04 |
| 3000 | 85.07 | 6.21 | 72.31 | 5.28 |
| 2000 | 56.71 | 4.14 | 48.21 | 3.52 |
| 1000 | 28.36 | 2.07 | 24.10 | 1.76 |
| 500 | 14.18 | 1.04 | 12.05 | 0.88 |
| **Per Cyl. RPM** | | | | |
| 11000 | 77.98 | 5.69 | 66.28 | 4.84 |
| 10000 | 70.89 | 5.18 | 60.26 | 4.40 |
| 9000 | 63.80 | 4.66 | 54.23 | 3.96 |
| 8000 | 56.71 | 4.14 | 48.21 | 3.52 |
| 7000 | 49.62 | 3.62 | 42.18 | 3.08 |
| 6000 | 42.53 | 3.11 | 36.15 | 2.64 |
| 5000 | 35.45 | 2.59 | 30.13 | 2.20 |
| 4000 | 28.36 | 2.07 | 24.10 | 1.76 |
| 3000 | 21.27 | 1.55 | 18.08 | 1.32 |
| 2000 | 14.18 | 1.04 | 12.05 | 0.88 |
| 1000 | 7.09 | 0.52 | 6.03 | 0.44 |
| 500 | 3.54 | 0.26 | 3.01 | 0.22 |

## 1.7 LITER ENGINE

| RPM | AIR FLOW @ 100% VOL. EFF. CFM | lb./min. | AIR FLOW @ 85% VOL. EFF. CFM | lb./min. |
|---|---|---|---|---|
| 11000 | 331.02 | 24.16 | 281.37 | 20.54 |
| 10000 | 300.93 | 21.97 | 255.79 | 18.67 |
| 9000 | 270.83 | 19.77 | 230.21 | 16.81 |
| 8000 | 240.74 | 17.57 | 204.63 | 14.94 |
| 7000 | 210.65 | 15.38 | 179.05 | 13.07 |
| 6000 | 180.56 | 13.18 | 153.47 | 11.20 |
| 5000 | 150.46 | 10.98 | 127.89 | 9.34 |
| 4000 | 120.37 | 8.79 | 102.31 | 7.47 |
| 3000 | 90.28 | 6.59 | 76.74 | 5.60 |
| 2000 | 60.19 | 4.39 | 51.16 | 3.73 |
| 1000 | 30.09 | 2.20 | 25.58 | 1.87 |
| 500 | 15.05 | 1.10 | 12.79 | 0.93 |
| **Per Cyl. RPM** | | | | |
| 11000 | 82.75 | 6.04 | 70.34 | 5.13 |
| 10000 | 75.23 | 5.49 | 63.95 | 4.67 |
| 9000 | 67.71 | 4.94 | 57.55 | 4.20 |
| 8000 | 60.19 | 4.39 | 51.16 | 3.73 |
| 7000 | 52.66 | 3.84 | 44.76 | 3.27 |
| 6000 | 45.14 | 3.30 | 38.37 | 2.80 |
| 5000 | 37.62 | 2.75 | 31.97 | 2.33 |
| 4000 | 30.09 | 2.20 | 25.58 | 1.87 |
| 3000 | 22.57 | 1.65 | 19.18 | 1.40 |
| 2000 | 15.05 | 1.10 | 12.79 | 0.93 |
| 1000 | 7.52 | 0.55 | 6.39 | 0.47 |
| 500 | 3.76 | 0.27 | 3.20 | 0.23 |

## 1.8 LITER ENGINE

| RPM | AIR FLOW @ 100% VOL. EFF. CFM | lb./min. | AIR FLOW @ 85% VOL. EFF. CFM | lb./min. |
|---|---|---|---|---|
| 11000 | 350.12 | 25.56 | 297.60 | 21.72 |
| 10000 | 318.29 | 23.23 | 270.54 | 19.75 |
| 9000 | 286.46 | 20.91 | 243.49 | 17.77 |
| 8000 | 254.63 | 18.59 | 216.44 | 15.80 |
| 7000 | 222.80 | 16.26 | 189.38 | 13.82 |
| 6000 | 190.97 | 13.94 | 162.33 | 11.85 |
| 5000 | 159.14 | 11.62 | 135.27 | 9.87 |
| 4000 | 127.31 | 9.29 | 108.22 | 7.90 |
| 3000 | 95.49 | 6.97 | 81.16 | 5.92 |
| 2000 | 63.66 | 4.65 | 54.11 | 3.95 |
| 1000 | 31.83 | 2.32 | 27.05 | 1.97 |
| 500 | 15.91 | 1.16 | 13.53 | 0.99 |
| **Per Cyl. RPM** | | | | |
| 11000 | 87.53 | 6.39 | 74.40 | 5.43 |
| 10000 | 79.57 | 5.81 | 67.64 | 4.94 |
| 9000 | 71.61 | 5.23 | 60.87 | 4.44 |
| 8000 | 63.66 | 4.65 | 54.11 | 3.95 |
| 7000 | 55.70 | 4.07 | 47.35 | 3.46 |
| 6000 | 47.74 | 3.49 | 40.58 | 2.96 |
| 5000 | 39.79 | 2.90 | 33.82 | 2.47 |
| 4000 | 31.83 | 2.32 | 27.05 | 1.97 |
| 3000 | 23.87 | 1.74 | 20.29 | 1.48 |
| 2000 | 15.91 | 1.16 | 13.53 | 0.99 |
| 1000 | 7.96 | 0.58 | 6.76 | 0.49 |
| 500 | 3.98 | 0.29 | 3.38 | 0.25 |

## 2.2 LITER ENGINE

| RPM | AIR FLOW @ 100% VOL. EFF. CFM | lb./min. | AIR FLOW @ 85% VOL. EFF. CFM | lb./min. |
|---|---|---|---|---|
| 11000 | 426.50 | 31.13 | 362.53 | 26.46 |
| 10000 | 387.73 | 28.30 | 329.57 | 24.06 |
| 9000 | 348.96 | 25.47 | 296.61 | 21.65 |
| 8000 | 310.19 | 22.64 | 263.66 | 19.25 |
| 7000 | 271.41 | 19.81 | 230.70 | 16.84 |
| 6000 | 232.64 | 16.98 | 197.74 | 14.44 |
| 5000 | 193.87 | 14.15 | 164.79 | 12.03 |
| 4000 | 155.09 | 11.32 | 131.83 | 9.62 |
| 3000 | 116.32 | 8.49 | 98.87 | 7.22 |
| 2000 | 77.55 | 5.66 | 65.91 | 4.81 |
| 1000 | 38.77 | 2.83 | 32.96 | 2.41 |
| 500 | 19.39 | 1.42 | 16.48 | 1.20 |
| **Per Cyl. RPM** | | | | |
| 11000 | 106.63 | 7.78 | 90.63 | 6.62 |
| 10000 | 96.93 | 7.08 | 82.39 | 6.01 |
| 9000 | 87.24 | 6.37 | 74.15 | 5.41 |
| 8000 | 77.55 | 5.66 | 65.91 | 4.81 |
| 7000 | 67.85 | 4.95 | 57.68 | 4.21 |
| 6000 | 58.16 | 4.25 | 49.44 | 3.61 |
| 5000 | 48.47 | 3.54 | 41.20 | 3.01 |
| 4000 | 38.77 | 2.83 | 32.96 | 2.41 |
| 3000 | 29.08 | 2.12 | 24.72 | 1.80 |
| 2000 | 19.39 | 1.42 | 16.48 | 1.20 |
| 1000 | 9.69 | 0.71 | 8.24 | 0.60 |
| 500 | 4.85 | 0.35 | 4.12 | 0.30 |

air. But under our new local conditions, the 420 cfm (140 x 3) only carries (.16 x 3 =) .48 lbs./sec. of air. That's only 88% of the mass flow needed to support 300 horsepower.

Since air/fuel ratios are, as we said above, based on 23% of the dry air weight being oxygen, the fuel mass flow will be too high. Here's how the numbers play out.

BSFC average of .5 requires .042 lbs./sec. of fuel [ (300 hp x .5)/3600 sec.). Local air only carries .48 lbs./sec. at 420 cfm limit of our engine. This gives you an air/fuel ratio (.48/.042) of 11.42:1. In terms of an oxygen to fuel ratio local conditions now yield .110 lbs./sec. oxygen and therefore a 2.62:1 oxygen to fuel ratio.

Definitely richer and because there is less oxygen available, the mixture produces less heat and pressure and therefore less power.

To figure out how much fuel you should flow you need to do a little algebra:

$$\frac{.48 \text{ lbs./sec. Air}}{X \text{ lbs./sec. Fuel}} = 12.85$$

Solving for X:

.48 = 12.85 * X

$$\frac{.48}{12.85} = X$$

.037 = X

That means for this air density, in order to make the most power the dry air oxygen content will support, we need to reduce mass fuel flow to .037 lbs./sec. or 2.22 lbs./min. fuel.

You can find an approximate power output by finding this fuel flow in the chart and checking the power level it supports at BSFC .5. You'll have to divide the number by whatever multiple of 100 horsepower you are working in. For example, dividing 2.22 by 3, since we are working with 300 horsepower, gives us .74 lbs./min. Referenced on the chart we see that flow rate supports 90 horsepower, not 100. That of course means we're 30 horsepower off the standard because 10 x 3 = 30.

So you can see that seemingly small changes end up being quite significant. The moral to this exercise, if there is one, would be that calculating air density to judge fuel ratios without taking humidity into account can put you way off the mark and that trip to the winner's circle will have to wait.

## MANAGING FUEL DELIVERY

### Carburetor Tuning Tactics

With carbureted cars, the carburetor is the source of naturally aspirated carbureted engine performance, in that it mixes fuel with air so that combustion can occur in the cylinders. Further, it must do so in a specified proportion we call the air to fuel ratio. A good working average air to fuel ratio (a/f ratio) that is accepted as safe and will produce the most acceleration from a high performance gasoline fueled internal combustion four-stroke engine is 12.8:1 or a brake specific fuel consumption (BSFC) of .50. Advanced engine tuners can run a/f ratio of 13:1 or .45 BSFC at certain RPM ranges to get the most steady state power from an engine. Such combinations are tuned right on the edge to the lean side of the fuel curve, and if the air becomes more dense without making tuning corrections you can get into detonation. By the way, these ratios are for full throttle high load situations. When you're cruising under low load conditions, you can run right at 14.7:1 or stoichiometric and lower without problems. As long as it's not too lean.

From a performance standpoint though, the job of a drag racing carburetor is to deliver to the engine a constant a/f ratio of 12.8:1 throughout the RPM range of the engine. However, there are physical obstacles to achieving the desired result.

The carburetor is a mechanical device that regulates the amount of air and fuel the engine receives to control RPM and power output. The carburetor allows the engine to idle, hold a certain RPM level, and to rev up to the limits (and sometimes beyond) of engine combination. It does this by the physical dimension or size of the throttle bores and the angle or opening of the throttle plates which control the amount of air flow; and the various sizes of orifices and jets that comprise the idle, acceleration, midrange, and high speed fuel metering circuits.

At times, air travels faster than sound within the carburetor and changes temperature, density, and humidity levels. Because of the subtle complexities of mixing fuel into air, it has so far been impossible to design a carburetor that will deliver a constant a/f ratio throughout the entire engine RPM range. If you graphed the fuel curve as the carburetor throttle blades are opened, as the engine RPM increases, and as the various fuel metering circuits come into play, you'd see it zigzag around.

What the manufacturers do is arrange to have the variations of the fuel curve to head toward the rich side. This is because less power is lost on the rich side of the curve and there is less potential for engine damage to occur. Custom carburetor builders and blueprinters take this one step further in that they increase the CFM capability of the carburetor and modify the fuel metering circuits and structures, so that the carburetor is able to deliver more controlled a/f ratio within specific RPM ranges where your particular engine combination performs best.

Unlike fuel-injection systems with baro sensors, carburetors don't adjust for increasing air density. You must become a diligent observer, note taker and tester in order to establish a baseline carburetor tune.

## HOW TO BASELINE YOUR CARBURETOR JETTING

To be consistent, you need to do research. Fortunately this kind of research is fun because you get to do it at the race track. The purpose of baselining your jetting is to establish a standard that you can refer to under varying weather conditions. Your baseline is a reference point to help you regain your bearings and proper tune for your car.

Baselining carburetor jetting is a simple but time-intensive task. The goal is to find the best jetting combination for your car at a specific air density. This is how you do it.

Start with a properly adjusted carburetor. For example, check that the throttle opens 100 percent, the linkage is satisfactory, float levels and fuel pressure are correct, etc., and

## DETONATION CHECK LIST

**Lean Fuel Mixture or Too Much Nitrous.** A lean mix may burn slower than a fat mixture, but the heat of combustion is higher. When you raise temperature you also raise the pressure and you're just asking to generate a second flame front and detonate your main bearings away.

**Too Much Ignition Timing.** Firing the cylinder too much before TDC means the piston is going to be dwelling at TDC when the cylinder reaches peak pressure. Because the piston isn't traveling down the bore yet to relieve the pressure, it builds to a point where the fuel self-ignites. BOOM! You have detonation. Retard the timing to a point where peak cylinder pressure occurs just after the piston starts down the bore and you not only stay out of detonation, you make lots of reliable horsepower.

**Compression Ratio** affects detonation, as we discussed above.

**Cam Choice.** The timing of closing the intake and exhaust valves controls the dynamic compression ratio of the cylinder and thus the cylinder pressure and potentially the tendency of a fuel to detonate. A cam with valve timing that fills the cylinder with more air and fuel promotes higher cylinder pressures and higher horsepower. It also increases the chances for detonation.

**Coolant/Engine Temperature.** You can get hotspots in the cylinder or combustion chamber from an inefficient or insufficient cooling system. Hot spots raise the temperature in the combustion chamber and, well, you know.

**Cylinder-to-Cylinder Distribution.** If an engine has uneven distribution of the air/fuel mixture between cylinders, the leaner cylinders are more likely to detonate. That means you've got to retard the timing for the mixture of the leanest cylinder. This most often occurs on carbureted cars but it also happens to fuel-injected cars as the injectors get clogged or just weren't built right at the factory.

**Carbon Buildup** on the piston, valves, and combustion chamber surfaces can cause a hot spot. Need we say more? If you really get a lot of carbon built up, it can raise the compression ratio.

**Oil in the combustion chamber**. If you get oil in the mix, from worn or broken rings, a bad guide, or ring flutter, your engine will detonate.

**Air Inlet Temperature.** High air inlet temperatures can push an engine on the edge of detonation right over the cliff. The higher the inlet air temperature, the more chance you have of detonating. Just one more reason not to put your air cleaner right by the exhaust pipes.

**Combustion Chamber Shape.** A pent-roof, or clover shaped, combustion chamber with a centrally located spark plug and lots of quench area has the least tendency to detonate. A hemi-head/pent-roof head allows for faster combustion, allowing less time for detonation to occur ahead of the flame front.

**Octane Number.** A high octane number is an indication of a particular blend of gasoline's resistance to detonation. If your engine has high compression, chances are it'll need a high octane number.

**Spark plug choice.** The proper heat range and spark plug type is a critical factor in keeping your engine from detonating, particularly on nitrous. See the Nitrous Tuning section about choosing the right spark plug.

---

jetting that you know is too rich for the altitude and temperature at the test site. (See above for specifics to determine actual air density, as opposed to altitude density.) The reason you start from the rich side, is because it's safer and because the power levels are not affected as much coming from a rich condition as coming from a lean condition. So when in doubt, go rich not lean.

If you're not sure of the current jetting and whether or not it is too rich, physically inspect the system and write down on the carb, firewall, even a piece of paper, the number or orifice size; then ask some of the faster racers at the track for guidance. Generally, the stock jetting is on the rich side, but if you're running a high RPM combination, heads ported with a massaged manifold, big cam, and headers, then you need to be at least two jet sizes up from what is considered stock.

Then run your car down the track, changing jets until you get the fastest MPH. It is best to stay in the same lane for your test runs in order to reduce variations in traction, even though the MPH at the end of the quarter-mile is the significant figure. While you are establishing a baseline, remember to only make one change at a time. Do not change timing or adjust the lash or any other tuning procedures. Simply change jets until you get the fastest speed in the quarter mile. The MPH at the end of the quarter mile indicates horsepower generated.

Once you find the fastest MPH in the quarter, note which jet sizes are installed. Take a temperature reading, in the shade with open air and make a note of it. Also check the wet-bulb temperature and note the pressure altitude of the test track with a barometer. Keep a log of the best jets for the pressure altitude, vapor pressure, and temperatures and it'll help you tune for various conditions. Of course, buying a weather station and racing computer is the best scenario, but good record keeping can create a firm database from which to make tuning decisions if you're on a tight budget.

### FUEL INJECTION TUNING

Presented here is a brief introduction to fuel injection theory. If you're

```
         0%   10%    25%         50%           75%  90%  100%
ON

OFF
                                                    One Cycle
```

$F_2 = \sqrt{P_2 / P_1} * F_1$

Where:
F2 = New Fuel Flow Rate
F1 = Original Fuel Flow Rate
P2 = New Fuel Pressure
P1 = Original Fuel Pressure

Duty cycle is how fuel injectors control fuel delivery. A 0% duty cycle is completely off; a 100% duty cycle is locked open. Duty cycle is a constantly changing amount of time controlled by the RPM of the engine. The injector has only so much time before the intake valve opens again. The limit to the injector is really how quickly it can close and open. The time unit is usually milliseconds. The Injector Time Schedule charts display the time cycles for RPM and duty cycle.

**This formula tells you the fuel flow rate increase from a pressure increase provided you know the original flow rates and pressure at the injector.**

### INJECTOR TIME SCHEDULE BATCH-FIRE: ONCE/REV

| RPM | Millisecs /RPM | 90% Duty | Time Closed | 80% Duty | Time Closed | Revs /Sec |
|---|---|---|---|---|---|---|
| 11000 | 5.45 | 4.91 | 0.55 | 4.36 | 1.09 | 183.33 |
| 10000 | 6.00 | 5.40 | 0.60 | 4.80 | 1.20 | 166.67 |
| 9000 | 6.67 | 6.00 | 0.67 | 5.33 | 1.33 | 150.00 |
| 8000 | 7.50 | 6.75 | 0.75 | 6.00 | 1.50 | 133.33 |
| 7000 | 8.57 | 7.71 | 0.86 | 6.86 | 1.71 | 116.67 |
| 6000 | 10.00 | 9.00 | 1.00 | 8.00 | 2.00 | 100.00 |
| 5000 | 12.00 | 10.80 | 1.20 | 9.60 | 2.40 | 83.33 |
| 4000 | 15.00 | 13.50 | 1.50 | 12.00 | 3.00 | 66.67 |
| 3000 | 20.00 | 18.00 | 2.00 | 16.00 | 4.00 | 50.00 |
| 2000 | 30.00 | 27.00 | 3.00 | 24.00 | 6.00 | 33.33 |
| 1000 | 60.00 | 54.00 | 6.00 | 48.00 | 12.00 | 16.67 |
| 500 | 120.00 | 108.00 | 12.00 | 96.00 | 24.00 | 8.33 |

### INJECTOR TIME SCHEDULE SEQUENTIAL: ONCE/INT VALVE OPEN

| RPM | Millisecs /Intake Opening | 90% Duty | Time Closed | 80% Duty | Time Closed | Revs /Sec |
|---|---|---|---|---|---|---|
| 11000 | 10.91 | 9.82 | 1.09 | 8.73 | 2.18 | 183.33 |
| 10000 | 12.00 | 10.80 | 1.20 | 9.60 | 2.40 | 166.67 |
| 9000 | 13.33 | 12.00 | 1.33 | 10.67 | 2.67 | 150.00 |
| 8000 | 15.00 | 13.50 | 1.50 | 12.00 | 3.00 | 133.33 |
| 7000 | 17.14 | 15.43 | 1.71 | 13.71 | 3.43 | 116.67 |
| 6000 | 20.00 | 18.00 | 2.00 | 16.00 | 4.00 | 100.00 |
| 5000 | 24.00 | 21.60 | 2.40 | 19.20 | 4.80 | 83.33 |
| 4000 | 30.00 | 27.00 | 8.40 | 13.71 | 16.29 | 66.67 |
| 3000 | 40.00 | 36.00 | 4.00 | 32.00 | 8.00 | 50.00 |
| 2000 | 60.00 | 54.00 | 6.00 | 48.00 | 12.00 | 33.33 |
| 1000 | 120.00 | 108.00 | 12.00 | 96.00 | 24.00 | 16.67 |
| 500 | 240.00 | 216.00 | 24.00 | 192.00 | 48.00 | 8.33 |

not very familiar with electronic fuel injection, you may wish to read the *High Performance Honda Handbook, Volume One*. It has a very extensive section on the basics of fuel injection systems.

Electronic Fuel Injection (EFI is based on a timed pulse of the injector. This occurs at specific intervals determined by key engine events such as the intake valve opening. The pulse time is known as the duty cycle. By varying the duty cycle, the pulse duration, or more properly, the pulse width, change to deliver a known quantity of fuel in proportion to a know quantity of air.

There are several methods of measuring air intake and density of the engine which we've discussed in the previous book so we won't here. The important point here is not the method really, but what they are measuring. Oxygen is what reacts with fuel in your engine, so it is really what is being measured, though indirectly, by the various intake air measurement schemes.

Whether you have a carburetor, or have the trickiest aftermarket sequential, phase sequential, or whatever injector firing scheme you care to name, the goal is to deliver precise amounts of fuel with precise amounts of air to achieve optimum cylinder pressure at all operating RPM. This is a very delicate job because an engine's air flow, and hence its demand, for fuel are mind-numbing variables. Even if you limit the discussion to wide open throttle conditions, where the intake pressure is fed by a constant pressure, the air flow is variable because the engine's volumetric efficiency changes throughout its RPM range. So to get it right, you have to have air flow values for all the engine RPM points under various load and throttle opening conditions and it must be done extremely quickly. Factory EFI systems use a table that corresponds these conditions for the computer. The table is developed on a dyno over many hours of testing.

Since we can't do that (or don't have to because we're running a stock computer with stock injectors), we need a model of the air flow and fuel demands of our engine that at least gets us close. That is why we can choose the

## FLOW RATES, POWER POTENTIAL & IDLE REQUIREMENTS OF REPRESENTATIVE LUCAS FUEL INJECTORS

| @psi/bar | 43.5/3.0 | 43.5/3.0 | 43.5/3.0 | 39.15/2.7 | 43.5/3.0 | 50.75/3.5 | 43.5/3.0 | 43.5/3.0 |
|---|---|---|---|---|---|---|---|---|
| lbs./hr | 52.07 | 42.29 | 37.27 | 35.81 | 26.43 | 21.41 | 21.28 | 19.82 |
| lb./min. | 0.87 | 0.70 | 0.62 | 0.60 | 0.44 | 0.36 | 0.35 | 0.33 |
| lb./millisec. | 0.00001446 | 0.00001175 | 0.00001035 | 0.00000995 | 0.00000734 | 0.00000595 | 0.00000591 | 0.00000551 |
| lb./sec. | 0.01446389 | 0.01174722 | 0.01035278 | 0.00994722 | 0.00734167 | 0.00594722 | 0.00591111 | 0.00550556 |
| max power @90% duty w/bfsc .5 per injector | 93.73 | 76.12 | 67.09 | 64.46 | 47.57 | 38.54 | 38.30 | 35.68 |
| @80% duty | 83.31 | 67.66 | 59.63 | 57.30 | 42.29 | 34.26 | 34.05 | 31.71 |
| CFM air req'd @90% duty for horsepower per injector | 149.96 | 121.80 | 107.34 | 103.13 | 76.12 | 61.66 | 61.29 | 57.08 |
| @80% duty | 133.30 | 108.26 | 95.4 | 91.67 | 67.66 | 54.81 | 54.48 | 50.74 |
| min CFM air req'd for idle a/f 12.25:1 | 2.43 | 1.97 | 1.74 | 1.67 | 1.23 | 1.00 | 0.99 | 0.92 |
| min lb./sec. air req'd for idle a/f 12.25:1 | 0.177 | 0.144 | 0.127 | 0.122 | 0.090 | 0.073 | 0.072 | 0.067 |
| Grams/min. | 394.00 | 320.00 | 282.00 | 271.00 | 200.00 | 162.00 | 161.00 | 150.00 |
| mg/pulse | 11.80 | 9.96 | 8.42 | 8.13 | 6.10 | 5.28 | 4.50 | 3.28 |

right size injectors for our combination as well as make other tuning adjustments such as high load, wide-open throttle enrichments for a custom intake or a turbo, supercharger, or nitrous.

If we assume that the air flow capacity of the engine is linear through its RPM range at wide-open throttle, we can then assume the fuel delivery requirements will rise in a linear fashion as well. Though this isn't the case in reality, the fact that an engine doesn't lose as much power if it is slightly rich gives us some leeway for tuning.

In reality, the engine goes through a million combinations of volumetric efficiency. At idle, for example, the throttle blade is closed and with most stock or near-stock cams and cam timing, the intake manifold absolute pressure (MAP) sensor will read around 35 kPa. (Since absolute pressure starts from 0 at a total vacuum, 35 kPa is roughly equivalent to 19 InHg. of vacuum.) So with only that amount of pressure forcing air into the cylinders, even though they are open a long time, they don't take in anywhere near their volume. You have to adjust for that when calculating the air flow at idle to size your injectors.

Assume 100 kPa is a standard atmosphere, (29.92 InHg, 14.7 psi). That's 35% of one atmosphere, so if we multiply the cfm flow at idle RPM, say 1000 rpm, we should be close to that actual CFM and lbs./min. air flow at idle. From here we can better determine whether or not an injector is able to deliver the small portion of fuel required at idle air flow as well as at high RPM high power output.

Use the air flow charts for the various engines sizes to help you calculate air flow at the various RPM ranges. This will help you decide on the injector size you need to reach your power target.

Another factor in determining injector size is the firing tactic of your fuel injection system. Some systems are sequential, meaning they fire the injector once per intake valve opening. The advantage of the sequential system is that the idle mixtures can be controlled to a finer degree, so emissions are reduced on street cars. For race cars, this gives the tuner very fine control over the fuel curve so he can optimize the efficiency of the engine, make impressive horsepower numbers and still idle through the pits.

Batch fire schemes fire the injectors once per crankshaft revolution. This means that an injector half the size of the one used on the sequential system

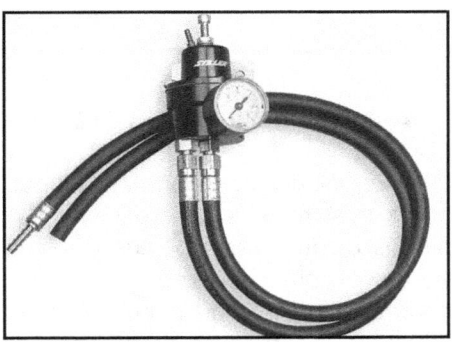

Stillen's R&D department has been analyzing ways to richen the fuel mixture for a power gain on vehicles equipped with intake, headers, and exhaust. Such equipment leans out a motor and the typical cure is to update the fuel delivery schedule hidden within the engine's computer. The Fuel Pressure Riser (FPR) offered by the company has proven to be the answer. Tested and tuned on a Honda Civic equipped with intake, headers, and exhaust, Stillen's FPR showed a maximum gain of 6 horsepower on the company's DynoJet. The billet aluminum component is shipped with gauge, clamps, hoses, fittings and instructions. The FPR installs in 30 minutes.

can deliver the same amount of fuel and make the same horsepower. The catch is on the idle side, however. Since it fires twice, it may deliver too much fuel at idle for the idle quality to be very good, let alone pass any emission standards.

# Honda Builder's HANDBOOK Vol. II
## NITROUS TUNING

**A BASIC NITROUS SYSTEM**

In its most basic form, a nitrous oxide system is a simple device. A nitrous oxide system begins with the bottle of nitrous itself. The most common bottle is an aluminum tank capable of containing 10 pounds of nitrous oxide. A bottle's weight is how you determine how much nitrous it contains. The bottle will have a label on it that tells you the weight of the bottle when empty and when full. The bottle has a safety pressure-relief disc mounted in the valve. This disc is required by law to relieve the pressure in the bottle if it gets too high. At room temperature, the pressure of a typical nitrous bottle is about 850 psi. The safety disc will rupture at somewhere around 1200 psi. Each bottle also carries a certification date stamped into it. When you get your bottle refilled, the refill vendor cannot legally refill your bottle if it's out of date. An out-of-date bottle has to pass a pressure test and get recertified before being refilled.

Inside each bottle is a tube that is attached to the bottle valve and extends to the bottom of the inside of the bottle. More nitrous can be transferred in liquid form than in gaseous form. This fact permits small hoses and lines to carry the nitrous toward the engine. The tube inside the bottle is called a siphon tube. It sucks up liquid nitrous until there is very little left. Each manufacturer supplies instructions for mounting the bottle. The instructions show how to properly position the siphon tube so the liquid nitrous flows during acceleration.

The bottle is usually mounted in the trunk for convenience — and also because it doesn't fit well anywhere else. A high pressure hose gets the nitrous from the bottle to the rest of the system under the hood. This is a special hose that has a Teflon inner liner and a braided-steel outer covering. The ends are power-crimped. Don't replace this hose with a standard neoprene-rubber-lined braided-steel hose, especially one that has screw-together type ends. These types of hoses cannot take the high pressures of nitrous, and they will become very brittle at the extremely low temperatures of nitrous.

The solenoids are the next step along the way. There is one for nitrous and one for fuel in most typical carburetor-style systems. There are some systems designed for factory fuel injection systems that don't use a fuel solenoid. These systems supply the additional fuel during nitrous-assisted operation by raising the fuel pressure to the fuel injectors. The solenoids are the valves that control the on/off operation of the system. These electro-mechanical valves use 12 volts to create a strong magnetic field, which in turn pulls open a small plunger. The solenoids are designed so that the supply pressure assists in keeping the valve closed. The arrangement works similar to a ball covering the drain in a bathtub. As the water gets deeper the pressure on the ball increases, thereby

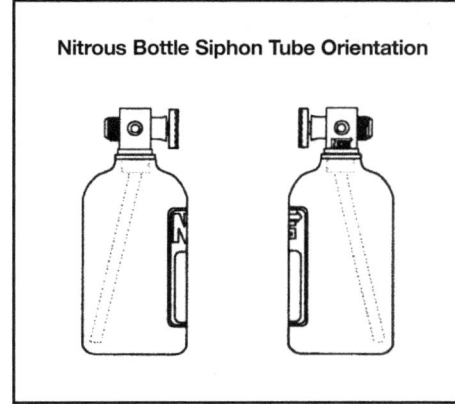

**You have to mount the bottle correctly if you want your nitrous system to function properly. This illustration shows the orientation of the siphon tube and valve. All NOS nitrous bottles are assembled so that the bottom of the siphon tube is at the bottom and opposite the label.**

increasing the sealing action. In a solenoid, the magnetism created by the wire windings of the coil must be strong enough to pull open the plunger. A solenoid is simply an electrically operated valve.

From the solenoids, the nitrous and the fuel — which are still completely separated from each other — travel to the small jets that set the calibration of the system. These jets are typically small brass inserts that are easily changed for tuning purposes. After passing through the jets, the nitrous and the fuel can then be introduced into the engine.

There are various schemes for introducing these substances to the engine. The most common method for carbureted applications involves a thin plate, which mounts below the carburetor and has thin brass tubes that are paired together. One tube is positioned over the other. The upper tube is usually nitrous and the lower tube is usually fuel. The high velocity of the nitrous as it comes out of the upper tube helps to atomize the fuel.

Another method of getting nitrous and fuel into the engine involves a mixer nozzle. This type of nozzle combines the nitrous and the fuel as they are injected into the engine. It can be used as a single nozzle for the entire engine or as individual nozzles per cylinder. The individual nozzles allow you to tune each cylinder differently if necessary.

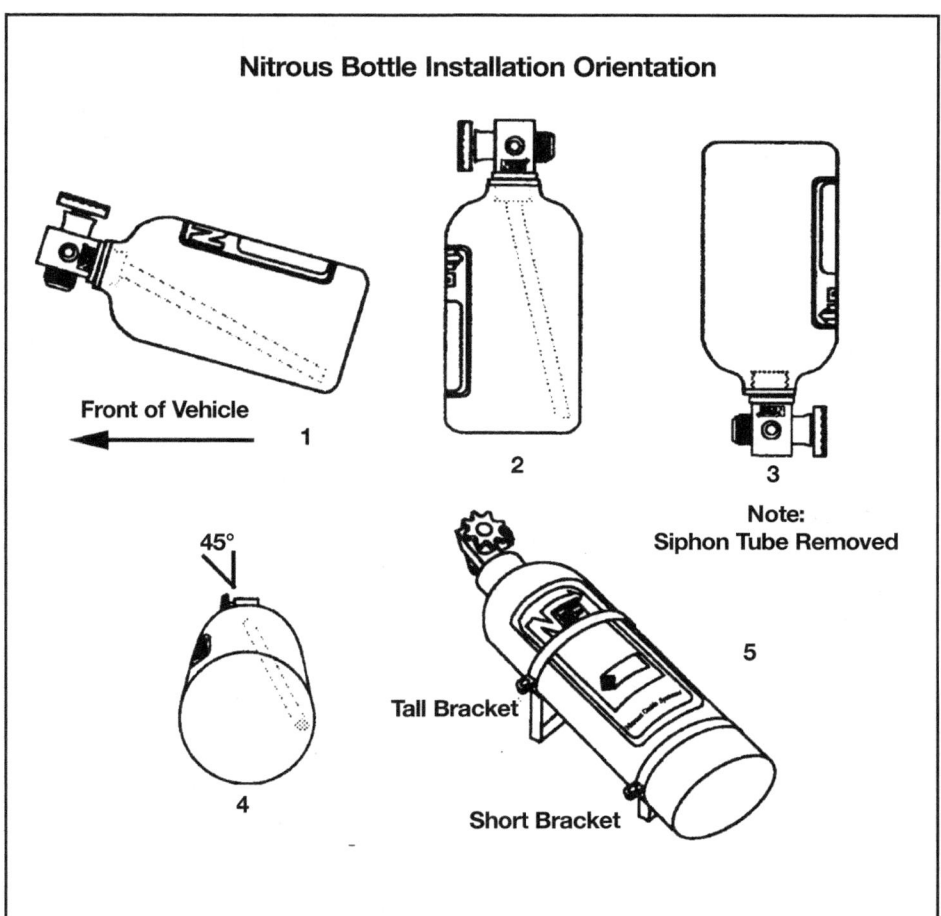

**Whenever the bottle is mounted in a lay-down position, the valve handle most be towards the front of the vehicle with the label facing up (1). If the bottle is mounted vertically, the valve handle and label must face toward the front of the vehicle (2). A bottle mounted upside-down must have the siphon tube removed before use (3). Non-siphon bottles can be specially ordered from NOS. If the bottle must be mounted parallel to the axles of the vehicle (sideways), the valve handle and label must be angled at approximately 45° toward the front of the vehicle (4). When using a bottle with a siphon tube, the tall bracket should be at the valve end of the bottle and the short bracket at the bottom (5). The most efficient mounting is the lay-down position (1) with the valve handle toward the front of the vehicle. This position allows the greatest amount of liquid to be used before the siphon tube begins to pick up gaseous nitrous oxide. This orientation will position the siphon tube at the back of the bottle where the liquid $N_2O$ will be during acceleration. DO NOT attempt to remove the siphon tube without completely emptying the bottle of all nitrous and pressure.**

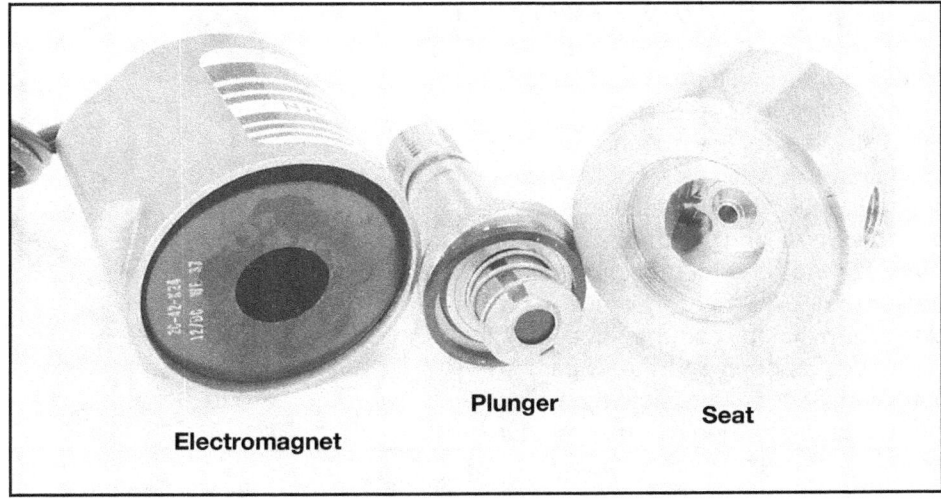

**A nitrous solenoid consists of an electromagnetic plunger and seat.**

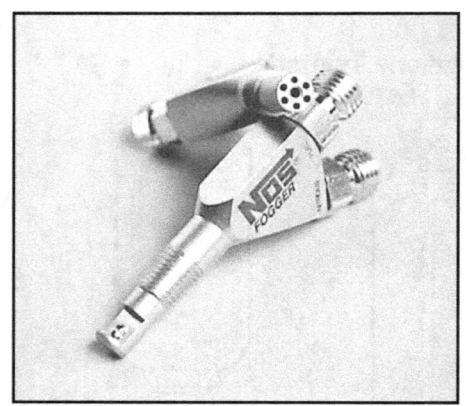

Direct port nozzles mix super cool nitrous oxide at 900 psi and fuel. One of the tricks of making power with nitrous is thoroughly mixing the nitrous and fuel into a vapor.

### BOTTLE WEIGHT CHART

The following is a list of the weights of NOS nitrous oxide cylinders.

| Bottle Size | Weight - Empty (Pounds) | Weight - Full (Pounds) |
|---|---|---|
| 10 oz. | 2.0 | 2.6 |
| 2 lb. | 4.3 or 3.7 | 6.3 or 5.7 |
| 5 lb.* | 8.3 or 9.7 | 6.3 or 5.7 |
| 10 lb.** | 15.0, 14.7 or 13.6 | 25.0, 24.7 or 23.6 |
| 15 lb. | 23.9 | 38.9 |
| 20 lb. | 27.0 | 47.0 |

\* NOS has produced two different weight 5 lb bottles. Visually, they appear the same. Regardless of what the bottle label says, always weigh the bottle completely empty to determine which unit you have before filling.

\*\*NOS has produced three different weight 10 lb bottles. The radiused neck bottle (6.2 inches in diameter) weighs 23.6 pounds full. The stepped neck bottle (6.2 inches in diameter) weighs 25.0 pounds full. The short, fat bottle (6.9 inches in diameter) weighs 24.7 pounds full.

The fuel supply from the fuel side of the system must be very reliable and stable. The calibration accuracy of any nitrous system depends on the ability of the fuel side to deliver a consistent flow of fuel at a consistent pressure. Most carbureted systems tap the fuel line into the carburetor to supply fuel to the fuel solenoid. This method is adequate up to a certain power level. At higher power levels, a separate fuel pump, usually electric, supplies an adequate amount of fuel. A fuel-pressure regulator, which keeps the fuel pressure at a constant level, may be required to maintain the calibration accuracy. A majority of the problems encountered with nitrous systems can be traced to the fuel supply.

### CONTROLLING THE SYSTEM

The most basic of bare-bones nitrous systems have only two switches between the battery and the solenoids. One, called the "arming switch," makes 12 volts from the battery available to the second switch. The second switch is a momentary, spring-loaded switch that is manually operated by hand. With the arming switch on and the momentary switch depressed, or squeezed (hence the slang ter-minology "on the squeeze"), the solenoids open and the system is activated. This style of actuation circuitry was used when nitrous systems were in their infancy years ago.

The next addition in the evolution was a switch mounted on the throttle linkage to sense wide-open throttle (WOT). This switch helps prevent the system from coming on at part throttle, but it is susceptible to activation without the engine running. Filling the engine with nitrous and fuel when it isn't running will cause amazing technicolor carburetor and hood removals if the engine is started within the next 15 minutes. If you accidentally activate the system without the engine running, remove the coil wire at the distributor end and ground it securely; open the throttle nearly wide-open and crank the engine for 10 seconds to clear out the nitrous.

A good way to avoid activating the system without the engine running is to wire the activation circuit through an oil-pressure switch. This setup assumes that if there is oil pressure, the engine is running and vice versa. All of this still leaves the ultimate timing of the system to the coordination of the driver, whose hand is holding the activation button. Accidental activation at too low an RPM or when the clutch is in could cause bad things to happen. So, unless you have the driving skills of a ProStock driver, don't try pushing a button while shifting a manual-transmission car.

The smoothest, no-thought-just-drive way of activating any nitrous system is to use an electronic RPM-activated on/off switch. When used in

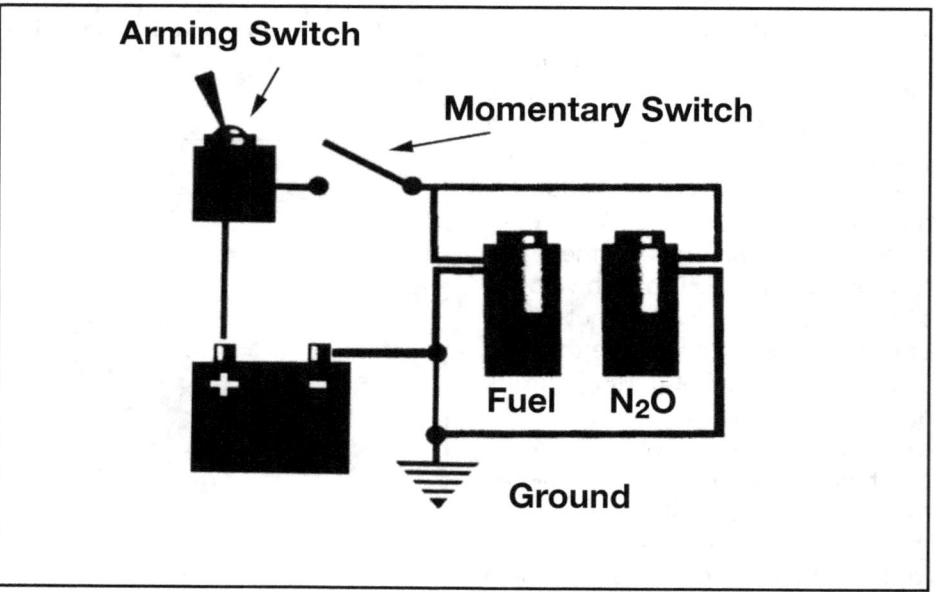

This is the most basic nitrous control circuit. All you have is an arming switch and a momentary switch to complete the circuit. The operator has total control and responsibility over when to activate and deactivate the system.

conjunction with WOT switches, an RPM switch makes the easiest and safest way to wire up your nitrous. The system can only come on when it is running at WOT and somewhere between a low- and high-RPM point. You can select the RPM at which the system comes on as well as the RPM at which it turns off. This setup prevents backfires caused by activating the system at too low an RPM and overrevving the engine while shifting gears. You just put your foot down and drive.

You should be aware that the electrical current draw, measured in amps, is a concern when wiring your nitrous system. Remember that the nitrous solenoid must generate a magnetic field strong enough to open the plunger against 850 psi. As a result, the nitrous-solenoid coil windings require 4 to 6 amps in the smaller solenoids and upwards of 16 to 18 amps in the largest solenoids currently available. Therefore it is always a good practice to use a power relay for the high-amperage circuit that feeds the voltage from the battery to the solenoids. The switches, the micro switches, the electronic boxes, and the connections could easily be damaged by the high-amperage draw of the solenoids. A power relay isolates the switch circuitry from the high-amperage circuits.

There are lots of goodies and extra add-ons for nitrous systems these days. Of all the parts available, the most important is a bottle heater. For example NOS' fully automatic, thermostatically controlled, strap-type heater maintains the bottle temperature at a toasty 75 degrees, even if the temperature outside is below zero. The bottle temperature is important because as the temperature of the bottle falls, so does the pressure. If the pressure in the bottle falls too low, the calibration of the system will be way off and most likely the system will run very poorly.

There are no other power-enhancing devices on the market that make it as easy to increase the power output of an engine so dramatically as a

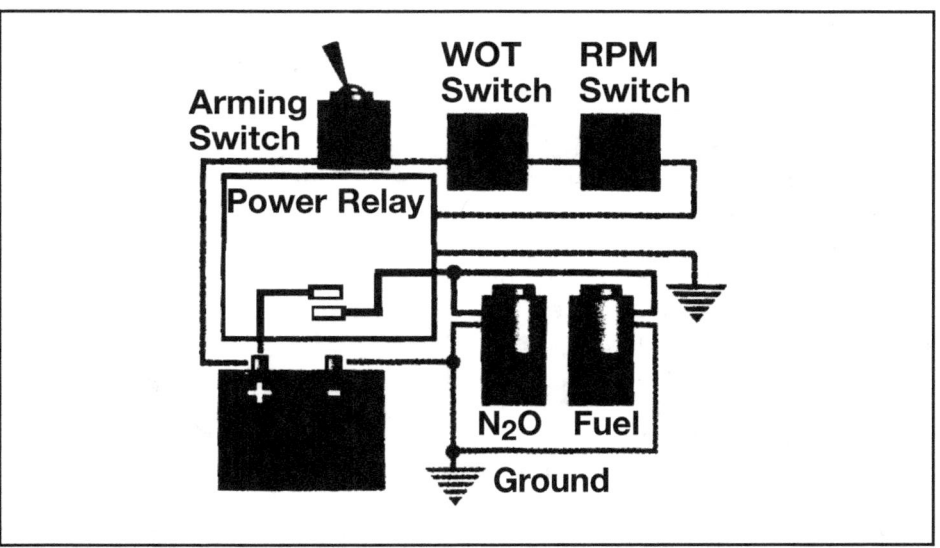

Here is the preferred control circuit. It has a lot of failsafe protection built in, so you can concentrate on driving and having fun.

nitrous system. It's easy to change those two tiny brass jets and get another 50 horsepower, so remember to exercise some discipline as well as common sense. This lack of restraint is exactly what has given nitrous oxide the reputation of destroying engines. The truth is, nitrous doesn't destroy engines; the fuel that was put in there and burned destroyed the engine. Nitrous does not make power; fuel does. Engines don't make power; they only release the potential energy in the fuel given to them. Nitrous oxide is simply a tool that allows you to adjust how much or how quickly the engine burns the fuel. If the fuel is there and a sufficient amount of oxygen is available to it, it will release its energy. It won't care if it's in an engine or a tin can, which leads us to our final point: the limitations of your engine.

Every engine has limitations. An engine will only take a certain amount of heat, stress, and abuse before it breaks. It's just a device. So before you bust out your cell phone for an emergency call to NOS to get your mega horsepower system, check out the section on engine building tips and read the following section about how nitrous works in your engine.

## HOW NITROUS MAKES POWER

The fundamentals of nitrous begin with this concept: An engine is a mechanical device that releases heat energy from fuel and captures some of that energy in the form of torque. Torque is the twisting force we put to work in our race cars through spinning gears and wheels. The important fact to remember is that without fuel, an engine creates no power or force.

Fuel, in so far as this discussion is concerned, is gasoline. Gasoline is a volatile liquid petroleum distillation that when atomized and heated to a high temperature wants to rapidly combine its atoms with oxygen atoms. A huge amount of heat is released during such a chemical reaction. The heat causes the gases in the combustion chamber to expand, thereby forcing the piston down the cylinder. This linear force of the piston is turned to a rotational force by the piston rods connected to the crankshaft.

## FUEL BURNS FASTER WITH MORE OXYGEN

The second concept is that "fuel burns faster when more oxygen is present and slower with less oxygen." It is through the mechanism of this observed behavior of gasoline that superchargers, turbochargers and nitrous oxide makes power. All three of these techniques put more oxygen and more fuel in the combustion chamber. The first two by mechanically forcing more fuel and atmosphere, and therefore more oxygen, into the chambers.

Nitrous, in contrast, uses chemistry and stored mechanical energy to insert more oxygen and fuel into an engine's combustion chambers. The stored mechanical energy I'm referring to is the fact that nitrous gas is so highly compressed that it takes liquid form. When released from the bottle it expands and is able to absorb heat, thus super-cooling the intake charge. By super-cooling the intake charge, the expanding nitrous gas increases the density, and therefore the oxygen content of the intake charge.

So, the bottom line is that nitrous works with an engine's fuel. It is not a fuel unto itself. In fact, nitrous is very similar to air. Earth's atmosphere is basically 80-percent nitrogen and 20-percent oxygen. (We're not going to break it down to all it's components, which includes carbon dioxide, carbon monoxide, and a number of other politically active ingredients.) Nitrous oxide by comparison is 33-percent oxygen and 66 percent nitrogen. In other words it is two-thirds nitrogen and one-third oxygen. This is expressed by its chemical name $N_2O$, which translates to one oxygen atom bound to two nitrogen atoms.

You might think if oxygen is so chock full of power potential, why not inject pure oxygen into an engine?

Dumping pure oxygen into your engine's combustion chambers without controlling the ratio, and then lighting it off would just burn a hole through the pistons. Pure oxygen can react with just about anything but it is really fond of aluminum. You know about the solid rocket boosters on the space shuttle? The solid part is powdered aluminum to which oxygen is added to create a very hot fire. And so more oxygen in an engine's combustion chambers means a hotter,

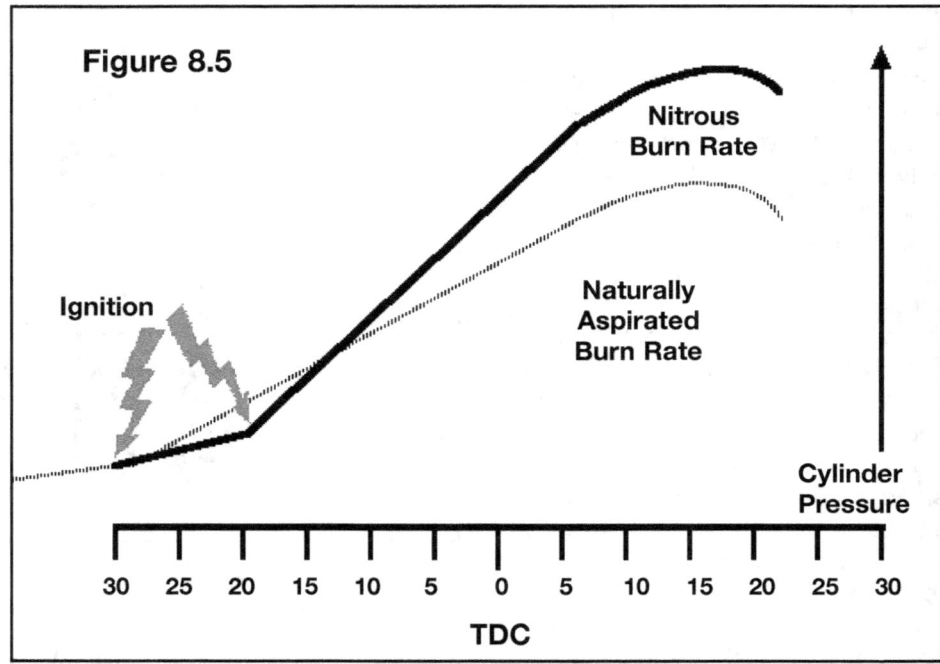

**Figure 8.5**

Timing maximum cylinder pressure is one of the most important tuning parameters. This is true with and without nitrous, though it's more of a concern with it since you're adding an oxidizer that increases the reaction rate of the fuel. That's why you need to retard timing in proportion to the amount of nitrous you are injecting.

as well as faster, burn. You must add more fuel to control the rate and temperature. For maximum performance, you have to control the burn rate and the temperature precisely. Here's why: First, is the optimum timing, in crankshaft degrees, of peak cylinder pressure. Second, is detonation. Detonation occurs when the fuel in the chamber develops one or more flame fronts and burns in an uncontrolled fashion. The rattling you sometimes hear during severe detonation is the flame fronts colliding and the resulting pressure spikes.

### THE IMPORTANCE OF TIMING MAX CYLINDER PRESSURE

The timing and control of peak pressure during the power stroke is the holy grail of engine tuners. Get the timing and burn rate right and the pressure builds gradually to force the piston down the cylinder with great intensity for a long time. It's a good thing to have the pressure build gradually. For one, a long controlled burn, by definition, inhibits detonation.

For another it lengthens the amount of time the expanding charge exerts the most force against the piston without destroying it. The longer and more intense you can make cylinder pressure at the right time, the more power an engine will produce.

Detonation destroys engines and while it is doing so does not create much power. A four-cycle gasoline fueled engine cannot capture much energy from detonation generated pressure spikes. All the energy of the intake charge is released too quickly, focusing the force on the top of the piston. It's sort of like the difference between driving a stake into the ground with a sledge hammer and shooting the end of the stake with a hunting rifle. There is so much force generated so quickly during detonation that it can crush the top of the piston, collapse the upper ring lands, punch holes through the pistons, destroy rod and main bearings...the list of bad things detonation can do to an engine just goes on and on. So it is very important to control how the fuel burns.

### ESTIMATED POWER/CYLINDER AT NOS FLOW RATES
### WITH DIRECT PORT SYSTEM (BOTTLE PRESSURE 900 - 925 PSI)

| $N_2O$ Jet | HORSEPOWER | BSFC = .5 | BSNC @ 5:1 | $N_2O$ lbs./min. | BSNC @ 6:1 | $N_2O$ lbs./min. |
|---|---|---|---|---|---|---|
| .016 | 6.00 | 3.00 | 15.00 | 0.25 | 18.00 | 0.30 |
| .018 | 12.50 | 6.25 | 31.25 | 0.52 | 37.50 | 0.62 |
| .022 | 18.75 | 9.37 | 46.87 | 0.78 | 56.25 | 0.93 |
| .024 | 25.00 | 12.5 | 62.50 | 1.04 | 75.00 | 1.25 |
| .026 | 31.50 | 15.75 | 78.75 | 1.31 | 94.50 | 1.57 |
| .028 | 37.50 | 18.75 | 93.75 | 1.56 | 112.50 | 1.87 |
| .032 | 43.75 | 21.875 | 109.37 | 1.82 | 131.25 | 2.18 |
| .034 | 50.00 | 25.00 | 125.00 | 2.08 | 150.00 | 2.50 |
| .036 | 60.00 | 30.00 | 150.00 | 2.50 | 180.00 | 3.00 |
| .047 | 100.00 | 50.00 | 250.00 | 4.16 | 300.00 | 5.00 |

## TECHNIQUES TO TIME MAX CYLINDER PRESSURE

Basically you have four techniques at your disposal to control burn rate (to avoid detonation) and peak pressure timing. First is the compression ratio of the engine. Second is the octane rating and chemistry of the fuel you choose. Third is the amount and ratio of oxygen to fuel present in the combustion chamber. And forth is ignition timing. Balancing these four factors is really the essence of tuning an engine.

## COMPRESSION RATIO

You have to decide on a compression ratio before you build your engine. If you're installing a nitrous system on a stock engine, or one that's already screwed together, you have to at least know what the compression ratio is. An engine's compression ratio is equal to the cylinder and combustion chamber volume divided by the combustion chamber volume. For example an engine with a combined cylinder and chamber volume of 100 cc at Bottom Dead Center (BDC) and only 10 cc at Top Dead Center (TDC) has a compression ratio of 10 to 1.

We need to discriminate between static compression and dynamic compression ratios. Static is just that — the volumes of the cylinder and combustion chambers mentioned above. Dynamic compression ratio is the real compression ratio achieved in the chambers with the engine running and making power. Once you get air moving in columns as it is in an intake manifold and in the exhaust headers, the air's inertia forces more air into the cylinder than the physical volume of the cylinder. In other words, charged air density is increased. So if there's more air in the cylinder at the start of the compression stroke, all other things being equal, you'll get a slightly higher compression ratio. Factors affecting volumetric efficiency, and therefore the dynamic compression ratio, of an engine include but are not limited to the intake runner design, head porting, and camshaft profile.

You might as well consider the dynamic compression ratio as the real compression ratio, since the static ratio is just a reference. You're more concerned with the state of the fuel mixture with the engine running than when it's stopped, right? How do you find the dynamic compression ratio? Well, it's pretty complicated and because there are so many variables calling it precisely is nearly impossible. Besides, the dynamic compression ratio changes through the RPM range of the engine as the volumetric efficiency changes. However, you can control the range of the dynamic compression ratio with cam choice. A cam that closes the intake valve early tends to increase dynamic compression thereby helping the engine make torque.

## CAM CONSCIOUSNESS

Nitrous engines respond better to different cam profiles than naturally aspirated engines. Choosing the right cam is one of your more important decisions to get the most from your engine combination.

Nitrous engines are very sensitive to dynamic compression ratio changes, so you have to be aware of how certain cam grinds and timing affect this parameter. In general, a cam with a shorter duration will yield a higher compression ratio than a cam with a longer duration. For an engine with a static compression ratio of 12:1, using a cam with less than about 240 degrees of duration measured at .050 lift can get you into detonation rather quickly.

Another consideration is exhaust duration. Nitrous engines receive a lot of fuel and oxygen. Once it is burned and expanded it needs to come out of the engine. Because of

| TEMP/PRESSURE CHART ||
|---|---|
| Bottle Temp. °F | Bottle Pressure (psi) |
| -30 | 67 |
| -20 | 203 |
| -10 | 240 |
| 0 | 283 |
| 10 | 335 |
| 20 | 387 |
| 32 | 460 |
| 40 | 520 |
| 50 | 590 |
| 60 | 675 |
| 70 | 760 |
| 80 | 865 |
| 97 | 1069 |

**Tech note:** As ambient temperature drops, so will bottle pressure which can cause a potentially fuel rich condition. Although usually not harmful to the engine, loss of optimal power can occur. On the other hand, very high ambient temperatures can lead to leaner burning conditions and possible engine damage.

this a cam with more exhaust duration than you'd normally use on a naturally aspirated engine consistently makes more horsepower with nitrous. Bear in mind, however, that simply increasing exhaust duration, (i.e., opening the valve earlier and closing it later) will change the overlap and therefore the dynamic compression ratio as well as the amount of time the intake and exhaust tracts communicate. Most engine tuners agree that nitrous engines respond better if the increased exhaustduration is gained by opening the exhaust valve earlier in the cycle. So for DOHC engines, advancing the exhaust cam by means of an adjustable cam gear is a sure way to make more power.

## OCTANE RATING

The reason we're concerned with compression ratio is because the charge — fuel mixed with air — can only be compressed so much before the mixture ignites prematurely, or detonates. Fuels are rated by their resistance to compression caused ignition or detonation. That's what an octane rating is. A

Since bottle pressure and fuel pressure control the amount of flow through a given jet size, you need to use the best gauges you can find. Large gauge faces give you finer resolution and are easier to read.

higher octane number corresponds to a fuel's greater resistance to reacting with oxygen from compression induced heat. High octane fuels are more resistant to detonation than lower octane fuels. As we discussed, detonation is detrimental to your engine's health and horsepower. Choosing an appropriate compression ratio and fuel octane is a way to avoid unwarranted detonation.

## AIR/FUEL RATIO

Assuming that you understand the affects of compression ratio and fuel octane on burn rate, let's move on. The next item is controlling the oxygen to fuel ratio. With a normally aspirated engine, the way you control the oxygen to fuel ratio is by mixing more or less fuel with the atmosphere as it travels down the intake manifold. Carburetor jetting, or changing the pulse duration for fuel injection motors is the usual channel for such adjustments. The key here is that fuel is added or subtracted from the mixture since the oxygen content of the atmosphere is pretty much stable at 19 percent.

When you're tuning your carburetor, the idea is to find the right amount of fuel that, depending on atmospheric conditions, will use the available oxygen to produce the most power. On most carbureted engines, 12.5 to 13 to one air to fuel ratios is where they make the most power. Any leaner (less fuel higher oxygen ratio), and the mixture burns hotter and quicker which can force detonation. It's also hard to ignite. That means peak pressure is difficult to control and usually displays as a loss of power.

## CONTROLLING IGNITION TIMING

Controlling the timing and duration of cylinder pressure is where all your engine's power is generated. Timing peak pressure correctly is a function of ignition timing and burn rate. Since it takes time for fuel to burn and the piston is traveling at a very high speed, you have to ignite the fuel before you want peak pressure. Look at Figure 8.5 and you can see graphically why you typically have advanced ignition curves. But with nitrous the burn rate of fuel accelerates. With the burn rate accelerated you have to retard the ignition timing to keep peak pressure in the engine's "sweet spot" around the 12 to 14 crankshaft degree mark.

We have explained the accelerated burn rate of the fuel as a consequence of adding oxygen. But merely accelerating the burn rate does not account for the increased power output of a nitrous-injected engine combination. Referring back to Figure 8.5, notice the cylinder pressure associated with a nitrous system. Where does the increase come from? The only way to increase pressure is to increase the temperature. And the only way to do that is to add more fuel. Nitrous supplies more oxygen so you can add more fuel. Mixed in the proper ratios, you get a desired burn rate plus more heat to raise cylinder pressure. The additional cylinder pressure results in more horsepower. It's as simple as that; no magic, just physics.

## TUNING YOUR NITROUS SYSTEM

The first step in tuning a nitrous system is tuning your engine combination. Get your engine running right without the nitrous system first because 90% of the time you'll be running on the motor alone. You don't want to jet the carburetor real rich or try to use such big injectors that it runs super rich off the bottle. You want all the additional fuel to come through the nitrous system unless you're using a dry manifold system.

With the engine tuned and running properly without nitrous, you can start tuning the nitrous system.

Typically, you should start with a conservative jetting combination and tune toward higher output. You don't want to start at the leanest jetting and break your engine right at the gate. If you don't have a reference point, then you're much better off starting conservative. It's just much more fun installing larger jets than sweeping up your engine.

Just keep putting in larger jet sizes, fuel and nitrous, or alternate between the two until the plugs read about like they would naturally aspirated. If you have the jetting correct, the plugs should read almost exactly like a naturally aspirated engine, only you're running nitrous and they see a lot more fuel. You don't have to run a nitrous system so rich the plugs are black.

While it's true that it's safer to run the mixture rich and some engines will make more power on the rich side than on the lean side, these observations come about from distribution problems not so much from the characteristics of the chemical reaction of fuel and nitrous.

## UNEVEN AIR/FUEL DISTRIBUTION AND DETONATION

Making sure each cylinder receives the same amount of fuel is very important when you are trying to get the last bit of power from your engine. If an engine has uneven distribution of the air/fuel mixture between cylinders, the leaner cylinders are more prone to detonate. That means you've got to, or the computer has to, retard the timing for the mixture of the leanest cylinder. This most often occurs on single carbureted cars but it also happens to throttle body-injected engines or to port fuel-injected cars as the injectors get clogged or just weren't built right at the factory. Basically if one cylinder is down on power, the rest of the cylinders are brought to that level by the computer as it retards timing.

A combination with poor distribution can easily turn into a broken engine once you hit it with nitrous. Be very careful about this. Dial up the power and always read the plugs. All of them. Don't just spot check. If one of the cylinders is going lean, you better know about it before putting more nitrous into the engine.

## CHOOSE THE RIGHT SPARK PLUG

Choosing the correct heat range for your spark plugs is paramount for proper performance of the nitrous system. Here's why. The ground strap on spark plugs is usually longer on stock engines because the combustion temperatures aren't that hot. The problem with running these types of plugs with nitrous is that the heat path is so long that the ground strap becomes red hot, the plug turns into a glow plug and then you get detonation. Even if you use a plug a few steps cooler like the nitrous kit manufacturers tell you to, you can still run into this problem. Again, it is the style of plug with a long ground strap that causes the problem not necessarily the heat range.

What you really need is a plug with a short, wide, and thick ground strap. You can even cut the ground strap so it isn't over the electrode so the spark can jump from the corner of the electrode. Keep the same gap but because this shortens the strap, it gets the heat out of the strap quicker and is less likely to force detonation. You'll find this same approach on racing plugs that have a very short ground strap mounted to the side of the electrode. On these plugs the ground strap is very short, thick, and wide so it more effectively transfers the heat to the cylinder head.

Choose the heat range of the plug for the type of duty the engine sees. If you go too cold then the plug won't clean itself and the cylinder won't fire. If you go too hot then you can get into detonation and even melt and crack the plug. With nitrous you don't have to use a non-projected style plug, such as a racing plug, but you do have to change the style of ground strap.

## ELECTRONIC ACTIVATION AND CONTROL FOR YOUR FWD HONDA

Several strategies to remove driver error from the activation loop have also evolved. A simple and quite popular method is to use an electronic RPM-activated on/off switch. When used in conjunction with WOT switches and pressure switches, they are the easiest and safest way to activate your nitrous system. The system can only come on when it is running at WOT and somewhere between a low- and high-RPM point. You can select the RPM at which the system comes on as well as the RPM at which it turns off. This setup prevents backfires caused by activating the system at too low an RPM and over revving the engine while shifting gears. You just put your foot down and drive.

With nitrous systems, it is sometimes far too easy to have an overly heavy foot. When the power comes, it comes with a vengeance. It can, and usually does, turn slicks into smoke as soon as you hit the button. And this is particularly true with front-drive cars. Enter the Nitrous Oxide Systems progressive controls. NOS makes two versions of this device. The first is a stand alone progressive nitrous controller; the second allows you to adjust the timing of how the power is applied.

The NOS Time Based Progressive Nitrous Oxide Injection Controller is designed to allow you to tune the rate at which power from your

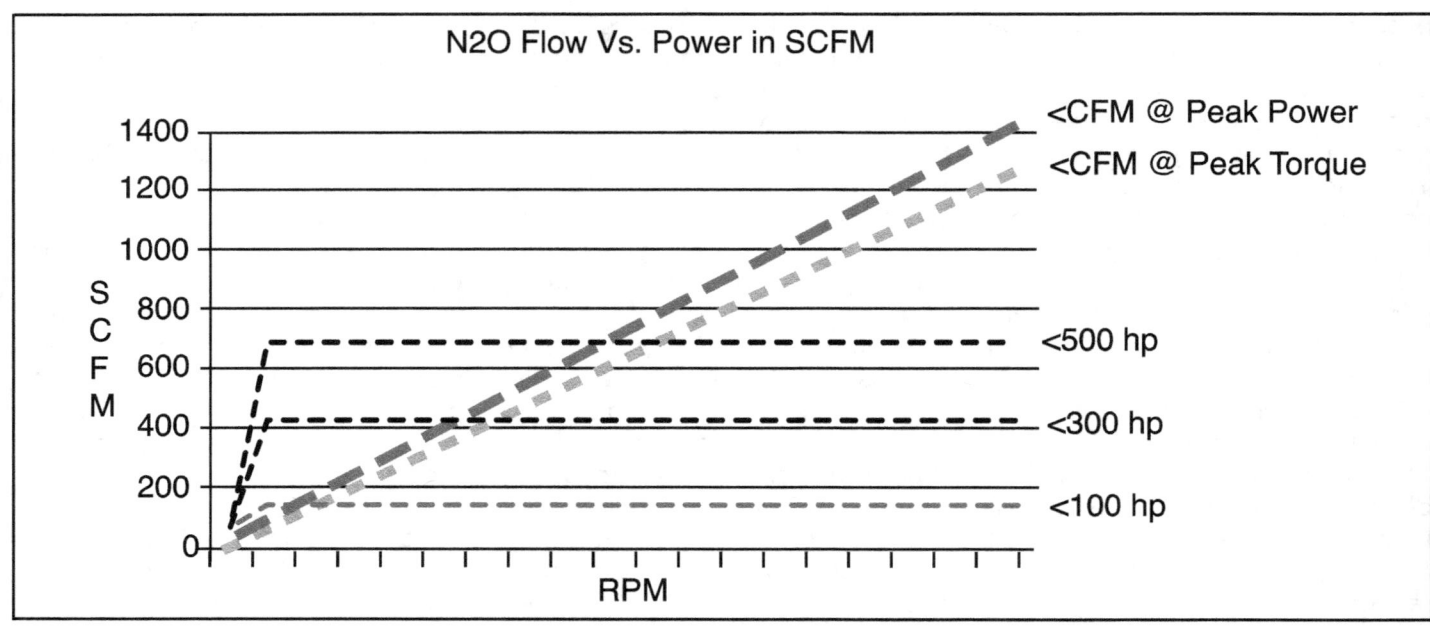

**Nitrous systems are flat flow devices; an engine is not. This chart compares flow rates of both.**

nitrous oxide injection kit is applied. Initial power is adjustable from 0 to 100%. The rate at which the remainder of the power is applied is adjustable from 0 to 5 seconds. Maximum power is adjusted through jetting changes, similar to a conventional nitrous oxide injection kit.

A secondary feature of this unit is its ability to function as a delay device. Length of delay is adjustable between 0 and 20% of the time setting selected on the "Time to Full Power" knob.

The time based progressive nitrous controller is applicable to a variety of vehicles using NOS nitrous oxide injection kits. The basic controller and operating principle is the same for your vehicle regardless of whether it is carbureted or equipped with electronic fuel injection. However, the mounting hardware necessary for a safe installation varies with application.

NOS makes three types of nitrous oxide injection kits. "Dry Manifold EFI Kits" are characterized by their use of two nitrous solenoids and no fuel solenoids. Vehicles which use this type of system are typically late model fuel-injected vehicles with return style fuel systems. No application kit is necessary to install electronic progressive controls in these vehicles.

"Wet Manifold Powershot/Super Powershot/Cheater/Big Shot Kits" are systems that use one fuel and one nitrous Super Powershot or Cheater solenoid. One installation kit P/N #00050 is required. "Wet Manifold Sportsman Fogger/ Pro Shot Fogger Kits" use two fuel and two nitrous Super Powershot/ Cheater/Big Shot solenoids. Two installation kits P/N #00050 are required.

### HOW THESE DEVICES WORK

On Dry Manifold Style NOS Systems, the flow of nitrous oxide into your engine is controlled using the technique known as "Pulse Width Modulation." This is the same principle employed on all factory fuel-injection systems. In simple terms, this means that the second (or downstream) solenoid is opened and shut 25 times per second. In Dry Manifold style NOS nitrous oxide injection kits, the #1, or upstream solenoid works as a safety solenoid. This prevents accidental leakage of nitrous oxide into the engine if the second solenoid (the unit being modulated) were to experience premature degradation of the solenoid plunger seat.

In Wet Manifold Carbureted and EFI Fogger Nozzle Style NOS Systems, the flow of nitrous oxide and supplemental fuel into your engine is also controlled by a microprocessor, using the technique known as "Pulse Width Modulation." Again a secondary or redundant solenoid must be used on the nitrous side of the system as a safety feature. When the timer is activated, the secondary solenoid opens 100% and stays open until the throttle switch is deactivated. Once the throttle switch is deactivated, this secondary solenoid also closes, preventing accidental leakage of nitrous oxide into the engine.

The advantage of these devices, is two-fold. First, they add power gradually, letting you tune to the limits of traction of your tires. Second, they let you tune consistently when the power is applied. Basically the driver is out of the loop except for the fact that he has to launch and drive the car, and of course, enjoy the ride.

### THROTTLE POSITION ACTIVATED PROGRESSIVE NITROUS CONTROLS

NOS offers two Progressive Nitrous Controls which are activated by throttle position sensing. These kits offer an excellent method of bringing in nitrous gradually as the throttle is brought toward wide open. Modifications may be required to mount the throttle position switch on your carburetor. The Progressive Control #15835-C may be used with virtually any nitrous systems using two solenoids and a TPS switch which produces a wide-open-throttle voltage between 4.7 and 5.0 volts. With the system armed, nitrous oxide and supplemental fuel begins to flow when TPS voltage reaches about 2.5 volts.

## RPM SWITCH

The NOS RPM-activated switch automatically turns your nitrous on and off under full throttle at predetermined RPM levels simply by plugging in interchangeable RPM chips ranging from 3000 to 8000 rpm. This is also excellent for use in conjunction with dual or multi-stage nitrous systems for activating a second stage. The NOS RPM switch will only allow the nitrous system to operate at wide open throttle within its pre-selected RPM range. It also acts as a nitrous "rev limiter" in that it shuts off the flow of nitrous and fuel at the high limit point. It includes 3000 & 6000 RPM chips.

## TURBOS AND NITROUS

A lot of Honda enthusiasts just aren't satisfied with a big turbo, or a nitrous system. They have to have both. You can use a nitrous system with a turbo or a supercharger successfully, if you design it right and use it right.

Designing the system really comes down to what we've been talking about all along. Delivering precise proportions of air and fuel to the combustion chamber and lighting it off at just the right crank angle, so when peak pressure occurs the piston is already on its way down the bore. The engine doesn't know that part of the oxygen and fuel is coming from a couple of jets in a nitrous system and through the turbo and fuel injectors.

So as long as the air fuel ratios are right (you're not beyond the compression limits of the fuel), and you've got the timing correct for your combination, it should perform correctly.

Assuming you've got that part of the system straightened out, we'll focus your attention on what we think is the best use of nitrous with a turbocharger and why.

If you have a turbocharger, or supercharger for that matter, the best use of nitrous is not for peak power. It is more adept at making low end torque, so why not use its natural talents. What we're suggesting is that you use nitrous to broaden the power curve, expand it, and make more power under the area of the curve.

If you look at the chart above, you can see a comparison of flow rates for an engine at peak torque and peak power with three theoretical nitrous systems. Notice that the nitrous systems are fixed flow devices whereas the engine is a dynamic flow device. The engine increases flow as RPM climbs. The nitrous systems simply flow at the rate decided by the jets, bottle, and fuel pressures.

This means that as the engine revs up, the percentage of nitrous oxide in the charge decreases. As that happens power drops off. Of course, a turbo doesn't start making boost and air flow until the engine starts to rev up under load. Remember, an engine makes power from burning fuel. It has to burn fuel to make the heat that expands the gasses that makes the power. So its natural talent starts showing itself once the engine starts making power and demanding air. It's more than willing to supply more air than the engine can use. That's what wastegates do — they bleed off excess air flow so you don't overtax the fuel system and get into detonation.

A nitrous system compliments a turbocharger particularly well on smaller engines. One of the facts of life for small twin cam, multi-valve engines such as those in Honda and Acura, is they don't make much power at lower RPM levels. You've got to rev them to make power, even with a turbo. But with a nitrous system working down low, it doesn't take long to spool up the turbo.

So the tactic is to use the nitrous at low RPM. But at what RPM should you activate it? We can't answer that question directly, because each combination is going to be different. But we can give you guidelines with which to approach the tuning.

We suggest you start conservative and work toward more aggressive tuning. For example, a reasonable RPM to activate the system is about 2000 rpm before the torque peak. So if you're seeing a torque peak at 5200 rpm on a 1.8 liter four-valve engine, activating the nitrous at 3200 rpm should be fine. One caveat — don't overdo it on the jetting. If you get too aggressive you can reach the limits of the fuel and start detonating. The reason this can happen is because at the lower RPM the nitrous oxide injection portion of the charge can be a much higher percent than at higher RPM. The valves are open longer but the intake and exhaust tuning aren't quite working yet to scavenge the cylinders and increase the volumetric efficiency. But the nitrous system will flow as much as you jet, and it gets there almost instantaneously. If you get too much fuel and oxygen in the cylinders, the cylinder pressure can reach the detonation limits of the fuel, because the piston is not traveling fast enough yet to avoid the condition. Be aware of this when you tune.

We've got a tuning strategy on activating the system, now we need to think about when to deactivate. Once again, because of the fix flow profile of nitrous systems, there's a point of diminishing returns. The percentage of the charge provided by the nitrous system rapidly becomes virtually insignificant. (This property of nitrous systems is why you have to run staged systems if you want to make power

## NITROUS OXIDE FLOW RATES AT 5:1 NITROUS TO FUEL RATIO
## WITH A .5 BSFC EQUIVALENT AIR/FUEL RATIO = 9.45:1

| Horse power | Gasoline lbs./hr. @ BSFC = .50 HP*.5 | Gasoline lbs./min. @ BSFC = .50 BSFC/60 | Nitrous lbs./min. @ 5/1 BSFC*5 | Oxygen lbs./min. @ 5/1 Nitrous lbs./min. * .36 | CFM @ 70°F Nitrous lbs./min. * 8.726 | Equivalent Atmosphere lbs./min. Oxygen lbs./min. / .19 | Equivalent Atmosphere CFM Atmosphere lbs./min. / .0762 |
|---|---|---|---|---|---|---|---|
| 100 | 50.00 | 0.83 | 4.17 | 1.50 | 36.36 | 7.89 | 103.61 |
| 95 | 47.50 | 0.79 | 3.96 | 1.43 | 34.54 | 7.50 | 98.43 |
| 90 | 45.00 | 0.75 | 3.75 | 1.35 | 32.72 | 7.11 | 93.24 |
| 85 | 42.50 | 0.71 | 3.54 | 1.27 | 30.90 | 6.71 | 88.06 |
| 80 | 40.00 | 0.67 | 3.33 | 1.20 | 29.09 | 6.32 | 82.88 |
| 75 | 37.50 | 0.62 | 3.12 | 1.12 | 27.27 | 5.92 | 77.70 |
| 70 | 35.00 | 0.58 | 2.92 | 1.05 | 25.45 | 5.53 | 72.52 |
| 65 | 32.50 | 0.54 | 2.71 | 0.97 | 23.63 | 5.13 | 67.34 |
| 60 | 30.00 | 0.50 | 2.50 | 0.90 | 21.82 | 4.74 | 62.16 |
| 55 | 27.50 | 0.46 | 2.29 | 0.82 | 20.00 | 4.34 | 56.98 |
| 50 | 25.00 | 0.42 | 2.08 | 0.75 | 18.18 | 3.95 | 51.80 |
| 45 | 22.50 | 0.38 | 1.88 | 0.67 | 16.36 | 3.55 | 46.62 |
| 40 | 20.00 | 0.33 | 1.67 | 0.60 | 14.54 | 3.16 | 41.44 |
| 35 | 17.50 | 0.29 | 1.46 | 0.52 | 12.73 | 2.76 | 36.26 |
| 30 | 15.00 | 0.25 | 1.25 | 0.45 | 10.91 | 2.37 | 31.08 |
| 25 | 12.50 | 0.21 | 1.04 | 0.38 | 9.09 | 1.97 | 25.90 |
| 20 | 10.00 | 0.17 | 0.83 | 0.30 | 7.27 | 1.58 | 20.72 |
| 15 | 7.50 | 0.12 | 0.62 | 0.22 | 5.45 | 1.18 | 15.54 |
| 10 | 5.00 | 0.08 | 0.42 | 0.15 | 3.64 | 0.79 | 10.36 |
| 5 | 2.50 | 0.04 | 0.21 | 0.07 | 1.82 | 0.39 | 5.18 |

## NITROUS OXIDE FLOW RATES AT 6:1 NITROUS TO FUEL RATIO
## WITH A .5 BSFC EQUIVALENT AIR/FUEL RATIO = 11.40:1

| Horse power | Gasoline lbs./hr. @ BSFC = .50 HP*.5 | Gasoline lbs./min. @ BSFC = .50 BSFC/60 | Nitrous lbs./min. @ 6/1 BSFC*6 | Oxygen lbs./min. @ 6/1 Nitrous lbs./min. * .36 | CFM @ 70°F Nitrous lbs./min. * 8.726 | Equivalent Atmosphere lbs./min. Oxygen lbs./min. / .19 | Equivalent Atmosphere CFM Atmosphere lbs./min. / .0762 |
|---|---|---|---|---|---|---|---|
| 100 | 50.00 | 0.83 | 5.00 | 1.80 | 43.63 | 9.47 | 124.33 |
| 95 | 47.50 | 0.79 | 4.75 | 1.71 | 41.45 | 9.00 | 118.11 |
| 90 | 45.00 | 0.75 | 4.50 | 1.62 | 39.27 | 8.53 | 111.89 |
| 85 | 42.50 | 0.71 | 4.25 | 1.53 | 37.09 | 8.05 | 105.68 |
| 80 | 40.00 | 0.67 | 4.00 | 1.44 | 34.90 | 7.58 | 99.46 |
| 75 | 37.50 | 0.62 | 3.75 | 1.35 | 32.72 | 7.11 | 93.24 |
| 70 | 35.00 | 0.58 | 3.50 | 1.26 | 30.54 | 6.63 | 87.03 |
| 65 | 32.50 | 0.54 | 3.25 | 1.17 | 28.36 | 6.16 | 80.81 |
| 60 | 30.00 | 0.50 | 3.00 | 1.08 | 26.18 | 5.68 | 74.60 |
| 55 | 27.50 | 0.46 | 2.75 | 0.99 | 24.00 | 5.21 | 68.38 |
| 50 | 25.00 | 0.42 | 2.50 | 0.90 | 21.82 | 4.74 | 62.16 |
| 45 | 22.50 | 0.38 | 2.25 | 0.81 | 19.63 | 4.26 | 55.95 |
| 40 | 20.00 | 0.33 | 2.00 | 0.72 | 17.45 | 3.79 | 49.73 |
| 35 | 17.50 | 0.29 | 1.75 | 0.63 | 15.27 | 3.32 | 43.51 |
| 30 | 15.00 | 0.25 | 1.50 | 0.54 | 13.09 | 2.84 | 37.30 |
| 25 | 12.50 | 0.21 | 1.25 | 0.45 | 10.91 | 2.37 | 31.08 |
| 20 | 10.00 | 0.17 | 1.00 | 0.36 | 8.73 | 1.89 | 24.87 |
| 15 | 7.50 | 0.12 | 0.75 | 0.27 | 6.54 | 1.42 | 18.65 |
| 10 | 5.00 | 0.08 | 0.50 | 0.18 | 4.36 | 0.95 | 12.43 |
| 5 | 2.50 | 0.04 | 0.25 | 0.09 | 2.18 | 0.47 | 6.22 |

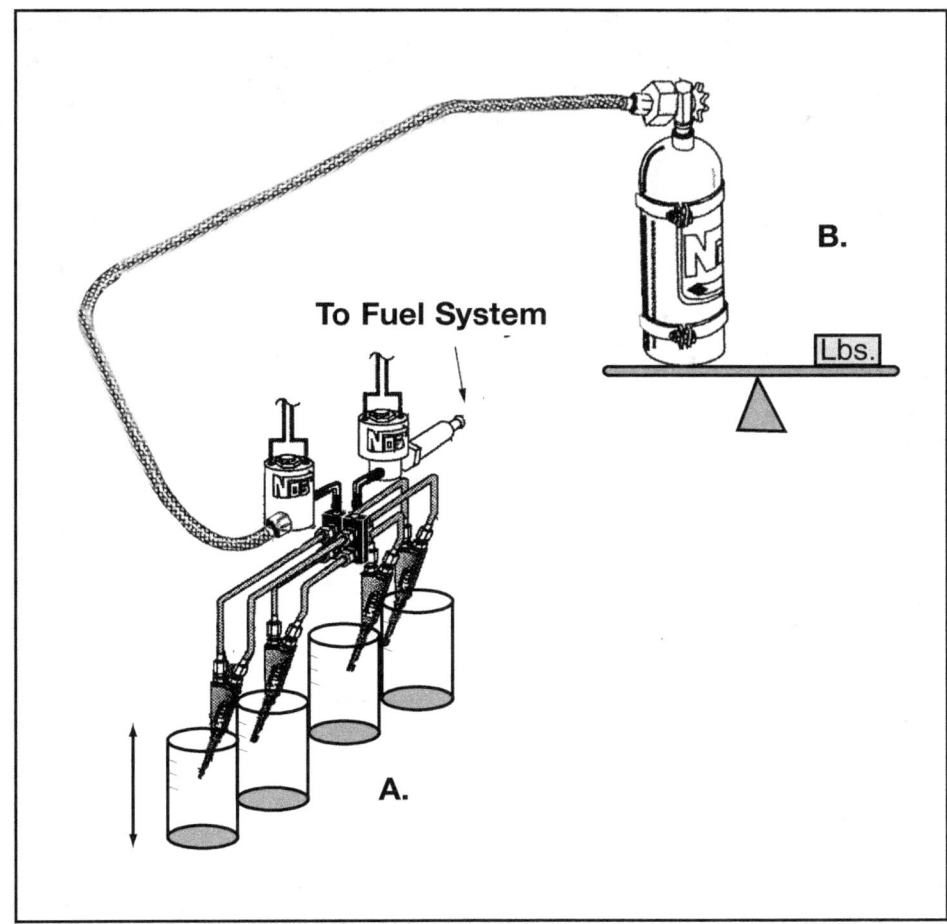

The only way to know for certain how much nitrous and fuel a system flows is by measuring it directly. Set your system up in a jig with graduated flasks (A) under each nozzle and measure the time it takes to flow a specific volume of fuel. Checking nitrous flow requires a weight scale, and again, measure the time it takes to flow a specific weight of nitrous. This method takes into the account friction in the lines and through the jets.

with nitrous throughout the rev range.) We feel you should deactivate the system right about when the boost comes on strong. There's no need to run the nitrous much longer, because the turbo's going to deliver more oxygen to the engine than the nitrous system can hope to, unless you're running a stock turbo, with limited boost. It the latter case, you may want to run it out a little longer depending on how much power you're flowing through the nitrous system. Always read all the plugs for signs of detonation before dialing in more nitrous.

Activation and deactivation are best handled with an RPM window switch. This device is available from MSD, as well as NOS and other outlets. The unit has RPM chips that let you chose RPM activation and deactivation in 500 rpm increments.

You may also find a boost switch handy for fine tuning the boost pressure at which the system stops flowing.

That is the essential information. It's not really difficult in concept, but you should approach tuning the system with care, making only one change at a time, and creep up on the maximum nitrous flow. Don't just slam in the biggest nitrous and fuel jets and hope for the best. You probably won't get it.

## HOW TO USE NITROUS TUNING TABLES

We use a Brake Specific Fuel Consumption rate (BSFC) of 1/2 pound of fuel per hour for each horsepower. We express this in decimal form as .5, i.e. 5/10th or 50/100th which are simply other ways of expressing 1/2. For example, to make 100 horsepower at a .5 BSFC means that the engine uses 50 lbs. of fuel per hour to generate 100 horsepower.

Why do we use .5 BSFC? This value has been found to be a good average number of fuel consumption in gasoline-fueled internal combustion engines. An engine doesn't really operate at .5 BSFC all the time. It will vary how much power it produces per unit of fuel consumed as it sweeps through its engine speed or RPM range. This observation is displayed graphically in the BSFC Map graphic. As you can see in the figure, the BSFC varies a great deal, but the average consumption is right near .5 lbs. of gasoline per hour per horsepower. It's just a convenient number that lets you calculate safe fuel needs for a given power output.

It may not be obvious, but you need a dynamometer to get BSFC numbers. We use them here mostly out of convenience, since we'll have to assume a power output level. For nitrous oxide users this is okay, since most kits are rated at a specific power output and using that number gives us a starting point.

Another concept we need to discuss is the relationship of air/fuel ratios to BSFC. The BSFC value is not the air fuel ratio but its magnitude is influenced by air/fuel ratios. The BSFC vs. MEP vs. A/F Ratio chart shows the relationship of air/fuel ratio to BSFC and average cylinder pressure. Engine tuners have found through experience that for gasoline-fueled engines, air/fuel ratios in the range of 12.5:1 to 13.3:1 make the most power but not the lowest BSFC. The dyno data comparing horsepower to BSFC show this relationship relative to the torque curve and BSFC. Notice that the highest torque output occurs at the lowest BSFC value. This is fairly typical of gasoline-fueled engines.

Essentially, this curve and the power/fuel consumption relationships hold true for each individual cylinder. The goal of an engine builder/tuner is to construct a combination that gives

# HOW TO FIND THE POWER LIMIT OF STOCK ENGINE COMBINATION WITH A DRY MANIFOLD NITROUS OXIDE SYSTEM

This question is responsible for at least 50% of the time you spend on hold if you call NOS's tech line. So we're going to try to answer it for you as clearly as possible. You have to have read the section on fuel and fuel injection to really understand this.

Here's the reasoning. A dry manifold system delivers a specific amount of nitrous by virtue of its jetting and bottle pressure. That amount of nitrous needs to be mixed with an additional amount of fuel, such that the appropriate oxygen to fuel ratios are maintained.

In a dry manifold system, the fuel injectors are the means to deliver the enrichment fuel. Instead of having a second fuel supply calibrated by pressure and jetting, the fuel injectors are called upon to deliver more fuel by increasing their fuel pressure.

The formula for this is given in the engine management chapter, but we'll repeat it here.

Since the power comes from the fuel, the limit in this case is going to be the stock fuel system. To find the approximate power limit of the stock system we can work from the rated power output of the engine and make a few assumptions about the fuel injectors. (At this point we need to refer you to the High Performance Honda Builder's Handbook, Volume One, and the section on fuel injection where Russ Collins tells you about most stock fuel injectors and their pressure limits and behaviors above 80-85% duty cycles.)

The assumptions we'll use, in addition to a BSFC of .5, is that the max duty cycle of the stock injector is 80% @ 7000 rpm and max fuel pressure is 65 psi with an increase limit of 30%.

Using a 1996 Acura Integra 1.8 liter RS as an example, we first note the power rating of the engine. It is rated at 142 horsepower at 6300 rpm. That means the engine makes approximately 35.5 horsepower per cylinder.

The formula for finding the power potential of an injector is:

HORSEPOWER = Flow rate x % duty cycle bsfc

For our case we have:

$35.5 = \frac{\text{Flow rate} \times .8}{.5}$

Which changes form when we solve for flow rate:

$\text{Flow Rate} = \frac{35.5 \times .5}{.8}$

Which is solved as:

Flow Rate = 22.19 lbs./hr. of fuel at max horsepower

This is the rate of flow for each injector at the maximum rated power of the engine. It is not the advertised flow rating of the injector. The flow rating is based on fuel flow through a lock open (100% duty cycle) injector at a specified fuel pressure. Ours is a working flow rate from which you can estimate the rated flow of the injector by adding 20%, which gives us a 26.6 lb./hr. injector.

Now that we know the naturally aspirated fuel flow rate, we can find the power limits of the stock fuel system with the required increase in fuel line pressure with a nitrous system.

Using the formula above to determine the potential fuel flow from the stock system, and therefore, the additional power it will support, we find:

P1 = 55 psi (assumed)

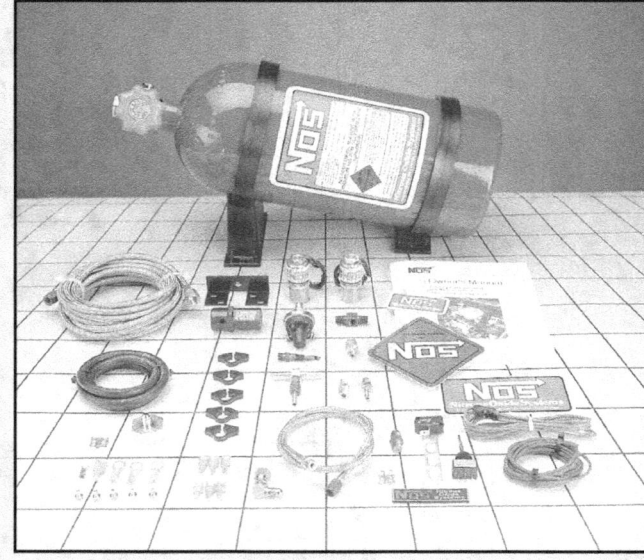

P2 = 71.5 (30% increase)

F1 = 22.19

F2 = 23.50

So you can raise the fuel pressure to 71.5 psi and deliver 23.5 lbs./hr. of fuel with a reasonable expectation of reliability from the fuel injectors.

The 23.5 lbs./hr. figures out thusly:
23.5/.5 = 47 horsepower.

Remember that's per cylinder. So with nitrous oxide, our 4 cylinder 1.8 liter engine with the stock fuel system has a potential of 188 horsepower or just over a 32% increase in total power. Per cylinder, we're up from 35.5 horsepower to 47 horsepower.

This is the limit if you want to maintain any assurance of reliability from the injectors. If you want to take a chance and step up the fuel pressure by 50%, 75%, or 100%, you're asking for an injector failure which could lean one or more cylinders and force detonation. We don't recommend it. But we'll run the numbers at 50% fuel pressure increase to see if it's worth the risk.

P1 = 55

P2 = 82.5

F1 = 22.19

F2 = 27.18

horsepower = 54.36 (54.36-47 = 7.36 horsepower/cyl)

We find a 7.36 power increase per cylinder or 217 total additional power. this is just over the suggested 50% increase in power for the engine combination (53%) and about 20% over the recommended increase for the fuel system. So we don't suggest going any further than this and this only if you understand the risks.

With this amount of fuel and nitrous, if one of the injectors acts funny and falls in flow rate, you could get detonation with sufficient force to crack a piston or worse.

each cylinder the same air/fuel ratio. In practice however, this is almost impossible. Port fuel-injected cars get very close, because the computer regulates the fuel injectors at each cylinder to deliver precise amounts of fuel. Any unequal fuel distribution is usually the result of varying flow rates between individual injectors.

Carbureted engines, especially ones with centrally located carburetors can have quite poor distribution. With unequal fuel distribution, instead of each cylinder performing at the point in the illustration, each cylinder gets a different air/fuel ratio and so produces more or less power as it consumes more or less fuel. You can have one, two, or more cylinders getting the proper 12:5:1 to 13.3:1 ratio, while two or three are slightly rich and two or three are slightly lean.

The cylinders on the rich side aren't as great a problem as the lean cylinders, and here's why. If you look at the mean effective pressure curve, you'll notice that it doesn't drop off as quickly on the rich side as it does on the lean side. This means that a slightly rich cylinder still makes good power but at a cost of consuming extra fuel. The lean cylinder on the other hand produces much less power, a trend that is aggravated as the cylinder gets leaner. With port fuel-injected engines or carbureted engine with a venturi for each cylinder and individual runners, you can just increase fuel delivered to that cylinder to bring it up to power. But on a centrally carbureted system, you have to enrich all the cylinders to get the individual cylinder to perform properly. That scenario usually puts more of the cylinders on the way-rich side, which increases fuel consumption and reduces power output. Still, you have to do it because the lean cylinder is most likely to experience detonation before the richer cylinders. Remember, with a multicylinder engine the sum of each cylinder's output is what moves the flywheel.

It's interesting to see how interdependent all of these measurements are. The air/fuel ratio directly influences mean effective pressure, which determines the torque for a given engine displacement, which influences how much horsepower is produced, which in turn influences BSFC, which is dependent on the air/fuel ratio. It's what tuning is all about.

These tables are here to help you dial in your nitrous combination. If you get totally lost, then you can use these tables as a map to get back to where you want to be; or you can use them to figure your next tuning move or in designing your next stage or nitrous system.

The tables are keyed from the horsepower level in the far-left column. The next column is a theoretical BSFC of .50 at that horsepower level. BSFC is calculated as the mass of the fuel flow divided by the horsepower. So if you're flowing 50 lbs./hr. of fuel and making 100 horsepower, you have a BSFC of .50. To convert that figure into lbs./min. we divide it by 60.

Next, we get the nitrous mass flow per minute at a 6:1 nitrous to fuel ratio by multiplying the BSFC/min figure by 6. In the next column we list the oxygen content, by weight, of the nitrous flow rate. This is done by multiplying the mass flow number in the preceding column by .36. (Nitrous is 36% oxygen by weight.) To convert our nitrous mass flow into a CFM rate, we use the specific volume of the gas at 70°F @ sea level or 8.726 cubic lbs./ft. Multiplying the lbs./min. figure by 8.726 gives an approximate expanded volume of that flow rate.

To get equivalent atmosphere flow rates we chose an oxygen content slightly less than that most commonly presumed. If you take the basic encyclopedic listing that the atmosphere is "23 something" percent oxygen, you tend to overestimate the actual oxygen in the air the engine ingests. We chose 19% because Ken Dutweiller, owner of Dutweiller Performance, told us that's a more realistic number. The great average oxygen content of the atmosphere may be almost 24 percent, but under most conditions it only contains around 19% oxygen. So multiplying the lb./min. @ 6:1 figure by .19 gives us an approximate equivalent rate. Then we take this figure and divide it by .0762 to convert the lbs./min. rate to CFM.

That's how we arrived at the values chosen for the tables. The reason we chose them can best be explained by an example.

Assume you have a nitrous kit that's calibrated to make 100 horsepower. The jetting guide says use X nitrous jet and Y fuel jet, each at a specified pressure. You can take the suggested jetting on faith, which for the most part you can do because the manufacturers are pretty accurate. But what if the combination doesn't perform as expected? What do you do then? What changes should you make in order to tune the system?

These tables are designed to give you reference points. Continuing our example, we know the kit is jetted to make 100 horsepower. That means at a BSFC of .5 it needs to deliver 50 lbs./hr. of fuel; or .83 lbs./min. of fuel. Right here you have something you can test that will verify if, in fact, the nitrous kit's fuel side is delivering the required fuel. You know X-jet at 7 psi doesn't tell you that. The same is true of the nitrous flow rate. You can weigh the bottle, verify bottle pressure, turn on the system for a specific length of time, and calculate the nitrous flow. If the system isn't delivering the required amount of nitrous, you'll know that too.

The atmosphere equivalents were included to show the relationship between air and nitrous. Because when you get to the core, fuel makes the power, not the nitrous. It also lets you establish an approximately equivalent air/fuel ratio. Just divide the equivalent atmosphere in lbs./min. by the BSFC in lbs./min. For example, at 100 horsepower the BSFC /min is .83- pounds and the equivalent atmosphere is 9.47 lbs/min. : 9.47/.83 = 11.40:1 equivalent air/fuel ratio. This puts the tuning in a more familiar format. From this you know you can put in a little more nitrous or take away some fuel if the plugs look like they need it.

# Honda Builder's HANDBOOK Vol. II
# ENGINE BUILDING

Building an engine to make more power is often a subtle exercise. Not everything that makes a difference is as easy to see as a brand new set of headers is. But if you want to use nitrous or install a turbo or supercharger, there are certain details that will make your engine more reliable and make more power as well.

Once again, we tapped the talent and expertise of Russ Collins. We followed along with him as he massaged the already super performing Honda del Sol 1.6 L VTEC engine. The engine in question was built to run naturally aspirated. But where appropriate, Russ clues us in on the correct choice of component and prep work for nitrous, turbo, and supercharged applications.

We begin with prepping the block.

### BLOCK PREP

The block has piston oilers that use the crankshaft oil supply and pressure to spray oil up on the bottom of the pistons. They are located at the bottom of the cylinder right off the main galley. The nozzles are aimed such that they miss the rods and hit the bottom of the piston. The oil temp in this motor is typically around 220 to 240 degrees F. The theory is that the oil will cool the piston and that will improve the volumetric efficiency of the engine by cooling the temperature in the chamber, which in turn cools the temperature of the incoming air. Russ's drag racing gut tells him that the less oil he gets on the piston the better. Why should the piston carry 5, 10 or 15 grams of oil on the down stroke? You don't want the rod and piston to be an oil pump, all you need is enough oil on them to keep them from sticking. And if the chamber temperature is too hot (in a racing application), put more fuel in it. That can't happen on an emissions controlled street engine because fuel mixtures are strictly controlled to meet emissions.

If you're driving your car on the street and want to keep the reliability of the engine, you'll want to keep the oil squirters. But for a racing engine, less oil on the reciprocating assembly means it is effectively lighter. It has less mass. That means the power that would otherwise be used to accelerate the heavier reciprocating assembly is now available to accelerate the car. It's your call.

Collin's experience with Mitsubishi turbo racing engines using the same stock oil squirting technique, is that in a racing engine where you can cool the combustion chamber with additional fuel, the motors live very well, tend to spawn heavy duty ponies, and they rev quicker off the corners.

The B16A3, like all modern Honda blocks, has lots of webbing and internal architecture supporting force loads as well as distributing heat and cooling.

Honda's quality control is superb, so if you go out looking for a block, don't get fooled by the "seasoned block" pitch. It might be a concern for low tech castings on domestic V-8s, but the newer Honda blocks are made from a high silicon content aluminum. When Honda gets through with them, they're treated. It's as hard as it's going to get.

In this view of the timing belt side of the block, you can see that the long skirting places the crankshaft high enough in the block to make room for the windage tray.

Honda locates the identification plate near the transaxle side of the block.

The siamesed cylinder set is common to all the late-model Honda 4-cylinder engines. This design feature is one of Honda's weakest performance links. The cylinders do not have the support of the block or head, so the cylinder walls are particularly prone to splitting under detonation.

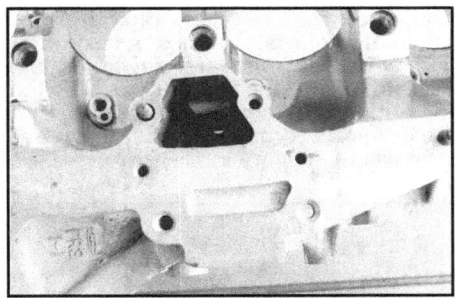

The block features ample main bearing webbing to support the crank and transfer heat into the cooling system. Notice the large drain-back holes. These DOHC engines move a lot of oil up top; plus they are positioned so the oil doesn't hit the crankshaft, which would cause parasitic loss of power.

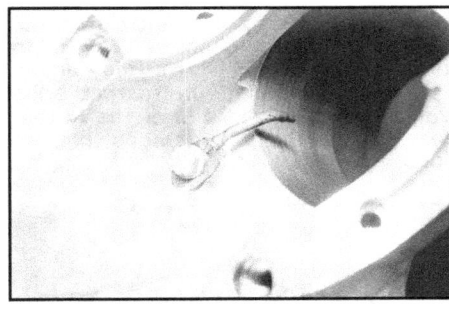

All the VTEC engines have oil jets that shoot a stream of oil on the bottom of the piston. This technique comes from the F1 program and is designed to help cool the piston and rod so that the rod and main bearings don't run overly hot. The oil around and through the crankshaft is very controlled so the pistons don't get splashed as in other engine designs.

## CHECKING MAIN BEARING CLEARANCE

The main bearing factory clearances on most Honda engines are pretty consistent, but they are pretty consistently tight. Collins says he knows why the Honda engineers do it this way — they have to make the engines last for 100,000 miles. But when you're building a racing motor you need looser clearances, so it can run strong right away without being broken in. When I build an IMSA or SCCA race motor, I think they'll last longer and run better than any stock motor. I don't do anything to hurt reliability. These engines have to last 24 hours at full throttle. And some race teams use the engine for the whole year — that says something about the motor you build. Whereas if you try to race a stock one, you probably wouldn't make it through the season unless you got lucky or broke it in correctly. If you took a brand new stock motor and raced it hard, right out of the box, you'd have trouble getting through the year. The main thing to avoid is a clearance that's so tight you don't have any room for the oil film and to allow the crank to flex.

This engine is going out of country, so Collins says he's choosing main clearances that are a little tighter than he would use if the engine was local. Honda color codes bearings to accommodate dimensional variations in the crankshaft, so you just have to measure and chose between the various color codes to get the clearances you want. Each color code varies by .035. Collins kept the rod bearing clearances standard, choosing "yellow" bearings instead of the original "green" bearing set. With the crank polished, he figures that gives him exactly the additional bearing clearance he wanted. Purely a happy coincidence.

## BOTTOM END DESIGN TACTICS

As for the bottom end build for strength and reliability, choose rod ratios to make power at some efficient point, somewhere between 6000 and 7000 rpm for engines with two valves per cylinder; and up to 8000 or so for 4-valve per cylinder engines. Most engines breathe well at these engine speeds and with nitrous there is no reason to twist it real tight and tear it up. With nitrous you don't have to rely on high RPM to do more work in less time, just put more nitrous and fuel into the engine and it will make as much power as your bottom end and the seal between the block and head will take. Even the Pro Mod creatures don't spend much time past 7000 rpm. They've found they don't have to. Just put more

## STROKE IT

RPS had a 1.8L crank welded to stroke the engine out to 2.0L. This is done by welding material on the far side of all the rod journals, then machining it to spec.

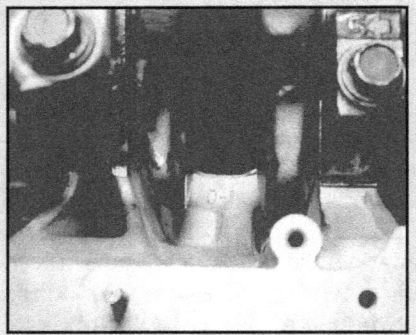

The stroked crank needs elbow room in the form of a notched block. It's a lot of work, but stroking a crank gives the piston/rod more leverage so it makes more torque. It also gives you more room to work with the piston dimensions.

With more room to work with, the ring pack gets spread out. This keeps the ring lands in a thick area with more material between them making the piston stronger. A domed piston raises compression because the builder wants to make power at high RPM.

nitrous and fuel and choose the right gear and put as many gears in the transmission as you can and go racing. Keep the engine in a very narrow power band and you can go very, very quick.

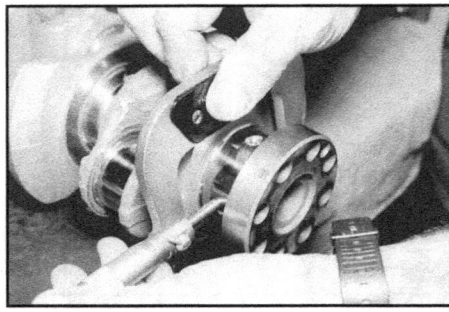

Measure the outside diameter of the main journals with a micrometer and write the numbers down. Collins says to check the dimension with the micrometer at several angles just to make sure it's round. If it is, the readings will all be very close.

Next, install the bearings and torque the main caps down to specs. Torque to factory spec, 58 lbs./ft. for this engine, unless you're using aftermarket bolts with a different tensile strength. In that case, follow the bolt maker's instructions.

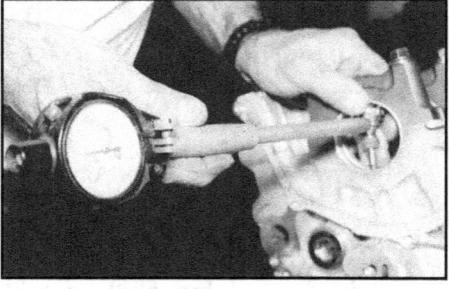

Measure the inner diameter of the main bearing bores with the bearing inserted with a bore gauge. Measure it vertically and horizontally and write these numbers down. Calculating the clearance is just a matter of subtracting the crank journal outer diameter numbers from the main bore inner diameter. Don't worry if the horizontal dimensions are a few thousandths over. They are supposed to be that way. This extra clearance keeps the tips of the bearing shells from bending in and scraping oil off the crank journal. Collins says he'll end up with .0017 - .0018 on the mains; probably the same on the rods. If it was a local drag racing motor, he suggests using looser clearances, probably .0022. Even with a road race motor, you can get it to rev quicker with .0020 main clearances.

Drop the crank into the bearing cradle. Lube everything. Collins uses VHT 701. He says there might be something better on the market but he's not aware of it. He's used some of the red jelly that Redline sells but he doesn't like it at all. He doesn't know exactly why the Redline product doesn't work for him as well as others, but VHT and Mobil One bring him back motors so clean he can eat off the insides of the valve covers. He says he's never seen any problems with these products.

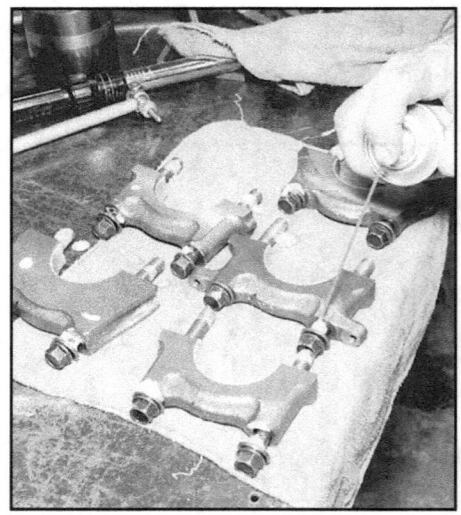

Lube everything before you assemble and torque down: the threads, shaft, and under the head of the bolt, even the bearing surfaces. When in doubt, lube it. No particular sequence to tighten the main bearings down, just don't forget any.

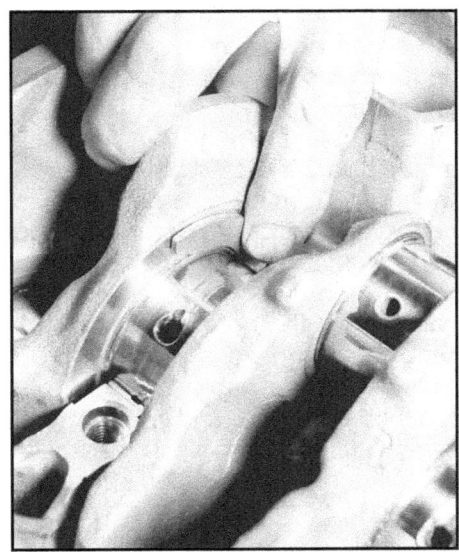

Install thrust bearings. If you're working on an engine with time on it and you're reusing some parts, it's a good idea to check the thrust with a dial indicator. Check with the factory manual for specs.

## ROD AND PISTON PREP

Rod bolts break from the inertial loading at overlap. That is the highest loading the rod bolts ever see. On the compression stroke they see pressure, helping to slow the rod down. On the power stroke the rod sees compression, the rod bolts aren't stressed, the load on the big end is on the rod side of the bearing. The rod bolt could fall out here and it wouldn't make a difference.

When the piston comes up on the exhaust stroke, there's still a little pressure as it pushes the exhaust gas out until it gets to top dead center. Then the intake valves open and the exhaust valves are just closing, releasing cylinder pressure that was cushioning the piston by absorbing some of the inertial energy. Now the only thing holding the rod and piston to the crank is — you guessed it — the rod bolts.

When you snap off the power at the end of a long straight or the quarter-mile, the butterfly is closed so there is no pressure coming through the intake. In fact, there's a slight vacuum on a naturally aspirated car. So in addition to the piston and rod wanting to continue in a straight line through the head, as the crankshaft starts pulling the rod and piston back down the bore, the inertia of the rod and piston combine with the opposing force of the crank rotation and can stretch the rod bolt. A few cycles of this and crunch, there goes your motor. If you're going to stretch a rod bolt, you can only stretch it at overlap. When else can you stretch it?

If a rod breaks in the middle of the beam just under the pin, that's a sign of too much power. That is a compression break, which is indicative of too much power for that rod. Severe detonation can also bend the rod.

This whole load of mass hits the top of the stroke and gets jerked right back down the cylinder. The problem is accentuated by a motor with a short rod ratio. The shorter the rod, the faster the piston has to slow down and the faster the crank throw will re-accelerate it. On a real long rod ratio motor, the piston hangs around top dead center forever. So the inertial energy of the piston and rod can dissipate a little before changing directions.

I've seen, through Dix, Motorsports Director at Honda, all the factory racing engines that have come back. Some privateers even send me parts, for failure analysis. I've seen broken rods and rod bolts from an army of race engines. With the new Preludes, or the new B series VTEC, they are torquing the rod bolts at 30-32 lbs. The only failure I've seen is where the rod bolt was missing or bent. It was bent because the other bolt went away. But it didn't break, it stripped the last four threads off the rod bolt and the nut came loose. The rod was either overtorqued and lost its tensile, or the nut wasn't tightened and it just backed off before the failure.

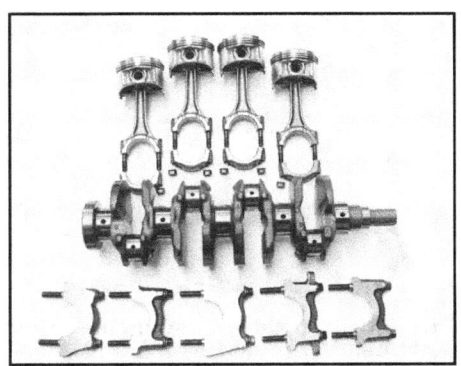

The crankshaft, rods and pistons are stout enough to handle the forces of 170 horsepower from 1.6 liters. However, if you're thinking of using small amounts of nitrous, a street blower, or turbocharger, you should at the very least install a set of quality forged aluminum pistons. If you think you may try to force more power through the engine, then a set of heavy duty forged rods in addition to the forged pistons is mandatory.

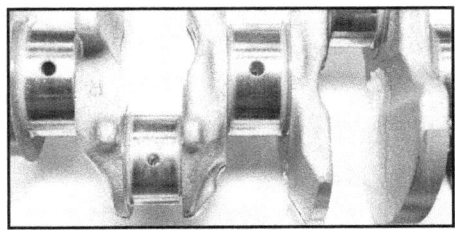

Crankshafts for these Honda engines (B16 & B18) are good for over 400 horsepower and perhaps 500 horsepower or more. (We know they're good for 477 horsepower. See RPS Turboclutch project car from *Honda Builder's Handbook, Volume One*.) There's plenty of overlap on this unit. The overlap between the crank main journals and rod journals is what determines the strength of a crankshaft.

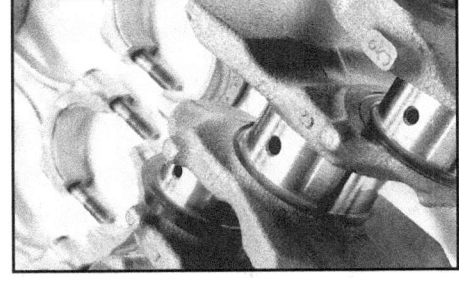

Collins says if he needed to find the last bit of horsepower from this engine, he'd knife edge the counter weights to cut down on aerodynamic drag. Engines with a windage tray, such as the VTEC 1.8 Integra, don't benefit as much from this technique since there's less oil fog to "knife through." If you polished the crank in every area possible, it would shed excess oil quicker so there would be less mass to accelerate, giving you more power at the flywheel. Plus, the oil is getting back to the pan and cooling faster.

*Honda Builder's Handbook Vol. 2*  **115**

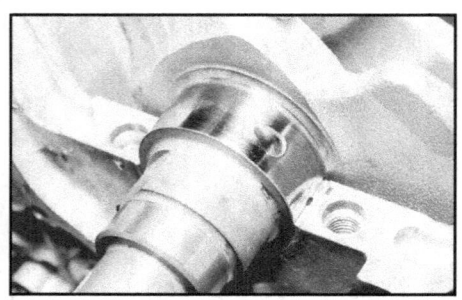

Russ Collins believes altering the crank main bearing oiling holes in this manner improves oiling. The extension of the hole is made in the direction of crank travel. It acts like the tunnel on an IndyCar, creating a low pressure area to pull oil into the oiling hole. Another factor helping flow is the oil doesn't have to make a 90 degree turn, as it would with the stock oil holes. Fluting the crank oiling holes is one way to have less oil backing up behind the main bearings.

Honda has world-class quality control, but if you're building a race engine you have to check everything. Collins suggests you may want to have the main bearing saddles honed to give you a few thousandths tighter bearing crush. It's commonly believed this resists "spinning a bearing." "Not true," says Collins. "The reason I do this on the mains and on the rod bearing is to get more surface area tightly fitted to make an efficient heat path." See "Honing Main and Rod Bearings" sidebar for more info.

## PISTON/RING DESIGN TIPS

The engine component most impacted by nitrous is the piston/ring assembly. The pistons and rings, among other things, have to seal cylinder pressure in *and* keep oil out. If you get oil in the combustion chamber, it lowers the octane of the fuel mixture leading to detonation. Even though this is a concern, you don't need to order special oil rings. We merely present it for your education.

However, while we are on the subject of rings, and by association, pistons, we have a few tips from the engineers at Federal-Mogul.

With high horsepower engines you need to be concerned with sinking the heat out of the crown of the piston. If you're using a heavy flow of nitrous and not a lot of RPM, then you don't need to go to a real thin ring. If you do, you are asking for trouble because a thin ring holds the heat in the crown. The heat in the piston crown has to go somewhere, and the only place it goes is out the side of the piston, through the rings into the cylinder case. Most people think the piston is cooled by oil splashing on the bottom of it. It is true this provides some cooling, but not nearly as much as is commonly supposed. In fact, most cooling of the piston top comes from the heat path through the rings into the cylinder case. This is why when you start losing ring seal you start losing pistons.

Unfortunately, this tends to be a common problem for nitrous users. When you get into detonation with nitrous, it easily bends the ring over the ring lands, and since the piston is really hot the pressure in the combustion chamber will bend the ring land down and start pinching the ring.

One of the more common solutions to this problem is to move the top ring down, away from the crown of the piston. But a better solution seems to be found in putting more space between the rings. Moving the second ring down puts more land material between the top and second ring and so provides more support for the top ring. This is important because the top ring is under tremendous pressure which tries to bend it down over the land. In severe cases, you can see a shiny ring on the bottom of the top ring that develops from the distortion. You can tell that the ring has been bent over from the pressure and has ridden on the sharp edge of the ring land. When this happens, the ring loses its seal because the ring face takes an angle to the cylinder wall instead of sitting flush.

The ring is still sealing, but what it is not doing is transferring the heat from the piston crown to the cylinder case as effectively as before. The reason is less surface area transferring heat. This causes the piston to heat to a point that it softens and the pressure forces the ring land to collapse on the second ring. What's weird is that the second ring binds, but the top ring remains free with no apparant problem.

So, if you are not spinning your motor past 7000 or 8000 rpm, use a wide ring. Even as wide as 5\64-inch ring would not be detrimental to performance. With nitrous you don't have to run thin rings in an effort to get that last few horsepower. So why keep wasting pistons and rings? Go wide and build reliability.

A nitrous motor and a pro stock engine are two very different animals. In a nitrous motor you don't have the cooling cycle that you do with a naturally aspirated engine. Nitrous motors have a longer burn time and more thermal loading of the pistons.

This same concept may apply to the technique of moving the whole ring pack down. Here's the theory: the cylinder pressure acts hydrostatically, i.e., the pressure will still be as great no matter how far down the piston you put the ring pack. It isn't necessarily a pressure problem, it is a heat problem.

If you were to design a stronger piston, one of the things to request is more material behind the rings. As you move the ring package down, you get into an area of the piston that is thinner. When that happens, the heat flows out of the small cross section of piston skirt and through the rings. So the small areas of the piston really take a high thermal load which tends to soften these areas allowing them to bend. It's like a bottle neck and pretty soon, as these areas soften, the whole top of the piston wants to come off.

Yet another tip the engineers from Federal-Mogul told us is that they want to see a little larger ring gap on the second ring than on the top ring. They say they find a better seal with this gap configuration in hot running conditions. Just how hot is hard to say, but you know the engine is too hot when the rings butt together. What happens in this case is the top ring closes more than the second ring. So even if you set both rings' end-gaps at .025, the top ring gap will be smaller than the second ring gap.

It is important for the gaps to be this way, because you want the pressure between the top ring and the second ring to go out the gap of the second ring faster and easier than it gets past the top ring gap. The Federal-Mogul engineers assert that you do not want the pressure to equalize before and after the top ring. If that happens, there is no pressure to force it against the cylinder wall and seal the bore. If the pressure is equal here, then all that's sealing the cylinder is the ring tension, which isn't nearly enough. You have to have a pressure difference above and below the top ring for it to work properly.

This happens far too often to guys running zero gap rings on nitrous engines. Zero gap rings, especially the second ring, are fine for pro stock engines where you want zero leak. But, it just doesn't make any sense because that takes the pressure off the top ring and you lose cylinder pressure. What's going on when you observe horsepower gains with zero gap rings is the friction of the top ring is eliminated which shows up on the dyno as more power at the flywheel. But the top ring is no longer sealing, so you better hope the second ring is very good because it now has to do all the sealing and heat transfer work.

### SHOULD YOU USE HYPERUETECTIC PISTONS IN YOUR NITROUS ENGINE?

You don't want to use hyperuetectic pistons in a nitrous engine. They'll take a lot of pressure — you can stand a mountain on them — and they won't break under the weight. But the minute you ring them with the frequency that nitrous causes when it detonates, they shatter like glass. They break; they don't melt.

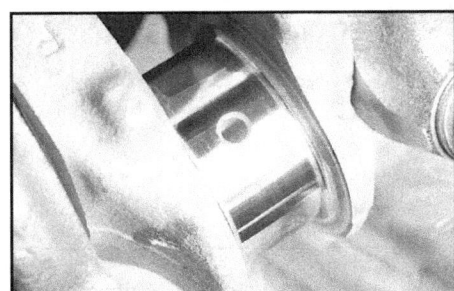

The rod bearing oiling holes are chamfered. You don't need to do much here, because the oil comes out of these. On the motorcycle engines, Collins would flute them in a cross pattern to spread the oil and get it to move across the rod bearing. But the loading on these rods isn't that great. If this engine combination was going to double the horsepower output, he'd have aluminum rods and more rod clearance. The side clearance is right at .010. They start at .080 to .090. He wants the oil to move across the rod bearing, not particularly the main. The mains are a problem because they have a double hole and a groove top bearing.

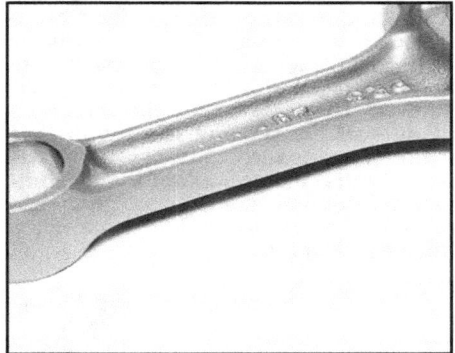

Collins had a shop do the old stress relieve and shot peen tune up on the rods. If you look at the stock rod you can see the forging flashing on the side of the beam. Grinding this smooth relieves a potential area where stress cracks can form. But grinding on the rod beam removes the surface tension of the factory shot peen process. So to restore the surface tension, the rods need to be shot peened. Shot peening compacts the surface of the metal, raising surface tension, which helps the metal resist cracking along the beam.

Tip: Use dummy rod bolts to hold the cap on while you're having the rod treated, shot peened, etc.

The big end of the rod is honed for the same reason the main bearing bores are — to get the right amount of bearing crush in order to facilitate heat transfer. Improving the heat path is a definite must in engine combinations using nitrous, turbos or superchargers. See the main bearing sidebar for more information.

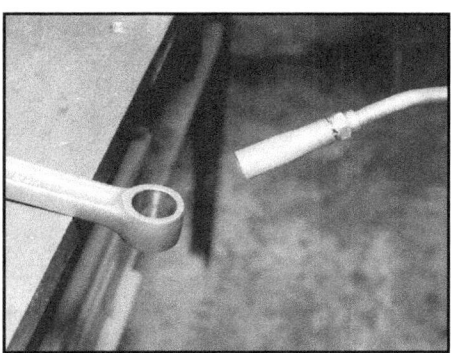

When installing the wrist pin in the rod, heat it up until the surface just turns color. The color is very subtle, sort of a light, brownish gray. Move the torch around the small end of the rod to heat it evenly. When you get the discoloration, put the pin in the piston rod assembly (which you've set up in a vice press) and slide it in. Do it in one quick motion and it'll cool right about the time the pin is centered. If not, gently slide it to center with a press.

Collins says he had all the sharp edges, particularly on the piston dome, removed to prevent hot spots which can cause pre-ignition or detonation. He had the valve pockets re-radiused to remove thin spots with the potential to retain enough heat to prematurely ignite the mixture. He also re-radiused the edges of the piston skirt. Again, these procedures are essential in nitrous, turbo, and supercharged engines. You should do this to the forged pistons you're installing.

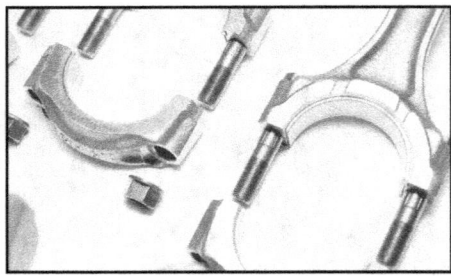

The stock rod has four (two each side) oil escape channels cast that splash oil up to the piston to oil the wrist pin. They want the oil to have a way to get out, and they want it to escape across the top of the bearing, not the bottom, because of all the inertia loading on the bottom and because overlap is pretty high, especially in RPM past the redline. Still most of the load from the power stroke is at the top, so by getting the oil to flow in this direction it stays cooler and more effectively lubricates the crank to rod interface. It may appear a little overkill to have four escape channels and the oil squirters. But this is the first Honda motor that feeds the crank oil from the top. All the other Honda motors fed the crank from the bottom.

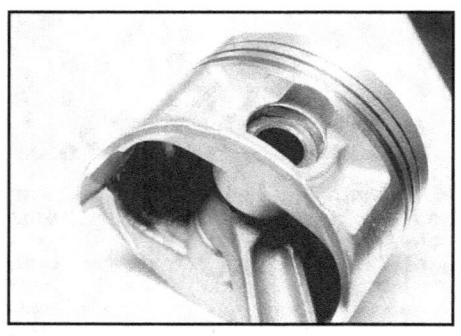

The stock rod does not have a pin oil hole in the small end to help lubricate the wrist pin. Collins says he'll probably put them in the rods. Notice the notches in the edges of the wrist pin opening. These help oil get between the piston and the pin. This was first done on Buick Indy Car engines. You could make the wrist pins a full-floater if you're willing the do the machine work and put clips in to retain the wrist pin.

### RING PACK AND CYLINDER WALL PREP

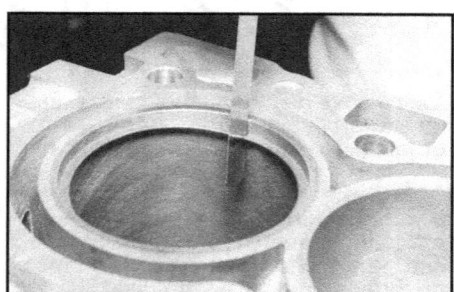

Check ring end gap with a feeler gauge after you make sure the ring is square to the centerline of the bore. You have to have a top ring gap, or you don't get pressure forcing the second ring, an oil control ring which is very important, against the cylinder wall. That's why gapless rings such as Total Seal aren't gapless on top. The tensile, or the spring of the rings don't seal the ring. The cylinder pressure seals the piston rings. Rings seal by having just enough clearance to let some of the cylinder pressure behind the ring to force it against the cylinder wall. So the width and depth of the ring land compared to the dimensions of the ring is critical. If it's too tight, no pressure gets behind it and you lose cylinder pressure. If it's too loose, the pressure bleeds off behind and again you lose cylinder pressure. Always use the dimensions the manufacturer recommends. Running a tight end gap, without knowing for sure that it works, is a mistake. Don't do it.

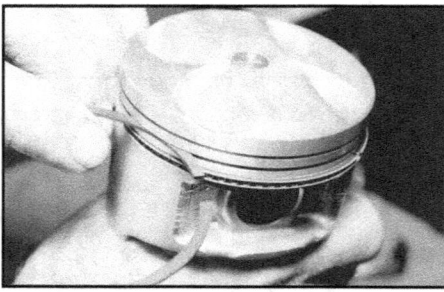

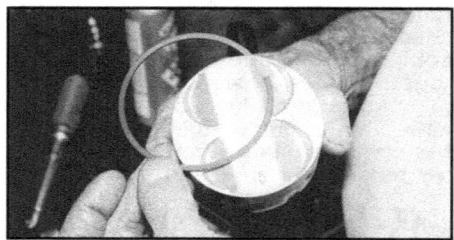

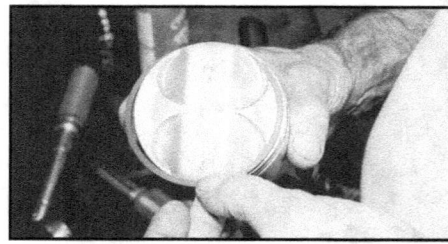

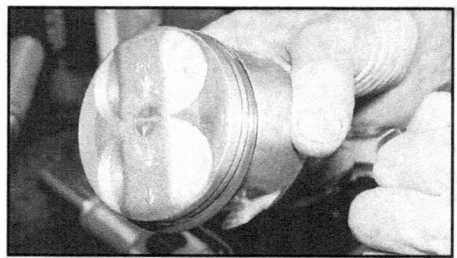

Honda rings are wonderful. Collins feels the stock Honda rings are more than adequate for most high performance endeavors. Installing rings: Put the bottom one in first, then work your way up. The quick technique is to screw the rings on as shown in this sequence.

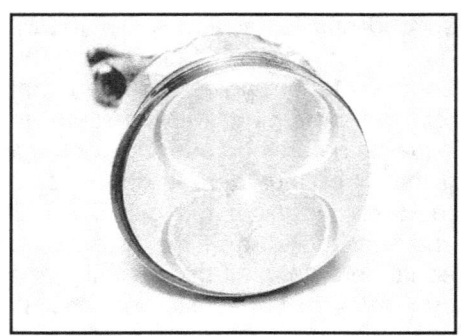

Here is where you want your ring gaps. Almost every piston ring in the world has a mark on it and they always go up.

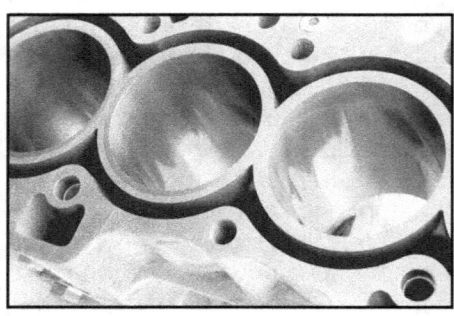

Collins used a 300 grit stone to hone the bores of this motor to get a .192 piston to wall clearance. The stock Honda rings are chromemoly so he polishes the bores with 600 grit sandpaper to help them seat. He says he uses different techniques for different applications. If you're building a street motor designed to run forever, grease up the bores and have a real fine finish on them and let it take 10,000 miles to wear in. Don't worry about burning a little oil, once the rings seat it'll run forever. If it's a race engine, that's going to be pushed hard as soon as it gets to temperature, then you need something different. It can't wait. The rings have to seat.

### ROD AND PISTON INSTALLATION

Lube the bearings and bolts before installing pistons. Tighten the ring compression tool around the piston. Slide it into the hole. You shouldn't have to worry about the rod bolts hitting the rod journals, but do be aware of any conflict. Tap the ring compression tool until it's flush against the cylinder deck.

Tap the piston in with the handle of a hammer. Russ uses an autobody hammer he's had forever. Tap the piston in by going around the edges as you gently tap it with the hammer handle. Don't hit it in the center, because if all of the ring surface sees the top of the cylinder at the same time, it's just too much, they bend or break. So if you walk it around, the piston will actually screw itself down in the hole. The tighter the clearance, the more important it is to do this.

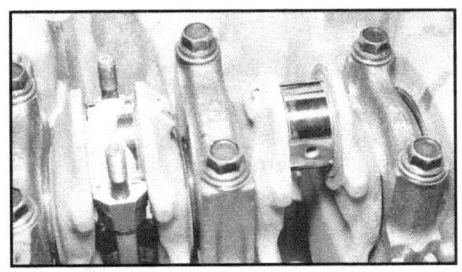

Oil the threads and nuts of the rod bolts before you torque them. If you torque them dry you'll get a false reading. The torque value on the rod bolts is the most important part of putting the motor together. Anything else, you've got room for a little bit of error. Notice how polished the crank is; micro polished for less friction.

If you miss the torque spec on the rod bolts, then you've broken your engine. If you get a rod bolt loose or overtight, if you stretch the rod bolt, which causes it to lose its tensile strength, it's gone, history, toasted. It's either going to pull apart and break, or it's going to unscrew and fall out. Start at 18 lbs./ft. then go to 24 lbs./ft. and finish with 30 lbs./ft. Don't jerk the wrench, move it slowly and deliberately until you get the desired torque spec. If you jerk it, you make it jump and overtorque the bolt.

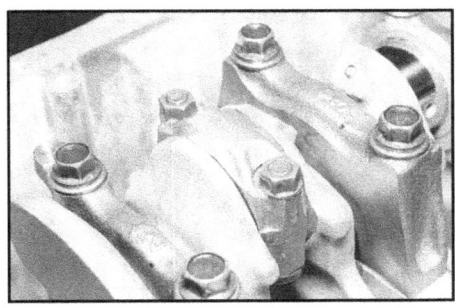

Collins says he can tell by the wobble of the rod on the bearing about how much clearance he has. You get a feel for this after building hundreds of racing engines. Get the right torque and make sure everything has assembly lube on it. And if you follow the book, you'll be all right.

## OIL PUMP AND WATER PUMP INSTALLATION

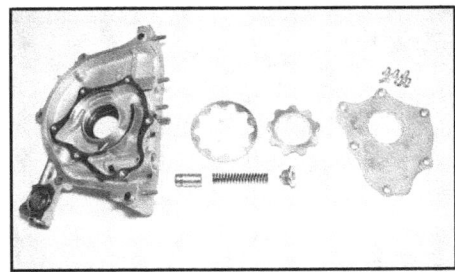

The oil pump is driven off the crankshaft nose and integrates into the front of the block. You can raise the oil pressure by shimming the relief valve spring. Sometimes this is a good idea, as it is when you're running looser main and rod clearances, and sometimes it's not. If you're running tighter clearances and you want to free up some power, reducing oil pressure is a tactic you may want to investigate with your machinist.

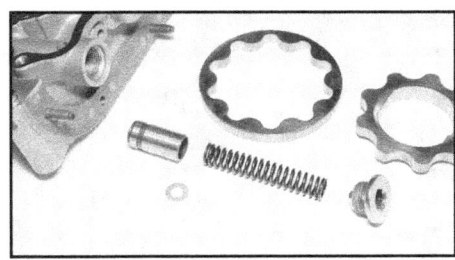

Collins used a 0.0040 - 0.0060 shim to bump up the pressure a bit. It's not a big deal.

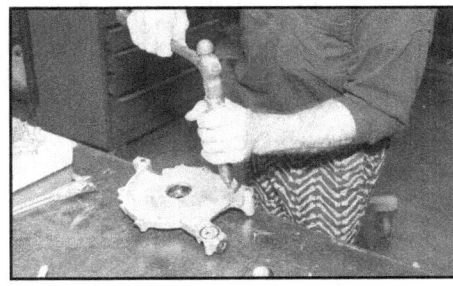

The pump gears fit inside each other in the housing. Then the cover goes on over. Pop it on with an impact driver. You don't want these coming loose.

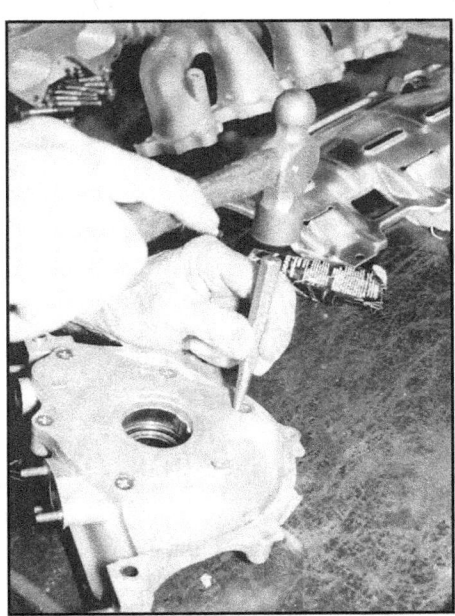

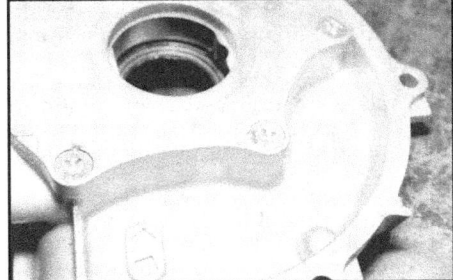

Collins prefers to dimple the metal to lock the fasteners in place. The more you control the variables, the less chance you have of breaking something.

Honda Builder's Handbook Vol. 2

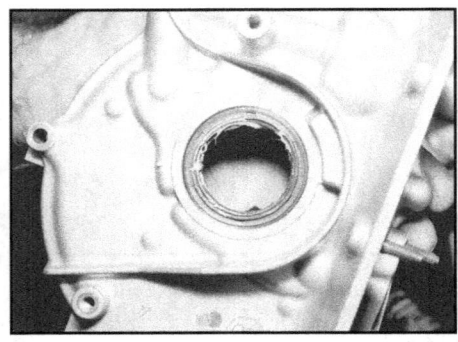

Get some grease in the seal so it won't wear the first time the motor spins. You also need to get these two flats and the crank lined up so the pump will fit over the nose of the crank.

Everything is cleaned. This is a race motor so we just can't take a chance that it will leak . . . so we put Honda Bond #4 everywhere.

Have a speed wrench like this and then have a torque wrench. Torque it to whatever is called for. Then go back over with the speed wrench. Pretty soon you'll find you can put an engine together with a speed wrench and the torque will be right there. If speed is any concern — and for race mechanics it is — there is always more work to do on a race car. You don't want to rush but can't make a hobby out of building the engine. If you want to go pro, work for Penske, Gurney or Foyt. Those aren't hobby shops; they need pro mechanics working at pro speeds to keep the racing stable on the track at full speed. After you get real good and know the feel of the metal and your air tools, you can use them to screw a motor together without over or undertorquing parts.

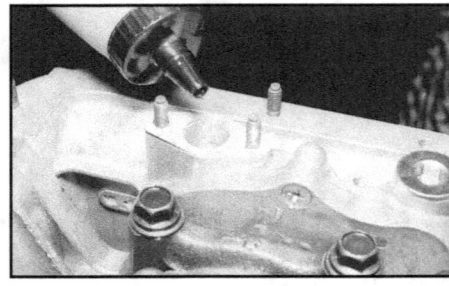

Collins uses gear oil to prime the oil pump because it will hang around forever. Some guys grease the oil pump to get it vacuuming up oil real quick. I want that oil to get up there as fast as it can when it first turns over. And always leave the plugs out until you see the oil pressure come up to spec.

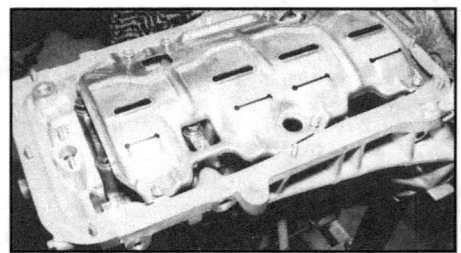

Install the windage tray before installing the oil pump pick up. This is simple — it goes on with 8 bolts.

## MILLING AND HONING CRANK SHAFT BEARINGS

Russ Collins says the only reason he hones a race engine main bearing bore is to get more crush on the bearings. The reason is to make sure the bearings fit tight with as much surface area contact to the block and cap as possible in order to conduct heat away from the mains into the block. The heat is then absorbed by the cooling system and finally injected into the atmosphere.

To do this right you have to mill the main cap and saddle to reduce the diameter. (See figure at right.) Then the cap is torqued to spec and the main bearing saddle is honed to the desired dimension.

Most racers think you do this to keep the bearing from spinning and to make sure the bores align perfectly with the crank's main journals. Actually, the crankshaft floats in a thin layer of oil, so the bearings and the crank main journal surfaces should never touch. If they do, basically that's the end of the engine. And as far as having a perfect alignment of the main bearing bores and the journals, once you start getting power strokes coming through the crank, it's going to flex anyway.

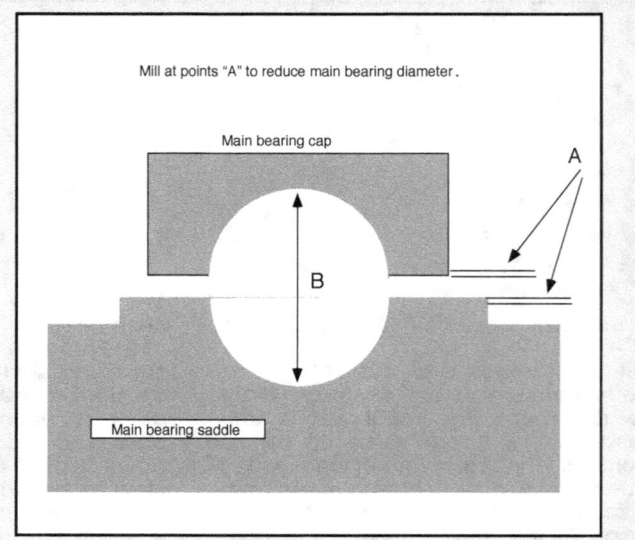

## THE ULTIMATE NATURALLY ASPIRATED POWER COMBO

Now that you've gone this far, why not step up to something really fast? RPS Performance Products built this 1.6L delSol engine equipping it with the right combination to make power at high RPM:

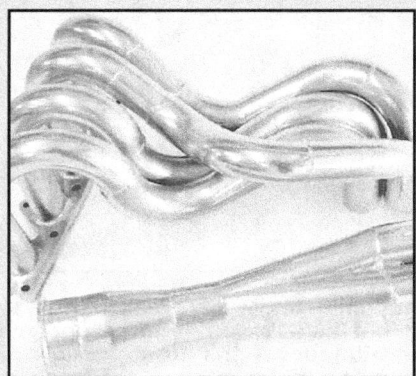
A swoopy set of step headers with large bends and gradually increasing diameter to keep the exhaust moving.

The four-into-one headers feed into a tuned collector that generates a low pressure pulse to increase cylinder scavenging and engine efficiency. Very cool.

The intake features a large plenum with straight velocity stacks welded to the stock flange. Its runner length is tuned with a computer modeling program. Fuel injectors are from RC Engineering.

The oil pickup bolts are the most important bolts on the motor (at least as important as the rod bolts). If these back off and you lose the oil pick up suction, you won't know it until you've ruined the engine. You get to the end of the straightaway, and your engine's dead meat. Use a drop of lock tite on the threads.

The oil pan is such that long left hand turns may get the oil pump sucking air. The pan has a lip on the trans side to help control oil, but for serious road racing you'll need to do something.

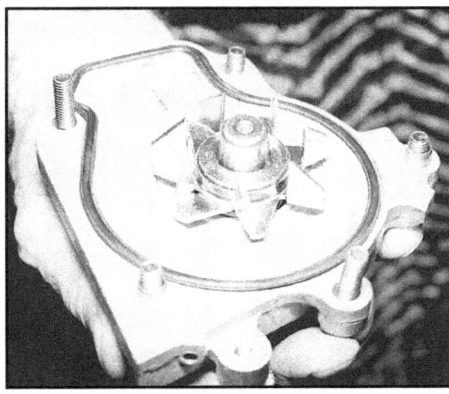

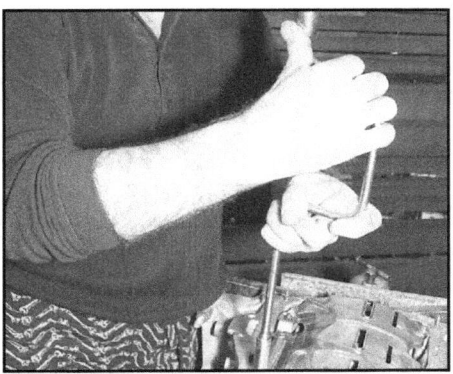
When you're working with a speed wrench, says Collins, you get more feel for what the metal is doing if you put your forearm across the handle. Then after you've torqued the bolts, do a final check with the tips of your fingers.

Don't forget to top off the oil pump pick up with a little extra gear oil.

If you know you'll need different size bolts to fasten certain components, such as the water pump, put them in the bolt holes on tear down. If nothing else, it reminds you that these bolts are special. Even if you drop them on the floor and lose their position, you are still alert to the fact that a particular sequence is called for.

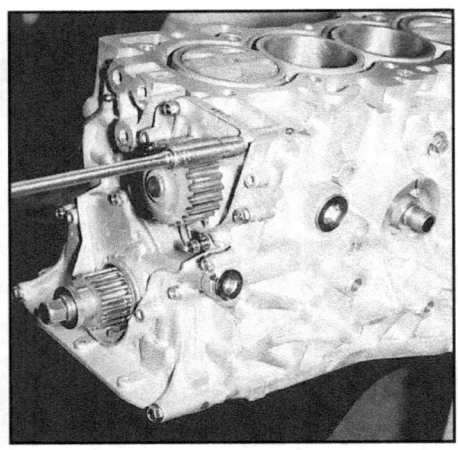

Installing the water pump. Just be sure all the bolt lengths match with the holes.

Installing the timing belt tensioner. You need as much slack on the belt as possible when you first install it. So press down on the tensioner and tighten it at that position.

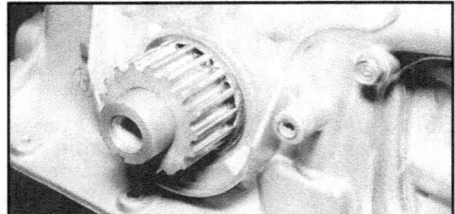

Install the crankshaft drive wheel.

## MILLING THE HEAD AND INSTALLING IT

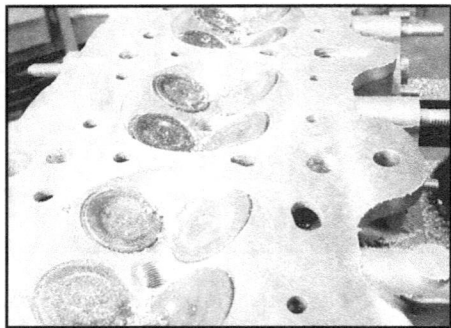

Collins milled .040 off the head. Milling the head reduces combustion chamber volume which raises the compression ratio. On overhead cam engines, milling the head changes the cam timing, since now that the head is thinner the cam drive is closer to the crankshaft. The tensioning mechanism takes up the slack but the result is retarded cam timing. The decision to mill or not depends on your combination. Nitrous isn't as affected by static compression increases as are turbos and superchargers. Unless you're running huge doses of nitrous, the amount of mass you're adding to be compressed doesn't make much difference. Unless you're already on the edge of detonation. See the fuel section for more information about compression ratio and detonation.

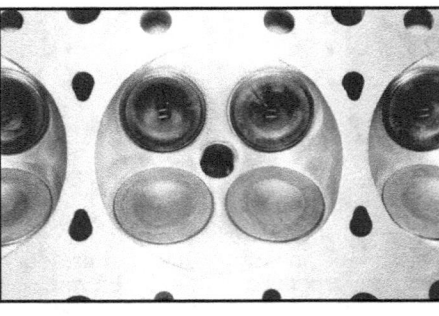

Checking piston to head clearance. As the piston comes up to TDC it has more chance to rock back and forth, and if you don't have enough clearance between the piston and the head they'll collide. Not good. When you mill the head, you have to check indentation of the squish areas, add that dimension to the gasket thickness and how far the piston travels up the bore plus a stretching factor. For example, if the gasket is .032 and the indentation of the cylinder head is only about, well in this engine it was .014, .016, .011 and .006. That's the inconsistency of the chambers when they're cast. The one that has .006 Collins says he worries about a little bit because he wants to see about .040 between the piston and the heads at all times, because the rods will stretch that much. He'll go with .032 minimum but he doesn't want to take a chance on this engine, since it is one of the first built for testing. And he has to have a combination that he can build with consistency and reliability.

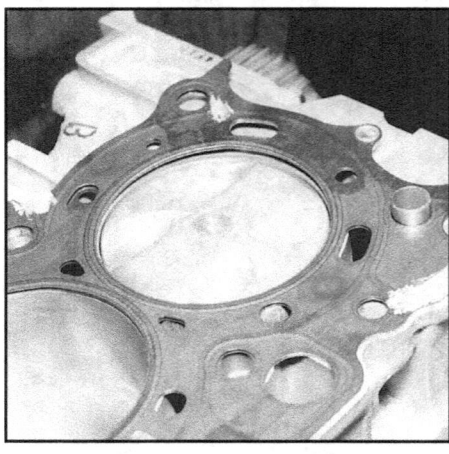

The head gaskets do not require any sealer on them whatsoever. So why is Collins putting sealer on the head gasket? Because it's a race motor and it's not going to get any break in. He'll start it, get the oil to temperature, and go full throttle down the front straight and hope no oil leaks on to the track. And because he has the Honda sealer he's going to use it. Well, actually the VTEC engine has a ton of oil in the head and he likes to take precautions against having to pull the engine out of the car to fix an oil leak. Now reportedly it doesn't need any. But since he's bumped up the oil pressure a bit, how does he know the gasket will hold? If you had to install the gasket right before a race, Collins says he wouldn't use the sealer. He'd install the gasket and hope for the best. But if he doesn't have to hope, why should he? If he uses Honda Bond he doesn't have to worry. Middle channel is for oil delivery. The other is the oil return.

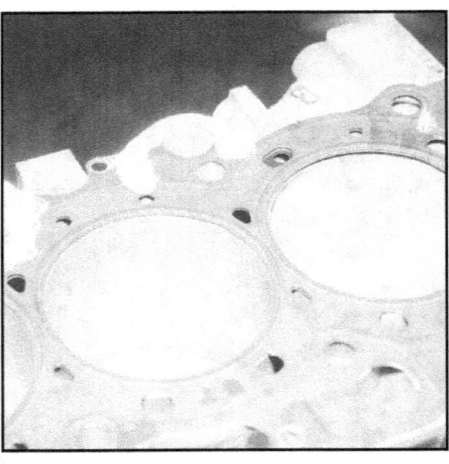

A word of caution. When you're ready to install the head, be aware that the oil drain back holes are large enough to let bolts fall directly to the oil pan. So keep focused when working around these so you don't inadvertently drop stuff in the motor. The locating dowels are particularly easy to drop in the motor, especially if there's a writer in the clean room. Lubricate the head bolts, thread, and head. Set the head on the block and install head bolts.

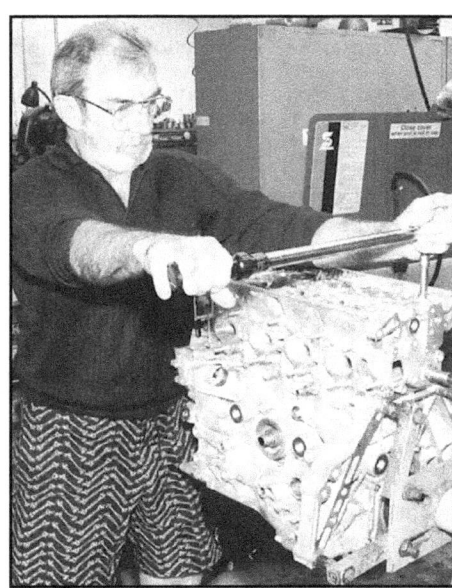

Torque the head. Snug it up and torque it with the same feeling as with the rod bolts or any other critical component. The book has a specific sequence but it's not exactly necessary. As for working from the center out, actually by the time you do the several center head bolts, there's no reason to go all the way across the head. Keep a routine. After you torque the head bolts check them by going up one side and down the other or whatever routine you've established.

## CAM AND VTEC MECHANISM INSTALLATION

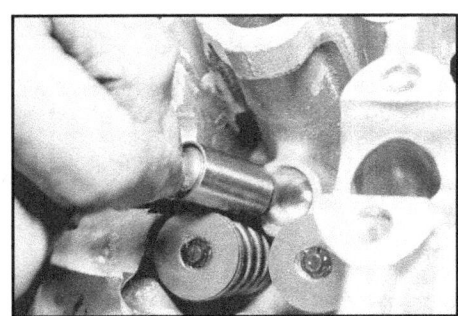

Install the loss motion devices. Do this before you install the VTEC shaft. The loss motion devices are really just noise suppressors. They keep the VTEC rocker arm from rattling when not in use.

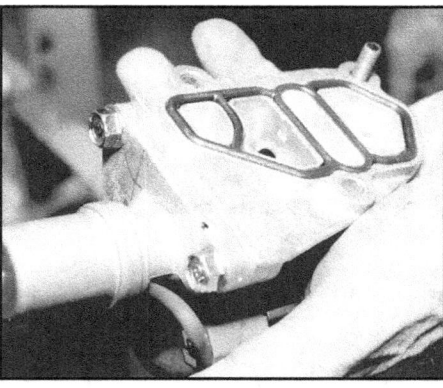

Make sure the VTEC controller screen is clean and clear and that the O-ring is good. This device controls the flow of oil and pressure to the Vtec shaft which activates the system. This sensor has to see 55 psi and this one has to be activated by the computer. So when the computer sees 55 psi and the RPM limit (5000 rpm), then it allows the oil pressure to activate the VTEC. (The computer might monitor road speed or in gear before activating.)

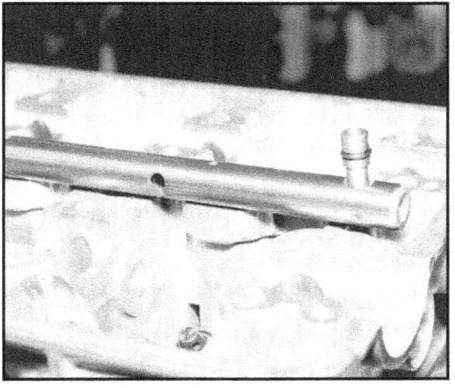

Collins installs the VTEC rocker arm shafts from this side of the head because then he only has to remove one plug. From the other he has to remove two plugs. These shafts fit in the head just below and inboard of the cams. See the oil hole? When VTEC engages, oil comes in there and pushes several pistons such that the three rocker arms for each intake and exhaust valve become locked together by the pin moving across.

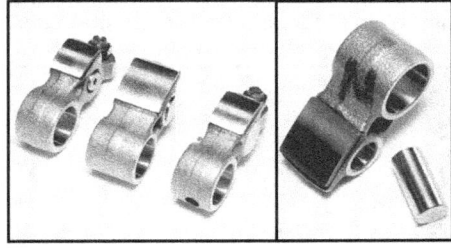

In normal operation the two outside lobes are working until the pin comes across. Then the middle lobe takes over and then the outside rockers aren't touching the camshaft, except for the base circle.

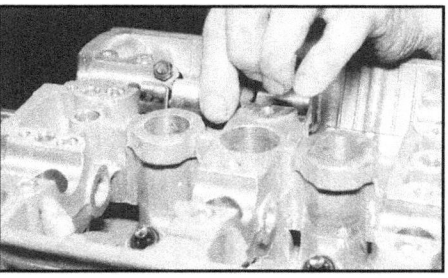

Honda suggests holding the three rockers with a rubber band to help installation. Russ says he likes to just hold them and work them on the shaft. You've got to be careful here because the VTEC pin can slip out and if you're unlucky fall down an oil drain back.

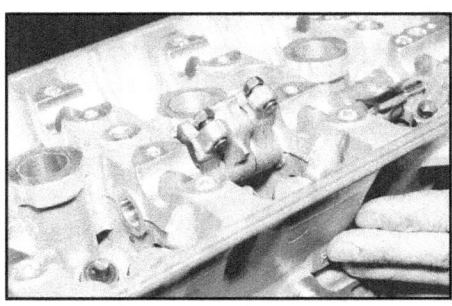

The VTEC rocker shaft is the same for both sides. Essentially the VTEC feed holes become rocker oiler holes when not matched to the VTEC rocker arm. Russ calculates there are 64 "leaks" in the rocker shaft, which is one of the reasons you need high oil pressures. But the leaks keep the valvetrain well lubricated. Notice the VTEC bleeder on this side. This is the exhaust rocker shaft that's going to be installed.

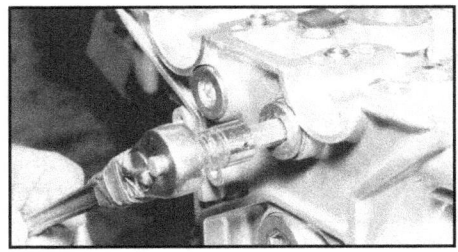

After you get all the lost motion devices and rockers and rocker shaft installed, button it up.

Now you're ready to install the cams. But first, Collins lays on a little more assembly lube. Just flow it over the cam bearings and the rockers.

*Honda Builder's Handbook Vol. 2* **123**

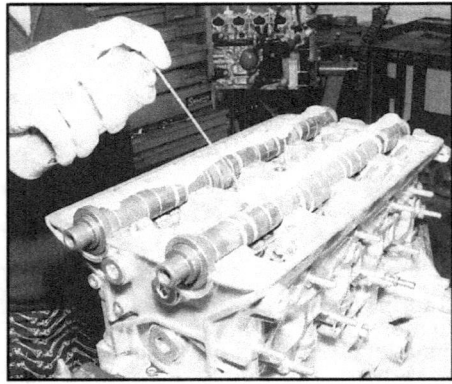

The easy way to install the cams is to put the cam drives on before you install them. After you lay the cams in the bearing saddles, lube them.

When you install the cam bearing caps and girdle, this area is one that's prone to binding and leaking. We provide this view of the seal for reference.

This is the distributor drive off the exhaust cam. The exhaust cam is on the transmission side.

On race engines, Collins is always searching out areas that might leak. One of the areas he backs up with a dab of Honda Bond is the cam seals.

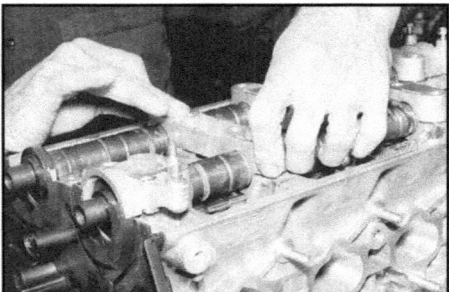

Install the cam girdle and torque the cam bearing caps. If you didn't loosen all the valve adjusters during the tear down, do it before you torque the cam bearing caps. You should loosen them to a point that no, repeat no, pressure is put on the valves. If you put pressure on the valves, you can skew the torque readings. The cams should be installed with the timing you wish to run. In this case, Russ is installing the cam straight up, but that will change because of the slight milling of the head.

Put the key in the cam key way and install cam drives. Put a drop of red lock tight on the cam drive fasteners before threading in. I know this is one of those "do as I say, not as I do" things, but it's best to torque the cam drives on the bench before you get all the caps and girdles in place. It's just easier that way.

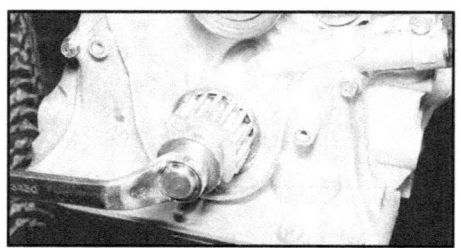

The crank is also at top dead center on numbers 1 and 4 cylinders. Let's get them out of the way. Just back the crankshaft off a few degrees to pull the pistons down the barrel. This is particularly important when you're installing a high lift racing cam. With high lift cams you do everything very slowly. Crank the engine slowly back to TDC, feel for valve bind, coil bind, anything that can hurt the engine.

Bring the cam fasteners down real slow, with your speed wrench, and watch everything. If you hear it groaning or feel a bind, stop and find out where it's coming from and resolve the conflict before proceeding.

Check the oil seal on the cam drive side. Sometimes, as you're tightening the cam bearing caps and girdle, it gets cocked to one side. If that happens use a blunt tool such as a bolt to work it back into place. If you can't get it with that, take the bearing cap off and position the seal correctly.

Using a wrench to run the bolts down before setting with a torque wrench. After you've torqued the main fasteners, tighten and torque the bolts at the extreme end of the head.

Tighten and torque the main fasteners on the cam and girdle. Leave the bolts at the extreme ends. Lubricate the heads and threads of all the bolts. These are only tightened to about 18 lbs./ft. and without the lube you can see 18 lbs./ft. because of drag, but you won't have any crush on the component.

Cams should go in there the way you're going to run them. With the crank set at TDC and these marks aligned you're at overlap.

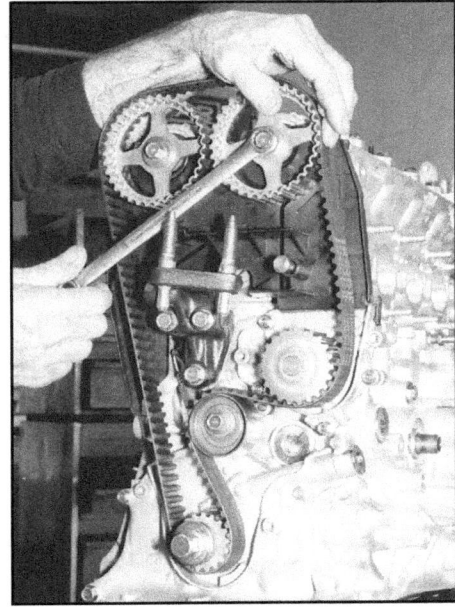

If the marks are lined up and go basically straight across with just a little slop in here, that's okay. That's the intake cam coming back, and when the tensioner is loosened, everything comes right back in. It's not adjusted correctly all the way yet, so we'll just snug it for now.

Adjusting timing belt tension; checking cam timing. Put number one cylinder at TDC by turning the crank in the direction of engine rotation. Right when you get to TCD while the tension on the belt is nice and tight, keep tension on the bottom pulley, or keep turning the engine if you want, that's when you set the belt tensioner. Push it against the belt and then cinch the fastener.

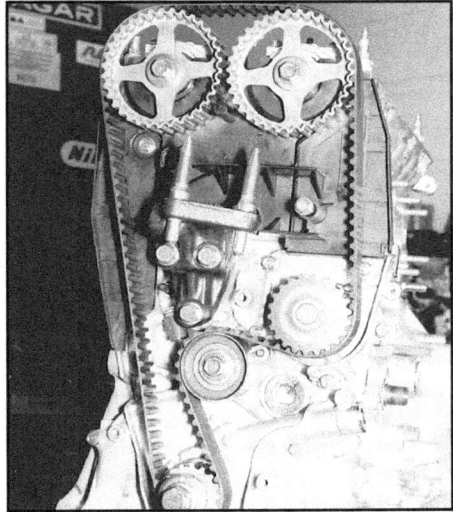

With the crank at TDC number one, the cams are about 3 degrees retarded. Milling the heads does this which shifts the power curve up in the RPM range. If you want a bottom end short track motor, an advanced cam puts the power curve farther down in the RPM band. Why? Cycle time is up; air speed is down. At high RPM, air is traveling as fast as it can, but the amount of time the valve is open is less. If you close the intake valve later (retard the cam timing), the engine has more time to breath in air. For low RPM torque and power, you want to close the intake valve a little sooner. Because you have all the time in the world to fill the cylinder and right at max torque, the air is at max velocity, mach .5 or so. When the valve opens, the cylinder gets full and you make power. If you added thickness to the heads, cam timing would be advanced.

## ADJUSTING VALVES

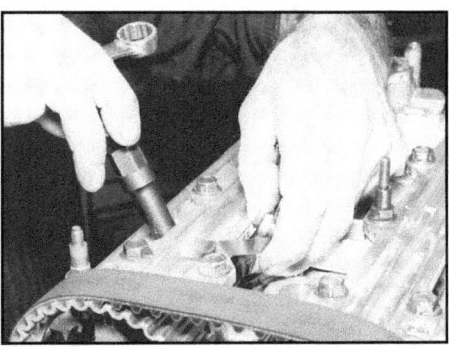

The feel in a valve adjustment should be more than .001. In fact it can be right on, zero-clearance (from lash spec) or you can be .001 loose. But if you're .001 tight, it should be apparent to you that you can't pull the damn feeler gauge out. Keep the feeler gauge in the gap while you tighten the jam nut. Many times you'll feel the adjusting screw turn when you tighten the jam nut. After you tighten, check the feel again. Sometimes what you're feeling is correct; sometimes not. But always check and double check. After you get through adjusting the valves, go back and check all of them. It's real easy to forget a valve when you're adjusting 16 of them.

The factory manual says you should adjust the valves one cylinder at a time. Bring the piston of the cylinder you're adjusting to TDC to adjust the valves. There is a quicker way, but it is a little confusing and so it's easier to miss adjusting a valve. Basically this involves finding a spot in the rotation of the engine where half the valves are fully closed. You adjust those valves, then rotate the crankshaft until the other half are closed. Usually this means rotating the crankshaft 360 degrees to put you in the proper location of the 4 cycle process so that the rocker arms you want to adjust are on the base circle of the cam.

*Honda Builder's Handbook Vol. 2*

## BUTTONING UP

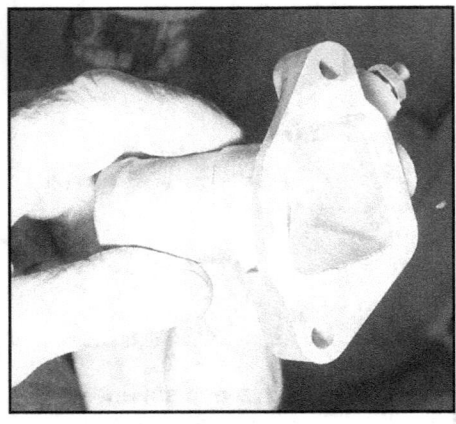

The plugs shouldn't be in the motor while you're installing the head and adjusting valves. But as soon as possible after these operations are complete, get plugs in the heads. Don't even attempt to install the cam and VTEC mechanisms without something in the plug hole. If you drop something, the VTEC pin for example, you'll probably have to take the head off to retrieve it. Honda's got a lot of courage to make a water transfer port like that with no gasket. No gasket, no O ring. They just know it'll work.

The VTEC controller installs on the trans end of the head. You can also see the water temp gauge and water temp computer sensor. The hole on the exhaust side is the sensor.

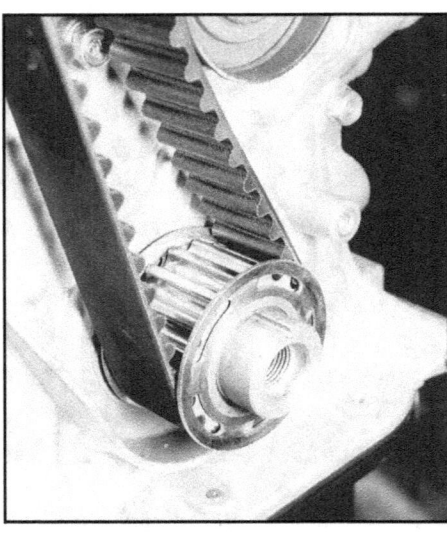

Remove the crankshaft drive bolt to install the timing belt guide.

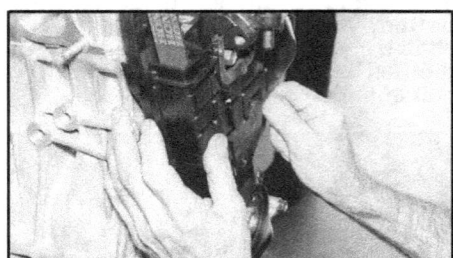

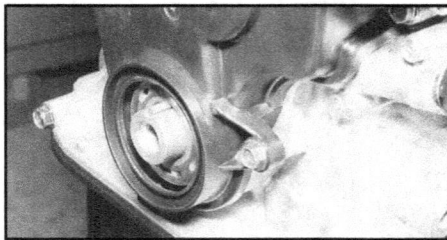

Install the lower cover and crankshaft accessory drive pulley.

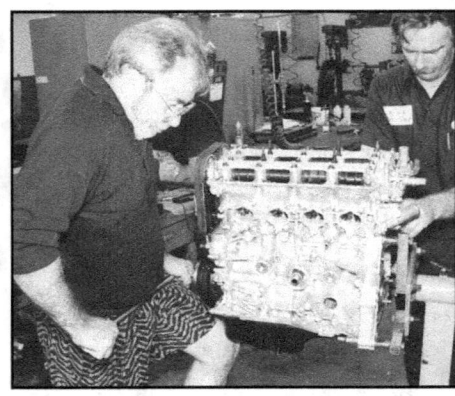

You'll need a partner to hold the crankshaft while you torque the drive fastener to spec.

Bolt on the middle portion of the timing belt cover.

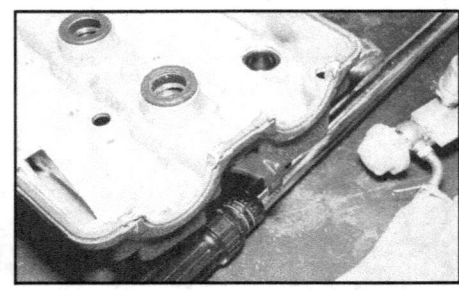

Dab Honda Bond on the corners of the valve cover gasket. This is where they tend to leak.

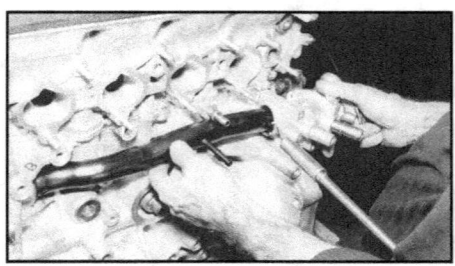

**Hot Tech Tip:**
If you grease the rubber O ring, installing the water return pipe correctly is very difficult. If you grease it, it gets so slippery it wants to slide out of the receiver groove while you're trying to insert the return pipe. It gets doubled up behind the back.

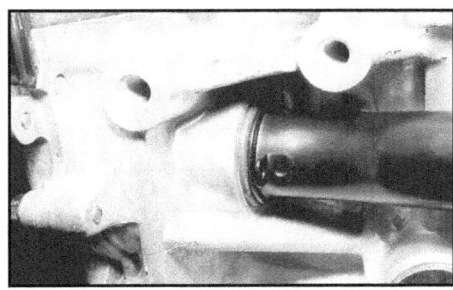

If you only grease the entrance to the hole and the rubber O ring is dry, then the O ring will stick to the dry steel and slip over the greased entry. It just pops in place.

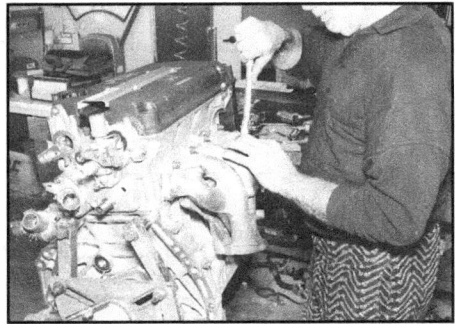

Don't forget the heat shield on the block side of the exhaust. Honda used to only shield the outside or radiator, but they found that they started to get a lot of heat in the motor from this source. When you turbo charge on these motors you should be careful of this. Russ says he's seen some turbo kits that put the turbo so close to the block that the oil in the center mains cooks and causes the engine to fail.

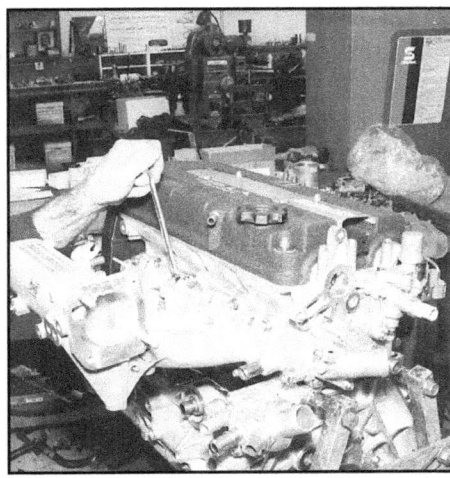

Collins says, as he tightens the fasteners on the intake, he likes to ship his engines without plugs, so that the customer has to think about firing up the engine. If he's thinking about firing up the engine, then he'll probably be thinking about spinning the motor up to oil pressure before firing. If he forgets and just tries to fire the motor without thinking about it, the tape will pop off the heads and at least the engine has a few rotations on it before being fired up.

Most of the time Collins has to leave his work unsigned and undetected. But this project is different. And you can bet he'll be sending a matched set of his injectors with the engine.

## HOW TO DEGREE YOUR CAM

There's a possibility of having so much camshaft timing retard (from milling the head) that Russ Collins thinks he might have to re-cut the pulley. What he'd do is take the crank pulley off and machine the keyway groove out and put a keyway in it. He'll just put a groove in it any where that gives the timing he wants.

To do that he'll degree the cam to find out how much it is actually retarded. Because it's still running the stock computer, he can't change the lobe centers much or he'd just change the keyways on the camshafts instead of the crankshaft. He says he'll put the engine together and see what the owner wants, depending on the purpose of the engine. For top end power, just leave the cams retarded; leave the lobe centers alone. If the owner plans on using an aftermarket computer, then Collins can put the lobe centers anyway he wants. He says he'd bring them down to 108 exhaust/106 intake. You could go tighter, 105 or 107 for more overlap and more top end power.

Using a degree wheel we can see the cams are late. And then the differential at the crankshaft will indicate exactly the degree of retard. So we're about three degrees retard for .040 off the head. That won't kill the performance of the motor, but it'd run better if it was two degrees advanced. So that means we need to put about five degrees advance on the bottom pulley to let it run two degrees advanced.

For most naturally aspirated engines, the magic number from Dale Armstrong, Austin Coil, or Russ Collins seems to be 2 degrees advanced with split overlap. So two degree differential in lobe centers between intake and exhaust would be higher. Exhaust would be a high number and the intake would be a low number because it opens sooner before TDC. With the lobe centers at 108 degrees (exhaust) and 106 degrees (intake), whichagain is two degrees advanced from split overlap, that would be equivalent to timing a single pattern cam at 107 degrees intake lobe center. Only the cam grinder can change the lobe centers for a push rod Chevy, for example. A common lobe center for that engine is 105 and then advance the cam two degrees. So now the cam timing numbers come out (exhaust/ intake) with a two degree differential. With twin cams you can do anything you want. You can change the lobe center relationship and the timing of either intake or exhaust valve timing events in relation to the camshaft.

Use a degree wheel and a dial indicator to determine max lift of intake valve at precise crankshaft degree. Use the stock lobe centerline angle of the del Sol 1.6 VTEC low RPM cam with max valve lift at 107.5 crankshaft degrees after top dead center. With the heads milled, max lift occurred at 110 degrees, or three degrees retarded.

Working with overhead cam engines means the max lift occurs when the valve travels farthest away from the dial indicator.

**NOTES:**